New Perspectives on

HTML and XHTML

D0086205

Introductory

3-43

New Perspectives on

HTML and XHTML

Introductory

Patrick Carey

Carey Associates, Inc.

THOMSON

* **COURSE TECHNOLOGY** ™

Australia • Canada • Mexico • Singapore • Spain • United Kingdom • United States

THOMSON

COURSE TECHNOLOGY

New Perspectives on HTML and XHTML—Introductory

is published by Course Technology.

Managing Editor:
Rachel Goldberg

Senior Product Manager:
Kathy Finnegan

Senior Technology Product Manager:
Amanda Young Shelton

Product Managers:
Karen Stevens, Brianna Germain

Associate Product Manager:
Emilie Perreault

Editorial Assistant:
Shana Rosenthal

Marketing Manager:
Joy Stark

Developmental Editor:
Sasha Vodnik

QA Manuscript Reviewers:
John Freitas, Burt LaFontaine,
Jeff Schwartz, Danielle Shaw

Senior Production Editor:
Aimee Poirier

Composition:
GEX Publishing Services

Text Designer:
Steve Deschene

Cover Designer:
Nancy Goulet

Cover Artist:
Helmick & Schechter Sculpture
www.handsart.net

Preface

Real, Thought-Provoking, Engaging, Dynamic, Interactive—these are just a few of the words that are used to describe the New Perspectives Series' approach to learning and building computer skills.

Without our critical-thinking and problem-solving methodology, computer skills could be learned but not retained. By teaching with a case-based approach, the New Perspectives Series challenges students to apply what they've learned to real-life situations.

Our ever-growing community of users understands why they're learning what they're learning. Now you can too!

See what instructors and students are saying about the best-selling New Perspectives Series:

"First of all, I just have to say that I wish that all of my textbooks were written in the style of the New Perspectives Series. I am using these titles for all of the courses that I teach that have a book available."
— Diana Kokoska, University of Maine at Augusta

"The New Perspectives format is a pleasure to use. The Quick Checks and the tutorial Review Assignments help students view topics from a real-world perspective."
— Craig Shaw, Central Community College—Hastings

"We have been using the New Perspectives Series for several years and are pleased with it. Step-by-step instructions, end-of-chaper projects, and color screenshots are positives."
— Michael J. Losacco, College of DuPage

...and about New Perspectives on HTML and XHTML:

"Outstanding! Working with inline styles throughout will be a big bonus for our students."
—George Jackson, Collin County Community College District

"For readability, no HTML title is in the same league as this one. I highly commend Carey for his writing and organizational styles and the way Course Technology formatted the materials."
—Zachary Wong, Sonoma State University, School of Business and Economics

www.course.com/NewPerspectives

Why *New Perspectives* will work for you

Context

Each tutorial begins with a problem presented in a "real-world" case that is meaningful to students. The case sets the scene to help students understand what they will do in the tutorial.

Hands-on Approach

Each tutorial is divided into manageable sessions that combine reading and hands-on, step-by-step work. Screenshots—now 20% larger for enhanced readability—help guide students through the steps. **Trouble?** tips anticipate common mistakes or problems to help students stay on track and continue with the tutorial.

Review

In New Perspectives, retention is a key component to learning. At the end of each session, a series of Quick Check questions helps students test their understanding of the concepts before moving on. And now each tutorial contains an end-of-tutorial summary and a list of key terms for further reinforcement.

Assessment

Engaging and challenging Review Assignments and Case Problems have always been a hallmark feature of the New Perspectives Series. Now we've added new features to make them more accessible! Colorful icons and brief descriptions accompany the exercises, making it easy to understand, at a glance, both the goal and level of challenge a particular assignment holds.

Reference

While contextual learning is excellent for retention, there are times when students will want a high-level understanding of how to accomplish a task. Within each tutorial, Reference Windows appear before a set of steps to provide a succinct summary and preview of how to perform a task. In addition, a complete Task Reference at the back of the book provides quick access to information on how to carry out common tasks. Finally, each book includes a combination Glossary/Index to promote easy reference of material.

Student Online Companion

This book has an accompanying online companion Web site designed to enhance learning. This Web site includes:

- Additional content for further exploration
- Student Data Files and PowerPoint presentations
- Links to Web sites for additional information
- Student Edition Labs—These online interactive labs offer students hands-on practice and reinforcement of skills and concepts relating to Web and Internet topics.

Review

Apply

Reference Window

Task Reference

www.course.com/NewPerspectives

New Perspectives offers an entire system of instruction

The New Perspectives Series is more than just a handful of books. It's a complete system of offerings:

New Perspectives catalog
Our online catalog is never out of date! Go to the catalog link on our Web site to check out our available titles, request a desk copy, download a book preview, or locate online files.

Coverage to meet your needs!
Whether you're looking for just a small amount of coverage or enough to fill a semester-long class, we can provide you with a textbook that meets your needs.

- Brief books typically cover the essential skills in just 2 to 4 tutorials.
- Introductory books build and expand on those skills and contain an average of 5 to 8 tutorials.
- Comprehensive books are great for a full-semester class, and contain 9 to 12+ tutorials.
- Power Users or Advanced books are perfect for a highly accelerated introductory class or a second course in a given topic.

So if the book you're holding does not provide the right amount of coverage for you, there's probably another offering available. Go to our Web site or contact your Course Technology sales representative to find out what else we offer.

Instructor Resources
We offer more than just a book. We have all the tools you need to enhance your lectures, check students' work, and generate exams in a new, easier-to-use and completely revised package. This book's Instructor's Manual, ExamView testbank, PowerPoint presentations, data files, solution files, figure files, and a sample syllabus are all available on a single CD-ROM or for downloading at www.course.com.

How will your students master Computer Concepts and Microsoft Office?
Add more muscle and flexibility to your course with SAM (Skills Assessment Manager)! SAM adds the power of skill-based assessment and the award-winning SAM classroom administration system to your course, putting you in control of how you deliver exams and training.

By adding SAM to your curriculum, you can:

- Reinforce your students' knowledge of key computer concepts and application skills with hands-on exercises.
- Allow your students to "learn by listening," with access to rich audio in their training
- Build hands-on computer concepts exams from a test bank of more than 200 skill-based concepts, windows, and applications tasks.
- Schedule your students' training and testing exercises with powerful administrative tools.
- Track student exam grades and training progress using more than one dozen student and classroom reports.

Teach your introductory course with the simplicity of a single system! You can now administer your entire Computer Concepts and Microsoft Office course through the SAM platform. For more information on the SAM administration system, SAM Computer Concepts, and other SAM products, please visit http://www.course.com/sam.

Distance Learning
Enhance your course with any of our online learning platforms. Go to www.course.com or speak with your Course Technology sales representative to find the platform or the content that's right for you.

www.course.com/NewPerspectives

About This Book

This book offers a case-based, problem-solving approach to learning introductory concepts of HTML and XHTML, from the basics of creating links through the use of frames and tables. Students learn how to hand-code Web sites using a simple text editor.

- All code is XHTML 1.0 compliant! Students learn well-formed code: all code is lowercase; all tags are closed; and correct syntax is used for empty elements.
- New! Students learn to use inline style from the beginning, instead of deprecated tags. Inline styles are used to format text and for page layout.
- New appendix covers Web accessibility and Section 508 guidelines!
- New Student Online Companion provides additional materials to enhance student learning.

New to this edition!

- Larger screenshots!
- Sequential page numbering!
- New end-of-tutorial material provides additional conceptual review of key terms and a tutorial summary.
- New labels and descriptions for the end-of-tutorial exercises make it easy for you to select the right exercises for your students.

Acknowledgments

I would like to thank the people who worked so hard to make this book possible. Special thanks to Sasha Vodnik for his excellent suggestions and ideas in developing this material and to Karen Stevens, the Product Manager who worked so hard in overseeing this project, keeping it on task and on target. Other people at Course Technology who deserve credit are Rachel Goldberg, Managing Editor; Emilie Perreault, Associate Product Manager; Aimee Poirier, Production Editor; and Quality Assurance Testers John Freitas, Burt LaFontaine, Jeff Schwartz, and Danielle Shaw.

Feedback is an important part of writing any book, and thanks go to the following reviewers for their ideas and comments: George Jackson, Collin County Community College; Allen Schmidt, Madison Area Technical College; Dorothy Harman, Tarrant County College; and Cheryl Jordan, San Juan College.

Special thanks also go to the members of our New Perspectives HTML Advisory Committee: Dr. Nazih Abdallah, University of Central Florida; Liz Drake, Santa Fe Community College; Ric Heishman, Northern Virginia Community College, Manassas Campus; George Jackson, Collin County Community College District; David Jampole, Bossier Parrish Community College; Eric Kisling, Indiana University; Diana Kokoska, University of Maine Augusta; William Lomerson, Northwestern State University—Natchitoches; Lisa Macon, Valencia Community College; David Ray, Jones County Junior College; Lo-An Tabar-Gaul, Mesa Community College; Sandi Watkins, Foothill College; and Zachary Wong, Sonoma State University.

I want to thank my wife Joan for her love and encouragement, and my six children: John Paul, Thomas, Peter, Michael, Stephen, and Catherine, to whom this book is dedicated.

—Patrick Carey

Brief Contents

Table of Contents

Level I

New Perspectives on
HTML and XHTML

Tutorial 1   **HTML 1.03**

Developing a Basic Web Page

Creating a Web Page for Stephen Dubé's Chemistry Classes

Tutorial 2   **HTML 1.55**

Developing a Basic Web Site

Creating a Chemistry Web Site

Read This Before You Begin: Tutorials 1–2

To the Student

Data Files

To complete the Level I HTML Tutorials (Tutorials 1 and 2), you need the starting student Data Files. Your instructor will either provide you with these Data Files or ask you to obtain them yourself.

The Level I HTML tutorials require the folders shown to complete the Tutorials, Review Assignments, and Case Problems. You will need to copy these folders from a file server, a standalone computer, or the Web to the drive and folder where you will be storing your Data Files.

Your instructor will tell you which computer, drive letter, and folder(s) contain the files you need. You can also download the files by going to www.course.com; see the inside back or front cover for more information on downloading the files, or ask your instructor or technical support person for assistance.

▼ **HTML**
Tutorial.01
Tutorial.02

To the Instructor

The Data Files are available on the Instructor Resources CD for this title. Follow the instructions in the Help file on the CD to install the programs to your network or standalone computer. See the "To the Student" section above for information on how to set up the Data Files that accompany this text.

You are granted a license to copy the Data Files to any computer or computer network used by students who have purchased this book.

System Requirements

If you are going to work through this book using your own computer, you need:

- **System Requirements** An Internet connection, a text editor and a Web browser that supports HTML 4.0 and XHTML 1.1 (for example, version 6.0 or higher of either Netscape or Internet Explorer). You may wish to

run an older browser version to highlight compatibility issues, but the code in this book is not designed to support those browsers.

- **Data Files** You will not be able to complete the tutorials or exercises in this book using your own computer until you have the necessary starting Data Files.

Developing a Basic Web Page

Creating a Web Page for Stephen Dubé's Chemistry Classes

Case

Stephen Dubé's Chemistry Classes

Stephen Dubé teaches chemistry at Robert Service High School in Edmonton, Alberta (Canada). In previous years, he has provided course information to students and parents with handouts. This year, he wants to put that information on the World Wide Web, where anyone can access it easily. Eventually, he hopes to post homework assignments, practice tests, and even grades on the Web site. Stephen is new to this technology and has asked you to help him create a Web page for his class.

Student Data Files

You can find a complete listing of the associated files in the comment section of each HTML file.

▼ **Tutorial.01**

▽ **Tutorial folder**
   dube.jpg

▽ **Review folder**
   chemtxt.htm
   logo.jpg
   flask.jpg

▽ **Case1 folder**
   childtxt.htm
   newborn.jpg

▽ **Case2 folder**
   euler.jpg
   eulertxt.htm
   pi.jpg

▽ **Case3 folder**
   flakes.jpg
   frosttxt.htm
   runner.jpg

▽ **Case 4 folder**
   logo.jpg
   smith.jpg
   smith.txt

Introducing the World Wide Web

Before you start creating a Web page for Stephen, it's helpful to first look at the history of the Web and how the HTML language was developed. To understand this history, we need to first become familiar with some of the basic features of networks.

A **network** is a structure linking computers together for the purpose of sharing resources such as printers and files. Users typically access a network through a computer called a **host** or **node**. A computer that makes a resource available to a network is called a **server**. A computer or other device that requests services from a server is called a **client**. Networks can be structured in many different ways. One of the most common structures is the **client-server network**, which is made up of several clients accessing information provided by one or more servers. You may be using such a network to access your data files for this tutorial from a network file server.

We can also classify networks based on their ranges. If the computers that make up a network are close together—for example, within a single department or building—then the network is referred to as a **local area network** or **LAN**. A network that covers a wider area, such as several buildings or cities, is called a **wide area network** or **WAN**. Wide area networks are typically built from two or more local area networks. The largest WAN in existence is the **Internet**.

In its early days in the late 1960's, the Internet was called the **ARPANET** and consisted of two network nodes located at UCLA and Stanford connected by a phone line. Today, the Internet has grown to include hundreds of millions of interconnected computers, cell phones, PDAs, televisions, and networks. The physical structure of the Internet uses fiber-optic cables, satellites, phone lines, and other telecommunications media, enabling a worldwide community to communicate and share information (see Figure 1-1).

Figure 1-1 ▶ **Structure of the Internet**

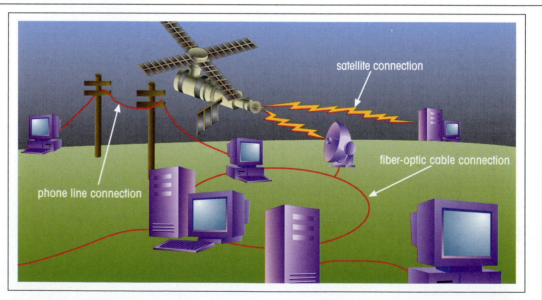

Most of the early Internet tools required users to master a bewildering array of terms, acronyms, and commands. Even navigating the network required users to be well-versed in both computers and network technology. Before the Internet could be accessible to the general public, it needed a simpler interface. This interface proved to be the World Wide Web.

The Development of the World Wide Web

The foundations for the **World Wide Web**, or the **Web** for short, were laid in 1989 by Timothy Berners-Lee and other researchers at the CERN nuclear research facility near Geneva, Switzerland. They needed an information system that would make it easy for their researchers to locate and share data, and which would require minimal training and support. To meet this need, they developed a system of interconnected hypertext documents that allowed their users to easily navigate from one topic to another. **Hypertext** is a method of organizing information that gives the reader control over the order in which the information is presented.

Properly used, hypertext provides quicker and simpler access to diverse pieces of information than traditional methods could. For example, when you read a book, you follow a linear progression, reading one page after another. With hypertext, you progress through those pages in whatever order best suits you and your objectives. Figure 1-2 illustrates the relationships of topics in linear and hypertext documents.

Linear versus hypertext documents | **Figure 1-2**

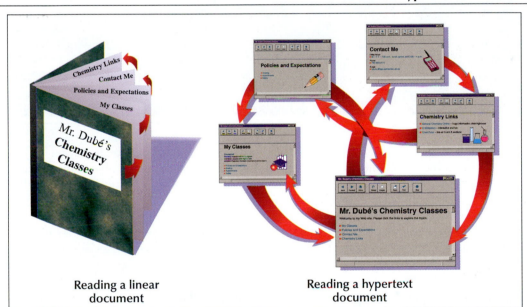

Reading a linear document

Reading a hypertext document

The key to hypertext is the use of **hyperlinks**, or **links**, which are the elements in a hypertext document that allow you to jump from one topic to another, often with a mouse click. A link may point to another section of the same document, or to another document entirely. A link can open a document on your computer or, through the Internet, a document on a computer anywhere in the world.

The hypertext approach was just what was needed to make the Internet accessible to the general public. The end user didn't need to know exactly where a document was stored, just how to get it. Since getting it was often no more difficult than clicking a mouse, access to any document anywhere was literally at every user's fingertips. The fact that the Internet and the World Wide Web are synonymous in many users' minds is a testament to the success of this approach.

An entire collection of linked documents is referred to as a **Web site**. The hypertext documents within a Web site are known as **Web pages**. Web sites have evolved from simple collections of text documents into complex sites where users can make purchases online, discuss a variety of topics, or access real-time stock market quotes. Individual pages can contain text, audio, video, and even programs that users can run remotely. While Web pages are primarily sources of information, they are increasingly becoming works of art in their own right.

Web Servers and Web Browsers

A Web page is stored on a **Web server**, which in turn makes it available to the network. To view a Web page, a client runs a software program called a **Web browser**, which retrieves the page from the server and displays it (see Figure 1-3).

Figure 1-3 | **Using a browser to view a Web document from a Web server**

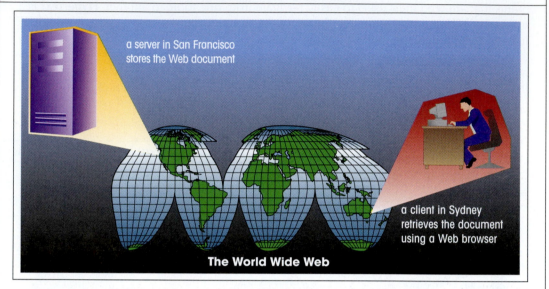

The earliest browsers, known as **text-based browsers**, were incapable of displaying images. Today most computers support **graphical browsers**, which are capable of displaying not only images, but also video, sound, animations, and a variety of graphical features. Cell phones can also connect to the Web to display sports scores or stock market tickers. Browsers can run on teletype machines, PDAs (personal digital assistants), Braille machines, and even information devices within a car. How does a Web page work with so many combinations of browsers and clients and devices? To understand, let's look at how Web pages are created.

HTML: The Language of the Web

A Web page is simply a text file written in a language called **Hypertext Markup Language** or **HTML**. We've already discussed hypertext, but what is a markup language? A **markup language** is a language that describes a document's structure and content. For example, if this tutorial were created using a markup language, that language would mark heading text, paragraph text, figure captions, and so forth.

Even though you can incorporate program code into an HTML file, HTML is not a programming language. HTML is also not a formatting language like those used by some desktop publishing programs. HTML does not necessarily tell you how a browser will display a document. If you want to format your document, the preferred method is to use styles. **Styles** are format descriptions written in a separate language from HTML that tell browsers how to render each element. We'll explore some of the basic styles as we create our first Web pages.

The History of HTML

Because the way HTML evolved impacts how you use it today, it's a good idea to review the language's history before going further into its details. The first version of HTML was created using the **Standard Generalized Markup Language (SGML)**. Introduced in the 1980's, SGML is a strong and highly flexible **metalanguage**, or a language used to create other languages. SGML is device- and system-independent, meaning that it can be applied to almost any type of document stored in almost any format. While powerful, SGML is also quite complex; for this reason, SGML is limited to those organizations that can afford the cost and overhead of maintaining complex SGML environments. However, SGML can also be used to create markup languages like HTML, which are tailored to specific tasks and are simpler to use and maintain.

In the early years after HTML was created, no one organization was responsible for the language. Web developers were free to define and modify HTML in whatever ways they thought best. While many rules were common, competing browsers, seeking to dominate the market, introduced some differences in the language. Such changes to the language were called **extensions**. The two major browsers during the 1990's, Netscape Navigator and Microsoft Internet Explorer, added the most extensions to HTML. These extensions were providing Web page authors with more options, but at the expense of complicating Web page development.

Web designers faced the challenge of determining which browser or browser version supported a particular extension, and creating a workaround for browsers that did not. By adding this layer of complexity to Web design, extensions, while often useful, diminished the promise of simplicity that made HTML so attractive in the first place.

Ultimately, a group of Web developers, programmers, and authors called the **World Wide Web Consortium**, or the **W3C**, created a set of **standards** or **specifications** that all browser manufacturers were to follow. The W3C has no enforcement power, but since a uniform approach to Web page creation is in the best interests of everyone, the W3C's recommendations are usually followed, though not always right away. The W3C also provides online tutorials, documentation, and quizzes that you can use to test your knowledge of HTML and other languages. For more information on the W3C and the services they offer, see their Web site at http://www.w3c.org.

Figure 1-4 summarizes the various versions of HTML that the W3C has released over the past decade. While you may not grasp all of the details of these versions yet, the important thing to understand is that HTML doesn't come in only one flavor.

Versions of HTML and XHTML — Figure 1-4

Version	Date	Description
HTML 1.0	1989–1994	The first public version of HTML which included browser support for inline images and text controls.
HTML 2.0	1995	The first version supported by all graphical browsers. It introduced interactive form elements such as option buttons and text boxes. A document written to the HTML 2.0 specification is compatible with almost all browsers on the World Wide Web.
HTML 3.0	1996	A proposed replacement for HTML 2.0 that was never widely adopted.
HTML 3.2	1997	This version included additional support for creating and formatting tables and expanded the options for interactive form elements. It also supported limited programming using scripts.
HTML 4.01	1999	This version added support for style sheets to give Web designers greater control over page layout. It added new features to tables and forms and provided support for international features. This version also expanded HTML's scripting capability and added increased support for multimedia elements.
XHTML 1.0	2001	This version is a reformulation of HTML 4.01 in XML and combines the strength of HTML 4.0 with the power of XML. XHTML brings the rigor of XML to Web pages and provides standards for more robust Web content on a wide range of browser platforms.
XHTML 1.1	2002	A minor update to XHTML 1.0 that allows for modularity and simplifies writing extensions to the language.
XHTML 2.0	2004–	The latest version, designed to remove most of the presentational features left in HTML.

When you create your Web pages you'll have to keep in mind not only what the W3C has recommended, but also what browsers currently in use actually support. This may mean dealing with a collection of approaches: some are new and meet the latest specifications, while some are older but still widely supported. Older features of HTML are often **deprecated**, or phased out, by the W3C. While deprecated features might not be supported in current or future browsers, that doesn't mean that you can't continue to use them—indeed, if you are supporting older browsers, you may *need* to use them. Because it's hard to predict how quickly a deprecated feature will disappear from the Web, it's crucial to be familiar with these features.

Future Web development is focusing increasingly on two other languages. **XML (Extensible Markup Language)** is a metalanguage like SGML, but without SGML's complexity and overhead. Using XML, document developers can create documents that obey specific rules for their content and structure. This is in contrast with a language like HTML, which included a wide variety of rules without a built-in mechanism for enforcing them. Indeed, one of the markup languages created with XML is **XHTML (Extensible Hypertext Markup Language)**, a stricter version of HTML. XHTML is designed to confront some of the problems associated with the different and competing versions of HTML, and to better integrate HTML with XML.

Even though XHTML shows great promise for the Web, HTML will not become obsolete anytime soon. HTML and XHTML overlap considerably, and the World Wide Web is still full of old HTML documents. In addition, we need to support those Web users who are still using older versions of Web browsers. In this book, we'll discuss the syntax of HTML 4.01 and XHTML 1.1, but we'll also bring in deprecated features and browser-supported extensions where appropriate.

Where does all of this leave you as a potential Web page author? A few guidelines are helpful:

- **Become well-versed in the history of HTML**. Unlike other languages, HTML history impacts how you write your code.
- **Know your market**. Do you have to support older browsers, or have your clients standardized on a particular browser or browser version? The answer affects how you write the code for your Web pages. Become familiar with what different browsers can and can't do.
- **Test**. If you have to support several types of browsers and several types of devices, get them and use them to view your documents. Don't assume that if your page works in one browser it will work in an older version of that same browser. In addition, a given browser version might even perform differently under different operating systems.

Tools for Creating HTML Documents

Because HTML documents are simple text files, you can create them with nothing more than a basic text editor such as Windows Notepad. However, specialized HTML authoring programs, known as HTML converters and HTML editors, are available to perform some of the rote work of document creation.

An **HTML converter** converts formatted text into HTML code. You can create the source document with a word processor such as Microsoft Word, and then use the converter to save the document as an HTML file. Converters free you from the laborious task of typing HTML code, and because the conversion is automated, you do not have to worry about introducing coding errors in your document. However, HTML code created using a converter is often longer and more complicated than it needs to be, resulting in larger-than-necessary files. Also, it is more difficult to edit HTML code directly in a file created by a converter.

An **HTML editor** helps you create an HTML file by inserting HTML codes for you as you work. HTML editors can save you a lot of time and can help you work more efficiently. Their advantages and limitations are similar to those of HTML converters. In addition, while HTML editors allow you to set up a Web page quickly, you will usually still have to work directly with the HTML code to create a finished document.

In the next session, you'll start creating your first HTML document using a simple text editor.

Session 1.1 Quick Check

1. What is a hypertext document?
2. What is a Web server? A Web browser? Describe how they work together.
3. What is HTML?
4. How do HTML documents differ from documents created with a word processor such as Word or WordPerfect?
5. What is a deprecated feature?
6. What are HTML extensions? What are some advantages and disadvantages of using extensions?
7. What software program do you need to create an HTML document?

Session 1.2

Creating an HTML Document

It's always a good idea to plan out a Web page before you start coding. You can do this by drawing a planning sketch or by creating a sample document using a word processor. The preparatory work can weed out errors or point to potential problems. In this case, the chemistry teacher, Stephen Dubé, has already drawn up a handout that he's used for many years with his students and their parents. The handout lists his classes and describes his class policies regarding homework, exams, and behavior. Figure 1-5 shows the current handout that Stephen is using.

Figure 1-5 The chemistry class handout

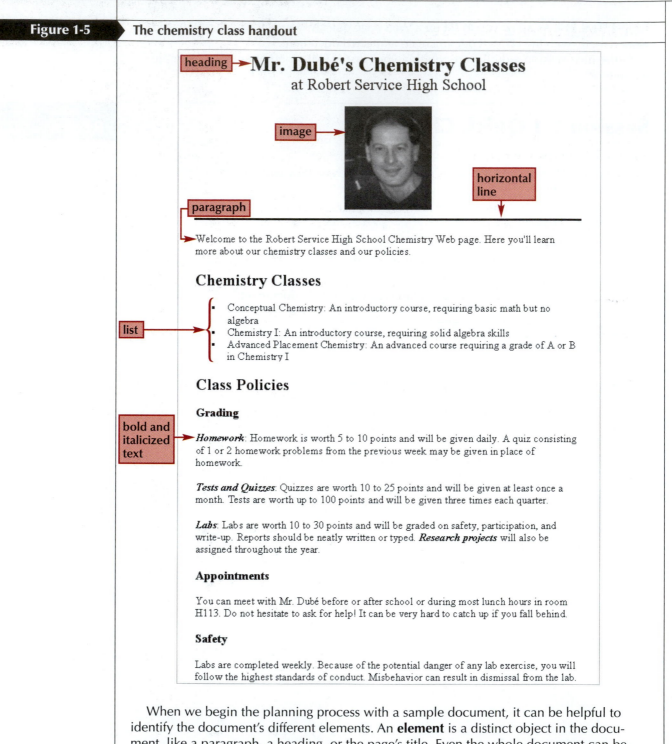

When we begin the planning process with a sample document, it can be helpful to identify the document's different elements. An **element** is a distinct object in the document, like a paragraph, a heading, or the page's title. Even the whole document can be considered an element. Stephen's handout includes several elements. A heading prominently displays his name, and beneath the heading, the document contains a photo and a horizontal line. The handout includes a brief introductory paragraph followed by two main sections: Chemistry Classes and Class Policies. The Chemistry Classes section lists the three classes he teaches. In the Class Policies section, three smaller headings list and describe his policies on Grading, Appointments, and Safety. We also want to take note of formatting features, such as text displayed in **boldfaced** font, and *italicized* text. As you recreate Stephen's handout as a Web page, you should periodically refer to Figure 1-5.

Marking Elements with Tags

The core building block of HTML is the **tag**, which marks each element in a document. Tags can be either two-sided or one-sided. A **two-sided tag** is a tag that contains some document content. The general syntax for a two-sided tag is:

```
<element>content</element>
```

where *element* is the name of the HTML element and *content* is any content it contains. For example, the following code marks the text, "Robert Service High School", with the <p> tag:

```
<p>Robert Service High School</p>
```

As you'll learn later, this indicates that a browser should treat "Robert Service High School" as a paragraph element.

In this book, the term "element" refers to an object in a Web page, and "tag" refers to the HTML code that creates the object. Thus we would say that we can create a p element in a Web page by inserting a <p> tag into the HTML file.

A two-sided tag's **opening tag** (<p>) and **closing tag** (</p>) should completely enclose its content. Earlier versions of HTML allowed designers to omit a closing tag if the surrounding code clearly indicated the tag's content, but this practice is no longer recommended. XHTML requires both an opening and closing tag.

HTML allows you to enter element names in either uppercase or lowercase letters. Thus you can type either <p> or <P> to indicate a paragraph. However, since XHTML strictly requires lowercase tag names, we will follow that convention here, and strongly recommend that you do likewise so that your Web pages will be consistent with current and future standards.

Unlike a two-sided tag, a **one-sided tag** contains no content. The general syntax for a one-sided tag is.

```
<element />
```

where *element* is once again the element name. HTML also allows you to enter one-sided tags using the syntax *<element>* (omitting the space and closing slash). However, XHTML does not support this form, so we once again strongly recommend that you include the space and the closing slash at all times. Elements that employ one-sided tags are called **empty elements** since they contain no content. One example of an empty element is a line break, which forces the browser to display the next set of characters on a new line. To create a line break you would use the one-sided tag:

```
<br />
```

Reference Window

Unless a Reference Window item is labeled "Deprecated," it is compliant with XHTML 1.0 standards.

Inserting Two-Sided and One-Sided Tags

- To create a two-sided tag, use the syntax:
  ```
  <element>content</element>
  ```
  where *element* is the name of the HTML and *content* is any content it contains. Element names should be lowercase.
- To create a one-sided tag, use the syntax:
  ```
  <element />
  ```

Deprecated

- Many browsers also accept one-sided tags written as:
  ```
  <element>
  ```
  This syntax is not recommend because it is not supported by XHTML and will probably not be supported by future browsers.
- Some browsers allow uppercase element names. This technique is not recommended because it is not supported by XHTML and probably not by future browsers.

A third type of tag is the **comment tag**, which you can use to add notes to your HTML code. While comments are not required and are not displayed or used by the Web browser, they are useful in documenting your HTML code for yourself and others. The syntax of the comment tag is:

```
<!-- comment -->
```

where *comment* is the text of your note. The following is an example of a comment tag that could describe the page you'll be creating for Stephen Dubé:

```
<!-- Chemistry page created for Robert Service High School -->
```

A comment can also be spread over several lines as follows:

```
<!-- Chemistry Class Web Page
     Created for Robert Service High School
-->
```

Reference Window

Inserting a Comment

- To insert a comment anywhere within your HTML file, enter:
  ```
  <!-- comment -->
  ```
  where *comment* is the text of your comment. Comments can extend over several lines.

White Space and HTML

The ability to extend a comment over several lines is not unique to the comment tag. You can do this with any tag. As simple text files, HTML documents are composed of text characters and **white space**—the blank spaces, tabs and line breaks within the file. HTML treats each occurrence of white space as a single blank space. Thus, as far as HTML is concerned, there is no difference between a blank space, a tab, or a line break. When a browser encounters consecutive occurrences of white space, it collapses them into a single occurrence. The following code samples are equivalent as far as HTML is concerned:

```
<p>This is an example of White Space</p>
<p>This is an example  of    White     Space</p>
<p>This is an example
   of    White
   Space</p>
```

Even though browsers ignore extra white space, you can use it to make your HTML documents more readable—for example, by indenting lines or by separating blocks of code from one another.

Element Attributes

Many tags contain **attributes** that control the behavior, and in some cases the appearance, of elements in the page. You insert attributes within the tag brackets using the syntax

```
<element attribute1="value1" attribute2="value2" .../>
```

for one-sided tags, and the syntax

```
<element attribute1="value1" attribute2="value2" ...>content</element>
```

for two-sided tags, where *attribute1*, *attribute2*, and so forth are the names of the attributes, and *value1*, *value2*, etc. are the values associated with those attributes. For example, you can identify an individual element using the id attribute. The following code assigns the id value of "title" to the paragraph "Robert Service High School", distinguishing it from other paragraphs in the document.

```
<p id="title">Robert Service High School</p>
```

You'll learn more about the id attribute in the next tutorial.

You can list attributes in any order, but you must separate them from one another with white space. As with element names, you should enter attribute names in lowercase letters. In addition, you should enclose attribute values within quotation marks. While many browsers still accept attribute values without quotation marks, you can ensure maximum compatibility by always including them. XHTML requires quotation marks for all attribute values.

Inserting Attributes

Reference Window

- To add attributes to an element, insert the following into the element's opening tag:
  `attribute1="value1" attribute2="value2"`
  where *attribute1*, *attribute2*, and so forth are the names of the attributes, and *value1*, *value2*, etc. are the values associated with each attribute.

Deprecated

- Some browsers accept attributes without quotation marks, as well as attribute names in uppercase. This syntax is not recommended because it is not supported by XHTML or will probably not be supported by future browsers.

The Structure of an HTML File

Now that we've studied the general syntax of HTML tags, we'll create our first HTML document. The most fundamental element is the HTML document itself. We mark this element using the two-sided <html> tag as follows:

```
<html>
</html>
```

The opening <html> tag marks the start of an HTML document, and the closing </html> tag tells a browser when it has reached the end of that HTML document. Anything between these two tags makes up the content of the document, including all other elements, text, and comments.

An HTML document is divided into two sections: the head and the body. The **head element** contains information about the document—for example, the document's title, or keywords that a search engine on the Web might use to identify this document for other users. The content of the head element is not displayed within the Web page, but Web browsers may use it in other ways; for example, Web browsers usually display a document's title in the title bar.

The **body element** contains all of the content to be displayed in the Web page. It can also contain code that tells the browser how to render that content.

To mark the head and body elements, you use the <head> and <body> tags as follows:

```
<html>

<head>
</head>

<body>
</body>

</html>
```

Note that the body element is placed after the head element.

The first thing we'll add to the document's head is the page title, also know as the **title element**. A given document can include only one title element. You create a title by inserting the two-sided <title> tag within the document's head. Since Stephen wants to give his page the title, "Mr. Dube's Chemistry Classes", our HTML code now looks like this:

```
<html>

<head>
<title>Mr. Dube's Chemistry Classes</title>
</head>

<body>
</body>

</html>
```

The technique of placing one element within another is called **nesting**. When one element contains another, you must close the inside element before closing the outside element, as shown in the code above. It would *not* be correct to close the outside element before closing the inside one, as in the following code sample:

```
<head><title>Mr. Dube's Chemistry Classes</head></title>
```

Now that you've seen how to insert HTML tags, let's start creating the chemistry Web page. In addition to the above code, we'll also add a comment that specifies the page's purpose and author, as well as the current date.

To create an HTML file:

1. Ensure that you can access your data files from your file server, CD-ROM, or floppy disk drive.

   Trouble? If you don't have access to your data files, talk to your instructor. See the Read This Before You Begin page at the beginning of the tutorials for further instructions.

2. Create a new document with a text editor.

   If you don't know how to locate, start, or use the text editor on your system, ask your instructor or technical support person for help.

3. Type the following lines of code in your document. Press the **Enter** key after each line. Press the **Enter** key twice for a blank line between lines of code. Insert your name in place of the text *your name* and the current date in place of *the date*.

   ```
   <html>

   <head>
   <!-- Chemistry Classes Web Page
        Author: your name
        Date:   the date
   -->
   <title>Mr. Dube's Chemistry Classes</title>
   </head>

   <body>
   </body>

   </html>
   ```

4. Using your text editor, save the file as **chem.htm** in the tutorial.01/tutorial folder where your Data Files are stored, but do not close your text editor. The text you typed should look similar to the text displayed in Figure 1-6.

Initial HTML code in chem.htm | **Figure 1-6**

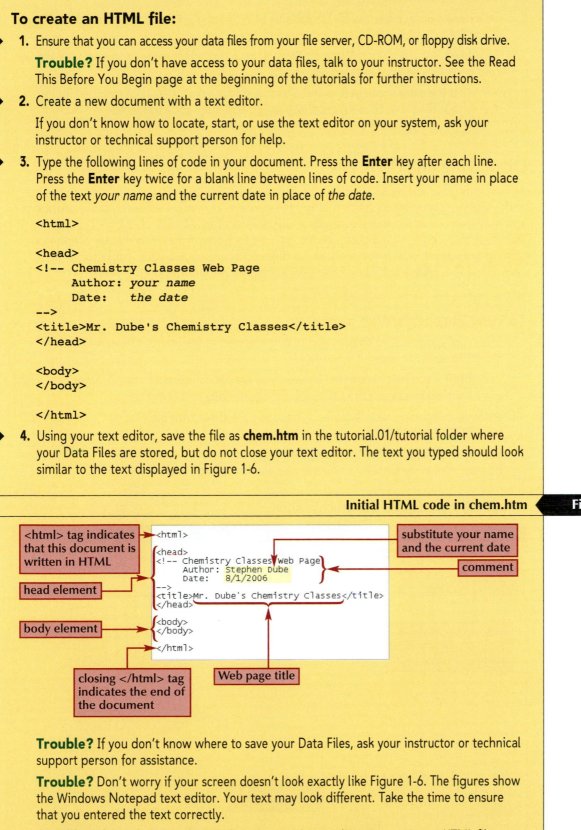

<html> tag indicates that this document is written in HTML

head element

body element

closing </html> tag indicates the end of the document

Web page title

substitute your name and the current date

comment

Trouble? If you don't know where to save your Data Files, ask your instructor or technical support person for assistance.

Trouble? Don't worry if your screen doesn't look exactly like Figure 1-6. The figures show the Windows Notepad text editor. Your text may look different. Take the time to ensure that you entered the text correctly.

Trouble? If you are using the Windows Notepad text editor to create your HTML file, make sure you don't save the file with the extension .txt, which is the default for Notepad. Instead, make sure you save the file with the file extension .htm or .html. Using an invalid file extension may make the file unreadable to Web browsers, which require .htm or .html as the file extension.

Trouble? If you are using Microsoft Word as your text editor, be sure to save your files as Web page files and not as Word documents.

Note that the extra space before and after the <body> tags is also not required, but it makes your file easier to read, especially as you add more code to the file.

Displaying an HTML File

As you continue adding to Stephen's Web page, you should occasionally view the page with your Web browser to verify that the file contains no syntax errors or other problems. You may even want to view the results using different browsers to check for compatibility. The steps and figures that follow use the Internet Explorer browser to display Stephen's page as you develop it. If you are using a different browser, ask your instructor how to view local files (those stored on your own computer rather than on the Web).

To view Stephen's Web page:

1. Start your browser. You do not need to be connected to the Internet to view local files stored on your computer.

   Trouble? If you try to start your browser and are not connected to the Internet, you might get a warning message. Click OK to ignore the message and continue.

2. After your browser loads its home page, open the **chem.htm** file that you saved in the tutorial.01/tutorial folder.

   Your browser displays the chemistry Web page, as shown in Figure 1-7. Note that the page title appears in the browser's title bar and not on the page itself.

Figure 1-7 **Initial Web page viewed in Internet Explorer**

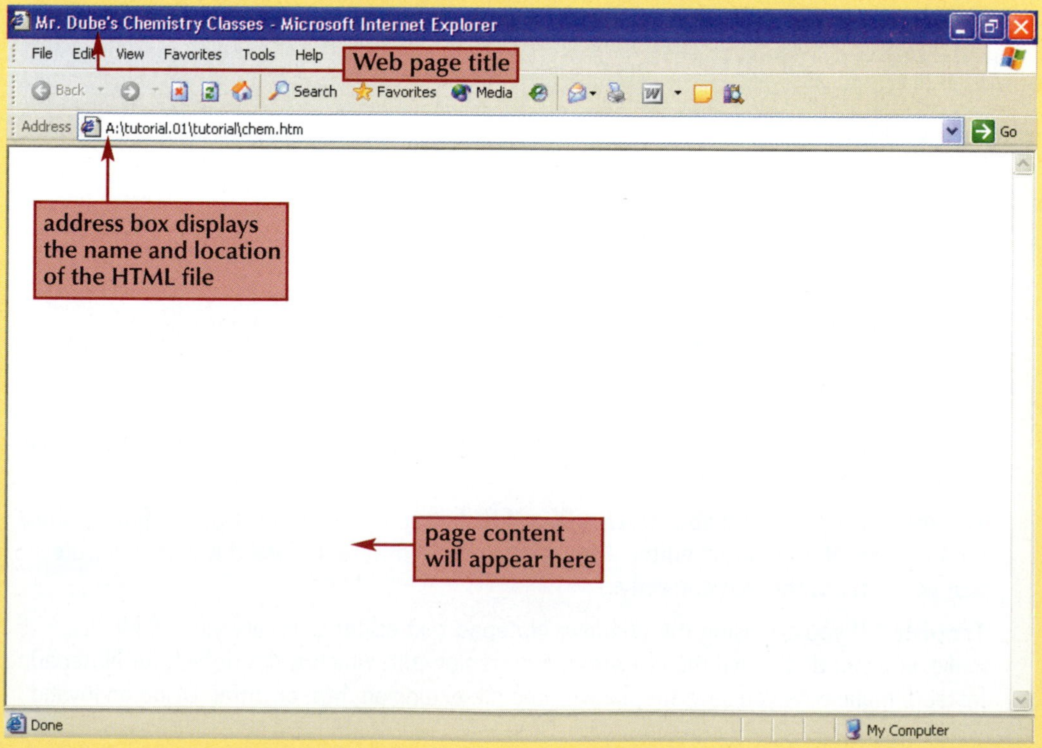

Mr. Dube's Chemistry Classes - Microsoft Internet Explorer

Web page title

Address A:\tutorial.01\tutorial\chem.htm

address box displays the name and location of the HTML file

page content will appear here

Trouble? To open a file in most browsers, click File on the menu bar, click Open, and click the Browse button to locate the file.

Trouble? Depending on the browser you're using, you may have to use a different command to open the file from your Data Files. Talk to your instructor or technical support person to find out how to open the file.

Trouble? If your browser displays something different, compare the code in your file to the code shown in Figure 1-6 and correct any errors. Save your changes, then return to your browser and click the Refresh or Reload button to view the new version of your Web page. So far, you have only entered a title for the Web page, which is why the main content area of the Web page is blank.

Working with Block-Level Elements

Now that you have created the basic structure of your document, you can start inserting the page's content. In a Web page, most content is marked as either a block-level element or an inline element. A **block-level element** contains content displayed in a separate section within the page, setting it off from other blocks. Paragraphs and headings are examples of block-level elements. An **inline element** is part of the same block as its surrounding content—for example, individual words or phrases within a paragraph.

Stephen's Web page includes several block-level elements. You will start adding page content by inserting the headings. You need to create a heading for the entire page and headings for each of two sections: Chemistry Classes and Class Policies. The Class Policies section includes three additional subheadings: Grading, Appointments, and Safety. You can mark all of these headings with HTML heading tags.

Creating Headings

HTML supports six heading elements, numbered h1 through h6. The h1 heading is reserved for the largest and most prominent headings, while the h6 element indicates a minor heading. The syntax for inserting a heading element is

```
<hy>content</hy>
```

where y is a heading number 1 through 6 and *content* is the content of the heading.

Figure 1-8 illustrates the general appearance of the six heading elements. Your browser might use slightly different fonts and sizes.

Figure 1-8 | **HTML headings**

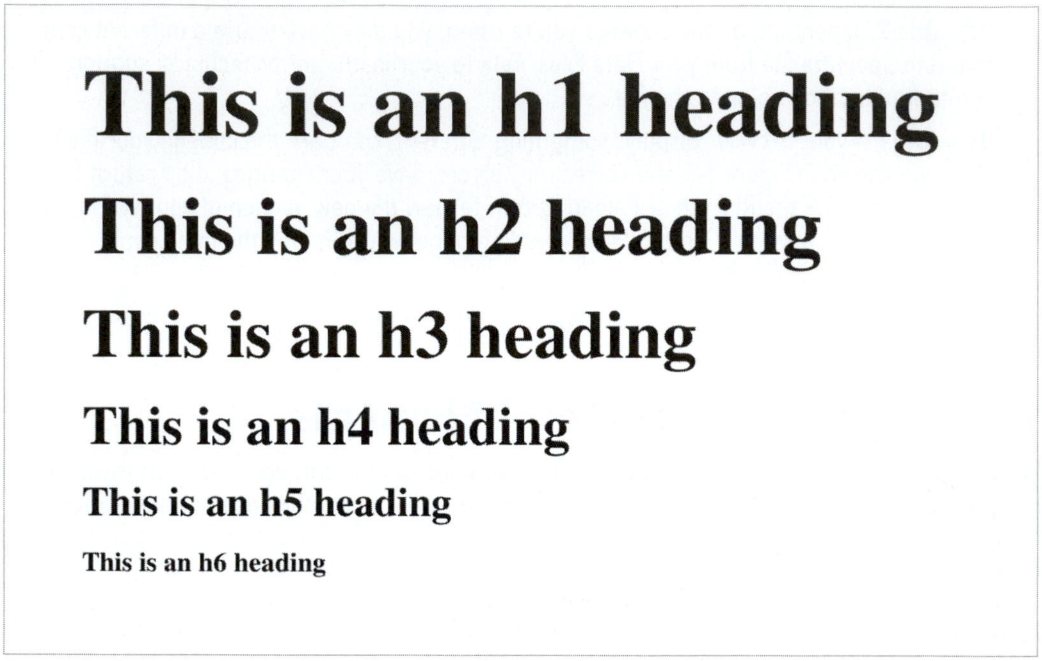

> # This is an h1 heading
>
> ## This is an h2 heading
>
> ### This is an h3 heading
>
> #### This is an h4 heading
>
> ##### This is an h5 heading
>
> ###### This is an h6 heading

Reference Window | **Inserting a Heading**

- To define a heading, use the syntax
  ```
  <hy>content</hy>
  ```
  where *y* is a heading number 1 through 6, and *content* is the content of the heading.

Inserting an Inline Style

By default, the contents of a heading are aligned with the left margin of the page. You notice that some of the headings in Stephen's handout are centered. To use styles to control the appearance of an element, such as text alignment, you use the style attribute. The syntax for inserting the style attribute into an HTML tag is

```
<element style="style1: value1; style2: value2; style3: value3; …">
```

where *element* is the element's name, *style1*, *style2*, *style3* and so forth are the names of styles, and *value1*, *value2*, *value3* and so on are the values associated with those styles. Styles specified as attributes in a tag are also referred to as **inline styles**. As you proceed in your study of HTML, you'll learn more about different styles and the many ways to apply them. For now, we'll focus on the text-align style.

Reference Window | **Inserting an Inline Style**

- To add an inline style to an element, insert the following attribute into the element's tag:
  ```
  style="style1: value1; style2: value2; style3: value3; …"
  ```
  where *style1*, *style2*, *style3*, and so forth are the names of the styles, and *value1*, *value2*, *value3*, etc. are the values associated with those styles.

Applying the Text-Align Style

The text-align style tells the browser how to horizontally align the contents of an element. The style has four values: left, right, center, and justify; the value "justify" tells a browser to spread the content to touch both the left and right margins of the element. To display the text "Chemistry Class" as a centered h1 heading, you would use the following code:

```
<h1 style="text-align: center">Chemistry Class</h1>
```

Most browsers also support the align attribute. Thus, you could also write

```
<h1 align="center">Chemistry Class</h1>
```

However, because the align attribute is a deprecated feature of HTML, you should probably not use it unless you need to provide backward-compatibility with older browsers. HTML attributes such as the align attribute are known as **presentational attributes**, meaning that they specify exactly how the browser should render an element. Remember that one of the goals of HTML is to separate content from design. HTML should inform the browser about the content of the document, but you should use styles to inform the browser how to render that content. For this reason, almost all presentational attributes have been deprecated in favor of styles.

Reference Window

Aligning the Contents of an Element

- To horizontally align the contents of an element, use the style:
  ```
  text-align: align
  ```
  where *align* is left, right, center, or justify.

Deprecated

- You can also align the contents of an element by adding the following attribute to the element's tag:
  ```
  align="align"
  ```
  where *align* is left, right, center, or justify. Not all elements support the align attribute. It is often used with paragraphs and headings.

To add headings to the chemistry file:

1. Using your text editor, open **chem.htm**, if it is not currently open.
2. Place the insertion point after the <body> tag, press the **Enter** key to move to the next line, and then type the following lines of code:

```
<h1 style="text-align: center">Mr. Dube's Chemistry Classes</h1>
<h2 style="text-align: center">at Robert Service High School</h2>
<h2>Chemistry Classes</h2>
<h2>Class Policies</h2>
<h3>Grading</h3>
<h3>Appointments</h3>
<h3>Safety</h3>
```

Figure 1-9 displays the revised code. To make it easier for you to follow the changes to the HTML file, new and modified text in the figures is highlighted in red. This will not be the case in your own text files.

Figure 1-9 | Entering heading elements

```
<html>

<head>
<!-- Chemistry Classes Web Page
     Author: Stephen Dube
     Date:    8/1/2006
-->
<title>Mr. Dube's Chemistry Classes</title>
</head>

<body>
<h1 style="text-align: center">Mr. Dube's Chemistry Classes</h1>
<h2 style="text-align: center">at Robert Service High School</h2>
<h2>Chemistry Classes</h2>
<h2>Class Policies</h2>
<h3>Grading</h3>
<h3>Appointments</h3>
<h3>Safety</h3>
</body>

</html>
```

centered headings

3. Save your changes to **chem.htm**. You can leave your text editor open.

Now view the revised page in your Web browser.

To display the revised version of the chemistry page:

1. Return to your Web browser. Note that the previous version of chem.htm probably appears in the browser window.

2. To view the revised page, click **View** on the menu bar, and then click **Refresh**. If you are using a Netscape browser, you will need to click **View** and then click **Reload**.

   Trouble? If you closed the browser or the file in the last set of steps, reopen your browser and the chem.htm file.

   The updated Web page looks like Figure 1-10.

Figure 1-10 | Headings as they appear in the browser

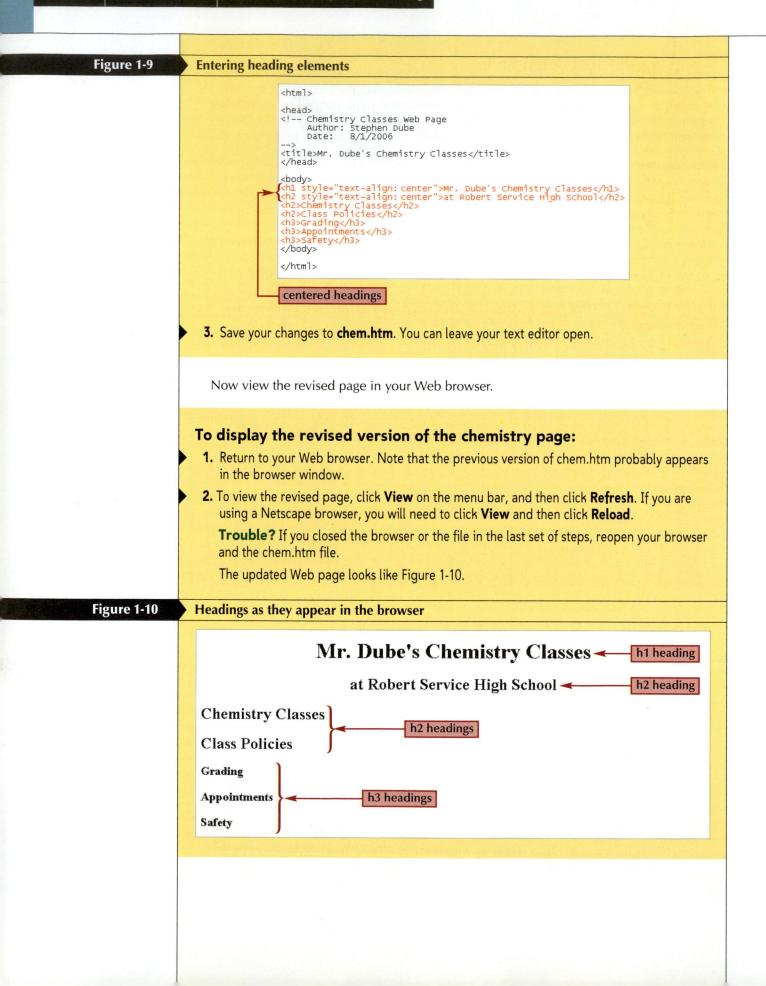

Creating Paragraphs

The next step is to enter text information for each section. As you saw earlier, you can insert a paragraph element using the <p> tag as follows:

<p>*content*</p>

where *content* is the content of the paragraph. When a browser encounters the opening <p> tag, it starts a new line with a blank space above it, separating the new paragraph from the preceding element. In earlier versions of HTML when standards were not firmly fixed, Web authors would often include only the opening <p> tag, omitting the closing tag entirely. While many browsers still allow this, your Web pages display more reliably if you consistently use the closing tag. Additionally, if you wish to write XHTML-compliant code then you must include the closing tag.

Reference Window

Creating a Paragraph

- To create a paragraph, use the syntax:
  <p>*content*</p>
  where *content* is the content of the paragraph.

To enter paragraph text:

1. Return to **chem.htm** in your text editor.

2. Place the insertion point at the end of the line that creates the h2 heading, "at Robert Service High School", and press the **Enter** key to create a blank line.

3. Type the following text:

<p>Welcome to the Robert Service High School Chemistry Web page.
Here you'll learn more about our chemistry classes and our policies.</p>

4. Press the **Enter** key to insert a blank line below the paragraph.

   Note that a blank line is not required for the text to display correctly in your browser. However, adding this space makes it easier for you to read the code by separating the first paragraph from the heading that follows. See Figure 1-11.

Inserting the first paragraph **Figure 1-11**

```
<body>
<h1 style="text-align: center">Mr. Dube's Chemistry Classes</h1>
<h2 style="text-align: center">at Robert Service High School</h2>
<p>Welcome to the Robert Service High School Chemistry Web page.
   Here you'll learn more about our chemistry classes and our
   policies.</p>

<h2>Chemistry Classes</h2>
<h2>Class Policies</h2>
<h3>Grading</h3>
<h3>Appointments</h3>
<h3>Safety</h3>
</body>
```

paragraph

5. Save your changes to **chem.htm**.

6. Using your Web browser, refresh or reload **chem.htm** to view the new paragraph. See Figure 1-12.

Figure 1-12 | **First paragraph in the browser**

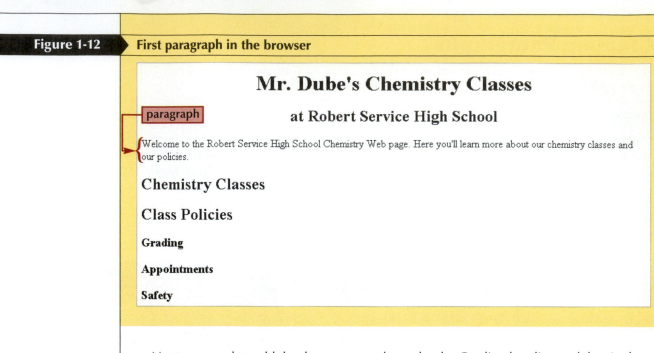

Next you need to add the three paragraphs under the Grading heading and the single paragraphs under both Appointments and Safety.

To enter the remaining paragraphs:

1. Return to the **chem.htm** file in your text editor.

2. Below the h3 heading "Grading," insert the following three paragraphs:

   ```
   <p>Homework: Homework is worth 5 to 10 points and will be given
   daily. A quiz consisting of 1 or 2 homework problems from the
   previous week may be given in place of homework.</p>

   <p>Tests and Quizzes: Quizzes are worth 10 to 25 points and will be
   given at least once a month. Tests are worth up to 100 points and
   will be given three times each quarter.</p>

   <p>Labs: Labs are worth 10 to 30 points and will be graded on
   safety, participation, and write-up. Reports should be neatly
   written or typed. Research projects will also be assigned throughout
   the year.</p>
   ```

   Note that because of how HTML handles white space, you can insert additional blank lines between the paragraphs or line breaks within paragraphs to make your code easier to read. This does not affect how a browser renders the paragraphs.

3. Below the h3 heading "Appointments," insert the following paragraph:

   ```
   <p>You can meet with Mr. Dube before or after school or during most
   lunch hours in room H113. Do not hesitate to ask for help! It can be
   very hard to catch up if you fall behind.</p>
   ```

4. Below the h3 heading " Safety," insert the following paragraph:

   ```
   <p>Labs are completed weekly. Because of the potential danger of any
   lab exercise, you will follow the highest standards of conduct.
   Misbehavior can result in dismissal from the lab.</p>
   ```

   Figure 1-13 shows the new code in the chem.htm file.

```
<h2>Chemistry Classes</h2>
<h2>Class Policies</h2>
<h3>Grading</h3>
<p>Homework: Homework is worth 5 to 10 points and will be given
daily. A quiz consisting of 1 or 2 homework problems from the
previous week may be given in place of homework.</p>

<p>Tests and Quizzes: Quizzes are worth 10 to 25 points and will be
given at least once a month. Tests are worth up to 100 points and
will be given three times each quarter.</p>

<p>Labs: Labs are worth 10 to 30 points and will be graded on safety,
participation, and write-up. Reports should be neatly written or
typed. Research projects will also be assigned throughout the
year.</p>

<h3>Appointments</h3>
<p>You can meet with Mr. Dube before or after school or during most
lunch hours in room H113. Do not hesitate to ask for help! It can be
very hard to catch up if you fall behind.</p>

<h3>Safety</h3>
<p>Labs are completed weekly. Because of the potential danger of any
lab exercise, you will follow the highest standards of conduct.
Misbehavior can result in dismissal from the lab.</p>

</body>
```

5. Save your changes to the file.

6. Return to your Web browser and refresh or reload **chem.htm** to view the new paragraphs. Figure 1-14 displays the revised version.

Mr. Dube's Chemistry Classes

at Robert Service High School

Welcome to the Robert Service High School Chemistry Web page. Here you'll learn more about our chemistry classes and our policies.

Chemistry Classes

Class Policies

Grading

Homework: Homework is worth 5 to 10 points and will be given daily. A quiz consisting of 1 or 2 homework problems from the previous week may be given in place of homework.

Tests and Quizzes: Quizzes are worth 10 to 25 points and will be given at least once a month. Tests are worth up to 100 points and will be given three times each quarter.

Labs: Labs are worth 10 to 30 points and will be graded on safety, participation, and write-up. Reports should be neatly written or typed. Research projects will also be assigned throughout the year.

Appointments

You can meet with Mr. Dube before or after school or during most lunch hours in room H113. Do not hesitate to ask for help! It can be very hard to catch up if you fall behind.

Safety

Labs are completed weekly. Because of the potential danger of any lab exercise, you will follow the highest standards of conduct. Misbehavior can result in dismissal from the lab.

Creating Lists

You still need to describe the three chemistry courses that the school offers. Rather than entering these in paragraph form, you'll use a list. HTML supports three kinds of lists: ordered, unordered, and definition.

Creating an Ordered List

You use an **ordered list** for items that must appear in a particular sequential order. You create an ordered list using the ol element in the following form:

```
<ol>
    <li>item1</li>
    <li>item2</li>
...
</ol>
```

where *item1*, *item2*, etc, are items in the list. Each <li> tag marks the content for a single list item. For example, if Stephen wants to list the three chemistry classes from the least difficult to the most difficult, the HTML code could look as follows:

```
<ol>
    <li>Conceptual Chemistry</li>
    <li>Chemistry I</li>
    <li>Advanced Placement Chemistry</li>
</ol>
```

By default, browsers display ordered lists as a series of sequentially numbered items. Based on the preceding HTML code, Stephen's list would appear in the following form:

1. Conceptual Chemistry
2. Chemistry I
3. Advanced Placement Chemistry

Reference Window

Creating an Ordered List

- To create an ordered list, use the syntax:
  ```
  <ol>
      <li>item1</li>
      <li>item2</li>
      ...
  </ol>
  ```
  where *item1*, *item2*, etc. are items in the list.

Creating an Unordered List

To display a list in which the items do not need to occur in any special order, you would create an **unordered list**. The structures of ordered and unordered lists are the same, except that the contents of an unordered list are contained within a <ul> tag:

```
<ul>
    <li>item1</li>
    <li>item2</li>
    ...
</ul>
```

By default, the contents of an unordered list are displayed as bulleted items. Thus, the code

```
<ul>
   <li>Introductory course</li>
   <li>No algebra required</li>
</ul>
```

would be displayed by a browser as

- Introductory course
- No algebra required

Creating an Unordered List

- To create an unordered list, use the syntax:
  ```
  <ul>
      <li>item1</li>
      <li>item2</li>
      ...
  </ul>
  ```
  where *item1*, *item2*, etc. are items in the list.

Creating a Nested List

One list can contain another. For example, it can sometimes be useful to combine two different types of lists, as in the following example:

1 Conceptual Chemistry

- Introductory course
- No algebra required

2 Chemistry I

- Introductory course
- Algebra required

3 Advanced Placement Chemistry

- Advanced course
- Requires an A or B in Chemistry I

You could create the preceding combination of ordered and unordered lists using the following HTML code:

```
<ol>
   <li>Conceptual Chemistry
      <ul>
         <li>Introductory course</li>
         <li>No algebra required</li>
      </ul>
   </li>
   <li>Chemistry I
      <ul>
         <li>Introductory course</li>
         <li>Algebra required</li>
      </ul>
   </li>
```

```
    <li>Advanced Placement Chemistry
       <ul>
           <li>Advanced course</li>
           <li>Requires an A or B in Chemistry I</li>
       </ul>
    </li>
</ol>
```

Note that some of the list items in this code contain lists themselves.

Applying a Style to a List

If you don't want your list items marked with either numbers or bullets, you can specify a different marker by applying the following style to either the ordered or unordered list:

```
list-style-type: type
```

where `type` is one of the markers listed in Figure 1-15.

Figure 1-15 ▶ **List style types**

List-Style-Type	Marker (s)
disc	•
circle	○
square	■
decimal	1, 2, 3, 4, …
decimal-leading-zero	01, 02, 03, 04, …
lower-roman	i, ii, iii, iv, …
upper-roman	I, II, III, IV, …
lower-alpha	a, b, c, d, …
upper-alpha	A, B, C, D, …
none	*no marker displayed*

For example, to create the following list:

   a. Conceptual Chemistry
   b. Chemistry I
   c. Advanced Placement Chemistry

you would enter the HTML code:

```
<ol style="list-style-type: lower-alpha">
   <li>Conceptual Chemistry</li>
   <li>Chemistry I</li>
   <li>Advanced Placement Chemistry</li>
</ol>
```

You can also substitute a graphic image for a list marker by using the style:

```
list-style-image: url(file)
```

where `file` is the name of an image file containing the marker. Figure 1-16 demonstrates how to use a graphic image named "flask.jpg" as a marker in a list.

Using a graphic list marker ▷ **Figure 1-16**

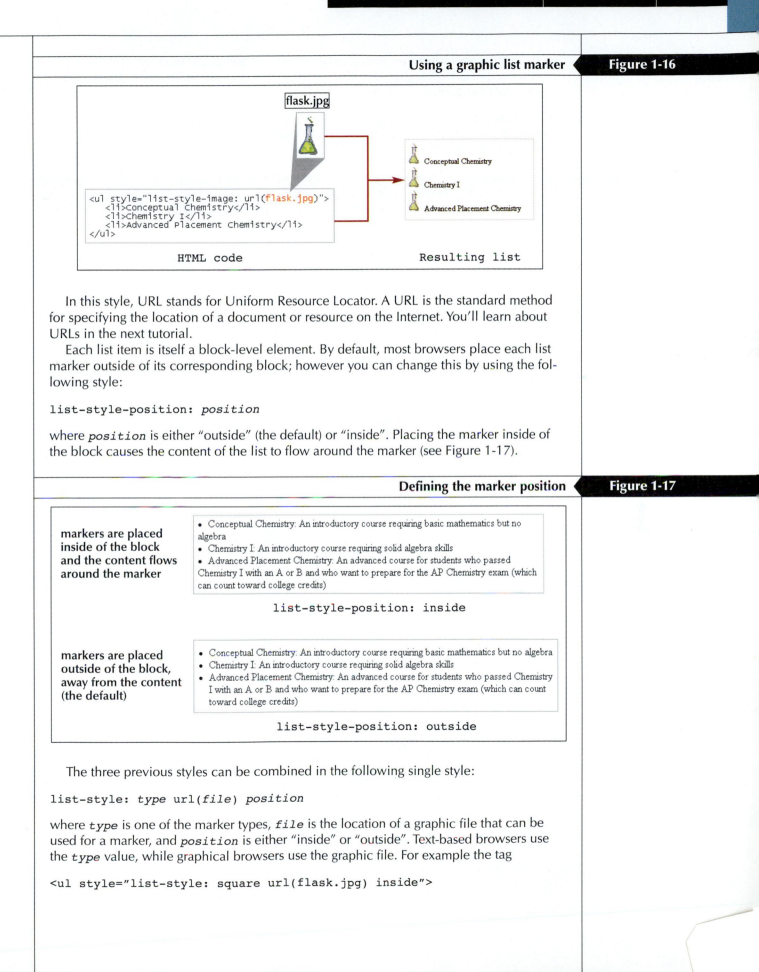

In this style, URL stands for Uniform Resource Locator. A URL is the standard method for specifying the location of a document or resource on the Internet. You'll learn about URLs in the next tutorial.

Each list item is itself a block-level element. By default, most browsers place each list marker outside of its corresponding block; however you can change this by using the following style:

```
list-style-position: position
```

where *position* is either "outside" (the default) or "inside". Placing the marker inside of the block causes the content of the list to flow around the marker (see Figure 1-17).

Defining the marker position ▷ **Figure 1-17**

markers are placed inside of the block and the content flows around the marker	• Conceptual Chemistry: An introductory course requiring basic mathematics but no algebra • Chemistry I: An introductory course requiring solid algebra skills • Advanced Placement Chemistry: An advanced course for students who passed Chemistry I with an A or B and who want to prepare for the AP Chemistry exam (which can count toward college credits)

```
list-style-position: inside
```

markers are placed outside of the block, away from the content (the default)	• Conceptual Chemistry: An introductory course requiring basic mathematics but no algebra • Chemistry I: An introductory course requiring solid algebra skills • Advanced Placement Chemistry: An advanced course for students who passed Chemistry I with an A or B and who want to prepare for the AP Chemistry exam (which can count toward college credits)

```
list-style-position: outside
```

The three previous styles can be combined in the following single style:

```
list-style: type url(file) position
```

where *type* is one of the marker types, *file* is the location of a graphic file that can be used for a marker, and *position* is either "inside" or "outside". Text-based browsers use the *type* value, while graphical browsers use the graphic file. For example the tag

```
<ul style="list-style: square url(flask.jpg) inside">
```

would create an unordered list with a square marker for text-based browsers and the flask.jpg image marker for graphical browsers. Whichever marker a browser uses appears inside of each list item.

For older browsers that don't support inline styles, you can use one of the presentational attributes that HTML provides for ordered and unordered lists. See the accompanying reference window for details.

Reference Window

Formatting a List

- To change the list marker, use the style:
  ```
  list-style-type: type
  ```
  where *type* is disc, circle, square, decimal, decimal-leading-zero, lower-roman, upper-roman, lower-alpha, upper-alpha, or none.
- To use a graphic image in place of a marker, use the style:
  ```
  list-style-image: url(file)
  ```
  where *file* is the name of the image file.
- To specify the location of the list marker, use the style:
  ```
  list-style-position: position
  ```
  where *position* is either inside or outside.

Deprecated

- You can also change the list marker by adding the following attribute to the <ol> or <ul> tag:
  ```
  type="type"
  ```
  For unordered lists, the *type* value can be circle, square, or disc. For ordered lists, *type* values are a (for lower-alpha), A (for upper-alpha), i (for lower-roman), I (for upper-roman), and 1 (for numeric).
- For ordered lists, you can specify the starting number of the first item in the list using the attribute:
  ```
  start="number"
  ```
  where *number* is the starting value. A start number of "2" starts the list with the second marker. For a numeric marker, this is the value '2', while for an alphabetical list, this is the letter "b" or "B".

Creating a Definition List

HTML supports a third list element, the **definition list**, which contains a list of definition terms, each followed by a definition description. The syntax for creating a definition list is:

```
<dl>
      <dt>term1</dt>
      <dd>definition1</dd>
      <dt>term2</dt>
      <dd>definition2</dd>
...
</dl>
```

where *term1*, *term2*, etc. are the terms in the list, and *definition1*, *definition2*, etc. are the definitions of the terms.

If Stephen wanted to create a list of his classes and briefly describe each one, he could use a definition list. The code might look as follows:

```
<dl>
    <dt>Conceptual Chemistry</dt>
    <dd>An introductory course requiring basic mathematics but no
        algebra</dd>
    <dt>Chemistry I</dt>
    <dd>An introductory course requiring solid algebra skills</dd>
    <dt>Advanced Placement Chemistry</dt>
    <dd>An advanced course for students who passed Chemistry I with an A
        or B and who want to prepare for the AP Chemistry exam (which can
        count toward college credits)</dd>
</dl>
```

Web browsers typically display the definition description below the definition term and slightly indented. Most browsers would display the definition list code shown above as:

Conceptual Chemistry
  An introductory course requiring basic mathematics but no algebra
Chemistry I
  An introductory course requiring solid algebra skills
Advanced Placement Chemistry
  An advanced course for students who passed Chemistry I with an A or B and who
  want to prepare for the AP Chemistry exam (which can count toward college credits)

Creating a Definition List

Reference Window

- To create a definition list, use the syntax:
  ```
  <dl>
      <dt>term1</dt>
      <dd>definition1</dd>
      <dt>term2</dt>
      <dd>definition2</dd>

      ...
  </dl>
  ```
  where *term1*, *term2*, etc. are the terms in the list, and *definition1*, *definition2*, etc. are the definitions of the terms.

Now that you've seen how you can use HTML to create different kinds of lists, you'll add an unordered list of classes to the chemistry Web page. You decide to use a square marker for each item. By default, the marker is placed outside of the block.

To add an unordered list to the chemistry page:

1. Return to the **chem.htm** file in your text editor.

2. Below the line "<h2>Chemistry Classes</h2>" insert the following code, as shown in Figure 1-18.

```
<ul style="list-style-type: square">
    <li>Conceptual Chemistry: An introductory course, requiring basic
        math but no algebra</li>
    <li>Chemistry I: An introductory course, requiring solid algebra
        skills</li>
```

```
        <li>Advanced Placement Chemistry: An advanced course requiring a
            grade of A or B in Chemistry I</li>
    </ul>
```

You can indent the lines using either tabs or blank spaces. Remember that indenting has no effect on the appearance of the list in a browser.

Figure 1-18   **Inserting an unordered list**

```
<body>
<h1 style="text-align: center">Mr. Dube's Chemistry Classes</h1>
<h2 style="text-align: center">at Robert Service High School</h2>
<p>Welcome to the Robert Service High School Chemistry Web page.
   Here you'll learn more about our chemistry classes and our
   policies.</p>

<h2>Chemistry Classes</h2>
<ul style="list-style-type: square">
    <li>Conceptual Chemistry: An introductory course, requiring basic
        math but no algebra</li>
    <li>Chemistry I: An introductory course, requiring solid algebra
        skills</li>
    <li>Advanced Placement Chemistry: An advanced course requiring a
        grade of A or B in Chemistry I</li>
</ul>
```

3. Save your changes to the file.

4. Using your Web browser, refresh or reload **chem.htm**. Figure 1-19 shows the latest version of the page.

Figure 1-19   **An unordered list in the browser**

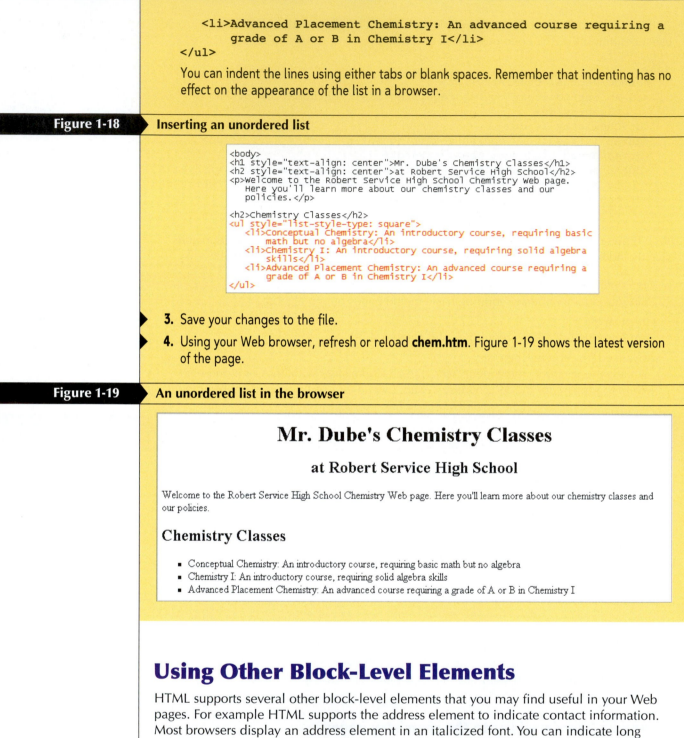

Mr. Dube's Chemistry Classes

at Robert Service High School

Welcome to the Robert Service High School Chemistry Web page. Here you'll learn more about our chemistry classes and our policies.

Chemistry Classes

- Conceptual Chemistry: An introductory course, requiring basic math but no algebra
- Chemistry I: An introductory course, requiring solid algebra skills
- Advanced Placement Chemistry: An advanced course requiring a grade of A or B in Chemistry I

Using Other Block-Level Elements

HTML supports several other block-level elements that you may find useful in your Web pages. For example HTML supports the address element to indicate contact information. Most browsers display an address element in an italicized font. You can indicate long quoted passages by applying the blockquote element. A browser encountering this element typically indents the quoted text. Figure 1-20 describes additional block-level elements and shows how they look in most browsers.

Block Level Element	Description	Visual Appearance
<address> ... </address>	Identifies contact information	*Italicized text*
<blockquote> ... </blockquote>	Identifies a long quotation	Plain text indented from the left and right
<center> ... </center>	Centers content horizontally within a block. **Deprecated**	Plain text, centered
<dd> ... </dd>	Identifies a definition description	Plain text
<dir> ... </dir>	Identifies a multicolumn directory list; superseded by the ul element. **Deprecated**	Plain text
<div> ... </div>	Identifies a generic block-level element	Plain text
<dl> ... </dl>	Identifies a definition list	Plain text
<dt> ... </dt>	Identifies a definition term	Plain text
<hy> ... </hy>	Identifies a heading, where y is a value from 1 to 6	**Boldfaced text of various font sizes**
<li> ... </li>	Identifies a list item in an ordered or unordered list	Bulleted or numbered text
<menu> ... </menu>	Identifies a single column menu list; superseded by the ul element. **Deprecated**	Plain text
<ol> ... </ol>	Identifies an ordered list	Plain text
<p> ... </p>	Identifies a paragraph	Plain text
<pre> ... </pre>	Retains all white space and special characters in preformatted text	`Fixed width text`
<ul> ... </ul>	Identifies an unordered list	Plain text

You'll have a chance to apply some of these other block-level elements in the case problems at the end of the tutorial.

Working with Inline Elements

As you compare your Web page with Figure 1-5, you notice that Stephen's original hand-out contains several words formatted in boldface or italics. In order to apply this formatting to the chemistry Web page, we need to use a set of HTML's inline elements known as **character formatting elements**, which allow us to format text characters. Figure 1-21 describes some character formatting elements that HTML supports.

Figure 1-21	Inline elements

Inline Element	Identifies	Visual Appearance
<abbr> ... </abbr>	an abbreviation	Plain text
<acronym> .. </acronym>	an acronym	Plain text
<b> ... </b>	boldfaced text	**Boldfaced text**
<big> ... </big>	big text	Larger text
<cite> ... </cite>	a citation	*Italicized text*
<code> ... </code>	program code text	`Fixed width text`
<del> ... </del>	deleted text	~~Strikethrough text~~
<dfn> ... </dfn>	a definition term	*Italicized text*
<em> ... </em>	emphasized content	*Italicized text*
<i> ... </i>	italicized text	*Italicized text*
<ins> ... </ins>	inserted text	<u>Underlined text</u>
<kbd> ... </kbd>	keyboard-style text	`Fixed width text`
<q> ... </q>	quoted text	"Quoted text"
<s> ... </s>	strikethrough text. **Deprecated**	~~Strikethrough text~~
<samp> ... </samp>	sample computer code text	`Fixed width text`
<small> ... </small>	small text	Smaller text
<span> ... </span>	a generic inline element	Plain text
<strike> ... </strike>	strikethrough text. **Deprecated**	~~Strikethrough text~~
<strong> ... </strong>	strongly emphasized content	**Boldfaced text**
_{...}	subscripted text	Subscripted $_{text}$
^{...}	superscripted	Superscripted ^{text}
<tt> ... </tt>	teletype text	`Fixed width text`
<u> ... </u>	underlined text. **Deprecated**	<u>Underlined text</u>
<var> ... </var>	programming variables	*Italicized text*

For example, if you wanted to mark a section of boldfaced text within a paragraph, you could enter the following HTML code:

```
<p>Welcome to our <b>Chemistry Classes</b></p>
```

resulting in the following paragraph in the Web page:

Welcome to our **Chemistry Classes**

To mark those same words as italicized text, you would use

```
<p>Welcome to our <i>Chemistry Classes</i></p>
```

If you want the phrase "Chemistry Classes" to be marked as both boldface and italics, you could use the code

```
<p>Welcome to our <b><i>Chemistry Classes</i></b></p>
```

which would be displayed as

Welcome to our ***Chemistry Classes***

Stephen's handout requires the use of character tags only in the Grading section, where he wants to highlight the name of each grading topic. You decide to use a combination of the <b> and <i> tags to display the key words in bold and italics.

To add character tags to the chemistry file:

▶ **1.** Return to the **chem.htm** file in your text editor.

▶ **2.** Type the <i> and <b> tags around the key words in the Grading section of the handout as follows:

```
<p><i><b>Homework</b></i>:Homework is worth …
<p><i><b>Tests and Quizzes</b></i>: Quizzes are worth …
<p><i><b>Labs</b></i>: Labs are worth …
<i><b>Research projects</b></i> will also be assigned …
```

See Figure 1-22.

Inserting boldfaced and italicized text ◀ **Figure 1-22**

```
<h2>Class Policies</h2>
<h3>Grading</h3>
<p><i><b>Homework</b></i>: Homework is worth 5 to 10 points and will be given
daily. A quiz consisting of 1 or 2 homework problems from the
previous week may be given in place of homework.</p>

<p><i><b>Tests and Quizzes</b></i>: Quizzes are worth 10 to 25 points and will be
given at least once a month. Tests are worth up to 100 points and
will be given three times each quarter.</p>

<p><i><b>Labs</b></i>: Labs are worth 10 to 30 points and will be graded on safety,
participation, and write-up. Reports should be neatly written or
typed. <i><b>Research projects</b></i> will also be assigned throughout the
year.</p>
```

▶ **3.** Save your changes to the file.

▶ **4.** Using your Web browser, refresh or reload **chem.htm**. The updated Grading section of your page should look like Figure 1-23.

Displaying boldfaced and italicized text ◀ **Figure 1-23**

Class Policies

Grading

Homework: Homework is worth 5 to 10 points and will be given daily. A quiz consisting of 1 or 2 homework problems from the previous week may be given in place of homework.

Tests and Quizzes: Quizzes are worth 10 to 25 points and will be given at least once a month. Tests are worth up to 100 points and will be given three times each quarter.

Labs: Labs are worth 10 to 30 points and will be graded on safety, participation, and write-up. Reports should be neatly written or typed. *Research projects* will also be assigned throughout the year.

▶ **5.** If you are continuing to Session 1.3, leave your text editor and browser open. Otherwise you can close them at this time.

Understanding Logical and Physical Elements

As you examine the tag list in Figure 1-21, you may notice some overlap in the way the content appears in the browser. For example, if you want to display italicized text you could use the <dfn>, <em>, <i>, or <var> tags, or if you want to italicize an entire block of text, you could use the <address> tag. Why does HTML support so many different ways of formatting text?

While HTML can control the way text appears, the language's main purpose is to create a structure for a document's contents. While some browsers render different elements in the same way, it's important to distinguish between how a browser displays an element and the element's purpose in the document. For this reason, page elements are therefore often organized into two types: logical elements and physical elements. A **logical element**, which might be created with tags like <cite> or <code>, describes the nature of the enclosed content, but not necessarily how that content should appear. A **physical element**, on the other hand, which you might create with tags like <b> or <i>, describes how content should appear but doesn't indicate the content's nature.

While it can be tempting to use logical and physical elements interchangeably, your Web pages benefit in several ways when you respect the distinction. For one, different browsers can and do display logical elements differently. For example, both Netscape's browser and Internet Explorer display text created with the <cite> tag in italics, but the text-based browser Lynx displays citation text using a fixed width font. Some browsers, like those that display Braille or convert HTML code into speech, don't even display formatted text. For example, an aural browser might increase the volume when it encounters emphasized text. In addition, Web programmers can also use logical elements to extract a page's content. For example, a program could automatically generate a bibliography from all of the citations listed within a Web site.

In general, you should use a logical element that accurately describes the enclosed content whenever possible, and use physical elements only for general content.

You have finished inserting the text of the chemistry Web page. In the next session, you will add additional elements to the page, including an image and a graphical line.

Review

Session 1.2 Quick Check

1. What are the two main sections of an HTML file?
2. What are empty elements?
3. What is the syntax for creating a centered heading 1 of the text, "Chemistry Classes"?
4. What is the difference between a block-level element and an inline element?
5. If you want to create an extra blank line between paragraphs, why can't you simply add a blank line in the HTML file?
6. What are presentational attributes? When should you use them?
7. What attribute would you add to the <ol> tag to display uppercase Roman numerals?
8. What attribute would you add to the <ul> tag to display the ball.gif image mark on the inside of the item block?
9. What is the difference between a logical element and a physical element? Which would probably be more appropriate for a non-visual browser, such as a Braille browser?

Session 1.3

Working with Empty Elements

In the last session, you worked exclusively with two-sided tags to create content for the chemistry Web page. Stephen also wants to add images and horizontal lines to the page. To create these objects, you use empty elements. We'll start by inserting a graphic into the Web page.

Inserting a Graphic

To display a graphic, you insert an inline image into the page. An **inline image**, which is another example of an inline element, displays a graphic image located in a separate file within the contents of a block-level element. While a variety of file formats are available for image files, inline images are most widely viewable in two formats: GIF (Graphics Interchange Format) or JPEG (Joint Photographic Experts Group). You can use an image editing application such as Adobe Photoshop to convert images to either the GIF or JPEG file format. To create an inline image, you use the img element as follows:

```
<img src="file" alt="text" />
```

where `file` is the name of the image file and `text` is an alternative text string that browsers can use in place of an image. It's important to include an alt attribute in all of your inline images. Some users run browsers that do not display images, meaning that you need to duplicate with text any information that an image conveys. HTML does not require you to use an alt attribute with your inline images, but XHTML does.

Reference Window

Inserting an inline image

- To insert an inline image, use the tag:
    ```
    <img src="file" alt="text" />
    ```
    where `file` is the name of the image file and `text` is alternative text that browsers can display in place of the image.

If the image file is located in the same folder as the HTML file, you do not need to include any file location path information along with the filename. However, if the image file is located in another folder or on another computer, you need to include the full location path along with the filename in the src attribute. The next tutorial discusses folder paths and filenames in more detail. For now, you can assume that Stephen's image file is located in the same folder that contains the HTML file.

The image file that Stephen wants you to use in place of the page's main heading is named **dube.jpg** and is located in the tutorial.01/tutorial folder on your data disk (see Figure 1-24).

Image for the top of the chemistry page   **Figure 1-24**

Stephen wants you to center the image on the page. Since the img element is an inline element, it does not support an alignment attribute. In order to center it, we need to place it within a block-level element like a paragraph. We can then center the contents of the paragraph, which in this case consists only of the image.

To add Stephen's image to the Web page:

1. If necessary, use your text editor to reopen **chem.htm**.
2. Near the top of the file, select the two lines of code just below the <body> tag (from the <h1> opening tag to the </h2 > closing tag), and then press the **Delete** key. This removes the first two headings from the document.

3. Insert the following code directly below the `<body>` tag (see Figure 1-25):

```
<p style="text-align: center">
   <img src="dube.jpg"
   alt="Mr. Dube's Chemistry Classes at Robert Service High School"
   />
</p>
```

| Figure 1-25 | Inserting an inline image |

source of the inline image

text displayed for non-graphical browsers

```
<body>
<p style="text-align: center">
   <img src="dube.jpg"
   alt="Mr. Dube's Chemistry Classes at Robert Service High School" />
</p>

<p>Welcome to the Robert Service High School Chemistry web page.
   Here you'll learn more about our chemistry classes and our
   policies.</p>
```

4. Save your changes to the file.

5. Open or refresh **chem.htm** in your Web browser. Figure 1-26 shows the placement of the image in the page.

| Figure 1-26 | Displaying an inline image |

inline image

Welcome to the Robert Service High School Chemistry Web page. Here you'll learn more about our chemistry classes and our policies.

Inserting Horizontal Lines

Stephen is pleased with the image's placement on the page. He would like you to add a horizontal line below the image, separating it from the page's text. To create a horizontal line, you use the one-sided tag

```
<hr />
```

To modify the line's size, you can use the styles

```
width: value; height: value
```

where *value* is a size measurement in pixels. A **pixel** is a dot on your computer screen that measures about 1/72" square. You can alternately specify a width value as a percentage of the page's width. The default width is 100% (the width of the Web page) and the default height is 2 pixels.

You can set a line's color using either of the two following styles:

```
color: color; background-color: color
```

where *color* is either the name of a color or an RGB color value. We'll study the issue of color in greater detail in a later tutorial. For now, know that browsers understand basic color names like red or blue or green.

While some browsers use the color style to assign a color to a horizontal line, other browsers use the background-color style. Therefore, if setting a line's color is an important aspect of your page's design, it's best to include both the color and background-color styles.

Reference Window

Inserting a Horizontal Line

- To insert a horizontal line, use the tag
  ```
  <hr />
  ```
- To change the color of the line, use the style
  ```
  color: color; background-color: color
  ```
  where *color* is either a recognized color name or an RGB color value.
- To change the width and height of the line, use the style
  ```
  width: value; height: value
  ```
  where *value* is the width or height of the line in pixels. You can also express the width value as a percentage of the page width. The default width is 100%, which is equal to the width of the Web page. The default height is usually 2 pixels.

Deprecated

- You can also format the appearance of your horizontal lines by adding the following attributes to the <hr /> tag:
  ```
  align="align" color="color" size="value" width="value"
  ```
  The align attribute specifies the alignment of the line on the page and can have the values left, right, or center (the default). The color attribute specifies the color of the line (Internet Explorer only). The size attribute specifies the height of the line in pixels. The width attribute specifies the width of the line in pixels.

For example, if Stephen wants to create a red horizontal line that is half the width of the page and 5 pixels high, he would enter the following tag into his HTML document:

```
<hr style="color: red; background-color: red; width: 50%; height: 5" />
```

The default rendering of a horizontal line is not standard across browsers. Typically the line extends across the complete width of the page at a height of 2 pixels. Some graphical browsers display the line in a solid black color, while others apply a chiseled or embossed effect. Text-based browsers display the line using dashes or underscores.

For the chemistry page, Stephen simply wants a red horizontal line, 2 pixels high. He'll let the line extend across the width of the page.

To add a horizontal line to the chemistry file:

1. Return to the **chem.htm** file in your text editor.

2. Below the paragraph containing the dube.jpg inline image, insert the following tag (see Figure 1-27):

```
<hr style="color: red; background-color: red; height: 2; width: 100%" />
```

Figure 1-27 ▶ **Inserting a horizontal line**

```
<body>
<p style="text-align: center">
    <img src="dube.jpg"
    alt="Mr. Dube's Chemistry Classes at Robert Service High School" />
</p>
<hr style="color: red; background-color: red; height: 2; width: 100%" />
<p>Welcome to the Robert Service High School Chemistry Web page.
    Here you'll learn more about our chemistry classes and our
    policies.</p>
```

▶ **3.** Save your changes to the file.

▶ **4.** Using your Web browser, refresh or reload the **chem.htm** file. Figure 1-28 shows the new horizontal line.

Figure 1-28 ▶ **Displaying a horizontal line**

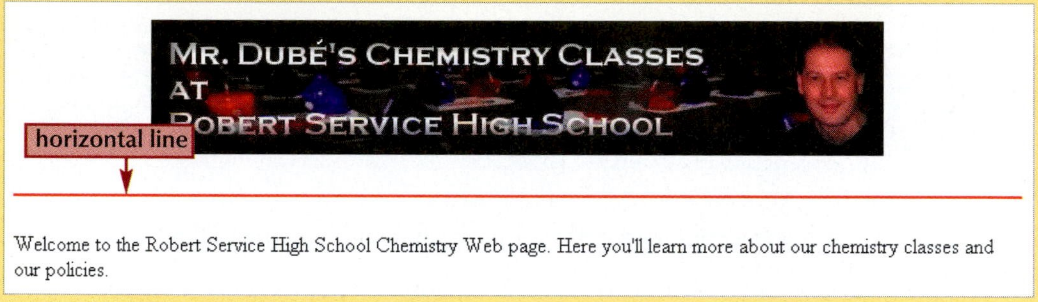

Most browsers still support several deprecated presentational attributes, which you can use in place of styles for your horizontal lines. See the "Inserting a Horizontal Line" reference window for more details.

Other Empty Elements

Other empty elements you may wish to use in your Web page include line breaks and meta elements. The <br /> tag creates a line break, which starts a new line within a paragraph. For example, the following code

```
<br />
<br />
<br />
```

creates three consecutive line breaks. You can use the <br /> tag to control the spacing of the different sections in your document.

Meta elements are placed in the document's head and contain information about the document that may be of use to programs that run on Web servers. You create a meta element using the one-sided <meta /> tag as follows:

```
<meta name="text" content="text" scheme="text" http-equiv="text" />
```

where the name attribute specifies the name of a property for the page, the content attribute provides a property value, the scheme attribute provides the format of the property value, and the http-equiv attribute takes the place of the name attribute for some Web servers. For example the following <meta /> tag stores the name of the Web page's author.

```
<meta name="author" content="Stephen Dube" />
```

Some Web sites, like Google, use search engines to create lists of Web pages devoted to particular topics. You can give extra weight to your Web page by including a description of the page and a list of keywords in <meta /> tags at the top of the document.

```
<meta name="description" content="Chemistry Class Web page" />
<meta name="keywords" content="chemistry, school, Edmonton, science" />
```

Note that a document's head can contain several meta elements.

Working with Special Characters

Occasionally, you will want to include special characters in your Web page that do not appear on your keyboard. For example, a page might require mathematical symbols such as β or μ, or you might need to include the copyright symbol © to show that an image or text is copyrighted.

Stephen's last name uses an accented letter, "é". His name appears three times in his Web page: in the title at the top of the page, again in the alt text for the inline image, and finally in a paragraph on making an appointment.

HTML supports the use of character symbols that are identified by a code number or name. The syntax for creating a special character is:

&*code*;

where *code* is either a code name or a code number. Code numbers are preceded by a pound symbol (#). Figure 1-29 shows some HTML symbols and the corresponding code numbers or names. The appendices include a more complete list of special characters. Some older browsers support only code numbers, not code names.

Inserting a Special Character

- To insert a special character, enter:
    &*code*;
  where *code* is either a code name or code number. Code numbers are preceded by a pound symbol (#).

Special characters and codes ◄ **Figure 1-29**

Symbol	Code	Name	Description
©	©	©	Copyright symbol
®	®	®	Registered trademark
•	·	·	Middle dot (bullet)
°	°	°	Degree symbol
			Nonbreaking space, used to insert consecutive blank spaces
<	<	<	Less than symbol
>	>	>	Greater than symbol
&	&	&	Ampersand

To add a character code to the chemistry page:

1. Return to the **chem.htm** file in your text editor.

2. Replace the **e** in Mr. Dubé's name in the page title, the img element, and the appointments paragraph with the code, **é** as shown in Figure 1-30.

Figure 1-30 ▶ **Inserting a special character**

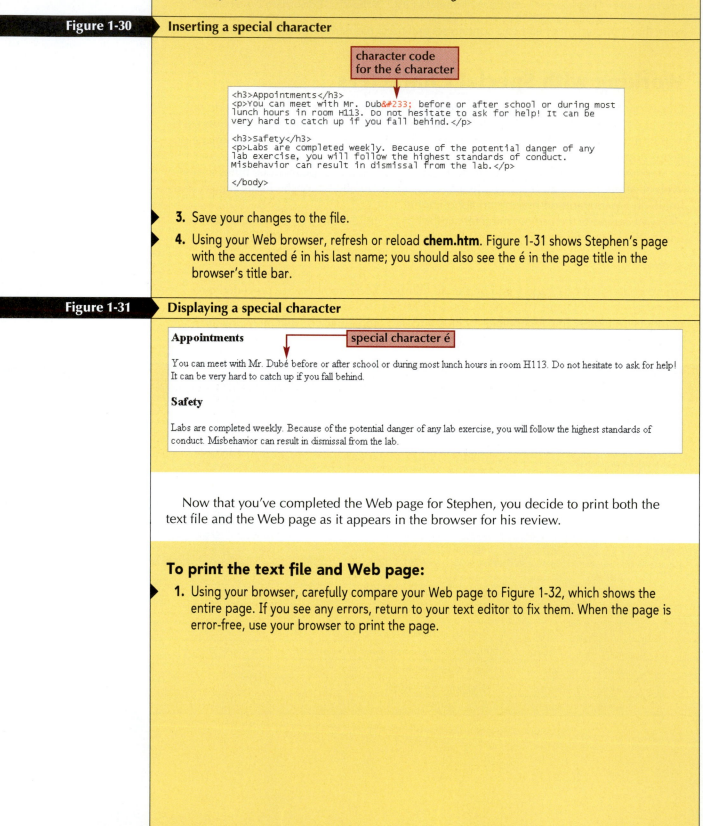

character code
for the é character

```
<h3>Appointments</h3>
<p>You can meet with Mr. Dub&#233; before or after school or during most
lunch hours in room H113. Do not hesitate to ask for help! It can be
very hard to catch up if you fall behind.</p>

<h3>Safety</h3>
<p>Labs are completed weekly. Because of the potential danger of any
lab exercise, you will follow the highest standards of conduct.
Misbehavior can result in dismissal from the lab.</p>

</body>
```

3. Save your changes to the file.

4. Using your Web browser, refresh or reload **chem.htm**. Figure 1-31 shows Stephen's page with the accented é in his last name; you should also see the é in the page title in the browser's title bar.

Figure 1-31 ▶ **Displaying a special character**

Appointments

special character é

You can meet with Mr. Dubé before or after school or during most lunch hours in room H113. Do not hesitate to ask for help! It can be very hard to catch up if you fall behind.

Safety

Labs are completed weekly. Because of the potential danger of any lab exercise, you will follow the highest standards of conduct. Misbehavior can result in dismissal from the lab.

Now that you've completed the Web page for Stephen, you decide to print both the text file and the Web page as it appears in the browser for his review.

To print the text file and Web page:

1. Using your browser, carefully compare your Web page to Figure 1-32, which shows the entire page. If you see any errors, return to your text editor to fix them. When the page is error-free, use your browser to print the page.

Final Web page | **Figure 1-32**

MR. DUBÉ'S CHEMISTRY CLASSES
AT
ROBERT SERVICE HIGH SCHOOL

Welcome to the Robert Service High School Chemistry Web page. Here you'll learn more about our chemistry classes and our policies.

Chemistry Classes

- Conceptual Chemistry: An introductory course, requiring basic math but no algebra
- Chemistry I: An introductory course, requiring solid algebra skills
- Advanced Placement Chemistry: An advanced course requiring a grade of A or B in Chemistry I

Class Policies

Grading

Homework: Homework is worth 5 to 10 points and will be given daily. A quiz consisting of 1 or 2 homework problems from the previous week may be given in place of homework.

Tests and Quizzes: Quizzes are worth 10 to 25 points and will be given at least once a month. Tests are worth up to 100 points and will be given three times each quarter.

Labs: Labs are worth 10 to 30 points and will be graded on safety, participation, and write-up. Reports should be neatly written or typed. *Research projects* will also be assigned throughout the year.

Appointments

You can meet with Mr. Dubé before or after school or during most lunch hours in room H113. Do not hesitate to ask for help! It can be very hard to catch up if you fall behind.

Safety

Labs are completed weekly. Because of the potential danger of any lab exercise, you will follow the highest standards of conduct. Misbehavior can result in dismissal from the lab.

2. Using your text editor, print chem.htm, and compare it to the complete code shown in Figure 1-33. When you are finished, you can close your text editor and browser unless you are continuing on to the assignments.

| Figure 1-33 | Final HTML code |

```html
<html>

<head>
<!-- Chemistry Classes Web Page
     Author: Stephen Dube
     Date:   8/1/2006
-->
<title>Mr. Dub&#233;'s Chemistry Classes</title>
</head>

<body>
<p style="text-align: center">
   <img src="dube.jpg"
    alt="Mr. Dub&#233;'s Chemistry Classes at Robert Service High School" />
</p>
<hr style="color: red; background-color: red; height: 2; width: 100%" />
<p>Welcome to the Robert Service High School Chemistry Web page.
   Here you'll learn more about our chemistry classes and our
   policies.</p>

<h2>Chemistry Classes</h2>
<ul style="list-style-type: square">
   <li>Conceptual Chemistry: An introductory course, requiring basic
       math but no algebra</li>
   <li>Chemistry I: An introductory course, requiring solid algebra
       skills</li>
   <li>Advanced Placement Chemistry: An advanced course requiring a
       grade of A or B in Chemistry I</li>
</ul>

<h2>Class Policies</h2>
<h3>Grading</h3>
<p><i><b>Homework</b></i>: Homework is worth 5 to 10 points and will be given
daily. A quiz consisting of 1 or 2 homework problems from the
previous week may be given in place of homework.</p>

<p><i><b>Tests and Quizzes</b></i>: Quizzes are worth 10 to 25 points and will be
given at least once a month. Tests are worth up to 100 points and
will be given three times each quarter.</p>

<p><i><b>Labs</b></i>: Labs are worth 10 to 30 points and will be graded on safety,
participation, and write-up. Reports should be neatly written or
typed. <i><b>Research projects</b></i> will also be assigned throughout the
year.</p>

<h3>Appointments</h3>
<p>You can meet with Mr. Dub&#233; before or after school or during most
lunch hours in room H113. Do not hesitate to ask for help! It can be
very hard to catch up if you fall behind.</p>

<h3>Safety</h3>
<p>Labs are completed weekly. Because of the potential danger of any
lab exercise, you will follow the highest standards of conduct.
Misbehavior can result in dismissal from the lab.</p>

</body>

</html>
```

Stephen is pleased with your work on his Web site and feels that it effectively captures the content of the original handout. You explain to him that the next step is to add hyperlinks to his Web page so that you can add contact information and create links to the interesting chemistry Web sites you've discovered. You'll do this in the next tutorial.

Tips for Good HTML Code

- Use line breaks and indented text to make your HTML file easier to read.
- Insert comments into your HTML file to document your work.
- Enter all tag and attribute names in lowercase.
- Place all attribute values in quotes.
- Close all two-sided tags.
- Make sure that nested elements do not cross.
- Use styles in place of presentational attributes whenever possible.
- Use logical elements to describe an element's content. Use physical elements to describe the element's appearance.

- Include the alt attribute for any inline image to specify alternative text for non-graphical browsers.
- Know your market and the types of browsers that your audience will use to view your Web page.
- Test your Web page on all relevant browsers and devices.

Review

Session 1.3 Quick Check

1. What is an inline image?
2. Why is it important to always include the alt attribute when inserting an inline image?
3. What code would you enter to display the inline image, logo.jpg, into your Web page? Assume that the alternate text for this image is "Chemistry Web Page".
4. What code would you enter to insert a blue horizontal line that is 200 pixels wide?
5. How does a text-based browser display a horizontal line?
6. How do you insert a line break into a Web page?
7. What tag would you add to your document to insert the meta information that the page author's name is "Diane Chou"?
8. What code would you use to insert the copyright symbol © into your page?

Review

Tutorial Summary

This tutorial introduced you to the basics of HTML. You learned about the history of the Internet, the Web, and HTML. You also studied the philosophy of HTML and learned how the language's standards and specifications were developed, and how they are maintained. You created your first HTML file through the use of two-sided and one-sided tags and learned how to use these tags to mark the various elements of your page, such as headings, paragraphs, and lists. You also learned how to use inline styles to provide formatting instructions for your browser. This tutorial also covered how to insert inline images and horizontal lines into a Web page. Finally, you learned how to use HTML to insert special characters and symbols.

Key Terms

ARPANET	Extensible Markup	inline style
block-level element	Language	Internet
body element	extension	LAN
character formatting	graphical browser	link
elements	head element	local area network
client	host	logical element
client-server network	HTML	markup language
closing tag	HTML converter	metalanguage
comment tag	HTML editor	nesting
definition list	hyperlink	network
deprecated	hypertext	node
element	Hypertext Markup	one-sided tag
empty element	Language	opening tag
Extensible Hypertext	inline element	ordered list
Markup Language	inline image	physical element

pixel	text-based browser	Web server
presentational attribute	title element	Web site
server	two-sided tag	white space
SGML	unordered list	wide area network
specification	W3C	World Wide Web
standard	WAN	World Wide Web
Standard Generalized	Web	Consortium
Markup Language	Web browser	XHTML
style	Web page	XML
tag		

Practice

Practice the skills you learned in the tutorial using the same case scenario.

Review Assignments

Data files needed for this Review Assignment: chemtxt.htm, flask.jpg, logo.jpg

Stephen has some time to study the Web page you created for him and has asked your help to make some additional revisions. In the Chemistry Classes section, he wants you to add a new class that he'll be offering next semester, and he would like the chemistry class names displayed in boldface. He also wants the list marker changed to a graphic image of a flask. He would like to you to indent the paragraphs on grading, office hours, and safety. He also wants you to add a numbered list in the Safety section listing his five main safety rules. He wants you to insert horizontal lines dividing the main sections of the page. Finally, he wants to add a whimsical sentence at the bottom of the site to let his students know that though he is serious about learning and safety, he wants his classes to be fun. He'd like the line to read: "Chemistry with Dubé is like medicine with a spoonful of $C_{12}H_{22}O_{11}$!" ($C_{12}H_{22}O_{11}$ is the formula for sugar.) Figure 1-34 shows a preview of the page you'll create.

Figure 1-34

MR. DUBÉ'S CHEMISTRY CLASSES AT ROBERT SERVICE HIGH SCHOOL

Welcome to the Robert Service High School Chemistry Web page. Read below to learn about our classes and policies.

Chemistry Classes

Conceptual Chemistry: An introductory course, requiring basic math but no algebra

Chemistry I: An introductory course, requiring solid algebra skills

Applied Chemistry: An introductory course requiring solid algebra skills and an interest in using critical thinking to solve real-world chemistry-related problems

Advanced Placement Chemistry: An advanced course requiring a grade of A or B in Chemistry I

Class Policies

Assignments and Grading

Homework: Homework is assigned after each class and is worth 5 to 10 points. A periodic quiz consisting of 1 or 2 homework problems may be given in place of homework.

Tests and Quizzes: Tests and quizzes are essential to check your understanding of the material. Quizzes are worth 10 to 25 points and will be given at least once a month. Tests are worth up to 100 points and will be given 3 times each semester.

Labs: Labs are worth 10 to 30 points and will be graded on safety, participation, and write-up. Your reports should be neatly written or typed.

Research projects: Research projects give you a chance to expand your knowledge beyond the classroom. There will be several research projects throughout the year.

Office Hours

You can meet with Mr. Dubé before or after school or during most lunch hours in room H113. Do not hesitate to ask for help! It is very hard to catch up if you fall behind.

Safety Rules

Because of the potential danger of any lab exercise, you will be held to the highest standards of behavior, and will be removed from the class if you pose a threat to yourself or other students.

1. Follow the instructor's written and oral directions carefully and immediately.
2. Never perform any procedure that the instructor does not specifically direct you to do.
3. No playful behavior is permitted in the lab.
4. You must wear safety equipment as directed at all times, even if you find it uncomfortable or unbecoming.
5. No food, drinks, or loose clothing are permitted in the lab.

Chemistry with Dubé is like medicine with a spoonful of $C_{12}H_{22}O_{11}$!

To complete this task:

1. Using your text editor, open **chemtxt.htm** located in the tutorial.01/review folder. Save the file as **chem2.htm** to the same folder.
2. Within the head element of the document, insert the Web page title, "Robert Service High School Chemistry". Also insert a comment that includes your name and the date.
3. Directly above each of the h2 headings (Chemistry Classes and Class Policies), insert a blue horizontal line that is 3 pixels high with a width equal to the width of the page.
4. In the unordered list section, after the line describing the Chemistry I class, add the following new list item:
   Applied Chemistry: An introductory course requiring solid algebra skills and an interest in using critical thinking to solve real-world chemistry-related problems
5. Display each of the four class names in the list in a boldfaced font. Change the markers to the graphic image found in the flask.jpg file in the tutorial.01/review folder.
6. Enclose the four paragraphs below the h3 heading, "Assignments and Grading" within a blockquote element (this will cause the text to appear indented in most browsers.) Also enclose the paragraph below the Office Hours heading and the paragraph below the Safety Rules heading in separate blockquote elements.
7. After the block quote describing Stephen's safety rules, create a numbered list with the following five list items:
   1. Follow the instructor's written and oral directions carefully and immediately.
   2. Never perform any procedure that the instructor does not specifically direct you to do.
   3. No playful behavior is permitted in the lab.
   4. You must wear safety equipment as directed at all times, even if you find it uncomfortable or unbecoming.
   5. No food, drinks, or loose clothes are permitted in the lab.
8. Enclose the numbered list you just created within a blockquote element.
9. Below the numbered list insert another blue horizontal line 3 pixels high and extending the width of the page.
10. Below the horizontal line, insert a centered paragraph containing the following text. (*Hint:* Use the <sub> tag to mark the numbers as subscripts and use a character code to display the character, é.)
    "Chemistry with Dubé is like medicine with a spoonful of $C_{12}H_{22}O_{11}$!"
11. Save your changes to chem2.htm.
12. Open your page in your Web browser and verify that it matches the page shown in Figure 1-34.
13. Submit your completed assignment to your instructor.

Apply

Use the skills you have learned to create a Web page for a childcare agency.

Case Problem 1

Data files needed for this Case Problem: childtxt.htm, newborn.jpg

ChildLink, Inc. You are an employee of ChildLink, Inc., a small, nonprofit agency in Las Cruces, New Mexico. ChildLink provides financial and emotional support for families with children who have newly discovered physical or mental disabilities. The agency received significantly more donations in the last year than expected, and it has decided to offer qualifying clients temporary help with housing and medical costs. The assistant director, Sandra Pauls, has asked you to post the eligibility requirements and application process on the Web. Figure 1-35 shows a preview of the page you'll create for ChildLink, Inc.

Figure 1-35

ChildLink of Las Cruces

A Loving Connection between Children with Disabilities and the Resources They Need

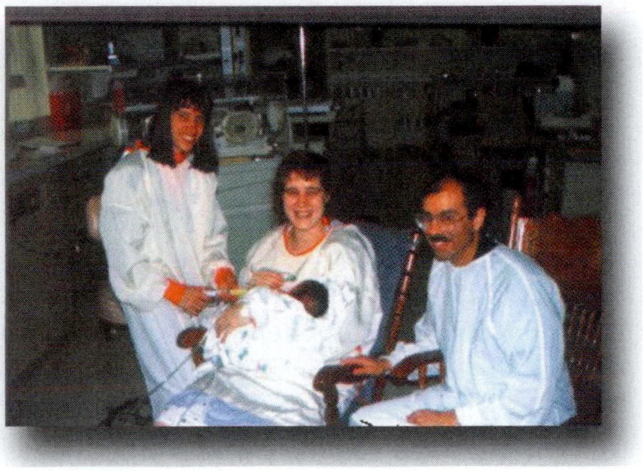

Temporary Financial Assistance Available

To be eligible for this program, you must meet the following criteria:

- Your child must have been diagnosed with a physical or mental disability within the last 6 months (the diagnosis can be prenatal or at any age)
- Your family must be at or below the State of New Mexico's poverty line

To apply, please complete the following steps:

1. Pick up an application from ChildLink (address below)
2. Assemble the following documents:
   a. Your completed application
   b. Doctor's record of your child's diagnosis
   c. Tax records or New Mexico Social Services certificate of your income level
   d. Your lease, mortgage, or medical bills, depending on which you need help with
3. Make an appointment with a ChildLink volunteer, available at the following times:
   a. Ida: MW 10:30 a.m. to 3:30 p.m.
   b. Juan: TR 9:00 a.m. to noon
   c. Chris: F 10:30 a.m. to 3:30 p.m.

ChildLink
1443 Cortnic Drive
Las Cruces, NM 88001
505-555-2371

To complete this task:

1. Use your text editor to open the file **childtxt.htm** from the tutorial.01/case1 folder, and save the file as **child.htm** to the same folder.
2. Within the head element, insert a comment containing your name and the date and insert the following Web page title: ChildLink Temporary Financial Assistance.
3. Within the body element, create an h1 heading containing the text "ChildLink of Las Cruces", and center the heading on the page.

4. Below the h1 heading, create an h3 heading containing the text "A Loving Connection between Children with Disabilities and the Resources They Need", and center the heading on the page.

5. Below the h3 heading, create an h2 heading containing the text "Temporary Financial Assistance Available", and center the heading.

6. Below the h2 heading, create an h4 heading containing the text "To be eligible for this program, you must meet the following criteria:" Leave this heading left-aligned.

7. Below the h4 heading, create a bulleted list with square bullets. Include the two list items shown in Figure 1-35.

8. Below the bulleted list, insert an h4 heading containing the text "To apply, please complete the following steps:" Leave this heading left-aligned.

9. Below the heading, insert an ordered list containing the three numbered items shown in Figure 1-35.

10. Within the "Assemble the following documents:" list item, create an ordered list containing the four items shown in Figure 1-35. Use the lower-alpha style to display a letter rather than a number next to each item.

11. Within the "Make an appointment" list item, create another ordered list containing the three volunteer names and times as shown in Figure 1-35; as in the previous step, display the items using letters rather than numbers.

12. Insert a horizontal line below the main numbered list.

13. Below the horizontal line insert the contact information shown in Figure 1-35 as an address element. Insert line breaks within the address, and display the word, "ChildLink" in a boldfaced font. Align the address with the right margin of the page.

14. After the h3 heading ("A Loving Connection…") near the top, insert a centered paragraph containing the inline image **newborn.jpg**. For text-based or non-visual browsers, display the alternative text, "We provide support for newborns".

15. Below this image, insert a horizontal line.

16. Save the file, view it in your browser, compare it to Figure 1-35, and then make any corrections necessary in your text editor. Submit your completed assignment to your instructor.

Case Problem 2

Data files needed for this Case Problem: euler.jpg, eulertxt.htm, pi.jpg

Mathematics Department, Coastal University Professor Laureen Coe of the Mathematics Department at Coastal University in Beachside, Connecticut is preparing material for her course on the history of mathematics. As part of the course, she has written short profiles of famous mathematicians. Laureen would like you to use content she's already written to create several Web pages that students can access on Coastal University's Web server. You'll create the first one in this exercise. Figure 1-36 previews this page, which profiles the mathematician Leonhard Euler.

Figure 1-36

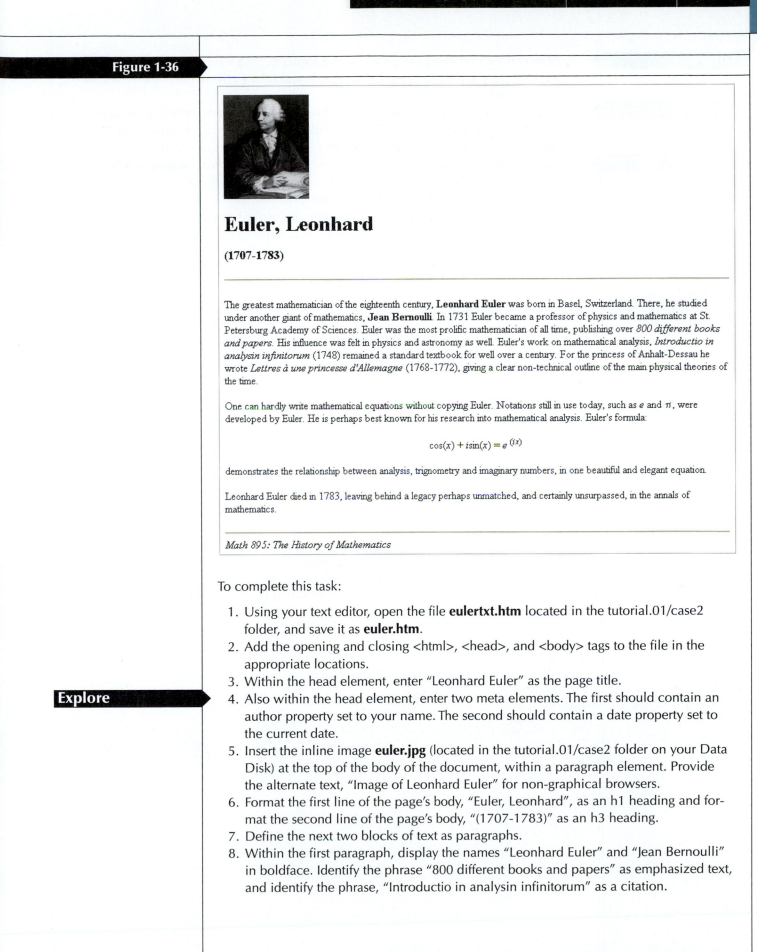

Euler, Leonhard

(1707-1783)

The greatest mathematician of the eighteenth century, **Leonhard Euler** was born in Basel, Switzerland. There, he studied under another giant of mathematics, **Jean Bernoulli**. In 1731 Euler became a professor of physics and mathematics at St. Petersburg Academy of Sciences. Euler was the most prolific mathematician of all time, publishing over *800 different books and papers*. His influence was felt in physics and astronomy as well. Euler's work on mathematical analysis, *Introductio in analysin infinitorum* (1748) remained a standard textbook for well over a century. For the princess of Anhalt-Dessau he wrote *Lettres à une princesse d'Allemagne* (1768-1772), giving a clear non-technical outline of the main physical theories of the time.

One can hardly write mathematical equations without copying Euler. Notations still in use today, such as e and π, were developed by Euler. He is perhaps best known for his research into mathematical analysis. Euler's formula:

$$\cos(x) + i\sin(x) = e^{(ix)}$$

demonstrates the relationship between analysis, trignometry and imaginary numbers, in one beautiful and elegant equation.

Leonhard Euler died in 1783, leaving behind a legacy perhaps unmatched, and certainly unsurpassed, in the annals of mathematics.

Math 895: The History of Mathematics

To complete this task:

1. Using your text editor, open the file **eulertxt.htm** located in the tutorial.01/case2 folder, and save it as **euler.htm**.
2. Add the opening and closing <html>, <head>, and <body> tags to the file in the appropriate locations.
3. Within the head element, enter "Leonhard Euler" as the page title.

Explore

4. Also within the head element, enter two meta elements. The first should contain an author property set to your name. The second should contain a date property set to the current date.
5. Insert the inline image **euler.jpg** (located in the tutorial.01/case2 folder on your Data Disk) at the top of the body of the document, within a paragraph element. Provide the alternate text, "Image of Leonhard Euler" for non-graphical browsers.
6. Format the first line of the page's body, "Euler, Leonhard", as an h1 heading and format the second line of the page's body, "(1707-1783)" as an h3 heading.
7. Define the next two blocks of text as paragraphs.
8. Within the first paragraph, display the names "Leonhard Euler" and "Jean Bernoulli" in boldface. Identify the phrase "800 different books and papers" as emphasized text, and identify the phrase, "Introductio in analysin infinitorum" as a citation.

Explore

9. In the phrase "Lettres a une princesse d'Allemagne," use the character code à to replace the one-letter word "a" with an à, and identify the name of the publication as a citation.

Explore

10. In the second paragraph, italicize the notation "e" and replace the word "pi" with the inline image **pi.jpg**, located in the case2 folder on your Data Disk. Provide the alternate text "pi" for non-graphical browsers.

Explore

11. Place the equation in a centered paragraph element and italicize each occurrence of the letters "x", "i", and "e" in the equation. Display the term "(ix)" as a superscript.
12. Format the next two blocks of text as paragraphs.
13. Define the name of the course at the bottom of the page as an address element.
14. Add horizontal lines before and after the biographical information.
15. Save your changes to the euler.htm file. Submit your completed assignment to your instructor.

Explore

Go beyond what you've learned in the tutorial by exploring how to use color and background images in a racing results Web page.

Case Problem 3

Data files needed for this Case Problem: flakes.jpg, frosttxt.htm, runner.jpg

Frostbite Freeze You are on the organizing committee for the Frostbite Freeze, a fun but competitive event held each January in Butte, Montana. You've volunteered to publish the results for Montana's craziest running race on the Web. You talk about the format of the page with Matt Turner, the chairman of the committee.

Matt wants you to include a snowflake background behind the text, which you can do using a graphic image. Such backgrounds are called tiled-image backgrounds because the browser repeats, or tiles, the image to cover the background of the entire page. You can create a tiled-image background with an image in either GIF or JPEG file format. To add a background image to an element, you apply the following style:

```
background-image: url(file)
```

where *file* is the name of the image file. Matt has given you two JPEG files to use for this Web page: **flakes.jpg**, which contains a snowflake pattern, and **runner.jpg**, which shows a Frostbite Freeze racer. Figure 1-37 shows a preview of the page you'll create.

Figure 1-37

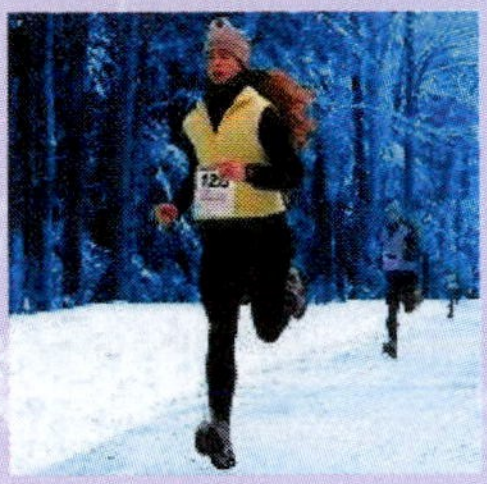

Frostbite Freeze

Montana's Craziest Footrace

The results are in ...

257 runners braved the -10° weather on January 19 and ran, in one fashion or another, the icy 5-kilometer course through downtown Butte. About half the runners sported costumes rather than serious running gear, and many runners posted good times (costumed or not). For many, this was the season's first run (not race – *run*), a motivational warm-up for the fun and work that lies ahead.

Awards were given for best time in four age categories for both sexes.

Girls 14-19
Jamie Harrington 19:33 · Sorcia Besay 20:06 · Rachel Stores 25:44

Boys 14-19
Bruce Bevin 18:55 · Endre Witthoeft 19:46 · Joe Wesevich 21:19

Women 20-39
Marie Sillers 17:45 · Denise Wortenhau 18:33 · Lorel Dwiers 18:56

Women 39-49
Jannie Gilbert 17:48 · Mia Saphi 19:23 · Dawn Severson 21:31

Women 50+
Julia Gent 21:09 · Mandy Reming 34:24 · Sung Bon 41:02

Men 20-39
Gary Cruz 17:11 · Lanny Sorla 18:40 · Kip Oestin 18:55

Men 40-49
Steve Jackson 18:50 · Jim Kostenberger 24:33 · Lee Whisten 27:18

Men 50+
Billy Tisa 18:22 · Alois Anderson 28:48 · Lyle Tolbor 35:46

To complete this task:

1. Using your text editor, open **frosttxt.htm** from the tutorial.01/case3 folder, and then save it as **frost.htm**.
2. Insert the <html>, <head>, and <body> tags in the appropriate locations.
3. Insert the Web page title "Frostbite Freeze Results" in the head element in the document and add a comment containing your name and the date.
4. **Explore** Apply a style to the body element to add flakes.jpg as the background image.
5. Mark the text "Frostbite Freeze" with as an h1 heading and center it on the Web page.
6. Mark the text "Montana's Craziest Footrace" as an h2 heading and center it on the page.

Explore

Explore

Explore

7. Insert a purple horizontal line below the h2 heading that is 50% of the width of the screen and 5 pixels high.

8. Mark the text "The results are in" as an h3 heading tag, leaving the text left aligned.

9. Add an ellipsis (…) after the text "The results are in" so it reads, "The results are in…" Use the character code for the ellipsis symbol, which you can find in appendices.

10. Add a degree symbol after "-10" in the first line of the first paragraph. (Use the character code for the degree symbol from the appendices.)

11. Identify the first two text blocks as paragraphs (one starts with "257 runners" and the other starts with "Awards were given").

12. Near the end of the first paragraph, display the word "run" in italics (see Figure 1-37).

13. Mark each of the eight age-sex categories (for example, "Girls 14-19") and the winners as eight individual paragraphs. Insert a line break between the category name and the winners.

14. Display the names of the eight age-sex categories in a boldfaced font.

15. Insert a middle dot symbol between each of the three names in each of the eight age-sex categories. Insert three nonbreaking spaces at the start of each line containing the winners to make the line appear indented on the page.

16. Insert the inline image **runner.jpg** (located in the case3 folder of the tutorial.01 folder on your Data Disk) between the top two headings, as shown in Figure 1-37. For non-graphical browsers, display the alternate text, "Race Results Page". Center the image within a paragraph.

17. Save your changes and view the completed page in your Web browser. Submit your assignment to your instructor.

Create

Test your knowledge of HTML by creating a product page for Body Systems.

Case Problem 4

Data files needed for this Case Problem: logo.jpg, smith.jpg, smith.txt

Body Systems Body Systems is one of the leading manufacturers of home gyms. The company recently hired you to assist in developing their Web site. Your first task is to create a Web page for the LSM400, a popular weight machine sold by the company. You've been given a text file, smith.txt, describing the features of the LSM400. You've also received two image files: logo.jpg, displaying the company's logo and smith.jpg, an image of the LSM400. You are free to supplement these files with any other resources available to you. You are responsible for the page's content and appearance.

To complete this task:

1. Create an HTML file named **smith.htm**, and save it in the tutorial.01/case4 folder.

2. In the head element, include an appropriate page title, along with a comment describing the purpose of the page, your name, and the date.

3. Include at least one example of each of the following in the document:

   - a heading
   - a paragraph
   - an ordered or unordered list
   - a character formatting element
   - an inline image
   - a horizontal line
   - a special character
   - a block-level element that is not a heading, paragraph, list, or horizontal line

4. Demonstrate your understanding of inline styles by including at least two different examples of an inline style.
5. Use proper HTML syntax at all times. Close all two-sided tags. Properly nest all tags. Use lowercase element and attribute names. Enclose attribute values in quotes. Include alternate text for non-graphical browsers with inline images.
6. Write your code so that it will be easy for your supervisor to read and understand.
7. Save your HTML file, and then view the resulting Web page in a browser.
8. Submit your completed assignment to your instructor.

Quick Check Answers

Session 1.1

1. A hypertext document is an electronic file containing elements that users can select, usually by clicking a mouse, to open other documents.
2. Web pages are stored on Web servers, which then makes those pages available to clients. To view a Web page, the client runs a software program called a Web browser, which retrieves the page and displays it.
3. HTML (Hypertext Markup Language) is the language in which Web pages are written.
4. HTML documents do not exactly specify the appearance of a document; rather they describe the purpose of different elements in the document and leave it to the Web browser to determine the final appearance. A word processor like Word exactly specifies the appearance of each document element.
5. Deprecated features and those features that are being phased out by the W3C, and which might not be supported by future browsers.
6. Extensions are special formats supported by a particular browser, but not generally accepted by all browsers. The advantage is that people who use that browser have a wider range of document elements to work with. The disadvantage is that the document will not work for users who do not have that particular browser, thus complicating the development process.
7. Because HTML documents are simple text files, you can create them with nothing more than a basic text editor such as Windows Notepad. However, specialized HTML authoring programs, known as HTML converters and HTML editors, are available to do some of the rote work of creating an HTML document.

Session 1.2

1. The head element which contains information about the document or instructions to the browser, and the body element which contains the content that the browser should render in the page.
2. Empty elements are elements that have no content. They are created using one-sided HTML tags.
3. `<h1 style="text-align: center">Chemistry Classes</h1>`
4. Block-level elements contain content that is displayed in a separate section within the page, such as a paragraph or a heading. An inline element is part of the same block as its surrounding content—for example, individual words or phrases within a paragraph.
5. HTML treats all white space (tabs, line breaks, blank spaces) as a single blank space and collapses consecutive occurrences of white space into a single occurrence. Thus, adding an extra blank line to your HTML file does not create an extra blank line in the rendered page.

6. Presentational attributes are HTML attributes that exactly specify how to the browser should render an HTML element. Most presentational attributes have been deprecated, replaced by styles. You should use presentational attributes when you need to support older browsers.

7. `style="list-style-type: upper-roman"`

8. `style="list-style-image: url(ball.gif); list-style-position: inside"`
   or
   `style="list-style: url(ball.gif) inside"`

9. Logical elements describe the nature of their enclosed content, but do not necessarily indicate how that content should appear. Physical elements describe how an element should appear, but provide little or no information about the nature of its content. Logical elements are more appropriate for a non-visual browser.

Session 1.3

1. An inline image is an inline element, used to display graphical images within the contents of a block-level element.

2. The alt attribute provides a text alternative to the image for non-graphical browsers.

3. `<img src="logo.jpg" alt="Chemistry Web Page" />`

4. `<hr style="color: blue; background-color: blue; width: 200" />`

5. Text based browsers display horizontal lines using dashes or underscores.

6. Use the `<br />` tag.

7. `<meta name="author" content="Diane Chou" />`

8. `&#169;` or `&copy;`

Objectives

Session 2.1
- Define links and how to use them
- Create element ids to mark specific locations within a document
- Create links to jump between sections of the same document
- Describe how to set and use anchors for backward compatibility with older browsers

Session 2.2
- List different types of Web site structures and how to employ them
- Create links between documents
- Create links to sections within a document
- Define absolute and relative paths

Session 2.3
- Interpret the structure and contents of a URL
- Link to a page on the Web
- Link to FTP servers, newsgroups, and e-mail addresses
- Open links in a secondary window
- Work with popup titles and access keys
- Create semantic links
- Create link elements

Developing a Basic Web Site

Creating a Chemistry Web Site

Case

Creating a Chemistry Web Site

In the last tutorial you created a basic Web page for Stephen Dubé, a chemistry teacher in Edmonton, Alberta. With your help, Stephen has made a few changes to the Web page, and he has ideas for additional content. Stephen notes that while the Web page's appearance reflects the course handout on which he originally based it, the Web page's layout is limiting. For example, students and their parents must scroll through the document window to find information about his classes. Stephen wants to make it as easy to navigate from topic to topic on his Web page as it is to scan the single-page handout.

Stephen also wants to put more information online, but he is concerned about making the original Web page too large and difficult to navigate. He'd like to list the ways students and parents can contact him (office hours, e-mail, phone numbers, and so forth). He would also like to share several helpful chemistry Web sites with his students.

Student Data Files

▼**Tutorial.02**

▽ **Tutorial folder**
- chemtxt.htm
- conttxt.htm
- linkstxt.htm
- +1 graphical file

▽ **Review folder**
- chemtxt.htm
- conttxt.htm
- glosstxt.htm
- linkstxt.htm
- +1 graphical file

▽ **Case1 folder**
- links.txt
- mpltxt.htm
- +1 graphical file

▽ Case2 folder	▽ Case3 folder	▽ Case 4 folder
glosstxt.htm	classtxt.htm	about.txt
hometxt.htm	indextxt.htm	bench.txt
m1txt.htm	memtxt.htm	cable.txt
m2txt.htm	+1 graphical file	contact.txt
m3txt.htm		lpress.txt
m4txt.htm		products.txt
+8 graphical files		smith.txt
		whybuy.txt
		+5 graphical files

Session 2.1

Working with Links

Since the last tutorial, you and Stephen have made some modifications to the layout and have added new content to the chemistry Web page. However, because the page is too long to fit in a browser window, a user opening the Web page sees only a small portion of the document. Of the document's four sections (Classes, Grading, Appointments, and Safety), a user initially sees only the class logo, the welcoming message, and the beginning of the class list (see Figure 2-1). To view the additional information, a user must scroll through the document. Stephen would like users to have a quicker way to access that information.

Figure 2-1 ▶ **Top of the chemistry Web page**

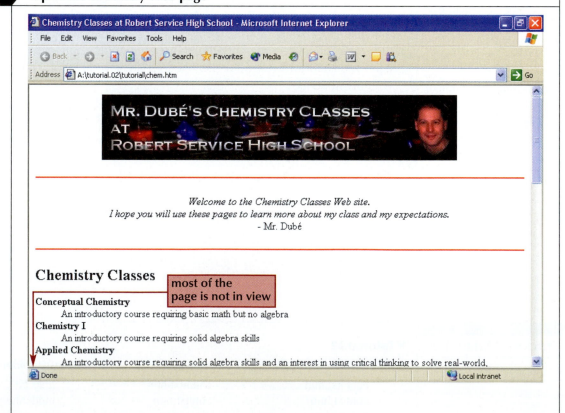

In the previous tutorial, you learned that a user can select a **link** in a Web page, usually by clicking it with a mouse, to view another topic or document, often called the link's **destination**. Stephen would like you to add links to his Web page that point to the different sections of the document. He would like you to list the four sections at the top of the page, and then format the names as links. When users open the chemistry page, they can click a link to move directly to the section of the page that interests them. You'll use the following steps to create these links in Stephen's page:

1. List the section names at the top of the document.
2. Mark each section in the HTML file using an id attribute. (You'll learn about this attribute shortly.)
3. Link the text you added in Step 1 to the sections you marked in Step 2.

Let's start by creating a list of the section names. We'll separate each section name with a • to make the text easier to read. You use the HTML character symbol · to create the • symbol.

To create a list of the section headings:

1. Use your text editor to open **chemtxt.htm** from the tutorial.02/tutorial folder. Save the file as **chem.htm**.

2. Enter *your name* and *the date* in the comment tag at the top of the file.

3. Directly above the first <hr /> tag, insert the following code:

```
<p style="text-align: center">
    Classes &#183;
    Grading &#183;
    Appointments &#183;
    Safety
</p>
```

See Figure 2-2.

Adding code for the text links ◄ **Figure 2-2**

```
<body>
<p style="text-align: center">
    <img src="dube.jpg"
     alt="Mr. Dub&#233;'s Chemistry Classes at Robert Service High School" />
</p>

<p style="text-align: center">
    Classes &#183;
    Grading &#183;
    Appointments &#183;
    Safety
</p>

<hr style="color: red; background-color: red; height: 2; width: 100%" />
```

4. Save your changes to the file, but leave your text editor open.

5. Start your Web browser and open **chem.htm** to verify your change, as shown in Figure 2-3.

Figure 2-3   **List of section heads**

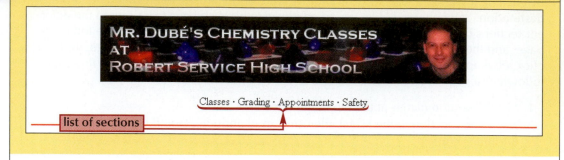

Creating Element ids

Now that you've listed the different sections of the Web page, you need a way to identify those elements in the HTML document. One way of doing this is through the id attribute, which uses the syntax:

```
id="id"
```

where *id* is the id name assigned to the element. For example, the code

```
<h2 id="classes">Chemistry Classes</h2>
```

assigns the id name "classes" to the h2 heading "Chemistry Classes". Note that id names must be unique. If you assign the same id name to more than one element in an HTML document, a browser will use only the first occurrence of the id name. In addition, if a browser finds duplicate id names in an XHTML document, it reports an error. Id names are not case sensitive, so browsers do not differentiate between ids named "classes" and "CLASSES", for example.

   For Stephen's Chemistry file, you decide to add ids to the h2 headings Chemistry Classes, Grading, Appointments, and Safety. You'll assign these tags the id names "classes", "grading", "app", and "safety".

To add id names to the section headings:

1. Return to the **chem.htm** file in your text editor.

2. Locate the <h2> tag for the heading "Chemistry Classes" and add the id attribute **id="classes"** as shown in Figure 2-4.

Adding id names　　　Figure 2-4

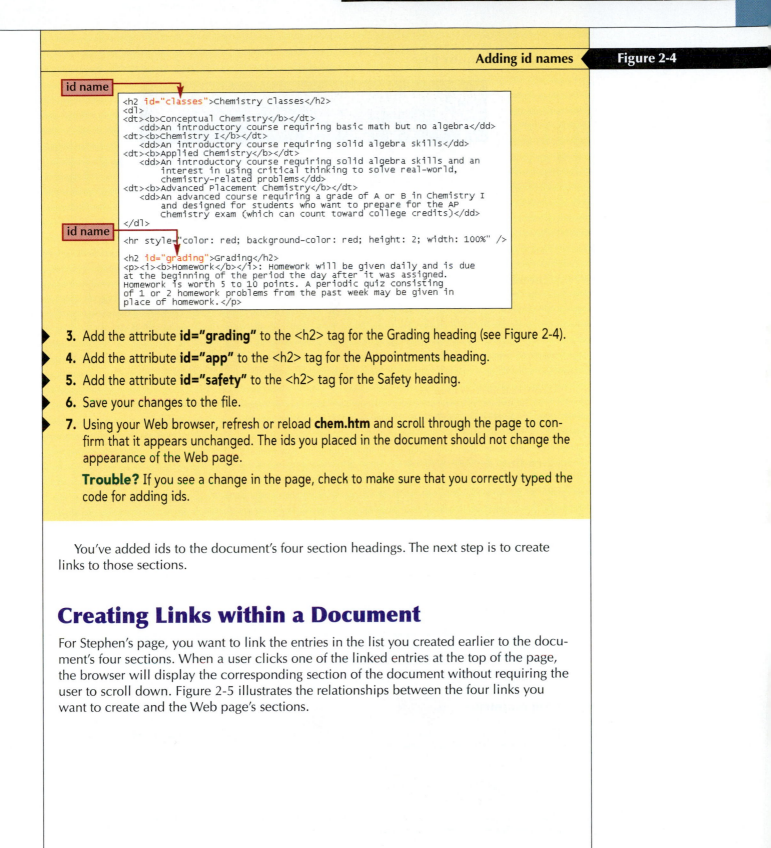

id name

```
<h2 id="classes">Chemistry Classes</h2>
<dl>
<dt><b>Conceptual Chemistry</b></dt>
    <dd>An introductory course requiring basic math but no algebra</dd>
<dt><b>Chemistry I</b></dt>
    <dd>An introductory course requiring solid algebra skills</dd>
<dt><b>Applied Chemistry</b></dt>
    <dd>An introductory course requiring solid algebra skills and an
        interest in using critical thinking to solve real-world,
        chemistry-related problems</dd>
<dt><b>Advanced Placement Chemistry</b></dt>
    <dd>An advanced course requiring a grade of A or B in Chemistry I
        and designed for students who want to prepare for the AP
        Chemistry exam (which can count toward college credits)</dd>
</dl>
```

id name

```
<hr style="color: red; background-color: red; height: 2; width: 100%" />

<h2 id="grading">Grading</h2>
<p><i><b>Homework</b></i>: Homework will be given daily and is due
at the beginning of the period the day after it was assigned.
Homework is worth 5 to 10 points. A periodic quiz consisting
of 1 or 2 homework problems from the past week may be given in
place of homework.</p>
```

3. Add the attribute **id="grading"** to the <h2> tag for the Grading heading (see Figure 2-4).

4. Add the attribute **id="app"** to the <h2> tag for the Appointments heading.

5. Add the attribute **id="safety"** to the <h2> tag for the Safety heading.

6. Save your changes to the file.

7. Using your Web browser, refresh or reload **chem.htm** and scroll through the page to confirm that it appears unchanged. The ids you placed in the document should not change the appearance of the Web page.

Trouble? If you see a change in the page, check to make sure that you correctly typed the code for adding ids.

You've added ids to the document's four section headings. The next step is to create links to those sections.

Creating Links within a Document

For Stephen's page, you want to link the entries in the list you created earlier to the document's four sections. When a user clicks one of the linked entries at the top of the page, the browser will display the corresponding section of the document without requiring the user to scroll down. Figure 2-5 illustrates the relationships between the four links you want to create and the Web page's sections.

Figure 2-5 Links in the Chemistry page

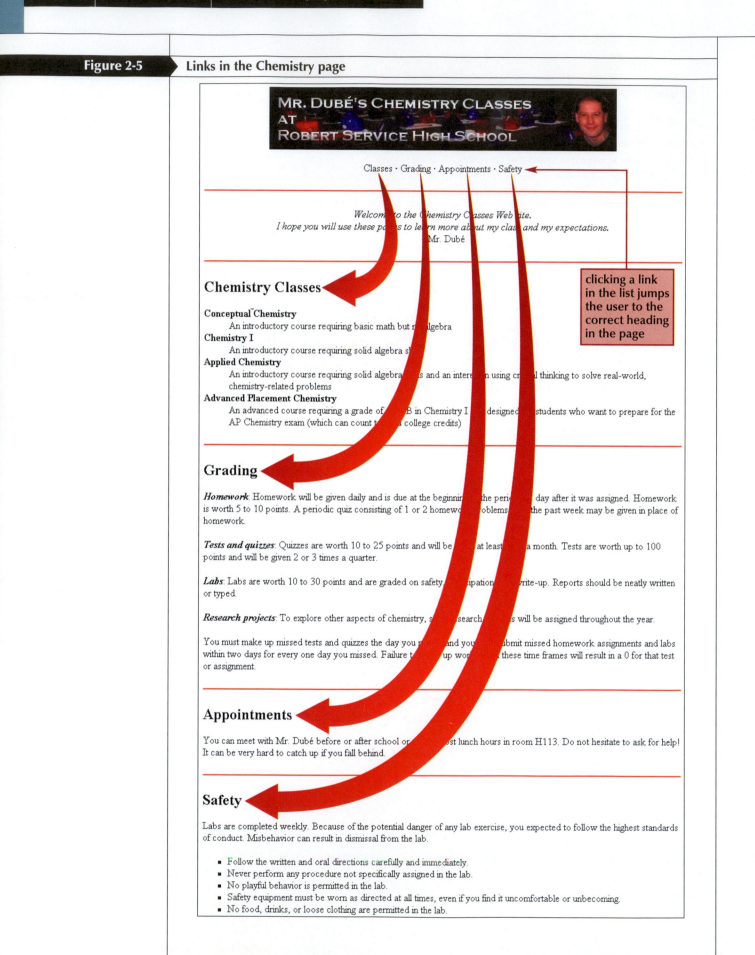

Classes · Grading · Appointments · Safety

clicking a link in the list jumps the user to the correct heading in the page

To create a link within a document, you enclose the content that you want to format as a link in an <a> tag, and use the href attribute (short for "Hypertext Reference") to identify the link target. The general syntax is

```
<a href="#id">content</a>
```

where *id* is the value of the id attribute for the destination and *content* is the content in the document that you want to act as a link. For example, to format the text "Classes" as a link pointing to the element named class, you would enter the code:

```
<a href="#classes">Classes</a>
```

In this example, the entire word "Classes" is defined as a link. When a user clicks on any part of the word, the browser jumps to the link's destination—in this case, the element whose id name is "classes".

Reference Window

Inserting and Linking to an Id

- To add an id name to an element, insert the following attribute into the element's tag:
  ```
  id="id"
  ```
  where *id* is the id name assigned to the element.
- To link to an element with an id, use the syntax:
  ```
  <a href="#id">content</a>
  ```
  where *content* is the content in the document that you want to act as a link.

A link's content is not limited to text. You can also format an inline image as a link, as in the following example:

```
<a href="#classes"><img src="dube.jpg" /></a>
```

In general, a link should not contain any block-level elements. Thus, if you want to change an h1 heading into a link, you should nest the link within the heading as follows:

```
<h2><a href="#classes">View Class List</a></h2>
```

rather than placing the heading within the link:

```
<a href="#classes"><h2>View Class List</h2></a>
```

While some browsers may accept this second form, others will reject it. XHTML will not accept any block level element placed within a link. Nor can you place one link inside of another. However, you can place most inline elements, including character-formatting elements, within a link. When in doubt, a good rule is to not place anything other than text and empty elements, such as inline images, within a link. This will ensure that your code is acceptable to all browsers and to XHTML.

Now that you've seen how to create a link, change the entries in the section list to links pointing to the document's different headings.

To create links in the chemistry page:

1. Return to **chem.htm** in your text editor.

2. Add opening and closing <a> tags to the list of sections at the top of the document as follows:

```
<p style="text-align: center">
    <a href="#classes">Classes</a> &#183;
    <a href="#grading">Grading</a> &#183;
    <a href="#app">Appointments</a> &#183;
    <a href="#safety">Safety</a>
</p>
```

See Figure 2-6.

Figure 2-6 | **Linking text to a destination**

id name in the current document

```
<p style="text-align: center">
    <a href="#classes">Classes</a> &#183;
    <a href="#grading">Grading</a> &#183;
    <a href="#app">Appointments</a> &#183;
    <a href="#safety">Safety</a>
</p>
```

3. Save your changes to the file.

4. Using your Web browser, refresh or reload **chem.htm**. The headings should now be a different color and be underlined. This is the standard formatting for links in most browsers. See Figure 2-7.

Figure 2-7 | **Links in the chemistry page**

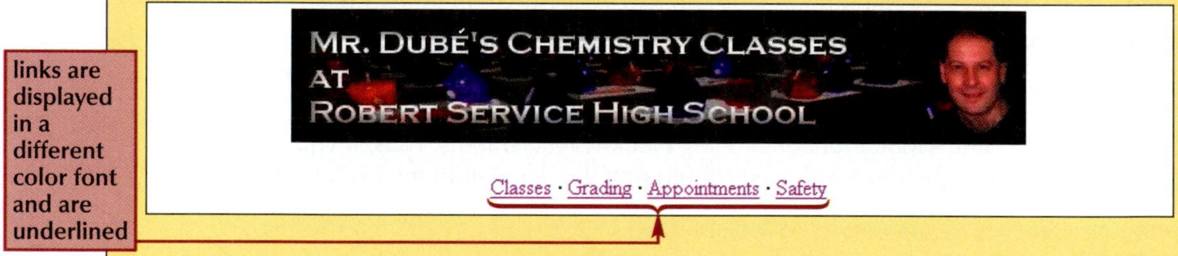

links are displayed in a different color font and are underlined

MR. DUBÉ'S CHEMISTRY CLASSES AT ROBERT SERVICE HIGH SCHOOL

Classes · Grading · Appointments · Safety

Trouble? If the headings do not appear as text links, check your code to make sure that you are using the <a> and </a> tags around the appropriate text, the href attribute within the tag, and the quotes and # symbols, as shown previously.

Before continuing, you should verify that the links work as you expect them to. To test a link, simply click it and verify that it jumps you to the appropriate destination.

To test your links:

1. Click one of the links. Your browser should display the section of the document indicated by the link. If it does not, check your code for errors by comparing it to Figure 2-6.

2. Click each of the other links, scrolling back to the top of the page after each test.

3. If you are continuing on to Session 2.2, leave your browser and text editor open. If you are not, you can close them at this time.

Trouble? The browser cannot scroll farther than the end of the page. Thus you may not see any difference between jumping to the Appointments section and jumping to the Safety section.

Creating Anchors

Older browser versions, such as Netscape Navigator 4.7 and Internet Explorer 4, do not support ids as link destinations. If you need to support these older browsers, you have to insert an anchor element into your document. An **anchor element** marks a specific location within a document. To create an anchor, you use the following syntax:

```
<a name="anchor">content</a>
```

where the name attribute provides the name of the anchor and `content` is the content (usually text) in the document that acts as the anchor. For example to add an anchor to the h2 heading, "Chemistry Classes", you could use the following HTML code:

```
<h2><a name="classes">Chemistry Classes</a></h2>
```

Since you create anchors with the same <a> tag you use to create links, anchor content can also include most inline elements and empty elements (like inline images); however, anchors cannot include block-level elements.

Once you create an anchor, the anchor's name acts just like an element id. Thus to link to the above anchor, you could create the following link:

```
<a name="#classes">Classes</a>
```

Inserting an anchor does not change your document's appearance in any way; it merely creates a destination within your document. Since anchors do not modify their content, you may be tempted to use them without content, as in the following example:

```
<a name="classes"></a><h2>Chemistry Classes</h2>
```

While many browsers will accept this form, some browsers expect every two-sided tag to contain some content and thus will reject this code. In practice, therefore, you should not create empty anchors.

Reference Window

Inserting and Linking to an Anchor

- To add an anchor to a document, use the syntax:
    ```
    <a name="anchor">content</a>
    ```
    where *anchor* is the name you want to give the anchor and *content* is the document content that will act as an anchor.
- To link to an anchor, use the syntax:
    ```
    <a href="#anchor">content</a>
    ```

You've completed your work adding links to the chemistry Web page. Stephen is confident that they will help his students and their parents to quickly navigate this lengthy page. In the next session, you'll learn how to create links to other documents on Stephen's Web site.

Session 2.1 Quick Check

Review

1. What is the HTML code for marking the h2 heading "Colorado State University" with the id name "csu"?
2. What is the HTML code for linking the text "Universities" to an element with the id, "csu"?
3. What is wrong with the following code?
    ```
    <a href="#info"><h3>For more information</h3></a>
    ```

4. What is the HTML code for marking an inline image, photo.jpg, with the anchor name "photo"?
5. What is the HTML code for linking the inline image button.jpg to an anchor with the name "links"?
6. When should you use anchors in place of ids for marking destinations within a document?

Session 2.2

Working with Web Site Structures

Stephen wants to add two more pages to his Web site: a page showing his contact information, and another listing his favorite chemistry links. Each page must contain links to the site's other pages, in order for users to be able to easily move around within the site. Figure 2-8 shows the three pages in Stephen's proposed site.

| Figure 2-8 | The three chemistry pages |

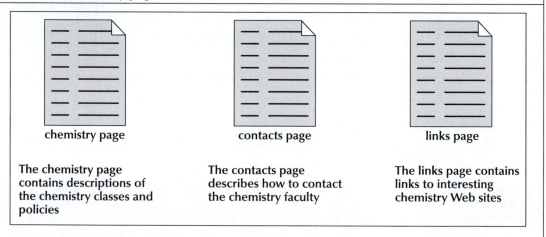

| chemistry page | contacts page | links page |

The chemistry page contains descriptions of the chemistry classes and policies

The contacts page describes how to contact the chemistry faculty

The links page contains links to interesting chemistry Web sites

Before you set up links to navigate a Web site, it's worthwhile to map out exactly how you want the pages to relate, using a common technique known as storyboarding. A **storyboard** is a diagram of a Web site's structure, showing all the pages in the site and indicating how they are linked together. Because Web sites use a variety of structures, it's important to storyboard your Web site before you start creating your pages in order to determine which structure works best for the type of information the site contains. A well-designed structure can ensure that users will able to navigate the site without getting lost or without missing important information.

The Web sites you commonly encounter as you navigate the Web use several different Web structures. Examining some of these structures can help you decide how to design your own sites.

Linear Structures

If you wanted to create an online version of a famous play, like Shakespeare's *Hamlet*, one method would be to create links between the individual scenes of the play. Figure 2-9 shows the storyboard of a **linear structure**, in which each page is linked with the pages that follow and precede it in an ordered chain. To read the online play, users move forward through the scenes (or backward if they wish to review the previous scenes).

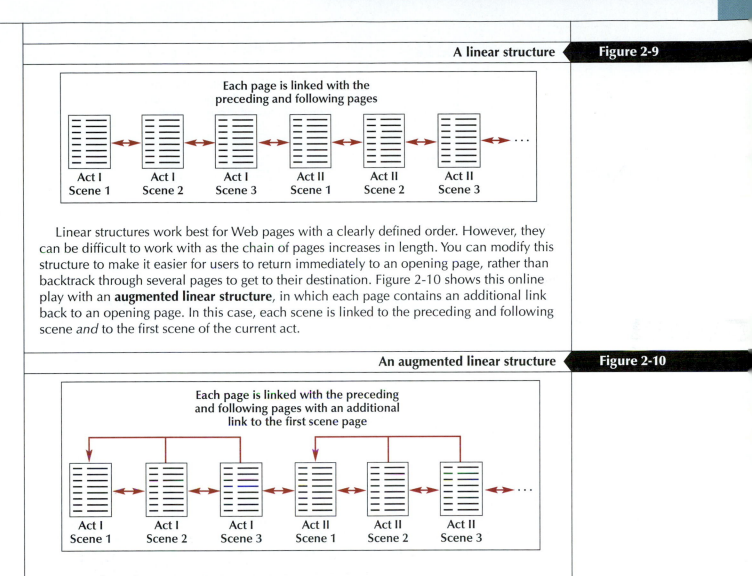

Linear structures work best for Web pages with a clearly defined order. However, they can be difficult to work with as the chain of pages increases in length. You can modify this structure to make it easier for users to return immediately to an opening page, rather than backtrack through several pages to get to their destination. Figure 2-10 shows this online play with an **augmented linear structure**, in which each page contains an additional link back to an opening page. In this case, each scene is linked to the preceding and following scene *and* to the first scene of the current act.

Hierarchical Structures

Another popular structure is the **hierarchical structure**, in which the pages are linked going from the most general page down to more specific pages. Those pages, in turn, can be linked to even more specific topics. In a hierarchical structure, users can easily move from general to specific and back again. In the case of our online play, we can link an introductory page containing general information about the play to pages that describe each of the play's acts, and within each act we can include links to individual scenes. With this structure, a user can move quickly to a specific scene within the page, bypassing the need to move through each scene in the play.

Figure 2-11 **A hierarchical structure**

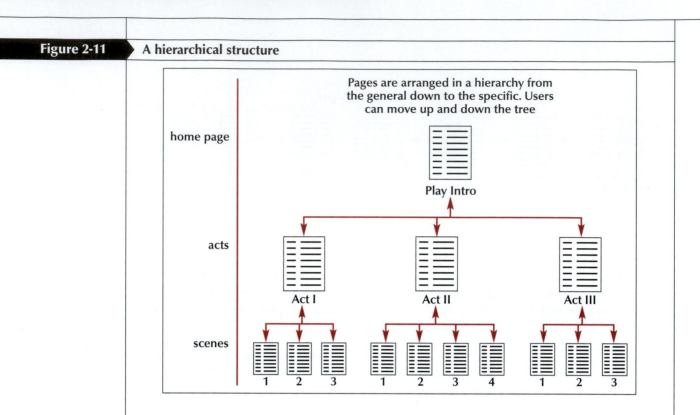

Mixed Structures

As your Web sites become larger and more complex, you often need to use a combination of several different structures. Figure 2-12 shows our online play using a mixture of different structures. The overall form is hierarchical, as users can move from a general introduction down to individual scenes; however, links also allow users to move through the site in a linear fashion, going from act to act and scene to scene. Note as well that each individual scene contains a link to the introductory page, allowing users to jump to the top of the hierarchy without moving through the different levels.

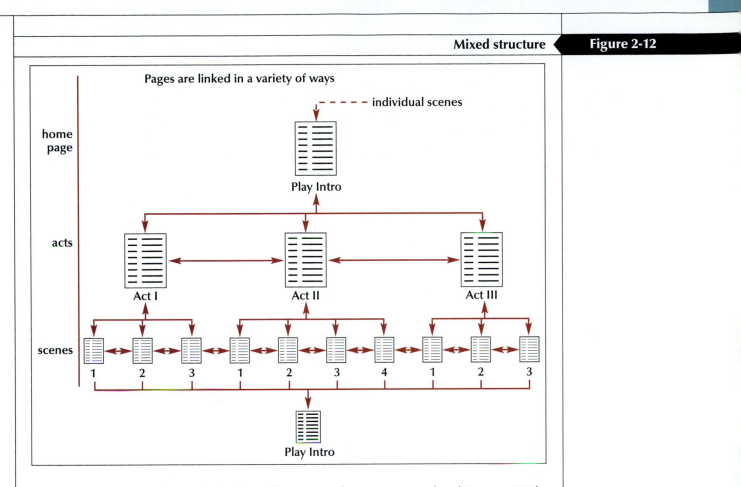

As these examples show, a little foresight can go a long way toward making your Web site easier to use. In addition, search results from a Web search engine such as Google or Alta Vista can point users to any page in your Web site, and they will need a way to quickly understand what your site contains and how to get at it. Thus, each page should contain at minimum a link to the site's home page, or to the relevant main topic page, if applicable. In some cases, you may want to supply your users with a **site index**, which is a page containing an outline of the entire site and its contents. Unstructured Web sites can be difficult and frustrating to use. Consider the storyboard of the site displayed in Figure 2-13.

Figure 2-13 Web site with no coherent structure

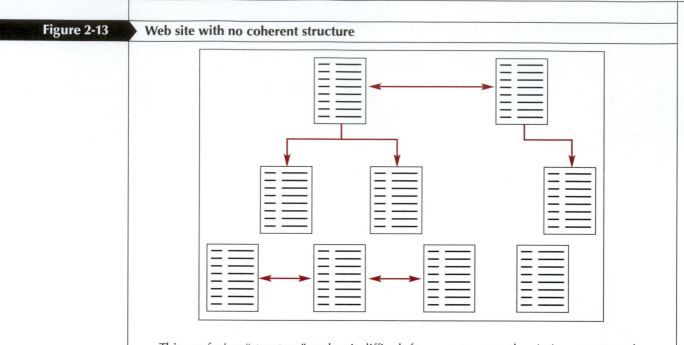

This confusing "structure" makes it difficult for users to grasp the site's contents and scope. The user might not even be aware of the presence of some pages because there are no connecting links (or the links only point in one direction). The Web is a competitive place and studies have shown that users who don't see how to get what they want within the first few seconds often leave a Web site. How long would a user hang around a site like the one shown in Figure 2-13?

Creating Links between Documents

Stephen wants students and their parents to be able to move effortlessly between the three documents in his Web site. To do that, you'll create links between each page and the other two pages. Figure 2-14 provides a storyboard for the simple structure you have in mind.

Figure 2-14 Storyboard for the chemistry Web site

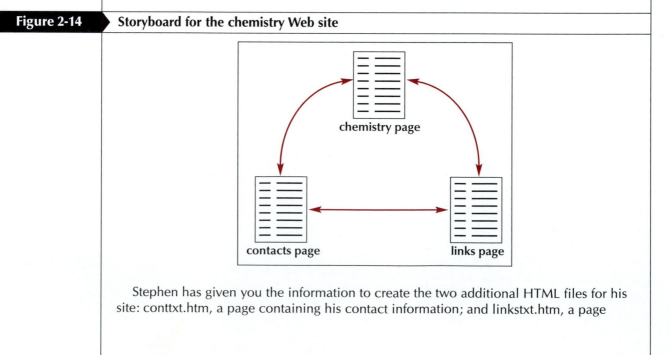

chemistry page

contacts page   links page

Stephen has given you the information to create the two additional HTML files for his site: conttxt.htm, a page containing his contact information; and linkstxt.htm, a page containing links to various chemistry Web sites that he has found particularly helpful to his students. These files are located in the tutorial folder in the tutorial.02 folder on your Data Disk. You should save these files with new names to keep the originals intact.

To rename the conttxt.htm and linkstxt.htm files:

1. Using your text editor, open **conttxt.htm** from the tutorial.02/tutorial folder. Enter *your name* and *the date* in the comment tag at the top of the file. Save the file as **contacts.htm**.

2. Using your text editor, open **linkstxt.htm** from the tutorial.02/tutorial folder. Enter *your name* and *the date* in the comment tag at the top of the file. Save the file as **links.htm**.

Linking to a Document

You begin by inserting links in the chemistry page to the contacts and links pages. To link to a page, you specify the name of the file using the href attribute of the <a> tag. For example, to link the phrase "Contact me" to the contacts.htm file, you enter the following HTML code:

```
<a href="contacts.htm">Contact me</a>
```

In order for the browser to be able to locate and open contacts.htm, it must be located in the same folder as the chem.htm file. You'll learn how to link to documents in separate folders shortly. Note that unlike creating links between elements on the same page, this process does not require you to create an id attribute or to set an anchor. The filename serves as the target.

Filenames are case sensitive on some operating systems, including the UNIX and Macintosh operating systems, but not on others, such as Windows and MS-DOS. For this reason, you may find that links you create on your computer may not work when you transfer your files to a Web server. To avoid this problem, the current standard is to use lowercase filenames for all files on a Web site, and to avoid using special characters such as blanks and slashes (/). You should also keep your filenames short, so that users are less apt to make typing errors when accessing your site.

To add links to the Contact and Links pages:

1. Using your text editor, reopen the **chem.htm** file that you worked on in Session 2.1 of this tutorial.

2. Locate the links you created in the last session, and then insert the following links at the top of the list, as shown in Figure 2-15.

```
<a href="contacts.htm">Contact Info</a> &#183;
<a href="links.htm">Chemistry Links</a> &#183;
```

Linking to other documents **Figure 2-15**

3. Save your changes to the file.

4. Open **chem.htm** in your Web browser. The two new, external text links appear to the left of the four internal links, as shown in Figure 2-16.

Figure 2-16 **Displaying links to other documents**

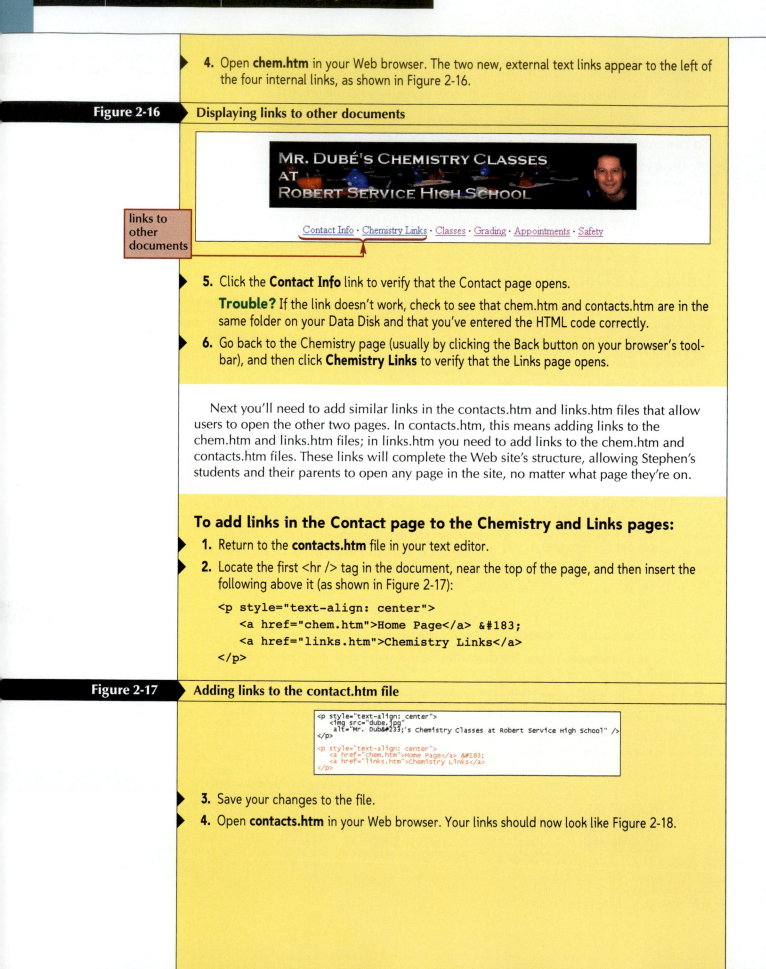

links to
other
documents

5. Click the **Contact Info** link to verify that the Contact page opens.

   Trouble? If the link doesn't work, check to see that chem.htm and contacts.htm are in the same folder on your Data Disk and that you've entered the HTML code correctly.

6. Go back to the Chemistry page (usually by clicking the Back button on your browser's tool-bar), and then click **Chemistry Links** to verify that the Links page opens.

Next you'll need to add similar links in the contacts.htm and links.htm files that allow users to open the other two pages. In contacts.htm, this means adding links to the chem.htm and links.htm files; in links.htm you need to add links to the chem.htm and contacts.htm files. These links will complete the Web site's structure, allowing Stephen's students and their parents to open any page in the site, no matter what page they're on.

To add links in the Contact page to the Chemistry and Links pages:

1. Return to the **contacts.htm** file in your text editor.

2. Locate the first <hr /> tag in the document, near the top of the page, and then insert the following above it (as shown in Figure 2-17):

```
<p style="text-align: center">
    <a href="chem.htm">Home Page</a> &#183;
    <a href="links.htm">Chemistry Links</a>
</p>
```

Figure 2-17 **Adding links to the contact.htm file**

```
<p style="text-align: center">
    <img src="dube.jpg"
    alt="Mr. Dub&#233;'s Chemistry Classes at Robert Service High School" />
</p>

<p style="text-align: center">
    <a href="chem.htm">Home Page</a> &#183;
    <a href="links.htm">Chemistry Links</a>
</p>
```

3. Save your changes to the file.

4. Open **contacts.htm** in your Web browser. Your links should now look like Figure 2-18.

Links in the Contacts page ◄ **Figure 2-18**

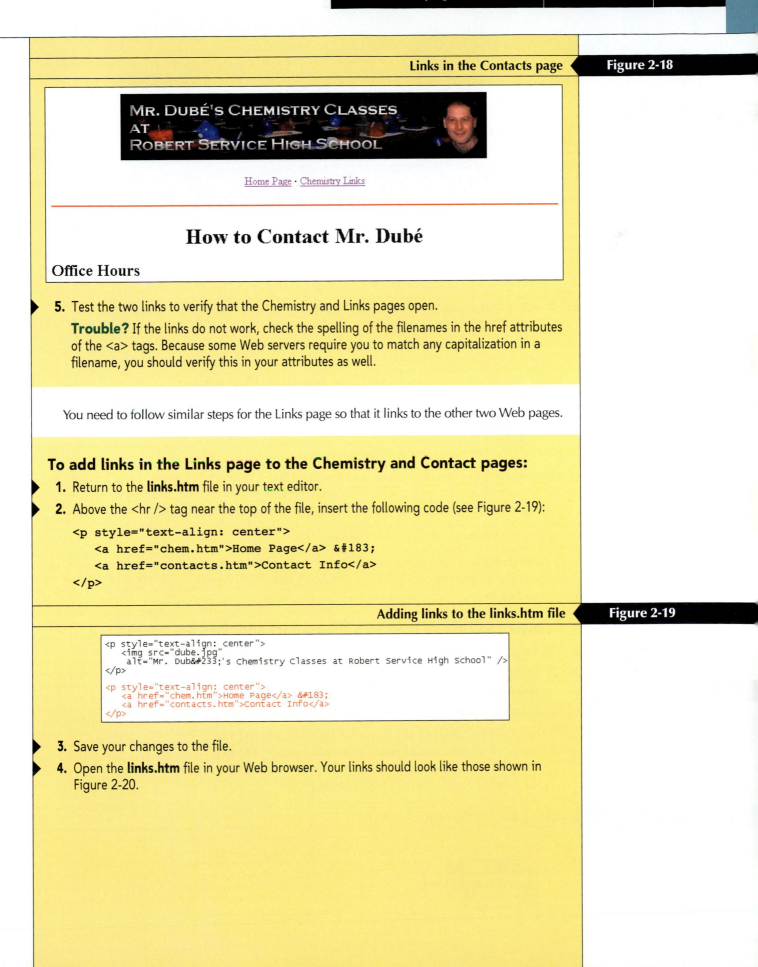

5. Test the two links to verify that the Chemistry and Links pages open.

   Trouble? If the links do not work, check the spelling of the filenames in the href attributes of the <a> tags. Because some Web servers require you to match any capitalization in a filename, you should verify this in your attributes as well.

You need to follow similar steps for the Links page so that it links to the other two Web pages.

To add links in the Links page to the Chemistry and Contact pages:

1. Return to the **links.htm** file in your text editor.

2. Above the <hr /> tag near the top of the file, insert the following code (see Figure 2-19):

```
<p style="text-align: center">
   <a href="chem.htm">Home Page</a> &#183;
   <a href="contacts.htm">Contact Info</a>
</p>
```

Adding links to the links.htm file ◄ **Figure 2-19**

```
<p style="text-align: center">
   <img src="dube.jpg"
   alt="Mr. Dub&#233;'s Chemistry Classes at Robert Service High School" />
</p>

<p style="text-align: center">
   <a href="chem.htm">Home Page</a> &#183;
   <a href="contacts.htm">Contact Info</a>
</p>
```

3. Save your changes to the file.

4. Open the **links.htm** file in your Web browser. Your links should look like those shown in Figure 2-20.

Figure 2-20 | Links on the Links page

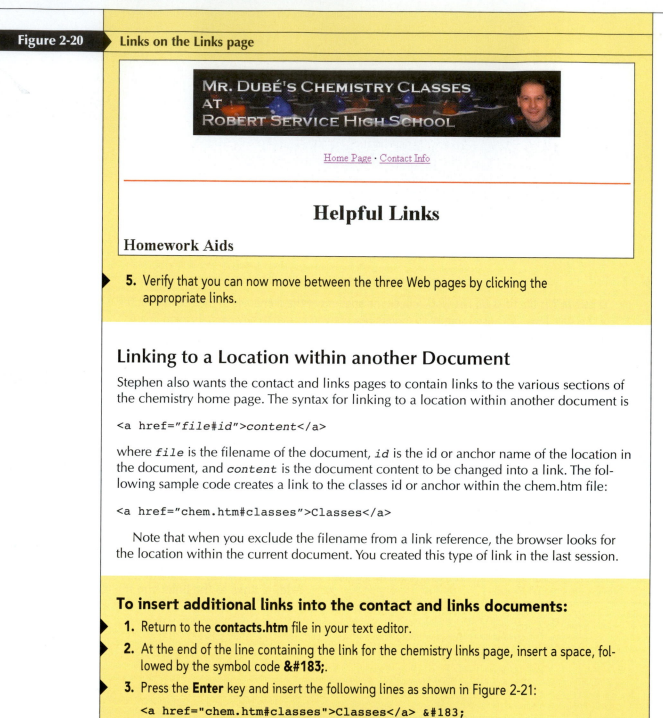

5. Verify that you can now move between the three Web pages by clicking the appropriate links.

Linking to a Location within another Document

Stephen also wants the contact and links pages to contain links to the various sections of the chemistry home page. The syntax for linking to a location within another document is

```
<a href="file#id">content</a>
```

where *file* is the filename of the document, *id* is the id or anchor name of the location in the document, and *content* is the document content to be changed into a link. The following sample code creates a link to the classes id or anchor within the chem.htm file:

```
<a href="chem.htm#classes">Classes</a>
```

Note that when you exclude the filename from a link reference, the browser looks for the location within the current document. You created this type of link in the last session.

To insert additional links into the contact and links documents:

1. Return to the **contacts.htm** file in your text editor.

2. At the end of the line containing the link for the chemistry links page, insert a space, followed by the symbol code **·**.

3. Press the **Enter** key and insert the following lines as shown in Figure 2-21:

```
<a href="chem.htm#classes">Classes</a> &#183;
<a href="chem.htm#grading">Grading</a> &#183;
<a href="chem.htm#app">Appointments</a> &#183;
<a href="chem.htm#safety">Safety</a>
```

Figure 2-21 | Adding links to the contact.htm file

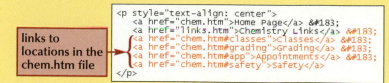

```
<p style="text-align: center">
    <a href="chem.htm">Home Page</a> &#183;
    <a href="links.htm">Chemistry Links</a> &#183;
    <a href="chem.htm#classes">Classes</a> &#183;
    <a href="chem.htm#grading">Grading</a> &#183;
    <a href="chem.htm#app">Appointments</a> &#183;
    <a href="chem.htm#safety">Safety</a>
</p>
```

links to locations in the chem.htm file

4. Save your changes to the file and then reopen **contacts.htm** in your Web browser. Verify that the list of links appears as shown in Figure 2-22 and that the browser displays the appropriate target when you click each link.

Final link list for the Contacts page | **Figure 2-22**

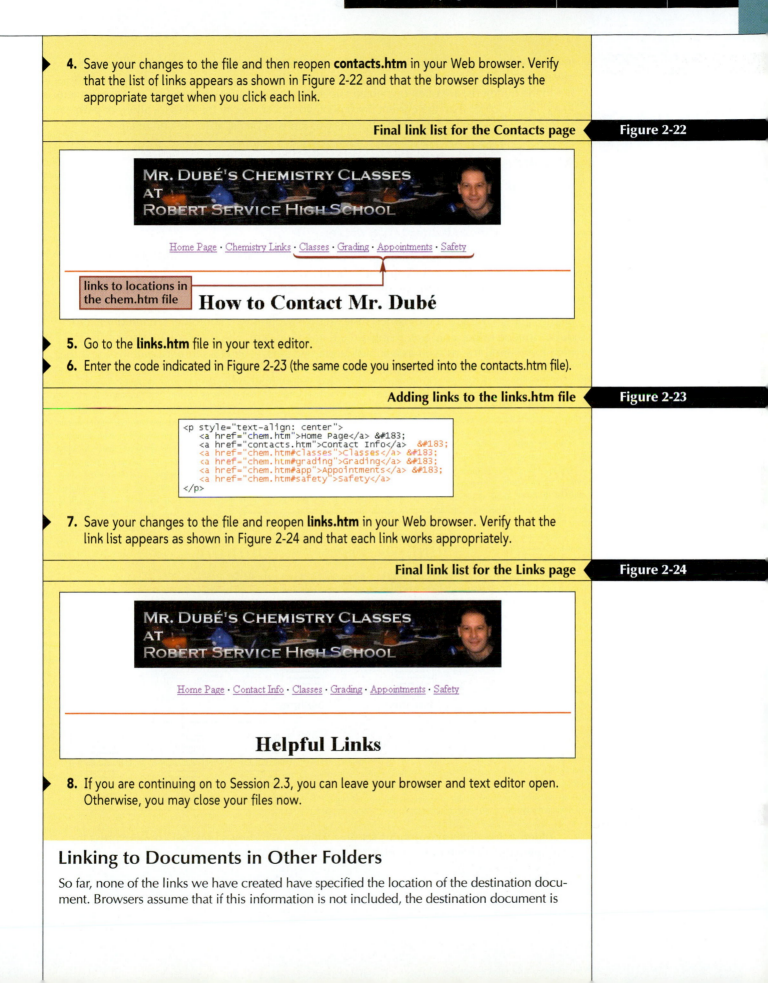

5. Go to the **links.htm** file in your text editor.

6. Enter the code indicated in Figure 2-23 (the same code you inserted into the contacts.htm file).

Adding links to the links.htm file | **Figure 2-23**

```
<p style="text-align: center">
   <a href="chem.htm">Home Page</a> &#183;
   <a href="contacts.htm">Contact Info</a>  &#183;
   <a href="chem.htm#classes">Classes</a> &#183;
   <a href="chem.htm#grading">Grading</a> &#183;
   <a href="chem.htm#app">Appointments</a> &#183;
   <a href="chem.htm#safety">Safety</a>
</p>
```

7. Save your changes to the file and reopen **links.htm** in your Web browser. Verify that the link list appears as shown in Figure 2-24 and that each link works appropriately.

Final link list for the Links page | **Figure 2-24**

8. If you are continuing on to Session 2.3, you can leave your browser and text editor open. Otherwise, you may close your files now.

Linking to Documents in Other Folders

So far, none of the links we have created have specified the location of the destination document. Browsers assume that if this information is not included, the destination document is located in the same folder as the document containing the link. However, these files are not always located in the same place. For instance, the files in a large Web site, which can number in the hundreds, are often organized into separate folders. To create a link to a file located in a different folder than the current document, you must specify the file's location, or **path**, so that browsers can find it. HTML supports two kinds of paths: absolute and relative.

Absolute Paths

An **absolute path** specifies a file's precise location within a computer's entire folder structure. Absolute pathnames employ the following syntax:

```
/folder1/folder2/folder3/... /file
```

where *folder1* is the topmost folder in the computer's folder tree, followed by *folder2*, *folder3*, and so forth, until you reach the file you want to link to.

Figure 2-25 shows a sample folder tree that might be used for the Web server at Stephen Dubé's school. In this case, the topmost folder in the tree is named faculty. The faculty folder contains a file named index.htm as well as two subfolders, named lee and dube. The lee folder contains a single file named bio.htm. The dube folder also contains a file named bio.htm, as well as a subfolder named class. The class folder contains the three files we've been working with in this session.

Figure 2-25 ▶ **A sample folder tree**

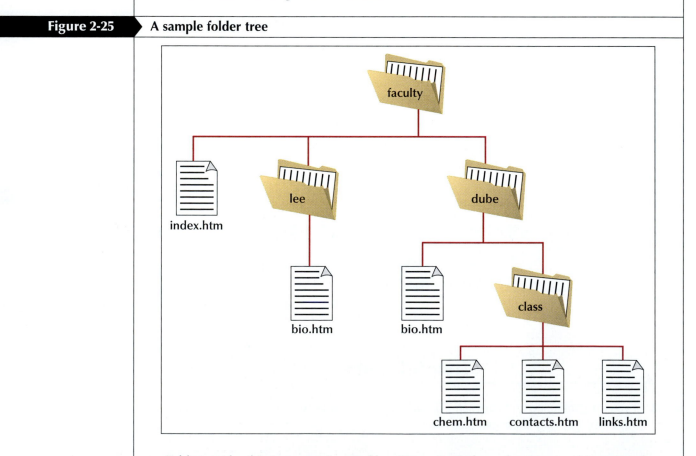

Folders aside, this tree contains six files. Figure 2-26 shows how we could express the absolute paths to each of these files.

Absolute Path	Interpretation
/faculty/index.htm	The index.htm file in the faculty folder
/faculty/lee/bio.htm	The bio.htm file in the lee subfolder
/faculty/dube/bio.htm	The bio.htm file in the dube subfolder
/faculty/dube/class/chem.htm	The chem.htm file in the dube/class subfolder
/faculty/dube/class/contacts.htm	The contacts.htm file in the dube/class subfolder
/faculty/dube/class/links.htm	The links.htm file in the dube/class subfolder

If files are located on different drives as well as in different folders, you must include the drive letter as follows:

`/drive|/folder1/folder2/folder3/... /file`

where `drive` is the letter assigned to the drive. For example the chem.htm file located on drive C in the /faculty/dube/class folder would have the absolute path:

`/C|/faculty/dube/class/chem.htm`

Remember that you don't have to include a drive letter if the destination document is located on the same drive as the document containing the link.

Relative Paths

When many folders and subfolders are involved, absolute pathnames can be cumbersome and confusing. For that reason, most Web designers prefer to use relative paths. A **relative path** specifies a file's location in relation to the location of the current document. If the file is in the same folder as the current document, you do not specify the folder name. If the file is in a subfolder of the current document, you have to include the name of the subfolder (forward slash is not required) followed by the file name. If you want to go one level up the folder tree, you start the relative path with a double period (..) and then provide the name of the file. To specify a different folder on the same level, known as a **sibling folder**, you move up the folder tree using the double period (..) and then down the tree using the name of the sibling folder.

For example, Figure 2-27 shows the relative paths to the six files in the tree from Figure 2-25, starting from a file stored in the /faculty/dube folder.

Relative Path from the faculty/dube folder	Interpretation
../index.htm	The index.htm file in the parent folder
../lee/bio.htm	The bio.htm file in the lee sibling folder
bio.htm	The bio.htm file in the current folder
class/chem.htm	The chem.htm file in the class subfolder
class/contacts.htm	The contacts.htm file in the class subfolder
class/links.htm	The links.htm file in the class subfolder

You should almost always use relative paths in your links. If you have to move your files to a different computer or server, you can move the entire folder structure without having to change the relative pathnames you created. If you use absolute pathnames, however, you must revise each link to reflect the new location of the folder tree on the computer.

Changing the Base

As we've noted, a browser resolves relative pathnames by default based on the location of the current document. You can change this behavior by specifying a different base in the document's head. The syntax for specifying the base is:

```
<base href="path" />
```

where *path* is the folder location that you want the browser to use when resolving relative paths in the current document.

The base element is useful when a document is moved to a new folder. Rather than rewriting all of the relative paths to reflect the document's new location, the base element can redirect browsers to the document's old location, allowing any relative paths to be resolved as they were before. The base element is also useful when you want to create a copy of a single page from a large Web site on another Web server. Instead of copying the entire site to the new location, you can copy the one file, but have the base point to the location of the original site. Any links in the copied page will behave the same as the links in the original page.

You've completed your work creating links between the three files in Stephen's Web site. In the next session, you'll learn how to create links that point to documents and resources located on the Internet.

Review

Session 2.2 Quick Check

1. What is storyboarding? Why is it important in creating a Web page system?
2. What is a linear structure? What is a hierarchical structure?
3. What code would you enter to link the text, "Sports Info", to the sports.htm file? Assume that the current document and sports.htm are in the same folder.
4. What code would you enter to link the text, "Basketball news", to the location with the id or anchor name of "bball" within a different file named sports.htm?
5. What's the difference between an absolute path and a relative path?
6. Refer to Figure 2-25. If the current file is in the /faculty/lee folder, what are the relative paths for the six files listed in the folder tree?
7. What is the purpose of the <base />tag?

Session 2.3

Linking to Resources on the Internet

In the links.htm file, Stephen has listed the names of some Web sites that have proved useful for him and his students. He would like you to change these names into links, so that his students can quickly access those sites from their browsers.

Understanding URLs

To create a link to a resource on the Internet, you need to know its URL. A **URL**, or **Uniform Resource Locator**, specifies the precise location of a resource on the Internet. The general form of a URL is:

```
scheme:location
```

where *scheme* indicates the type of resource that the URL is referencing, and *location* is the location of that resource. For Web pages the location is a document stored in a folder on a Web server, but for other resources, the location could be an identifying name. For example, an e-mail URL would have a location pointing to an e-mail address.

The name of the scheme is taken from the protocol used to access the Internet resource. A **protocol** is a set of rules defining how information is exchanged between two devices. Your Web browser communicates with Web servers using the **Hypertext Transfer Protocol** or **HTTP**. Thus, the URLs for all Web pages must start with the scheme "http". This tells a browser to use http to communicate with the Web server you specify. Other Internet resources, described in Figure 2-28, use different protocols and thus have different scheme names.

Common communication protocols ◄ **Figure 2-28**

Protocol	Used to
file	access documents stored locally on a user's computer
ftp	access documents stored on an FTP server
gopher	access documents stored on a gopher server
http	access Web pages stored on the World Wide Web
mailto	open a user's e-mail client and address a new message
news	connect to a Usenet newsgroup
telnet	open a telnet connection to a specific server
wais	connect to a Wide Area Information Server database

Linking to a Web Page

The URL for a Web page has the general form:

```
http://server/path/filename#id
```

where *server* is the name of the Web server storing a specific file, *path* is the path to the file on that server, *filename* is the name of file, and if necessary, *id* is the name of an id or anchor within the file. A Web page URL can also contain specific programming instructions for a browser to send to the Web server, but we won't deal with that topic here. Figure 2-29 shows the URL for a sample Web page with all of the parts identified.

A sample URL for a Web page ◄ **Figure 2-29**

You may have noticed that a URL like http://www.course.com doesn't include any path or file name. If a URL includes no path, then it indicates the topmost folder in the server's directory tree. If a URL does not specify a filename, the server searches for a file named "index.html" or "index.htm" in the specified location. This file is often the Web site's home page. Thus, a URL like http://www.course.com is equivalent to http://www.course.com/index.html.

Stephen has listed six Web pages that he wants students to be able to access. He's provided you with the URLs for these pages, which are shown in Figure 2-30.

Figure 2-30 ▶ **Links to chemistry sites on the Web**

Site	URL
Carnegie Library	http://www.carnegielibrary.org/subject/homework
Discovery Schools	http://school.discovery.com
Frostburg State	http://antoine.frostburg.edu/chem/senese/101
Yahoo	http://dir.yahoo.com/Science/chemistry
Los Alamos	http://pearl1.lanl.gov/periodic
Visual Elements	http://www.chemsoc.org/viselements

To link to these Web pages, you specify each URL as the href attribute value for the appropriate <a> tag as follows:

```
<a href="http://school.discovery.com">Discovery Schools</a>
```

Use the information that Stephen has given you to create links to all six of the Web sites listed in Figure 2-30.

To add links to the Chemistry Links page:

1. If necessary, use your text editor to reopen the **links.htm** file from the tutorial.02/tutorial folder.

2. Locate the text "Carnegie Library" and insert the following link:

```
<a href="http://www.carnegielibrary.org/subject/homework">
   Carnegie Library
</a>
```

3. Locate "Discovery Schools" and insert the link:

```
<a href="http://school.discovery.com ">
   Discovery Schools
</a>
```

4. Locate "Frostburg State" and insert the link:

```
<a href="http://antoine.frostburg.edu/chem/senese/101">
   Frostburg State
</a>
```

5. Locate "Yahoo" and insert the link:

```
<a href="http://dir.yahoo.com/Science/chemistry">
   Yahoo
</a>
```

6. Locate "Los Alamos" and insert the link:

```
<a href="http://pearl1.lanl.gov/periodic">
   Los Alamos
</a>
```

7. Locate "Visual Elements" and insert the link:

```
<a href="http://www.chemsoc.org/viselements">
   Visual Elements
</a>
```

Figure 2-31 shows the revised code.

Inserting links to the chemistry sites

Figure 2-31

```
<blockquote><p>
<b><a href="http://www.carnegielibrary.org/subject/homework">Carnegie Library</a></b>:
Homework resources from the Carnegie Library of Pittsburgh.</p></blockquote>

<blockquote><p>
<b><a href="http://school.discovery.com">Discovery Schools</a></b>:
Get homework help from the school sponsored by the Discovery Channel.</p></blockquote>

<h2>Chemistry Resources</h2>

<blockquote><p>
<b><a href="http://antoine.frostburg.edu/chem/senese/101">Frostburg State</a></b>:
View articles, tutorials, and online quizzes from the chemistry
department at Frostburg State University in Maryland.</p></blockquote>

<blockquote><p>
<b><a href="http://dir.yahoo.com/Science/chemistry">Yahoo</a></b>:
Yahoo's list of chemistry resources on the web.</p></blockquote>

<h2>The Periodic Table</h2>

<blockquote><p>
<b><a href="http://pearl1.lanl.gov/periodic">Los Alamos</a></b>:
An interactive periodic table of the elements presented by the
National Laboratory's Chemistry Division at Los Alamos.</p></blockquote>

<blockquote><p>
<b><a href="http://www.chemsoc.org/viselements">Visual Elements</a></b>:
A stunning visual representation of the periodic table by the
RSC's chemical science network.</p></blockquote>
```

1

8. Save your changes to the file.

9. Reload **links.htm** in your Web browser. Figure 2-32 shows the revised appearance of the page. Click each of the links in the page and verify that the appropriate Web site opens.

Links in the Links page

Figure 2-32

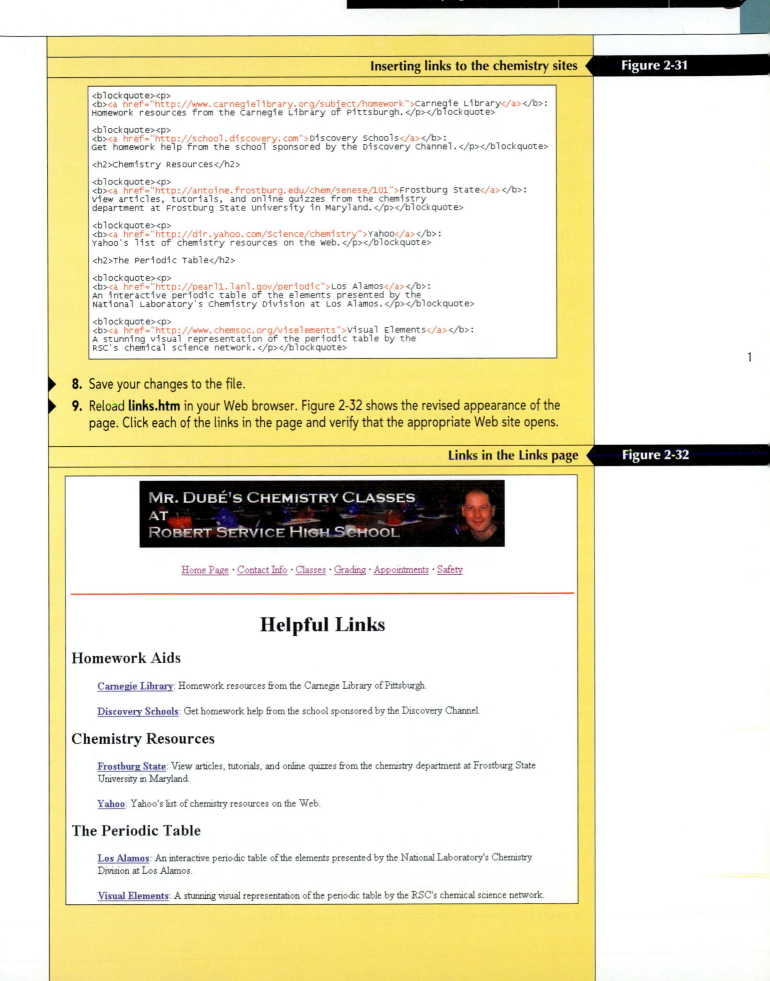

MR. DUBÉ'S CHEMISTRY CLASSES
AT
ROBERT SERVICE HIGH SCHOOL

Home Page · Contact Info · Classes · Grading · Appointments · Safety

Helpful Links

Homework Aids

Carnegie Library: Homework resources from the Carnegie Library of Pittsburgh.

Discovery Schools: Get homework help from the school sponsored by the Discovery Channel.

Chemistry Resources

Frostburg State: View articles, tutorials, and online quizzes from the chemistry department at Frostburg State University in Maryland.

Yahoo: Yahoo's list of chemistry resources on the Web.

The Periodic Table

Los Alamos: An interactive periodic table of the elements presented by the National Laboratory's Chemistry Division at Los Alamos.

Visual Elements: A stunning visual representation of the periodic table by the RSC's chemical science network.

Trouble? To open these sites you must be connected to the Internet. If you are still having problems, compare your code to the URLs listed in Figure 2-30 to confirm that you have not made a typing error. Also keep in mind that because the Web is constantly changing, the URLs for some of these links may have changed, or a site may have disappeared entirely since this book was printed.

Web pages are only one type of resource that you can link to. Before continuing work on the chemistry Web site, let's explore how to access some of these other resources.

Linking to FTP Servers

FTP servers are one of the main resources for storing files on the Internet. FTP servers transfer information using a communications protocol called **File Transfer Protocol**, or **FTP** for short. The URL for a file stored on an FTP server follows the general format:

```
ftp://server/path/filename
```

where *server* is the name of the FTP server, *path* is the folder path on the server, and *filename* is the name of the file you want to retrieve. If you omit the path and filename information, your Web browser will likely display the folders contained on the FTP server, which you can then navigate to download the file or files of interest (see Figure 2-33). Note that different browsers can display the contents of an FTP site in different ways. Figure 2-33 shows what a site might look like in Internet Explorer.

Figure 2-33 ▶ **An FTP site as it appears in Internet Explorer**

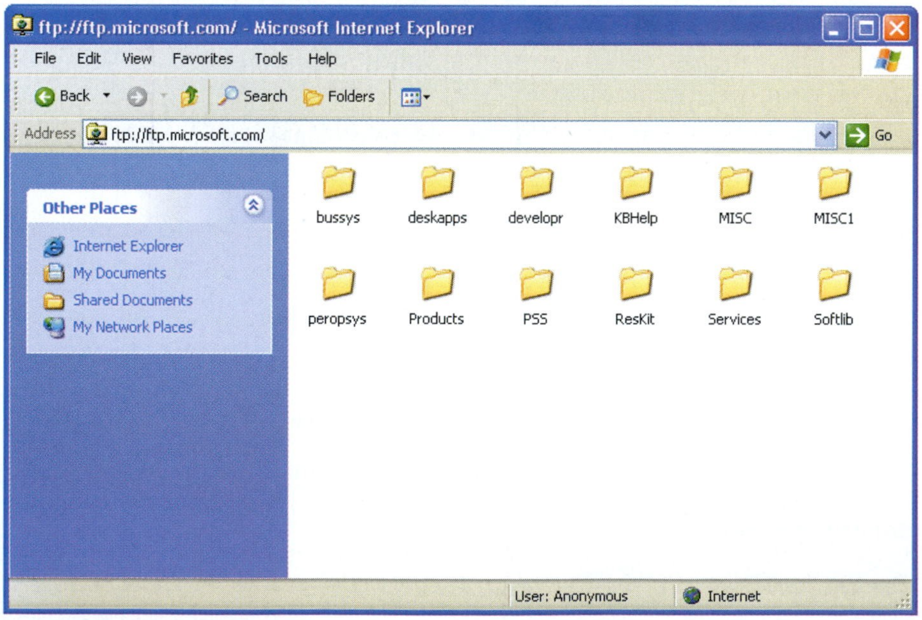

An FTP server requires each user to enter a password and a username to access its files. The standard username is "anonymous", which requires no password. Your browser supplies this information for you automatically, so in most situations you don't have to worry about passwords and usernames. However, some FTP servers do not allow anonymous access. In these cases, either your browser prompts you for the username and the password, or you can supply a username and password within the URL using the following format:

```
ftp://username:password@hostname/path/filename
```

where *username* and *password* are a username and password that the FTP server recognizes. It is generally *not* a good idea, however, to include usernames and passwords in URLs, as it can allow others to view your sensitive login information. It's better to let the browser send this information, or use a special program called an **FTP client**, because those programs can encrypt or hide this information during transmission.

Linking to Usenet News

Usenet is a collection of discussion forums called **newsgroups** that let users publicly exchange messages with each other on a wide variety of topics. The URL for a Usenet newsgroup has the form:

```
news:newsgroup
```

where *newsgroup* is the name of the group you want to access. For example, to access the surfing newsgroup alt.surfing, you would use the URL news:alt.surfing. When you click a link to a newsgroup, your computer opens a program for reading newsgroups, known as a **newsreader**, displaying the latest messages from the newsgroup. Figure 2-34 shows the contents of the alt.surfing newsgroup as displayed by the Outlook Express newsreader.

A sample newsreader ◄ **Figure 2-34**

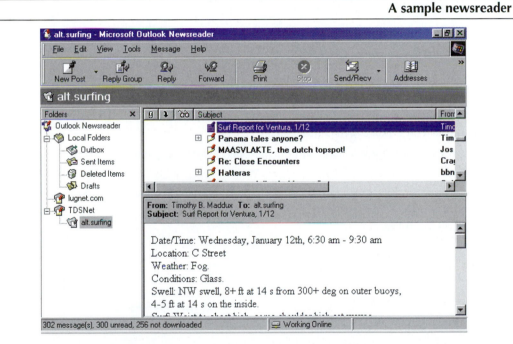

Linking to a Local File

On occasion, you may see the URL for a file stored locally on your computer or local area network. The form of this URL is:

```
file://server/path/filename
```

where *server* is the name of the local server, *path* is the path on that server to the file, and *filename* is the name of the file. This form is rarely used in Web pages, but it might appear in the address toolbar of your browser if you attempt to load a page off of your computer or LAN. If you're accessing a file from your own computer, the server name might be omitted and replaced by an extra slash (/). Thus, a file from the documents/chemistry folder might have the URL:

```
file:///documents/chemistry/chem.htm
```

If the file is on a different disk within your computer, the hard drive letter would be included in the URL as follows:

```
file://D:/documents/chemistry/chem.htm
```

Unlike the other URLs we've examined, the "file" scheme in this URL does not imply any particular communication protocol; instead, the browser retrieves the document using whatever method is the local standard for the type of file specified in the URL.

Linking to E-mail

Many Web sites use e-mail to allow users to communicate with a site's owner, or with the staff of the organization that runs the site. You can turn an e-mail address into a link, so that when a user clicks an address, the browser starts an e-mail program and automatically inserts the address into the "To" field of a new outgoing message. The URL for an e-mail address follows the form:

```
mailto:address
```

where *address* is the e-mail address. While the mailto: protocol is not technically an approved communication protocol, it is so widely supported that you should have no problem using it.

Stephen wants you to add to a link to his e-mail address on the chemistry Web site. Students and their parents can use this link to quickly send him messages about his classes. Format the e-mail address on Stephen's Contact page as a link.

To add an e-mail link to Stephen's Contact page:

1. Using your text editor, open **contacts.htm**.

2. Go to the bottom of the file and add the following link to the e-mail address, as shown in Figure 2-35.

   ```
   <a href="mailto:sdube@eps.edmonton.ab.ca">sdube@eps.edmonton.ab.ca</a>.
   ```

Figure 2-35 | **Creating an e-mail link**

```
<h2>E-mail</h2>
<p>E-mail is a great way to reach me. I answer e-mails from students
and parents within one school day of receiving the e-mail.
My address is :</p>

<blockquote><p>
<a href="mailto:sdube@eps.edmonton.ab.ca">sdube@eps.edmonton.ab.ca</a>.
</p></blockquote>
```

3. Save your changes to the file.

4. Using your Web browser, open **contacts.htm**.

5. Scroll to the bottom of the page and verify that the e-mail address is now displayed as a link (see Figure 2-36).

Figure 2-36 | **E-mail link in the Contact page**

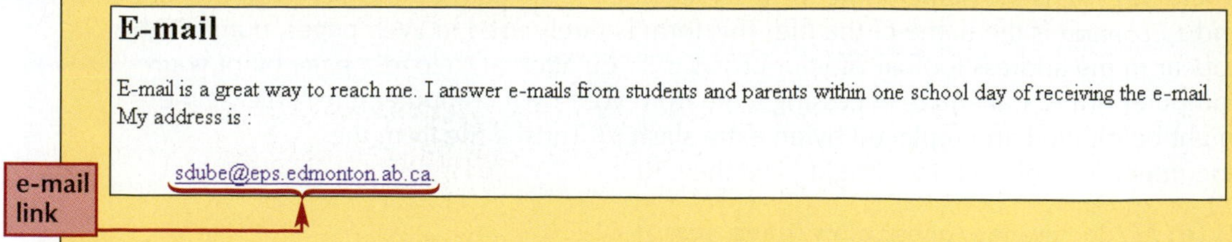

E-mail

E-mail is a great way to reach me. I answer e-mails from students and parents within one school day of receiving the e-mail. My address is :

> sdube@eps.edmonton.ab.ca

e-mail link

Trouble? Some browsers do not support the mailto: URL. If you use a browser other than Netscape Navigator or Internet Explorer, check to see if it supports this feature.

6. Click the e-mail address and verify that an e-mail message window, similar to the one in Figure 2-37, opens.

Testing the e-mail link **Figure 2-37**

mail message window opens with Stephen's e-mail address already inserted

Trouble? Your e-mail window may look different, depending on the mail program you are using.

7. Cancel the mail message by clicking the window's Close button. This e-mail address is a fictional one for illustration purposes only.

You should be aware that there are problems with placing an e-mail link in a Web page. A user may not know how to use an e-mail client, or a user's browser may open the wrong e-mail client when the user clicks the link.

Of more concern is the effect of e-mail links on increasing spam. **Spam** is unsolicited junk e-mail sent to large numbers of people, promoting products, services and in some cases, pornographic Web sites. Spammers create their e-mail lists through scanning Usenet postings, stealing Internet mailing lists, and using programs called **e-mail harvesters** that scan HTML code on the Web looking for the e-mail addresses contained in mailto URLs. Many Web developers are removing e-mail links from their Web sites in order to foil these harvesters, replacing the links with Web forms that submit e-mail requests to a secure server. If you need to include an e-mail address in your Web page, you can take a few steps to reduce problems with spam:

• Replace all e-mail addresses in your page text with inline images of those addresses.
• Write a program in a language like JavaScript to scramble any e-mail addresses in the HTML code. Users can then run the program to unscramble those addresses.

- Replace the characters of the e-mail address with character codes. You can replace the "@" symbol with the code @ replace blank spaces with the code   and so forth.
- Replace characters with words in your Web page's text—for example, replace the "@" symbol with the word "at".

There is no quick and easy solution to this problem. Fighting spammers is an ongoing battle and they have proved very resourceful in overcoming some of the traps people have written for e-mail harvesters. As you develop your Web site, you should carefully consider how you wish to handle e-mail and review the most current methods for safeguarding that information.

Reference Window	**Linking to Different Resources**

- The URL for a Web page has the form:
    `http://server/path/filename#id`
    where *server* is the name of the Web server, *path* is the path to a file on that the server, *filename* is the name of the file, and if necessary, *id* is the name of an id or anchor within the file.
- The URL for a FTP site has the form:
    `ftp://server/path/filename`
    where *server* is the name of the FTP server, *path* is the folder path, and *filename* is the name of the file.
- The URL for a Usenet newsgroup has the form:
    `news:newsgroup`
    where *newsgroup* is the name of the Usenet group.
- The URL for an e-mail address has the form:
    `mailto:address`
    where *address* is the e-mail address.
- The URL to reference a local file on your computer is:
    `file://server/path/filename`
    where *server* is the name of the local server or computer, *path* is the path to the file on that server, and *filename* is the name of the file. If you are accessing a file on your own computer, the server name would be replaced by another slash (/).

Working with Hypertext Attributes

HTML provides several attributes to control the behavior and appearance of your links. Let's study a few of these to see whether they would be effective in Stephen's Web site.

Opening a Secondary Window

By default, each new page you open replaces the contents of the previous page in the browser window. This means that when Stephen's students click on the six external links listed on the links page, they leave the chemistry Web site. To return to the chemistry Web site, a student would have to click their browser's Back button.

Stephen would prefer that the contents of his Web site stay open in the original browser window, and that any links to external Web sites be displayed in a second window. This arrangement would allow students and parents continued access to his chemistry Web site, even as they're browsing other sites.

To force a document to appear in a new window, you add the target attribute to the <a> tag. The general syntax is:

```
<a href="url" target="window">content</a>
```

where *window* is a name assigned to the new browser window. The value you use for the target attribute doesn't affect the appearance or content of the window; it's simply used by the browser to identify the different browser windows currently open. You can choose any name you wish for the target. If several links have the same target name, they all open in the same window, replacing the window's previous content. HTML also supports several special target names, described in Figure 2-38.

Target names for browser windows ◄ **Figure 2-38**

Target Name	Description
"*target*"	Opens the link in a new window named *target*
"_blank"	Opens the link in a new, unnamed, window
"_self"	Opens the link in the current browser window

Stephen suggests that all of the external links be opened in a browser window identified with the name "new".

To specify a target window for a link:

► 1. Return to the **links.htm** file in your text editor.

► 2. Locate the six links you created earlier that point to external sites. Within each of the six links, add the attribute **target="new"** as shown in Figure 2-39.

Adding a target to a link ◄ **Figure 2-39**

```
<blockquote><p>
<b><a href="http://www.carnegielibrary.org/subject/homework" target="new">Carnegie Library</a></b>:
Homework resources from the Carnegie Library of Pittsburgh.</p></blockquote>

<blockquote><p>
<b><a href="http://school.discovery.com" target="new">Discovery Schools</a></b>:
Get homework help from the school sponsored by the Discovery Channel.</p></blockquote>

<h2>Chemistry Resources</h2>

<blockquote><p>
<b><a href="http://antoine.frostburg.edu/chem/senese/101" target="new">Frostburg State</a></b>:
View articles, tutorials, and online quizzes from the chemistry
department at Frostburg State University in Maryland.</p></blockquote>

<blockquote><p>
<b><a href="http://dir.yahoo.com/Science/chemistry" target="new">Yahoo</a></b>:
Yahoo's list of chemistry resources on the web.</p></blockquote>

<h2>The Periodic Table</h2>

<blockquote><p>
<b><a href="http://pearl1.lanl.gov/periodic" target="new">Los Alamos</a></b>:
An interactive periodic table of the elements presented by the
National Laboratory's Chemistry Division at Los Alamos.</p></blockquote>

<blockquote><p>
<b><a href="http://www.chemsoc.org/viselements" target="new">Visual Elements</a></b>:
A stunning visual representation of the periodic table by the
RSC's chemical science network.</p></blockquote>
```

► 3. Save your changes to the file.

► 4. Reopen **links.htm** in your Web browser. Click each of the six external links and verify that the external sites all open within the same secondary window.

If you want all of the links in your document to point to a new window, you can add the target attribute to the <base /> tag in the document's header. The target name you specify will be applied to all of the Web page's links. You should use the target attribute sparingly in your Web site. Creating secondary windows can clog up the user's desktop and because the page is placed in a new window, users cannot use the Back button to return to the previous page in that window. This may confuse some users and annoy others. Note that the target attribute is not supported in strict XHTML-compliant code.

Reference Window	**Opening a New Browser Window**

- To open a link in a new browser window, add the following attribute to the <a> tag:
  `target="window"`
  where *window* is a name assigned to the new window. The value of *window* can be "_self" to open the link in the current window, "_blank" to open the link in a new, unnamed window or any other name to open the link in a named window.

Creating a Popup Title

If you want to provide additional information to your users, you can add a popup title to your links. A **popup title** is descriptive text that appears whenever a user positions the mouse pointer over a link. Figure 2-40 shows an example of a popup title applied to one of the links in the chemistry Web site.

Figure 2-40	Adding a popup title to a link

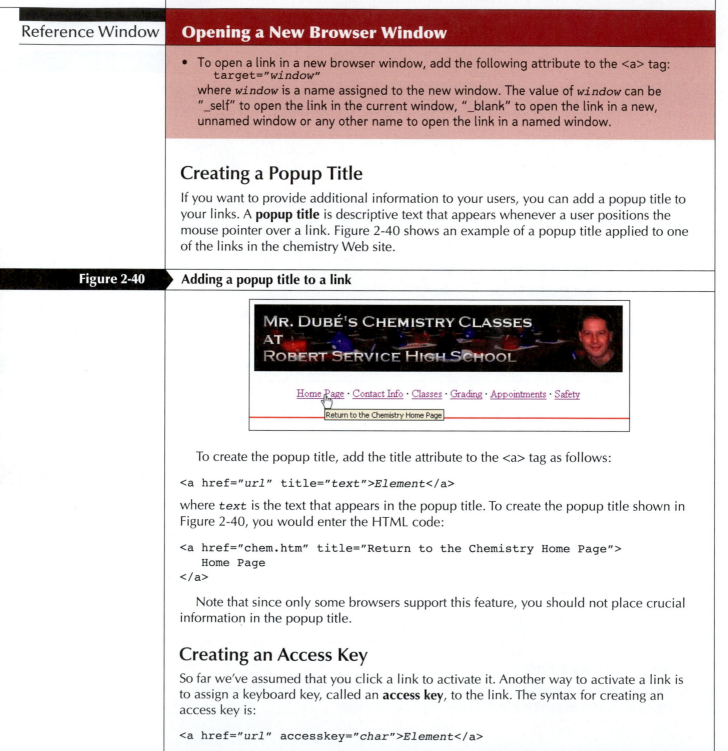

To create the popup title, add the title attribute to the <a> tag as follows:

```
<a href="url" title="text">Element</a>
```

where *text* is the text that appears in the popup title. To create the popup title shown in Figure 2-40, you would enter the HTML code:

```
<a href="chem.htm" title="Return to the Chemistry Home Page">
   Home Page
</a>
```

Note that since only some browsers support this feature, you should not place crucial information in the popup title.

Creating an Access Key

So far we've assumed that you click a link to activate it. Another way to activate a link is to assign a keyboard key, called an **access key**, to the link. The syntax for creating an access key is:

```
<a href="url" accesskey="char">Element</a>
```

where *char* is a single keyboard character. To use an access key you hold down an **accelerator key** (usually the Alt key in Windows or the Ctrl key on a Macintosh) and then press the specified access key. For example, if you modify the chem.htm link as follows:

```
<a href="chem.htm" accesskey="i">Home Page</a>
```

you can activate this link by pressing Alt+i (in Windows) or Ctrl+i (on a Macintosh). Access keys sound like a good idea, but they've proved to be impractical in most situations. One problem is that most access keys are already reserved by the browser. For example you can't use the "f" key because the browser uses it to access the File menu. In addition, it is difficult to indicate to the user which access key to press in order to activate a given link. The usual practice is to underline the access key in the Web page; however, by convention, underlining is reserved for indicating links.

Creating a Semantic Link

Two attributes, rel and rev, allow you to specify the relationship between a link and its destination. The rel attribute describes the contents of the destination document. For example, if Stephen wanted to link to a glossary of chemistry terms, he could insert the following link into his Web page:

```
<a href="terms.htm" rel="glossary">Chemistry Glossary</a>
```

The rev attribute complements the rel attribute: rev describes the contents of the source document as viewed from the destination document's perspective. For example, to go from the chemistry home page to the glossary, we might include the following rev attribute to describe where the user is coming from:

```
<a href="terms.htm" rel="glossary" rev="home">Chemistry Glossary</a>
```

Links containing the rel and rev attributes are called **semantic links** because the tag contains information about the relationship between the link and its destination. This information is not designed for the user, but rather for the browser. A browser can use the information that these attributes provide in many ways—for example, to build a custom toolbar containing a list of links specific to the page being viewed. Few browsers currently take advantage of these attributes, but future browsers may do so.

While rel and rev are not limited to a fixed set of attribute values, the specifications for HTML and XHTML include a proposed list of rel and rev names. Figure 2-41 shows some of these proposed relationship values.

Link types   **Figure 2-41**

Link Types	Description
alternate	References a substitute version of the current document, perhaps in a different language or in a different medium
stylesheet	References an external style sheet
start	References the first document in a collection of documents
next	References the next document in a linear sequence of documents
prev	References the previous document in a linear sequence of documents
contents	References a table of contents
index	References an index
glossary	References a glossary
appendix	References an appendix
copyright	References a copyright statement
chapter	References a document serving as a chapter in a collection of documents
section	References a document serving as a section in a collection of documents
subsection	References a document serving as a subsection in a collection of documents
help	References a Help document
bookmark	References a bookmark

Using the Link Element

Another way to add a link to your document is to add a link element to the document's head. Link elements are created using the one-sided tag

```
<link href="url" rel="text" rev="text" target="window" />
```

where the `href`, `rel`, `rev`, and `target` attributes serve the same purpose as in the `<a>` tag. Link elements are intended only for the browser's use. Because they are placed within a document's head, they do not appear in the browser window. A document head can contain several link elements.

Link elements have primarily been used to connect to style sheets. Browsers have only recently started using them for other purposes. For example, the Opera browser uses link elements to generate custom toolbars containing links based on the document's relationships. Figure 2-42 shows how Opera interprets some `<link />` tags to create such a toolbar.

Figure 2-42	Using link elements

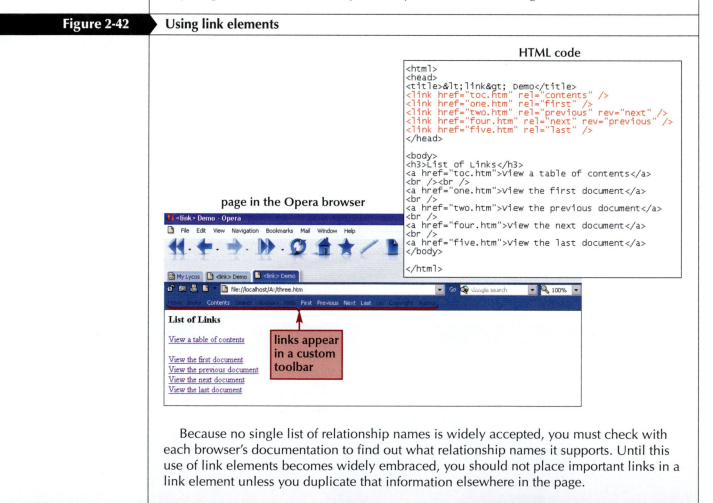

Because no single list of relationship names is widely accepted, you must check with each browser's documentation to find out what relationship names it supports. Until this use of link elements becomes widely embraced, you should not place important links in a link element unless you duplicate that information elsewhere in the page.

Reference Window

Creating a Link Element

- To create a link element, add the following tag to the document head:
  ```
  <link href="url" rel="text" rev="text" target="window" />
  ```
  where the `href`, `rel`, `rev`, and `target` attributes all serve the same purpose that they do in the `<a>` tag.

You show Stephen the final versions of the three Web pages you have been collaborating on. He's pleased with the results. You explain to him that the next step is to contact the school's Information Technology Department to place his site on the school's Web server. When that's done, Stephen's Web site will be available online to anyone with Internet access. You can now close any open files or editors.

Tips for Creating Effective Links

- Storyboard your Web site before you create it.
- Make sure that users can easily navigate your site by linking each page to the site's home page and a page containing a site index.
- Avoid using text like "click here" in your links. Make sure your linked text describes what the destination contains.
- Never place two links immediately adjacent to one another; separate them with text or extra spaces or a symbol.
- Avoid long pages; instead break up each page into a sequence of linked pages.
- If you do create a long page, create links to different sections of the page. Include links throughout the page that users can click to jump to the top of the page.
- Use only lowercase filenames for all of your documents.
- Use anchors if you need your internal document links to work with older browsers.
- Use care when inserting an e-mail link or address into a Web page. Research the latest tools and traps to thwart e-mail harvesters and spammers.

Review

Session 2.3 Quick Check

1. What are the five parts of a URL?
2. What tag would you enter to link the text "White House" to the URL http://www.whitehouse.gov, with the destination document displayed in a new unnamed browser window?
3. What tag would you enter to link the text "Washington" to the FTP server at ftp.uwash.edu?
4. What tag would you enter to link the text "Boxing" to the newsgroup rec.sports.boxing.pro?
5. What tag would you enter to link the text "President" to the e-mail address president@whitehouse.gov?
6. What attribute would you add to display the popup title, "Glossary of chemistry terms"?
7. What attribute would you add to a link specifying that the destination is the next page in a linear sequence of documents?
8. What tag would you add to a document's head to create a link to the file "toc.htm"? Include information telling the browser that the current document is a chapter document and the link's destination is a table of contents.

Review

Tutorial Summary

In this tutorial, you learned how to create and use links. You first saw how to create links within a single document. You learned two ways of marking a location within a document: using ids and using anchors. In the second session, you practiced creating links between documents within a Web site. The session also discussed how to build effective Web site structures and emphasized the importance of storyboarding. You also learned how to reference files in different folders using relative and absolute paths. The third session showed how to connect to different resources on the Internet, including Web pages, FTP servers, newsgroups, and e-mail addresses. The session also discussed how to use HTML attributes to open links in new windows, display popup titles, create access keys, and specify link relationships. The tutorial concluded with a presentation of the link element.

Key Terms

absolute path	FTP server	protocol
accelerator key	hierarchical structure	relative path
access key	HTTP	semantic link
anchor element	Hypertext Transfer Protocol	sibling folder
augmented linear structure	linear structure	site index
destination	link	spam
e-mail harvester	newsgroup	storyboard
File Transfer Protocol	newsreader	Uniform Resource Locator
FTP	path	URL
FTP client	popup title	Usenet

Practice

Practice the skills you learned in the tutorial using the same case scenario.

Review Assignments

Data files needed for this Review Assignment: chemtxt.htm, conttxt.htm, glosstxt.htm, linkstxt.htm, logo.jpg

Stephen has had some more work done on the chemistry Web site, including the following modifications:

- The contacts page includes a new contact for the lab assistant, Karen Cole.
- The links page contains two new Internet resources for students to explore.
- The site includes a new page, which contains a glossary of chemistry terms.

The new glossary page is very long, so Stephen wants to add a linked list of the letters of the alphabet at the top of the page so that users can click a letter to jump to the entries starting with that letter. Because of the page's length, Stephen also wants to add links that students can click to jump back to the top of the page. Figure 2-43 shows a preview of part of the completed glossary page.

Figure 2-43

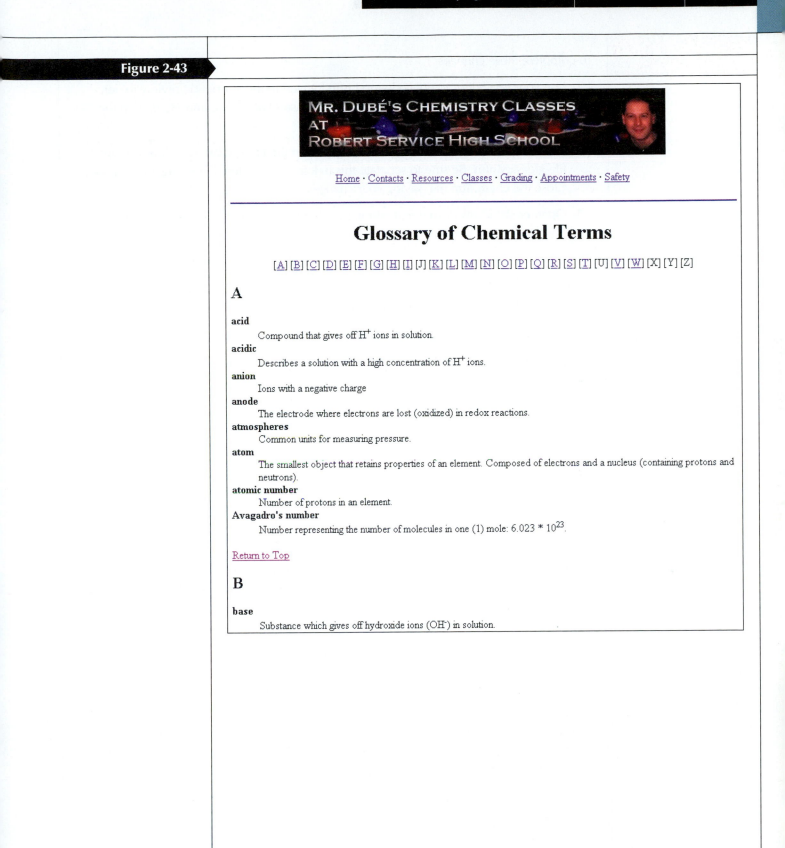

MR. DUBÉ'S CHEMISTRY CLASSES
AT
ROBERT SERVICE HIGH SCHOOL

Home · Contacts · Resources · Classes · Grading · Appointments · Safety

Glossary of Chemical Terms

[A] [B] [C] [D] [E] [F] [G] [H] [I] [J] [K] [L] [M] [N] [O] [P] [Q] [R] [S] [T] [U] [V] [W] [X] [Y] [Z]

A

acid
Compound that gives off H^+ ions in solution.
acidic
Describes a solution with a high concentration of H^+ ions.
anion
Ions with a negative charge
anode
The electrode where electrons are lost (oxidized) in redox reactions.
atmospheres
Common units for measuring pressure.
atom
The smallest object that retains properties of an element. Composed of electrons and a nucleus (containing protons and neutrons).
atomic number
Number of protons in an element.
Avagadro's number
Number representing the number of molecules in one (1) mole: $6.023 * 10^{23}$.

Return to Top

B

base
Substance which gives off hydroxide ions (OH$^-$) in solution.

To complete these changes:

1. Use your text editor to open **chemtxt.htm** located in the tutorial.02/review folder. Save the file as **chem.htm** to the same folder. Insert *your name* and *the date* in the comment tag at the top of the file.

2. After the Safety link at the top of the page, insert the text, "Glossary", linked to the file glossary.htm. Be sure to separate this link from the Safety link using a middle dot. Close the **chem.htm** file, saving your changes.

3. Open **conttxt.htm** in your text editor, saving it as **contacts.htm**. Enter *your name* and *the date* in the comment tag at the top of the file.

4. As you did in the chem.htm file, insert a link to the glossary.htm file after the Safety link at the top of the page.

5. Change Karen Cole's e-mail address into a link.

6. Close **contacts.htm**, saving your changes.

7. Open **linkstxt.htm** in your text editor, saving it as **links.htm**. Enter *your name* and *the date* in the comment tag.

8. Insert a link to the glossary.htm file after the Safety link at the top of the page.

9. At the bottom of the file, change the text "collegeboard.com" into a link pointing to the URL **www.collegeboard.com/student/testing/ap/subjects.html** and opening in a window named "new".

10. Close **links.htm**, saving your changes.

11. Open **glosstxt.htm** in your text editor, saving it as **glossary.htm**. Enter *your name* and *the date* in the comment tag.

12. Change the entries in the topic list at the top of the page into links pointing to the appropriate documents and document sections in the chemistry Web site. (*Hint:* Use the other files in this Web site as examples.)

13. Assign the first paragraph on this page (the one containing the inline image) the id name "top".

14. Locate the h2 headings containing the letters of the alphabet. Assign each heading a lowercase id name equal to the letter. For example the "A" heading should have an id name of "a" and so forth.

15. Locate the occurrences of the text, "Return to Top". Change this text to a link pointing to the element with the id name, "top".

16. Go to the letter list at the top of the page. Change each letter to a link pointing to the heading containing the appropriate id element in the document. Note that some letters do not have corresponding headings in the document. You do not have to change these letters into links.

17. Close **glossary.htm**, saving your changes.

18. Open **chem.htm** in your Web browser. Verify that you can navigate the entire Web site by clicking the appropriate list. Verify that you can move up and down the sections of the glossary page by clicking the letter links and the "Return to Top" links.

19. Submit the completed Web site to your instructor.

Apply

Use the skills you have learned to create a Web page listing government Web sites.

Case Problem 1

Data files needed for this Case Problem: links.txt, mpllogo.jpg, mpltxt.htm

Monroe Public Library You've recently been hired by the Monroe Public Library of Monroe, Iowa. The MPL is currently setting up Internet kiosks with computers linked to the World Wide Web. Monica Vinson, who is in charge of this project, has asked you to work on developing some Web pages for the kiosks. Your first task is to create a Web page containing links to various government Web sites. Monica has given you a text file containing the URLs of 19 executive, legislative, and judicial sites. She's also created the Web page, but without the links. Monica wants you to add the links to the page. She would like the links to open in a secondary browser window, so that the MPL Web page remains available to users in the original window. Figure 2-44 shows a preview of the finished page.

Figure 2-44

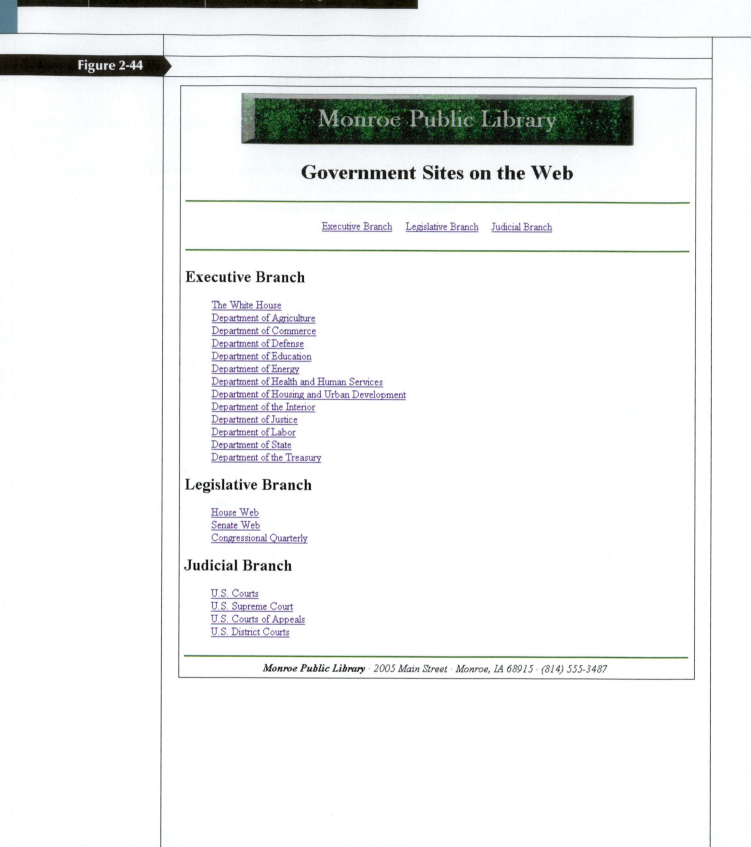

To complete this task:

1. Use your text editor open the file **mpltxt.htm** from the tutorial.02/case1 folder. Save the file as **mpl.htm**. Enter *your name* and *the date* in the comment tag at the top of the file.

2. Open the **links.txt** file in your text editor.

3. Convert each of the government sites listed in the mpl.htm file to a link using the URLs listed in the links.txt file. (*Hint*: Use the copy and paste feature of your text editor to copy the URLs from the list.txt file into the mpl.htm file).

Explore

4. Add a <base /> tag to the head of the mpl.htm file, specifying that all links in this page will, by default, open in a secondary window with the target name, "window2".

5. Add the id names "eb", "lb", and "jb" to the h2 headings Executive Branch, Legislative Branch, and Judicial Branch, respectively.

6. Link the list of branches at the top of the page to the headings.

Explore

7. For each of the three linked branches listed at the top of the page, change the target to "_self" so that these links open in the same browser window rather than in a secondary window.

8. Save your changes to **mpl.htm**.

9. Open **mpl.htm** in your Web browser. Test each of the links, verifying that each of the government sites opens in the same window (*Hint*: Change the size of the main browser window and the secondary window so that you can view each on your desktop at the same time). Verify that the links to the different sections of the document display those sections in the main browser window.

10. Submit the completed Web site to your instructor.

Explore

Broaden your knowledge and test your skills by exploring how to use inline images as links in a music history Web site.

Case Problem 2

Data files needed for this Case Problem: b9m1.jpg, b9m2.jpg, b9m3.jpg, b9m4.jpg, blank.jpg, hometxt.htm, glosstxt.htm, left.jpg, lvb.jpg, m1txt.htm, m2txt.htm, m3txt.htm, m4txt.htm, right.jpg

Western College for the Arts You're a graduate assistant in the Department of Music at Western College for the Arts. Professor Lysander Coe has asked your help in developing a Web site for his course on sonata forms. He is working on a presentation of Beethoven's Ninth Symphony and needs assistance in creating the links between the various pages in the site. The site will contain six pages: a home page, a glossary, and four pages describing each of the four movements of the Ninth Symphony. Professor Coe would like students to be able to navigate forward and backward through the movement pages, and to be able to jump to the site's home page and glossary at any time. He is also interested in using inline images as links to enhance the visual appearance of the site. Finally, the university is looking toward using more semantic links in their Web pages, so Professor Coe would like you to add semantic links to his Web site. Figure 2-45 shows a preview of one of the completed pages in the site you'll create.

Figure 2-45

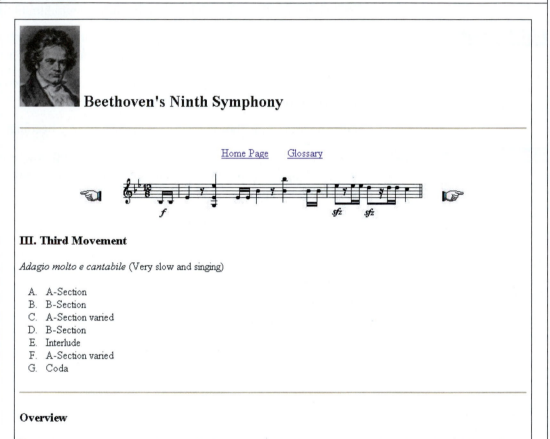

To complete the Web site:

1. Use your text editor to open the **hometxt.htm**, **glosstxt.htm**, **m1txt.htm**, **m2txt.htm**, **m3txt.htm**, and **m4txt.htm** files from the tutorial.02/case2 folder. Enter *your name* and *the date* in the comment tag at the top of each file. Save these files as: **b9home.htm**, **b9gloss.htm**, **b9m1.htm**, **b9m2.htm**, **b9m3.htm**, and **b9m4.htm** respectively.

2. Within the **b9home.htm** file, link the list entries First Movement, Second Movement, Third Movement, and Fourth Movement to the b9m1.htm, b9m2.htm, b9m3.htm, and b9m4.htm files. Link "Glossary" to the b9gloss.htm file.

Explore ▶ 3. Within the head element, add a link element pointing to the file b9gloss.htm. Add the rel attribute to the link with a value indicating that b9gloss.htm is a glossary.

4. Go to the file **b9gloss.htm**, and change the text "Home Page" to a link pointing to b9home.htm. Add a link element to the document's head referencing the home page. Use the rel attribute to specify that this link points to a chapter document.

5. Go to the file **b9m1.htm**. This file contains information about the symphony's first movement. Change the entries "Home Page" and "Glossary" into links pointing to the files b9home.htm and b9gloss.htm. Also add semantic link information to the document heading. Use the rel attribute to indicate that these links point to a chapter and a glossary page, respectively. Create two additional link elements: "next" pointing to b9m2.htm (the second movement) and "last" pointing to b9m4.htm (the last movement).

Explore ▶ 6. Locate the code for the inline image right.jpg. Link this image to the file b9m2.htm. Because browsers surround linked images with a blue or purple border by default, add the attribute style="border-width:0" to the <img /> tag to remove the border.

7. Within the file **b9m2.htm**, change "Home Page" and "Glossary" into links. Add link elements to the document head that point to the home and glossary pages, as well as the first movement in the symphony, the last movement, the previous movement, and the next movement. Add rel attributes to all of these link elements. Link the inline image left.jpg to the file b9m1.htm. Link right.jpg to the file b9m3.htm. Be sure to use the border-width style to hide the borders around these images.

8. Within the file **b9m3.htm**, change "Home Page" and "Glossary" into links. Add link elements to the document head that point to the home page, glossary, first movement, last movement, previous movement, and next movement. Link the image left.jpg to b9m2.htm. Link the image right.jpg to b9m4.htm.

9. Within the file **b9m4.htm**, change "Home Page" and "Glossary" into links. Add link elements to the document head pointing to the home page, glossary, first movement, and previous movement. Link the image left.jpg to the b9m3.htm file.

10. Save your changes to all six files.

11. Open **b9home.htm** in your Web browser. Verify that you can use the links and the linked inline images to navigate through the contents of this site.

Explore

12. Draw a storyboard of the Web site you created. Show all of the pages and the links between them. Do not include the link elements in this storyboard.

Explore

13. Using a browser that supports semantic links, such as Opera, open the Web site and test whether you can use the semantic links in the browser-built toolbar.

14. Submit the completed site to your instructor.

Explore

Broaden your knowledge and test your skills by exploring how to use anchors and popup titles in a health club Web site.

Case Problem 3

Data files needed for this Case Problem: classtxt.htm, indextxt.htm, memtxt.htm, logo.jpg

Diamond Health Club, Inc. You work for Diamond Health Club, a family-oriented health club in Seattle, Washington that has been serving active families for 25 years. The director, Karen Padilla, has asked you to help create a Web site for the club containing three pages:: the home page describing the club, a page listing classes offered, and a page describing the various membership options. You need to add links within the main page and add other links connecting the pages. Because this Web site will need to support older browsers, you will have to use anchors to mark specific locations in the three documents. Karen would also like you to create popup titles for some of the links in the site. Figure 2-46 shows a preview of the completed home page.

Figure 2-46

Home Page · Facilities · Classes · Memberships · Staff · Hours

Welcome

At Diamond Health Club, you can stay healthy year-round and have fun doing it! We offer something for everyone. Our state-of-the-art facilities can challenge the most seasoned athlete, while remaining friendly to our first-time users. Be sure to check out our great classes for everyone from children and teens to adults and seniors. No matter who you are, DHC offers a class for you.

DHC also provides several different membership options. You can register as an individual or a family. We also provide special couples plans. Planning to visit Seattle a few days, weeks, or a month? Our great temporary plans are tailored to meet the needs of any visitor. Temporary memberships also make great Christmas gifts.

Facilities

- 2 workout rooms
- Olympic size pool with at least 3 lanes always open
- Warm, 3-foot deep therapeutic pool
- 2 gymnasiums with full size basketball courts
- Five exercise rooms for private and class instruction
- Climbing gym
- 3 racquetball courts
- On-site child care

Hours

Mon. - Fri. : 5 a.m. to 11 p.m.
Sat. : 7 a.m. to 8 p.m.
Sun. : 8 a.m. to 5 p.m.

For More Information, E-mail our Staff

Ty Stoven, General Manager
Yosef Dolen, Assistant Manager
Sue Myafin, Child Care
James Michel, Health Services
Ron Chi, Membership
Marcia Lopez, Classes

Diamond Health Club · 4317 Alvin Way · Seattle, WA 98102 · (877) 555-4398
Your Year-Round Source for Fun Family Health

To complete this task:

1. Use your text editor to open the **indextxt.htm**, **classtxt.htm** and **memtxt.htm** files from the tutorial.02/case3 folder. Enter *your name* and *the date* in the comment tag at the top of each file. Save these files as: **index.htm**, **classes.htm**, and **members.htm** respectively.

Explore

2. Within the file **index.htm**, add the anchor names fac, hours, and staff to the h3 headings: "Facilities", "Hours", and "For More Information, E-mail our Staff" respectively.

Explore

3. Within the file **members.htm**, add anchor names to the h3 headings: "Individual memberships", "Family memberships", and "Temporary Memberships". Name these anchors: ind, fam, and temp.

Explore

4. Within the file **classes.htm**, add anchor names to the h3 headings: "Senior Classes", "Adult Classes", "Teen Classes", and "Children's Classes". Name these anchors: senior, adult, teen, and child.

5. Return to the **index.htm** file. In the list at the top of the page, change the text, "Home Page" into a link pointing to index.htm. Change "Facilities" into a link that points to the fac anchor within index.htm. Change "Classes" into a link pointing to classes.htm. Change "Membership" into a link pointing to members.htm. Change "Staff" into a link that points to the staff anchor within index.htm. Change "Hours" into a link that points to the hours anchor with index.htm.

Explore

6. Add the popup title "Return to the DHC Home Page" to the Home link. Add the popup title "Learn more about our facilities" to the Facilities link. Add the popup title "View our class list" to the Classes link. Add the popup title "Choose a membership plan" to the Membership link. Add the popup "Meet the DHC staff" to the Staff link. Add the popup title "View the DHC hours of operation" to the Hours link.

7. Repeat steps 5 and 6 for the entries listed at the top of **members.htm** and **classes.htm**.

8. Return to **index.htm**. Go to the staff list at the bottom of the page. Format each name as a link that points to the individual's e-mail address. The e-mail addresses are:

Ty Stoven:	tstoven@dmond-health.com
Yosef Dolen:	ydolen@dmond-health.com
Sue Myafin:	smyafin@dmond-health.com
James Michel:	jmichel@dmond-health.com
Ron Chi:	rchi@dmond-health.com
Marcia Lopez:	mlopez@dmond-health.com

9. Within the first paragraph of index.htm, link the word "children" to the child anchor in the classes.htm file. Link the word "teens" to the teen anchor in the classes.htm file. Link the word "adults" to the adult anchor in classes.htm. Finally, link "seniors" to the senior anchor in classes.htm.

10. Within the second paragraph of index.htm, link the word "individual" to the ind anchor in the members.htm file. Link the word "family" to the fam anchor in members.htm. Finally, link the first occurrence of the word "temporary" to the temp anchor in members.htm.

11. Go to the **classes.htm** file. Format the phrase, "e-mail Marcia Lopez" in the first paragraph as a link pointing to Marcia Lopez's e-mail address.

12. Go to the **members.htm** file. Format the phrase, "e-mail Ron Chi" in the first paragraph as a link pointing to Ron Chi's e-mail address.

13. Save your changes to the **index.htm**, **classes.htm**, and **members.htm** files.

14. Open **index.htm** in your Web browser. Verify that all of your links work correctly, including the links that point to sections within documents. Verify that popup titles appear as you move your mouse pointer over the six links at the top of each page.

15. Submit the completed site to your instructor.

Create

Test your knowledge of HTML by creating a Web site for Body Systems.

Case Problem 4

Data files needed for this Case Problem: about.txt, bench.jpg, bench.txt, cable.jpg, cable.txt, contact.txt, logo.jpg, lpress.jpg, lpress.txt, products.txt, smith.jpg, smith.txt, whybuy.txt

Body Systems You've been working for a few weeks as a Web site developer with Body Systems, one of the leading manufacturers of home exercise equipment. You've been asked to put together a sample Web site highlighting several Body System products. You've been given several text files containing descriptions of these products, as well as contact information for the company, and a file describing the company's history and philosophy. In addition, you've been given several image files of the products, along with an image file of the company logo. You are free to supplement these files with any other resources available to you. Your job is to use this information to create an effective Web site describing the products and the company for interested consumers.

To complete this task:

1. Locate the text files and image files in the tutorial.02/case4 folder of your Data Disk. Review the content of the text files and view the image files. Note that the files cover four products: the Linear Smith machine, the Cable Crossover machine, the Free Weight bench, and the Leg/Press Squat machine. Information about these products is stored in the smith.txt, cable.txt, bench.txt, and lpress.txt files, respectively.

Explore

2. Use one of the search sites on the Web to locate Web pages on strength training tips and advice.

3. Once you become familiar with all of the material available for your Web site, create a storyboard for the site. In the storyboard include all of the filenames of the Web pages and indicate any links between the pages. The Web site should contain at least one example of each of the following:

   - A link within a single document pointing to another section of the same document
   - A link between the documents in the Web site
   - A link to a section of another document
   - A link to an e-mail address

Explore

   - A link to at least one Web site on strength training tips and advice. Be sure to include explanatory text about the link or links you decide to include.

   Make sure that your site is easy to navigate.

4. Create the site you outlined in your storyboard. The design of the Web pages is up to you, but your code should follow correct HTML syntax rules and should be easy for others to read and interpret.

5. Within each file, include comments that document the page's content and purpose. Include your name and the current date in your comments.

6. Submit the completed site to your instructor.

Review

Quick Check Answers

Session 2.1

1. `<h2 id="csu">Colorado State University</h2>`
2. `<a href="#csu">Universities</a>`
3. Anchor tags should be placed within other tags such as the <h3> heading tag.
4. `<a name="photo"><img src="photo.jpg" /></a>`
5. `<a href="#links"><img src="button.jpg" /></a>`
6. Anchors should be used to support older browsers that do not recognize the id attribute.

Session 2.2

1. Storyboarding is the process of diagramming a series of related Web pages, taking care to identify all links between the various pages. Storyboarding is an important tool in creating Web sites that are easy to navigate and understand.

2. A linear structure is one in which Web pages are linked from one to another in a direct chain. Users can go to the previous page or the next page in the chain, but not to a page in a different section of the chain. A hierarchical structure is one in which Web pages are linked from general to specific topics. Users can move up and down the hierarchy tree.

3. `<a href="sports.htm">Sports Info</a>`

4. `<a href="sports.htm#bball">Basketball news</a>`

5. An absolute path indicates the location of the file based on its placement with the computer. A relative path indicates the location of the file relative to the location of the current document.

6. ../index.htm
   bio.htm
   ../dube/bio.htm
   ../dube/class/chem.htm
   ../dube/class/contacts.htm
   ../duble/class/links.htm

7. The `<base />` tag is designed to specify the location from which the browser should resolve all relative paths.

Session 2.3

1. The protocol, the hostname, the folder name, the filename, and the anchor name or id.

2. `<a href="http://www.whitehouse.gov" target="_blank">White House</a>`

3. `<a href="ftp://ftp.uwash.edu">Washington</a>`

4. `<a href="news:rec.sports.boxing.pro">Boxing</a>`

5. `<a href="mailto:president@whitehouse.gov">President</a>`

6. `title="Glossary of Chemistry Terms"`

7. `rel="next"`

8. `<link href="toc.htm" rel="contents" rev="chapter" />`

New Perspectives on

HTML and XHTML

Read This Before You Begin: Tutorials 3–5

To the Student

Data Files

To complete the Level II HTML Tutorials (Tutorials 3–5), you need the starting student Data Files. Your instructor will either provide you with these Data Files or ask you to obtain them yourself.

The Level II HTML tutorials require the folders shown to complete the Tutorials, Review Assignments, and Case Problems. You will need to copy these folders from a file server, a standalone computer, or the Web to the drive and folder where you will be storing your Data Files. Your instructor will tell you which computer, drive letter, and folder(s) contain the files you need. You can also download the files by going to www.course.com; see the inside back or front cover for more information on downloading the files, or ask your instructor or technical support person for assistance.

▼ **HTML**
    Tutorial.03
    Tutorial.04
    Tutorial.05

Student Online Companion

The Student Online Companion can be found by going to www.course.com and searching for this title. It contains additional information to supplement what you are learning in the text, as well as links to downloads, shareware, and other tools.

To the Instructor

The Data Files are available on the Instructor Resources CD for this title. Follow the instructions in the Help file on the CD to install the programs to your network or standalone computer. See the "To the Student" section above for information on how to set up the Data Files that accompany this text.

You are granted a license to copy the Data Files to any computer or computer network used by students who have purchased this book.

System Requirements

If you are going to work through this book using your own computer, you need:

- **System Requirements** An Internet connection, a text editor and a Web browser that supports HTML 4.0 and XHTML 1.1 (for example, version 6.0 or higher of either Netscape or Internet Explorer). You may wish to run an older browser version to highlight compatibility issues, but the code in this book is not designed to support those browsers.

- **Data Files** You will not be able to complete the tutorials or exercises in this book using your own computer until you have the necessary starting Data Files.

Objectives

Session 3.1
- Learn how HTML handles colors, and how to use colors effectively
- Create foreground and background colors using styles
- Select different font styles and designs using styles
- Align text with surrounding content using styles
- Control spacing between letters, words, and lines using styles

Session 3.2
- Learn about the different graphic formats supported on the Web and how to use them effectively
- Understand how to use transparent images and animated graphics
- Apply a background image to an element
- Float an image on the right or left page margin
- Set the margin size around an element

Session 3.3
- Understand image maps and how to use them
- Create image map hotspots and link them to destination documents
- Apply an image map to an inline image
- Remove the border from a linked image

Designing a Web Page

Working with Fonts, Colors, and Graphics

Case

Arcadium Amusement Park

Arcadium is a new amusement park located in northern Georgia. The park contains a wealth of rides, including roller coasters, water rides, go-kart racetracks, and gentler rides more appropriate for young children. Tom Calloway is the director of advertising for the park. In addition to radio, newspaper, and television spots, Tom is also overseeing the development of the park's Web site. He has asked you to join his Web site development team.

The team has already determined the site's content and structure. Tom wants you to concentrate on the site's design. He wants the design to convey a sense of fun and excitement to the reader. The Web pages you create should be colorful and should include a variety of images, along with animation, if possible. Tom has provided some of the graphic files you'll need to complete the site's design.

Student Data Files

▼Tutorial.03

▽ Tutorial folder
- abouttxt.htm
- indextxt.htm
- kartstxt.htm
- maptxt.htm
- ridestxt.htm
- watertxt.htm
- + 3 demo pages
- + 10 graphic files

▽ Review folder
- abouttxt.htm
- indextxt.htm
- kartstxt.htm
- maptxt.htm
- ridestxt.htm
- toddtxt.htm
- watertxt.htm
- + 10 graphic files

▽ Case1 folder
- dc100txt.htm
- dc250txt.htm
- dc500txt.htm
- indextxt.htm
- pixaltxt.htm
- + 7 graphic files

▽ Case2 folder
- kingtxt.htm
- + 7 graphic files

▽ Case3 folder
- crypttxt.htm
- + 5 graphic files

▽ Case4 folder
- midwest.txt
- + 9 graphic files

Session 3.1

Working with Color in HTML

The start of another tourist season is approaching and Tom has called you to discuss the appearance of the park's Web site. Other Web site developers have already worked on the site's structure and the content of the pages. Figure 3-1 shows the structure of the Arcadium Web site.

Figure 3-1   **Structure of the Arcadium Web site**

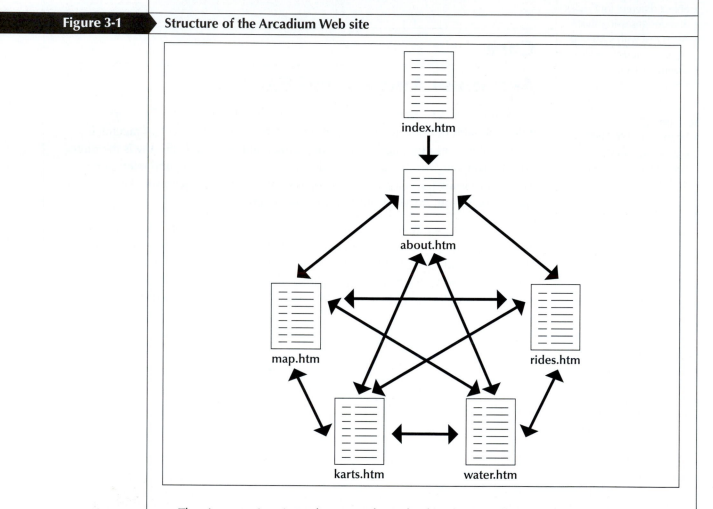

The site contains six Web pages. The index.htm page contains an introduction to Arcadium. This page acts as a **splash screen**, displaying the park logo and an interesting animated graphic, but no substantial content. The splash screen links users to the About page, which contains information about the park. The Karts, Water, and Rides pages all describe specific attractions at Arcadium. The Map page contains a map of the park. Aside from the splash screen page, the Web pages are all linked to one another, allowing users to roam freely around the site. In this case, you'll work only with the index.htm, about.htm, and map.htm files. The other files are provided to complete the Web site for you. The first page you'll work on is the About page.

To open the about.htm file:

1. Use your text editor to open **abouttxt.htm** from the tutorial.03/tutorial folder in your Data Files. Save the file as **about.htm**.

2. Enter *your name* and *the date* in the comment tag at the top of the file.

3. Save your changes to the file, but leave your text editor open.

4. Start your Web browser and open **about.htm**. Figure 3-2 shows the current format of the page.

The About Web page | Figure 3-2

ARCADIUM

About Arcadium   Park Map   Water Rides   Go Karts   Roller Coasters

Welcome

Exciting adventures await you at Arcadium, your affordable family fun center. The park is located 5 miles northwest of Derby - close to many of Georgia's scenic wonders. Arcadium offers over 50 rides, including some of the state's most exciting roller coasters and water rides. There's also plenty of fun for the younger kids, including two separate kiddie pools and special rides for the kids.

Arcadium is open seven days a week:

- April 1 up to Memorial Day weekend: 10am to 5pm
- Memorial Day weekend through Labor Day: 9am to 11pm
- The day after Labor Day through October 31: 10am to 5pm
- November 1 through March 31: closed

Arcadium is easy on your budget. Compare our low daily rates to the big chain parks. You can choose to purchase a gold ticket for any twenty rides, a platinum ticket for thirty rides, or for best value, a full-day pass to ride as many times as you want, wherever you want. Special off-season and large group rates are available.

Arcadium • Hwy 12, Exit 491 • Derby, GA 20010 • 1 (800) 555-5431

Tom is satisfied with the page's content, but he wants you to work on the appearance. He wants to see more color and the use of different fonts in the page. He also wants you to add photographs of people enjoying themselves at the park. Tom wants a visually pleasing page that will draw users into the site and give a good impression of the park.

You decide to start this project by creating an overall color scheme for the page. The first step is to learn how HTML handles colors. If you've worked with graphics software, you've probably made your color choices without much difficulty due to the interfaces that those applications employ. These interfaces, known as WYSIWYG (what you see is what you get), allow you to select colors visually. Selecting color with HTML is somewhat less intuitive, because HTML is a text-based language and requires you to define your colors in textual terms. This can be done in two ways: by specifying either a color value or a color name. Let's start by looking at color values.

Using Color Values

A **color value** is a numerical expression that precisely describes a color. To better understand how numbers can represent colors, it helps to review some of the basic principles of color theory and how they relate to the colors that your monitor displays.

White light is made up of three primary colors (red, green, and blue) mixed at equal intensities. By adding only two of the three primary colors we can generate a trio of complementary colors: yellow, magenta, and cyan (see Figure 3-3). To generate a wider range of colors, we simply vary the intensity of the red, green, and blue light. For example, orange is created from a high intensity of red light, a moderate intensity of green light, and an absence of blue light.

Figure 3-3 | **Primary color model for light**

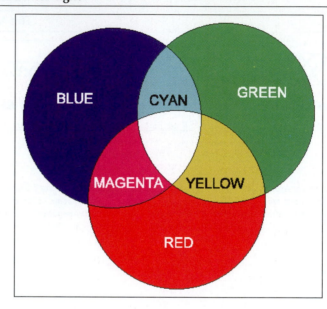

Your computer monitor generates colors by emitting red, green, and blue light at different intensities. Software programs, such as your Web browser, instruct your monitor to create colors mathematically. Each color is represented by a triplet of numbers called an **RGB triplet**, whose values are based on the strength of its red, green, and blue components. This triplet has the form

```
rgb(red, green, blue)
```

where red, green, and blue are the intensity values of the red, green, and blue components. The intensity values range from 0 (absence of color) to 255 (highest intensity). For example, the RGB triplet for white is (255, 255, 255), indicating that red, green, and blue are equally mixed at the highest intensity. Orange has the triplet (255, 165, 0) because it results from a mixture of high-intensity red, moderate-intensity green, and no blue. You can also enter each component value as a percentage, with 100% representing the highest intensity. In this form, you would specify the color orange with rgb (100%, 65%, 0%). The percentage form is less commonly used than RGB values. RGB triplets can specify 256^3 (16.7 million) possible colors, which is more colors than the human eye can distinguish.

In most software programs, you make your color choices using visual clues, sometimes without being aware of underlying RGB triplets. Figure 3-4 shows a typical color dialog box in which users make color selections based on a color's appearance, with the RGB values appearing alongside the color selection.

A typical colors dialog box   **Figure 3-4**

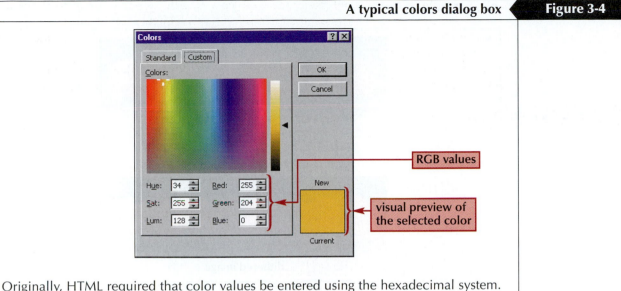

Originally, HTML required that color values be entered using the hexadecimal system. A **hexadecimal** is a number expressed in base 16 rather than in the base 10 form we use every day. In base 10 counting, you use combinations of 10 characters (0 through 9) to represent numerical values. The hexadecimal system includes six extra characters: A (for 10), B (for 11), C (for 12), D (for 13), E (for 14), and F (for 15). For values above 15, you use a combination of those 16 characters. To represent a number in hexadecimal terms, you convert the value to multiples of 16, plus a remainder. For example, 16 is equal to $(16 \times 1) + 0$, so its hexadecimal representation is "10." A value of 21 is equal to $(16 \times 1) + 5$, for a hexadecimal representation of 15. The number 255 is equal to $(16 \times 15) + 15$, or FF in hexadecimal format (remember that F = 15 in hexadecimal). In the case of the number 255, the first F represents the number of times 16 goes into 255 (which is 15), and the second F represents the remainder of 15. A color value represented as a hexadecimal number has the form

`#redgreenblue`

where `red`, `green`, and `blue` are the hexadecimal values of the red, green, and blue components. Thus, the color yellow could be represented either by the RGB triplet (255,255,0) or in the hexadecimal form #FFFF00.

At this point you might be wondering if you have to become a math major before you can start adding color to your Web pages. Fortunately, this is not the case. You can specify most colors in your Web pages with styles that use RGB triplets rather than the hexadecimal form. However, you may see HTML code that sets a color value to something like #FFA500, and now you know what that means, even if you can't tell at a glance that it represents the color orange.

While RGB triplets can distinguish over 16.7 million colors, the number of colors that a browser actually displays depends on the user's monitor. Some monitors are capable of displaying only 256 different colors, and thus browsers on these computers are limited to a smaller **palette**, or selection, of colors. When a browser encounters a color not in its palette, it attempts to render the color using a process called **dithering**, in which the browser combines similar colors from its palette to approximate the original color's appearance. Dithering can result in an image in which individual pixels stand out, and which appears fuzzy when compared to the original (see Figure 3-5).

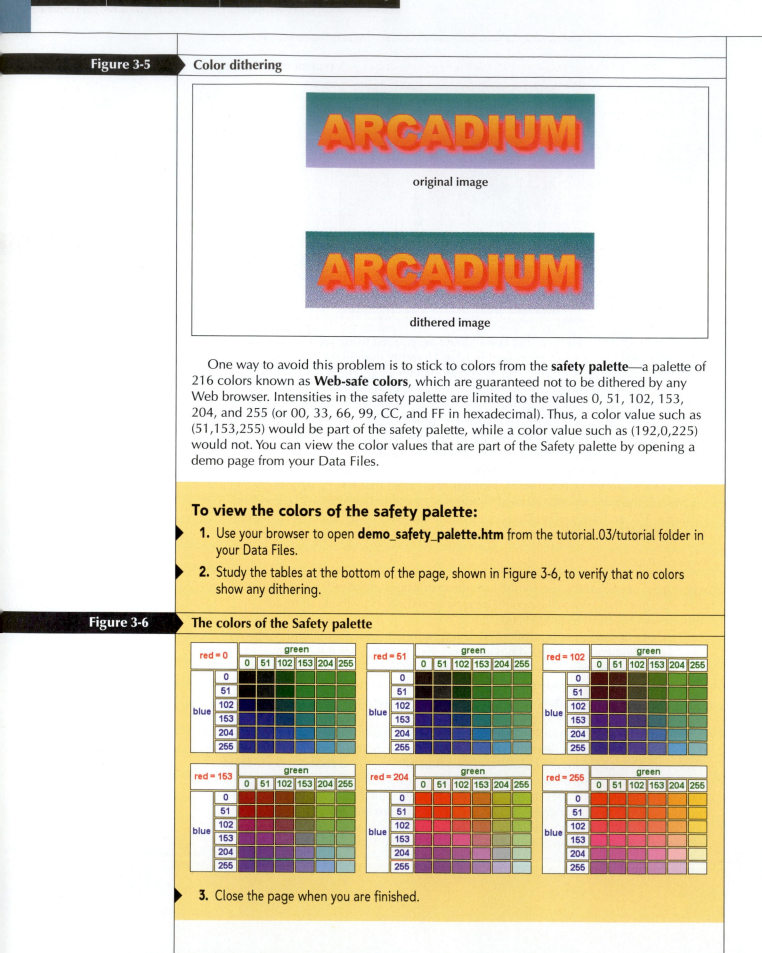

Figure 3-5 ▶ Color dithering

original image

dithered image

One way to avoid this problem is to stick to colors from the **safety palette**—a palette of 216 colors known as **Web-safe colors**, which are guaranteed not to be dithered by any Web browser. Intensities in the safety palette are limited to the values 0, 51, 102, 153, 204, and 255 (or 00, 33, 66, 99, CC, and FF in hexadecimal). Thus, a color value such as (51,153,255) would be part of the safety palette, while a color value such as (192,0,225) would not. You can view the color values that are part of the Safety palette by opening a demo page from your Data Files.

To view the colors of the safety palette:

1. Use your browser to open **demo_safety_palette.htm** from the tutorial.03/tutorial folder in your Data Files.

2. Study the tables at the bottom of the page, shown in Figure 3-6, to verify that no colors show any dithering.

Figure 3-6 ▶ The colors of the Safety palette

3. Close the page when you are finished.

By limiting your color selections to the colors of the safety palette, you can be assured that your images will appear the same to all users regardless of monitor resolution. However, because monitors now commonly support higher color resolutions, the need for the safety palette is not as great as it once was.

Using Color Names

If you don't want to use color values, you can also specify colors by name. HTML and XHTML support the 16 color names displayed in Figure 3-7. You've already used some of these color names in previous tutorials to insert colored lines into your pages.

The 16 basic color names ◄ **Figure 3-7**

Color Name	RGB Triplet	Hexadecimal	Color Name	RGB Triplet	Hexadecimal
Aqua	(0,255,255)	00FFFF	Navy	(0,0,128)	000080
Black	(0,0,0)	000000	Olive	(128,128,0)	808000
Blue	(0,0,255)	0000FF	Purple	(128,0,128)	800080
Fuchsia	(255,0,255)	FF00FF	Red	(255,0,0)	FF0000
Gray	(128,128,128)	808080	Silver	(192,192,192)	C0C0C0
Green	(0,128,0)	008000	Teal	(0,128,128)	008080
Lime	(0,255,0)	00FF00	White	(255,255,255)	FFFFFF
Maroon	(128,0,0)	800000	Yellow	(255,255,0)	FFFF00

Sixteen colors are not a lot, so most browsers support an extended list of 140 color names, including such colors as crimson, khaki, and peachpuff. While this extended color list is not part of the specification for either HTML or XHTML, you can feel confident that your users' browsers will support it.

To view the extended color list:

1. Use your browser to open **demo_color_names.htm** from the tutorial.03/tutorial folder in your Data Files.

2. The tables display the list of 140 extended color names, along with their color values expressed both as RGB triplets and in hexadecimal form (see Figure 3-8). The 16 color names supported by HTML and XHTML are highlighted in the table. Web-safe colors are displayed in boldface.

Figure 3-8   **A partial list of extended color names**

Sample	Name	RGB	Hexadecimal
	aliceblue	(240,248,255)	#F0F8FF
	antiquewhite	(250,235,215)	#FAEBD7
	aqua	**(0,255,255)**	**#00FFFF**
	aquamarine	(127,255,212)	#7FFFD4
	azure	(240,255,255)	#F0FFFF
	beige	(245,245,220)	#F5F5DC
	bisque	(255,228,196)	#FFE4C4
	black	**(0,0,0)**	**#000000**
	blanchedalmond	(255,235,205)	#FFEBCD
	blue	**(0,0,255)**	**#0000FF**
	blueviolet	(138,43,226)	#8A2BE2
	brown	(165,42,42)	#A52A2A
	burlywood	(222,184,135)	#DEB887

▶ **3.** Close the page when you are finished.

Depending on the design requirements of your site, you may sometimes need to use color values to get exactly the right color; however if you know the general color that you need, you can usually enter the color name without having to look up its RGB value.

Defining Foreground and Background Colors

With HTML you can define the foreground and background color for each element on your page. The foreground color is usually the color of the text in an element, although in the case of horizontal lines, it defines part of a line's color. The style to define the foreground color is

```
color: color
```

where *color* is either the color value or the color name. The style to define the background color is

```
background-color: color
```

If you do not define an element's color, it takes the color of the element that contains it. For example, if you specify red text on a gray background for the Web page body, all elements within the page inherit that color combination unless you specify different styles for specific elements.

Tom suggests that you change the text color in the About page from the default black to a shade of brown. You decide to use the Web-safe color value (153,102,102). You'll also set the background color of the page to white. While most browsers assume a white background color by default, it's a good idea to make this explicit in case some users have different settings. Because you're applying the color change to the entire page, you'll add the inline style to the body element.

To set the page's foreground and background colors:

▶ **1.** Return to the **about.htm** file in your text editor.

▶ **2.** Locate the <body> tag and insert the inline style:

```
<body style="color: rgb(153,102,102); background-color: white">
```

See Figure 3-9.

Setting page foreground and background colors ◀ **Figure 3-9**

foreground color   background color

```
<body style="color: rgb(153,102,102); background-color: white">
<p style="text-align: center">
    <img src="logo.gif" alt="ARCADIUM" />
    <br />
    <a href="about.htm">About Arcadium</a>    
    <a href="map.htm">Park Map</a>    
    <a href="water.htm">Water Rides</a>    
    <a href="karts.htm">Go Karts</a>    
    <a href="rides.htm">Roller Coasters</a>
</p>
```

▶ **3.** Save your changes to the file.

▶ **4.** Reload or refresh **about.htm** in your Web browser and verify that the text color has changed to a medium brown.

You can apply foreground and background colors to any page element. Tom suggests that the "Welcome" title might look better if it was formatted as white text on a medium brown background. The brown background would then act as a divider between the Arcadium logo and the main page body. To change the color, you add an inline style to the h1 element containing the text.

To change the color scheme for the h1 heading:

▶ **1.** Return to **about.htm** in your text editor.

▶ **2.** Locate the <h1> tag and insert the following inline style as shown in Figure 3-10.

```
<h1 style="color: white; background-color: rgb(153,102,102)">
```

Setting the colors for an h1 heading ◀ **Figure 3-10**

foreground color   background color

```
<h1 style="color: white; background-color: rgb(153,102,102)">
    Welcome
</h1>
```

Tom would also like you to change the color of the horizontal line at the bottom of the page to match the page's new color scheme.

▶ **3.** Locate the <hr /> tag at the bottom of the file and insert the inline style shown below:

```
<hr style="color: rgb(153,102,102); background-color:
rgb(153,102,102)" />
```

▶ **4.** Save your changes to the file.

▶ **5.** Refresh **about.htm** in your Web browser and verify that the color scheme for the h1 heading and the horizontal line has changed (see Figure 3-11).

Figure 3-11 **Setting foreground and background colors**

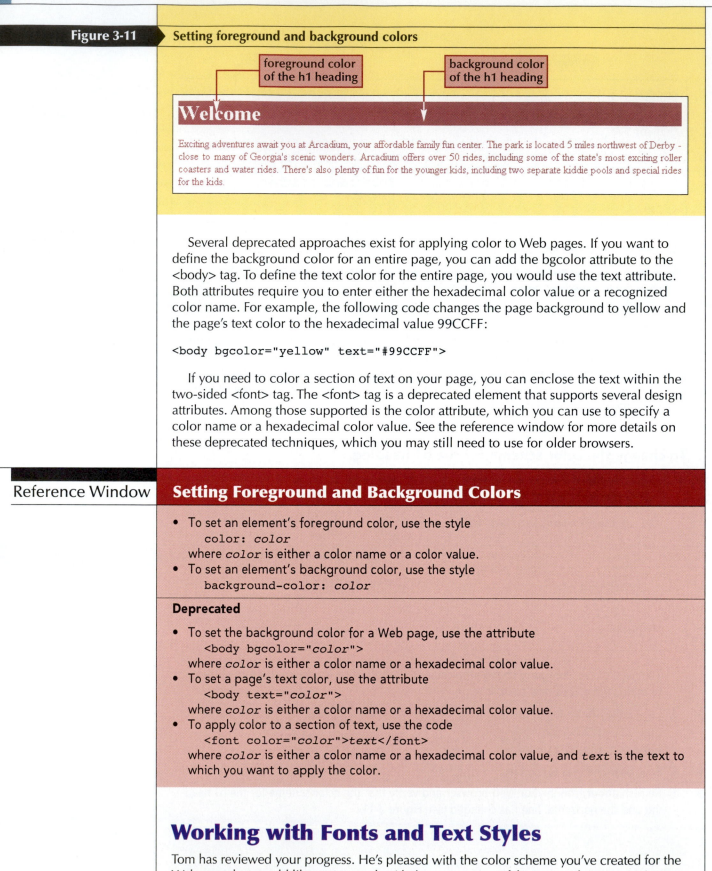

Several deprecated approaches exist for applying color to Web pages. If you want to define the background color for an entire page, you can add the bgcolor attribute to the <body> tag. To define the text color for the entire page, you would use the text attribute. Both attributes require you to enter either the hexadecimal color value or a recognized color name. For example, the following code changes the page background to yellow and the page's text color to the hexadecimal value 99CCFF:

```
<body bgcolor="yellow" text="#99CCFF">
```

If you need to color a section of text on your page, you can enclose the text within the two-sided <font> tag. The <font> tag is a deprecated element that supports several design attributes. Among those supported is the color attribute, which you can use to specify a color name or a hexadecimal color value. See the reference window for more details on these deprecated techniques, which you may still need to use for older browsers.

Reference Window

Setting Foreground and Background Colors

- To set an element's foreground color, use the style
  ```
  color: color
  ```
  where color is either a color name or a color value.
- To set an element's background color, use the style
  ```
  background-color: color
  ```

Deprecated

- To set the background color for a Web page, use the attribute
  ```
  <body bgcolor="color">
  ```
  where color is either a color name or a hexadecimal color value.
- To set a page's text color, use the attribute
  ```
  <body text="color">
  ```
  where color is either a color name or a hexadecimal color value.
- To apply color to a section of text, use the code
  ```
  <font color="color">text</font>
  ```
  where color is either a color name or a hexadecimal color value, and text is the text to which you want to apply the color.

Working with Fonts and Text Styles

Tom has reviewed your progress. He's pleased with the color scheme you've created for the Web page, but would like you to work with the appearance of the text on the page. He's concerned that all of the text on the page is displayed in the same typeface. He would also like to see more variety in the page fonts.

Choosing a Font

By default, browsers display Web page text in a single font, usually Times New Roman. You can specify a different font for any page element using the style

```
font-family: fonts
```

where *fonts* is a comma-separated list of fonts that the browser can use in the element. Font names can be either specific or generic. A **specific font** is a font such as Times New Roman, Arial, or Garamond, which is actually installed on a user's computer. A **generic font** is a name for the general description of a font's appearance. Browsers recognize five generic fonts: serif, sans-serif, monospace, cursive, and fantasy. Figure 3-12 shows examples of each. Note that each generic font can represent a wide range of designs.

Generic fonts ◄ **Figure 3-12**

One issue with generic fonts is that you cannot be sure which font a given user's browser will use. For this reason, HTML and XHTML allow you to specify a list of fonts. You list the specific fonts you want the browser to try first, in order of preference, and then end the list with the generic font. If the browser cannot find any of the specific fonts you list, it substitutes the generic font. For example, to specify a sans-serif font, you could enter the following style:

```
font-family: Arial, Helvetica, sans-serif
```

This style tells the browser to first look for the Arial font; if Arial is not available, it tells the browser to look for Helvetica; if neither of those fonts is available, it tells the browser to use the generic sans-serif font defined by the user's system.

To see how the generic fonts appear on your browser, a demo page on text styles has been prepared for you.

To view your browser's generic fonts:

1. Use your browser to open the **demo_text_styles.htm** file from the tutorial.03/tutorial folder of your Data Files.

   This demo page contains a collection of the styles you'll be learning about in this session. Initially, the Preview box displays the sample text in the default text style of your Web browser. You can specify different sample text by selecting the default text and editing it. You can select different style values using the input boxes and drop-down list boxes on the left side of the page. Entering or selecting "default" in an input or drop-down list box causes the page to use the default style. Pressing the tab key activates a style change. The code for the new style appears in the page's lower-right corner.

2. In the upper-right corner box, insert the text **Arcadium**, press the **Enter** key, and then type **Amusement Park**. Press the **Tab** key.

3. Enter the rgb value **255**, **255**, **255** into the three color input boxes and **153**, **102**, **102** into the three background-color input boxes. Press the **Tab** key.

4. Select **fantasy** from the font-family drop-down list box. Figure 3-13 shows the formatted sample text with the style code (your formatted text may look different).

Figure 3-13 | **Viewing the fantasy font**

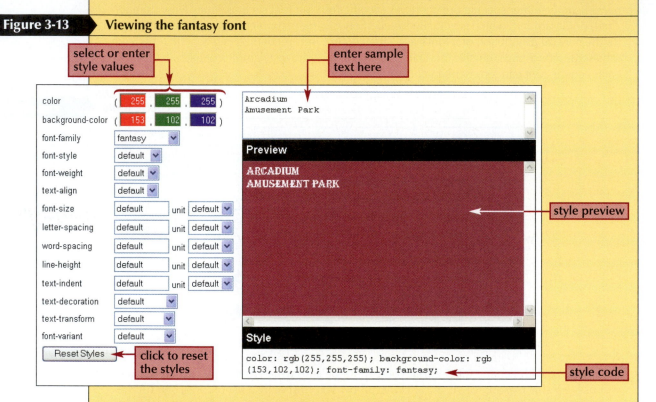

We'll work with this demo page throughout the rest of the session. You may want to keep the page open as you explore other styles.

Trouble? This demo page may look slightly different depending on your browser.

It's generally good practice not to use more than two different font faces within a single page, unless you're trying to create an interesting and striking visual effect. Serif fonts are best read in large blocks of text like paragraphs. Sans-serif fonts can work well either as paragraph text or as headings and subheads. You'll apply this principle to the About page by changing the font for the h1 heading and the list of links to a serif font.

To change the fonts for the heading and list of links:

1. Return to **about.htm** in your text editor.

2. Locate the first <p> tag in the file and insert the following inline style:

```
font-family: Arial, Helvetica, sans-serif
```

Be sure to use a semicolon to separate this new style from the text-align style already entered.

3. Go to the <h1> tag, and add the following style:

```
font-family: Arial, Helvetica, sans-serif
```

Be sure to use a semicolon to separate this style from the previous styles you entered. You may want to insert this style on a separate line to make your code more readable. Figure 3-14 shows the revised code.

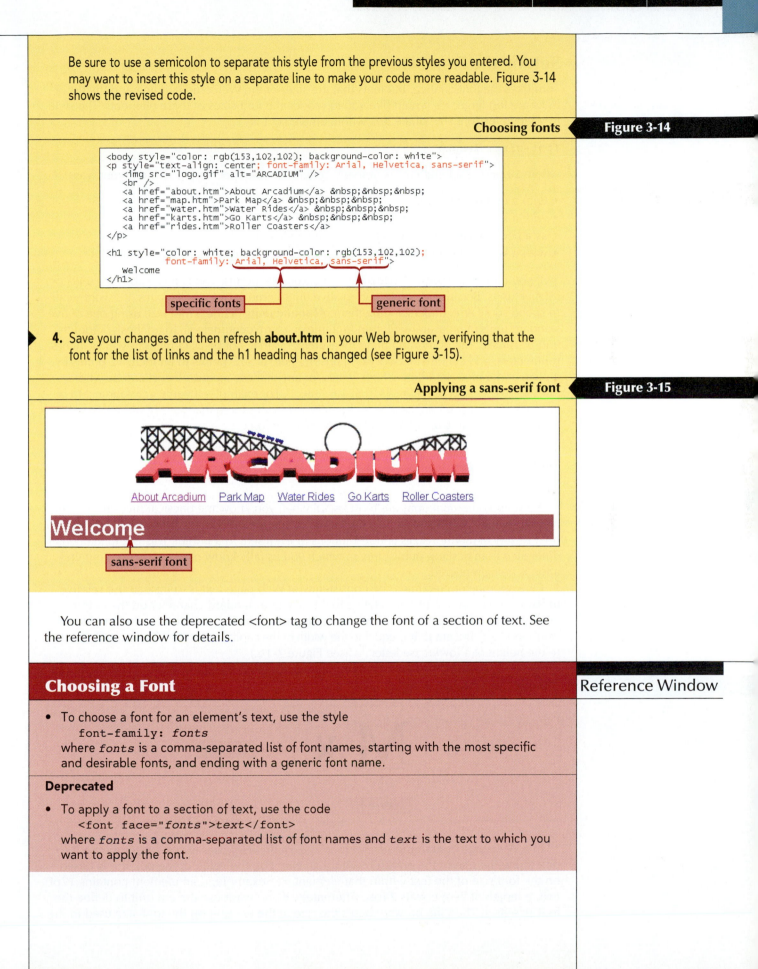

Choosing fonts — Figure 3-14

```
<body style="color: rgb(153,102,102); background-color: white">
<p style="text-align: center; font-family: Arial, Helvetica, sans-serif">
    <img src="logo.gif" alt="ARCADIUM" />
    <br />
    <a href="about.htm">About Arcadium</a>    
    <a href="map.htm">Park Map</a>    
    <a href="water.htm">Water Rides</a>    
    <a href="karts.htm">Go Karts</a>    
    <a href="rides.htm">Roller Coasters</a>
</p>

<h1 style="color: white; background-color: rgb(153,102,102);
        font-family: Arial, Helvetica, sans-serif">
    welcome
</h1>
```

specific fonts   generic font

4. Save your changes and then refresh **about.htm** in your Web browser, verifying that the font for the list of links and the h1 heading has changed (see Figure 3-15).

Applying a sans-serif font — Figure 3-15

sans-serif font

You can also use the deprecated <font> tag to change the font of a section of text. See the reference window for details.

Choosing a Font   Reference Window

• To choose a font for an element's text, use the style

    `font-family: fonts`

where *fonts* is a comma-separated list of font names, starting with the most specific and desirable fonts, and ending with a generic font name.

Deprecated

• To apply a font to a section of text, use the code

    `<font face="fonts">text</font>`

where *fonts* is a comma-separated list of font names and *text* is the text to which you want to apply the font.

Setting the Font Size

Tom likes the font change, but feels that the sizes of the Welcome heading and the list of links are too large. He would like you to reduce the font sizes of these elements. The style to change the font size of the text within an element is

```
font-size: length
```

where *length* is a length measurement. Lengths can be specified in four different ways:

- with a unit of measurement
- with a keyword description
- as a percentage of the size of the containing element
- with a keyword expressing the size relative to the size of the containing element

If you choose to specify lengths using measurement units, you can use absolute units or relative units. Because absolute and relative units come up a lot with styles, it's worthwhile to spend some time understanding them. **Absolute units** define a font size using one of five standard units of measurement: mm (millimeters), cm (centimeters), in (inches), pt (points), and pc (picas). The points and picas measurements may not be as familiar to you as inches, millimeters, and centimeters. For comparison, there are 72 points in an inch, 12 points in a pica, and 6 picas in an inch. Size values for any of these measurements can be whole numbers (0, 1, 2 ...) or decimals (0.5, 1.6, 3.9 ...). For example, if you want your text to be 1/2 inch in size, you can use any of the following styles (note that you should not insert a space between the size value and the unit abbreviation):

```
font-size: 0.5in
font-size: 36pt
font-size: 3pc
```

These measurement units are most useful when you know the physical properties of the output device. Of course this may not be the case with a Web page that could be displayed on a variety of monitor sizes and resolutions or even sent to a printer. This is a fundamental difference from desktop publishing, in which you usually know on what device your creation is being rendered.

One approach to retaining the consistency of Web page text is to instead use **relative units**, which express font size relative to the size of a standard character on the output device (whatever that may be). The two common typesetting standards are referred to as "em" and "ex." The **em unit** is equal to the width of the capital letter "M". The **ex unit** is equal to the height of a lowercase letter "x" (see Figure 3-16.)

| Figure 3-16 | The em and ex units |

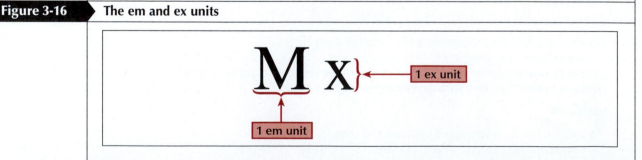

In a Web page containing several font sizes, a browser uses two different methods to determine the size of the em unit. Within an element, the value of the em unit is based on the font size of the text within that element. For example, if an element contains 12pt text, a length of 2em equals 24pts. Alternately, if you want use the em unit to define the font size itself, then the browser bases the size of the em unit on the font size used in the containing element. If the page body is set to a 10pt font, for example, a paragraph within the page set to a font size of 0.8em appears as 8pt font. The ultimate containing element is the browser itself, which has its own default font size for body text. Setting the body text to 0.8em reduces the font size to 80% of the browser's default font size.

You can use relative units to make your page **scalable**, which allows the page to be rendered the same way no matter how a user's output device is configured. For example, one user may have a large monitor with the default font size for body text set to 18pt. Another user may have a smaller monitor and a default font size of 12pt. You want your heading text to be about 50% larger than the body text for either user. Although you can't predict the default font size for a given user's output device, using a value of 1.5em for the heading ensures that it is sized appropriately on either monitor. Note that you can achieve the same effect by expressing a font size as a percentage of an element's default font size. For example, the style

```
font-size: 150%
```

causes the heading to appear 50% larger than the default size. Even though point size is the most commonly used unit in desktop publishing, the benefits of scalability often lead Web designers to opt for the em unit over points or other absolute units.

The final unit of measurement we'll examine is the **pixel**, which represents a single dot on the output device. Because the pixel is the most fundamental unit, for most length measurements, the browser assumes that a value is expressed in pixels if no unit is specified. Thus, to set the font size to 20 pixels, you could use either of the following styles:

```
font-size: 20px
font-size: 20
```

Be aware that the exact size of a pixel depends on the output device. Different devices have different resolutions, which are typically expressed in terms of **dots per inch** or **dpi**. For example, a 600dpi printer has six times more pixels per inch than a typical computer monitor. While you might assume that this would cause a 100 pixel length to appear shorter when you print a page, browsers adjust pixel sizes to ensure that a printout matches the computer screen image. Thus, not all pixels are equal!

Finally, you can express font sizes using seven descriptive keywords: xx-small, x-small, small, medium, large, x-large, or xx-large. Each browser is configured to display text at a particular size for each of these keywords, which enables you to achieve some uniformity across browsers. You can also use the relative keywords "larger" and "smaller" to make a font one size larger or smaller. For example, if a browser had been configured to display an element's text in the small size, you could move it to the medium size by using either of the following styles:

```
font-size: medium
font-size: larger
```

Armed with an almost dizzying array of possible font size values, you're ready to apply your knowledge to the list of links and the h1 heading. Recall that Tom wanted the text in these elements to be smaller. You decide to set the font size of the list of links to 0.8em (80% the size of the body text) and the font size of the h1 heading to 1.5em (50% larger than body text).

To change the font size for the heading and list of links:

1. Return to **about.htm** in your text editor.

2. Add the following style to the first <p> tag. Be sure to separate this new style from the previous ones with a semicolon.

```
font-size: 0.8em
```

3. Go to the <h1> tag, and add the following style:

```
font-size: 1.5em
```

Figure 3-17 shows the revised code.

Figure 3-17 Setting the font sizes

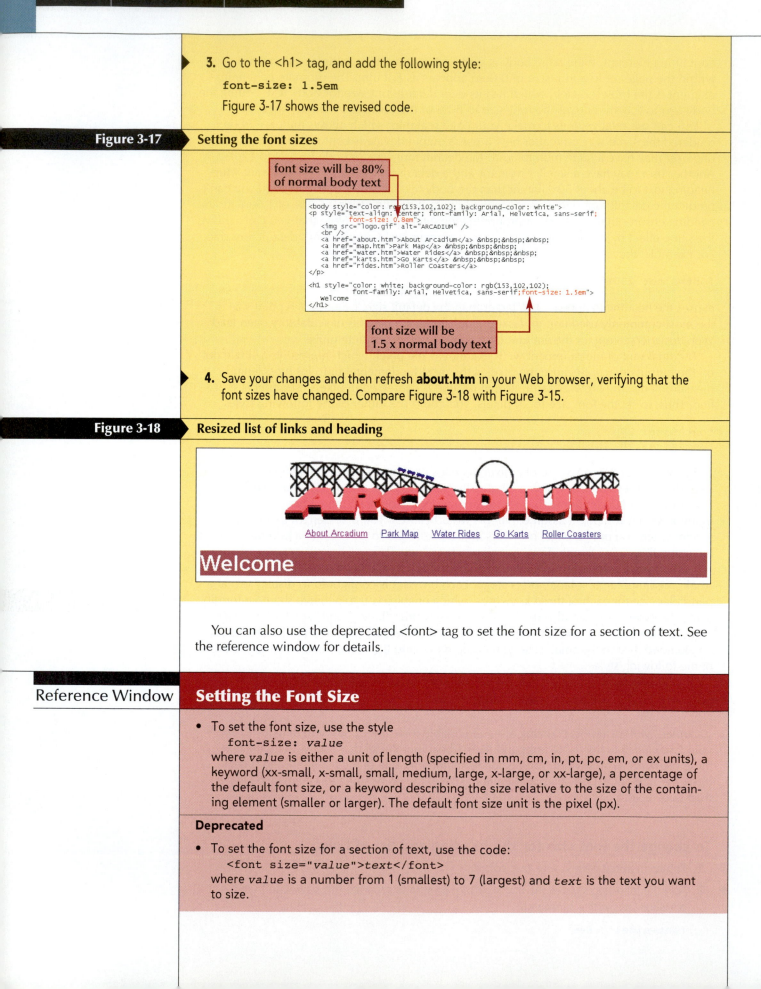

font size will be 80% of normal body text

```
<body style="color: rgb(153,102,102); background-color: white">
<p style="text-align: center; font-family: Arial, Helvetica, sans-serif;
        font-size: 0.8em">
    <img src="logo.gif" alt="ARCADIUM" />
    <br />
    <a href="about.htm">About Arcadium</a>    
    <a href="map.htm">Park Map</a>    
    <a href="water.htm">Water Rides</a>    
    <a href="karts.htm">Go Karts</a>    
    <a href="rides.htm">Roller Coasters</a>
</p>

<h1 style="color: white; background-color: rgb(153,102,102);
        font-family: Arial, Helvetica, sans-serif;font-size: 1.5em">
    Welcome
</h1>
```

font size will be
1.5 x normal body text

4. Save your changes and then refresh **about.htm** in your Web browser, verifying that the font sizes have changed. Compare Figure 3-18 with Figure 3-15.

Figure 3-18 Resized list of links and heading

About Arcadium   Park Map   Water Rides   Go Karts   Roller Coasters

Welcome

You can also use the deprecated <font> tag to set the font size for a section of text. See the reference window for details.

Reference Window

Setting the Font Size

- To set the font size, use the style
  ```
  font-size: value
  ```
  where *value* is either a unit of length (specified in mm, cm, in, pt, pc, em, or ex units), a keyword (xx-small, x-small, small, medium, large, x-large, or xx-large), a percentage of the default font size, or a keyword describing the size relative to the size of the containing element (smaller or larger). The default font size unit is the pixel (px).

Deprecated

- To set the font size for a section of text, use the code:
  ```
  <font size="value">text</font>
  ```
  where *value* is a number from 1 (smallest) to 7 (largest) and *text* is the text you want to size.

Controlling Spacing and Indentation

Tom feels that the text for the Welcome heading looks too crowded on the medium brown background. He would like you to spread it out more across the width of the page. He also would like to see more space between the first letter, "W," and the left edge of the brown background.

HTML and XHTML support styles that allow you to perform some basic typographic tasks, such as kerning and tracking. The amount of space between pairs of letters is referred to as the **kerning**, while the amount of space between words and phrases is called **tracking**. The styles to control an element's kerning and tracking are

```
letter-spacing: value
word-spacing: value
```

where `value` is the size of space between individual letters or words. You specify these sizes with the same units that you use for font sizing. As with font sizes, the default unit of length for kerning and tracking is the pixel (px). The default value for both kerning and tracking is 0 pixels. A positive value increases the letter and word spacing. A negative value reduces the space between letters and words.

To see how modifying these values can affect the appearance of your text, return to the text styles demo page.

To view kerning and tracking in action:

1. Return to the **demo_text_styles.htm** file in your Web browser.

2. Click the **Reset Styles** button and then change the text in the upper-right box to **Family Fun Park** and press the **Tab** key.

3. Select **sans-serif** from the font-family drop-down list box.

4. Change the value in the font-size box to **32**, the letter-spacing value to **6**, and the word-spacing value to **32**.

   Figure 3-19 shows the revised view of the sample text.

Changing the kerning and tracking   **Figure 3-19**

Another typographic feature that you can set is **leading**, which is the space between lines of text. The style to set the leading for the text within an element is

```
line-height: length
```

where `length` is a specific length, or a percentage of the font size of the text on those lines. If no unit is specified, a browser interprets the number to represent the ratio of the line height to the font size. The standard ratio is 1.2:1, which means that the line height is 1.2 times the font size. If Tom wanted his text to be double-spaced, you could apply the following style to the text:

```
line-height: 2
```

A common technique is to create multi-line titles with large fonts and small line heights in order to give title text more impact. Let's use the demo page to see how this works.

To view kerning and tracking in action:

1. Click the **Reset Styles** button, delete the text in the text Input box, type **Arcadium**, press **Enter**, type **Amusement Park**, and press **Tab**.

2. Select **sans-serif** from the font-family drop-down list box and choose **center** from the text-align drop-down list box.

3. Enter **32** in the font-size input box and select **px** from the font-size unit drop-down list box.

4. Enter **24** in the line-height input box and select **px** from the line-height unit drop-down list box.

Figure 3-20 shows how modifying the line height affects the impact of the title.

Figure 3-20 **Changing the line height**

An additional way to control text spacing is to set the indentation for the first line of a text block. The style is

```
text-indent: value
```

where `value` is either a length expressed in absolute or relative units, or a percentage of the width of the text block. For example, an indentation value of 5% indents the first line by 5% of the width of the block. The indentation value can also be negative, extending the first line to the left of the text block to create a **hanging indent**. Note that this technique is not well supported by many browsers.

Now you can use what you've learned about spacing to make the changes that Tom has suggested. You'll increase the kerning of the Welcome heading to 1em. This has the effect of putting one blank space between each letter. You'll also set the indentation to 1em, moving the text of the Welcome heading one space to the left.

To change the spacing of the heading:

1. Return to **about.htm** in your text editor.

2. Add the following style to the h1 heading (don't forget to include a semicolon to separate these new styles from the previous styles). You may wish to place the new styles on a separate line to make your code easier to read. See Figure 3-21.

```
letter-spacing: 1em; text-indent: 1em
```

Setting the kerning and indentation ◀ **Figure 3-21**

```
<h1 style="color: white; background-color: rgb(153,102,102);
        font-family: Arial, Helvetica, sans-serif;font-size: 1.5em";
        letter-spacing: 1em; text-indent: 1em">
   Welcome
</h1>
```

kerning will be set to 1 space	the Welcome text will be indented 1 space

3. Save your changes and refresh the About page in your Web browser. Verify that the spacing of the Welcome heading has changed (see Figure 3-22).

Revised spacing in the heading ◀ **Figure 3-22**

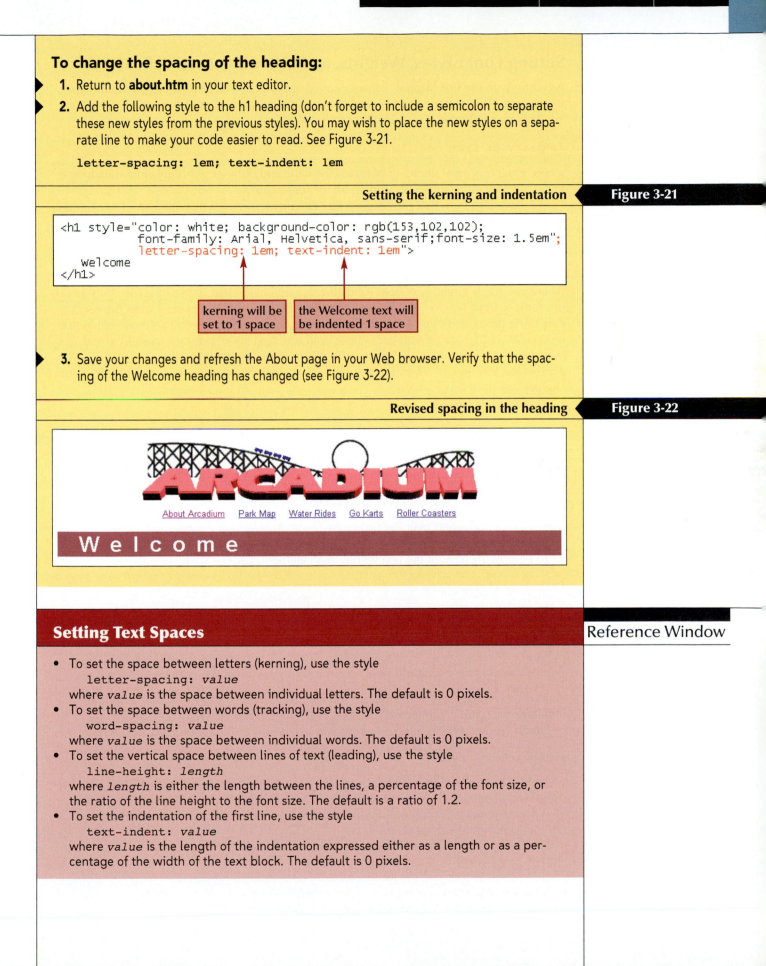

Reference Window

Setting Text Spaces

- To set the space between letters (kerning), use the style
    `letter-spacing: value`
  where *value* is the space between individual letters. The default is 0 pixels.
- To set the space between words (tracking), use the style
    `word-spacing: value`
  where *value* is the space between individual words. The default is 0 pixels.
- To set the vertical space between lines of text (leading), use the style
    `line-height: length`
  where *length* is either the length between the lines, a percentage of the font size, or the ratio of the line height to the font size. The default is a ratio of 1.2.
- To set the indentation of the first line, use the style
    `text-indent: value`
  where *value* is the length of the indentation expressed either as a length or as a percentage of the width of the text block. The default is 0 pixels.

Setting Font Styles, Weights, and other Decorative Features

As you saw in the first tutorial, browsers often apply default font styles to particular types of elements. Text marked with an <address> tag, for example, usually appears in italics. You can specify font styles yourself using the style

```
font-style: type
```

where *type* is normal, italic, or oblique. The italic and oblique styles are similar in appearance, but may differ subtly depending on the font in use.

You have also seen that browsers render certain elements in heavier fonts. For example, most browsers render headings in a boldfaced font. You can control the font weight for any page element using the style

```
font-weight: weight
```

where *weight* is the level of bold formatting applied to the text. You express weights as values ranging from 100 to 900, in increments of 100. In practice, however, most browsers cannot render nine different font weights. For practical purposes, you can assume that 400 represents normal (unbolded) text, 700 is bold text, and 900 represents extra-bold text. You can also use the keywords "normal" or "bold" in place of a weight value, or you can express the font weight relative to the containing element, using the keywords "bolder" or "lighter".

Another style you can use to change the appearance of your text is

```
text-decoration: type
```

where *type* is none (for no decorative changes), underline, overline, line-through, or blink. You can apply several decorative features to the same element. For example, the style

```
text-decoration: underline overline
```

places a line under and over the text in the element. Note that the text-decoration style cannot be applied to non-textual elements, such as inline images.

To control the case of the text within in an element, use the style

```
text-transform: type
```

where *type* is capitalize, uppercase, lowercase, or none (to make no changes to the text case). For example, if you want to capitalize the first letter of each word in the element, you could use the style

```
text-transform: capitalize
```

To display each letter in lowercase, you can use the text-transform value "lowercase". Similarly, the setting "uppercase" displays each letter in uppercase.

Finally, you can display text in uppercase letters and a small font using the style

```
font-variant: type
```

where *type* is normal (the default) or small caps (small capital letters). Small caps are often used in legal documents, such as software agreements, in which the capital letters indicate the importance of a phrase or point, but the text is made small so as to not detract from other elements in the document.

To see the impact of these different styles, you can use the demo page.

To view the different font styles:

1. Return to the **demo_text_styles.htm** page in your Web browser and click the **Reset Styles** button.
2. Enter **32** in the font-size input box.
3. Select **italic** from the font-style drop-down list box and select **bold** from the font-weight drop-down list box.
4. Select **underline** from the text-decoration drop-down list box and **small-caps** from the font-variant drop-down list box.

Figure 3-23 shows the impact of these style changes on the text.

Changing font styles ◄ **Figure 3-23**

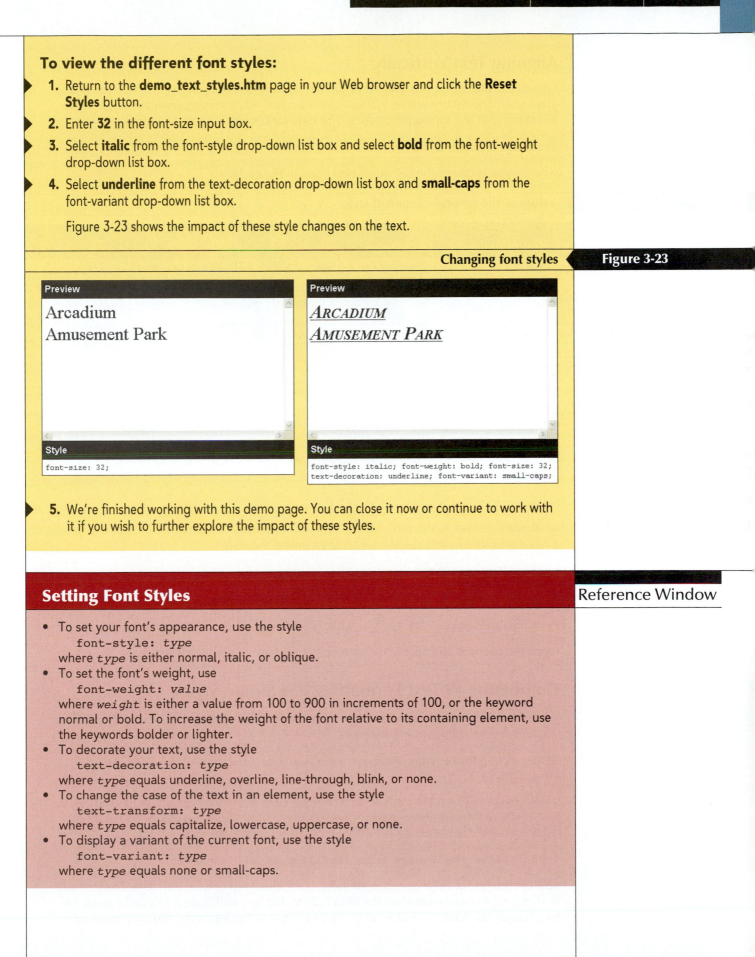

5. We're finished working with this demo page. You can close it now or continue to work with it if you wish to further explore the impact of these styles.

Setting Font Styles

Reference Window

- To set your font's appearance, use the style
    font-style: *type*
  where *type* is either normal, italic, or oblique.
- To set the font's weight, use
    font-weight: *value*
  where *weight* is either a value from 100 to 900 in increments of 100, or the keyword normal or bold. To increase the weight of the font relative to its containing element, use the keywords bolder or lighter.
- To decorate your text, use the style
    text-decoration: *type*
  where *type* equals underline, overline, line-through, blink, or none.
- To change the case of the text in an element, use the style
    text-transform: *type*
  where *type* equals capitalize, lowercase, uppercase, or none.
- To display a variant of the current font, use the style
    font-variant: *type*
  where *type* equals none or small-caps.

Aligning Text Vertically

One of the first styles you learned in Tutorial 1 was the text-align style, which you use to align text horizontally within a block-level element. You can also vertically align inline elements with the surrounding block. The style for setting vertical alignment is

```
vertical-align: type
```

where *type* is one of the keywords described in Figure 3-24.

Figure 3-24 **Values of the vertical-alignment style**

Vertical Alignment	Description
baseline	Aligns the element with the bottom of lowercase letters in surrounding text. (the default)
bottom	Aligns the bottom of the element with the bottom of the lowest element in surrounding content.
middle	Aligns the middle of the element with the middle of the surrounding content.
sub	Subscripts the element.
super	Superscripts the element.
text-bottom	Aligns the bottom of the element with the bottom of the font of the surrounding content.
text-top	Aligns the top of the element with the top of the font of the surrounding content.
top	Aligns the top of the element with the top of the tallest object in the surrounding content.

Instead of using keywords, you can specify a length or a percentage for the element to be aligned relative to the surrounding content. A positive value moves the element up and a negative value lowers the element. For example, the style

```
vertical-align: 50%
```

raises the element by half of the line height of the surrounding content, while the style

```
vertical-align: -100%
```

drops the element an entire line height below the baseline of the current line.

Combining all Text Formatting in a Single Style

We've covered a lot of different text and font styles. You can combine most of them into a single style declaration, using the form

```
font: font-style font-variant font-weight font-size/line-height
font-family
```

where *font-style* is the font's style, *font-variant* is the font variant, *font-weight* is the weight of the font, *font-size* is the size of the font, *line-height* is the height of each line, and *font-family* is the font face. For example, the style

```
font: italic small-caps bold 16pt/24pt Arial, sans-serif
```

displays the text of the element in an italic, bold, and Arial or sans-serif font. The font size is 16pt, and the space between the lines is 24pt. The text will appear in small capital letters. You do not have to include all of the properties of the font style; the only required properties are size and font-family. A browser assumes the default value for any omitted property. However, you must place any properties that you do include in the order indicated above. For example, the following would be a correct style declaration to specify a 16pt, bold, monospace font:

```
font: bold 16pt monospace
```

However, it would *not* be correct to switch the order, placing the font-family property before the style and weight properties:

```
font: monospace bold 16pt
```

Tom feels that the size of the address text at the bottom of the page is too large, and he feels that it would look better in a normal sans-serif font rather than in italics. Make these changes now using the font style.

To change the style of the address element:

1. Return to **about.htm** in your text editor.

2. Add the following style to the address element at the bottom of the file (be sure to separate all style declarations with a semicolon). See Figure 3-25.

   ```
   font: normal 8pt Arial, Helvetica, sans-serif
   ```

Using the font style | Figure 3-25

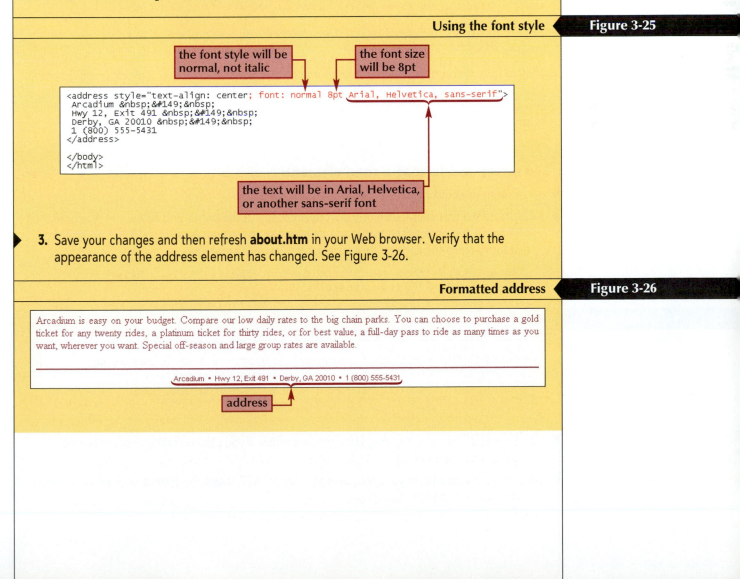

the font style will be normal, not italic

the font size will be 8pt

```
<address style="text-align: center; font: normal 8pt Arial, Helvetica, sans-serif">
Arcadium  &#149; 
Hwy 12, Exit 491  &#149; 
Derby, GA 20010  &#149; 
1 (800) 555-5431
</address>

</body>
</html>
```

the text will be in Arial, Helvetica, or another sans-serif font

3. Save your changes and then refresh **about.htm** in your Web browser. Verify that the appearance of the address element has changed. See Figure 3-26.

Formatted address | Figure 3-26

Arcadium is easy on your budget. Compare our low daily rates to the big chain parks. You can choose to purchase a gold ticket for any twenty rides, a platinum ticket for thirty rides, or for best value, a full-day pass to ride as many times as you want, wherever you want. Special off-season and large group rates are available.

Arcadium • Hwy 12, Exit 491 • Derby, GA 20010 • 1 (800) 555-5431

address

Reference Window

Using the font Style

- To combine all font properties in a single declaration, use the style
  ```
  font: font-style font-variant font-weight font-size/line-height
  font-family
  ```
  where `font-style` is the style, `font-variant` is the variant, `font-weight` is the weight, `font-size` is size, `line-height` is the height of the lines, and `font-family` is the font face. You may omit any of the properties except for font-size and font-family, but they must be entered in this order.

Using the Span Element

Tom wants to make one more change to the font styles on the page. He would like the word "Arcadium" in the first paragraph to be prominently displayed in bold and perhaps in Arial or Helvetica font, setting it off from the rest of the text in paragraph. To make this change, you first need a way of marking that single word within the paragraph. You can do that with the span element. The syntax is

```
<span>content</span>
```

where `content` is the content to be marked. The span element is just a marker; browsers do not format the content unless you also add a style to the element. For example, to display the word "Arcadium" in Arial or Helvetica, you would enter the code

```
<span style="font-family: Arial, Helvetica, sans-serif">
Arcadium</span>
```

The span element is an inline element and must be placed within a block-level element, such as a paragraph or a heading. HTML supports another marker, the div element, which is a generic block-level element. We will talk about the uses of the div element in a later tutorial.

To insert and format a span element:

1. Return to **about.htm** in your text editor.

2. Locate the first occurrence of the word Arcadium in the paragraph below the Welcome heading and enclose the text in the following span element (see Figure 3-27). You might want to place the code on its own separate line for readability.

   ```
   <span style="font-weight: bold; font-family: Arial, Helvetica,
   sans-serif">Arcadium</span>
   ```

Figure 3-27 Creating a span element

```
<p style="text-align: justify">
Exciting adventures await you at
<span style="font-weight: bold; font-family: Arial, Helvetica, sans-serif">Arcadium</span>,
your affordable family fun center. The park is located 5 miles northwest of
Derby - close to many of Georgia's scenic wonders. Arcadium offers over 50 rides,
including some of the state's most exciting roller coasters and water rides.
There's also plenty of fun for the younger kids, including two separate
kiddie pools and special rides for the kids.</p>
```

3. Save your changes. You may close the text editor if you plan on taking a break before going on to Session 3.2.

4. Reload **about.htm** in your Web browser. Figure 3-28 shows the format applied to the word Arcadium in the first paragraph.

Formatted text in the About page | Figure 3-28

span element

Welcome

Exciting adventures await you at **Arcadium**, your affordable family fun center. The park is located 5 miles northwest of Derby - close to many of Georgia's scenic wonders. Arcadium offers over 50 rides, including some of the state's most exciting roller coasters and water rides. There's also plenty of fun for the younger kids, including two separate kiddie pools and special rides for the kids.

5. Close your Web browser if you intend to take a break before starting Session 3.2.

Using the span element   Reference Window

- To create a generic inline element, use the HTML code
  ```
  <span>content</span>
  ```
  where *content* is the content of the inline element.

You've completed your work with colors and text in the About page. Tom is pleased with your work. He now wants you to examine how you can use graphics to improve the site's appearance. You'll tackle this task in the next session.

Session 3.1 Quick Check   Review

1. What style settings would you use to change the font color to yellow and the background color to the value (51,102,51)?
2. What are Web-safe colors and why would you use them in your Web pages?
3. What style setting would you use to display text in Courier New font, or in any monospace font if that specific font is not available?
4. What style setting would you use to set the font size to 16 points?
5. What is the em unit, and why would you want to use it with your Web page text?
6. What is kerning, and what style setting would you use to set an element's kerning to 2em?
7. What style would you use to make text double spaced?
8. What style settings would you use to create bold italic text?
9. What is the span element?

Session 3.2

Choosing an Image Format

Now that you've finished working with the Arcadium Web site's colors and fonts, Tom wants you to start working on the site's graphics. Most Web browsers support two image file formats: GIF and JPEG. Choosing the appropriate image format is an important part of Web page design. You must balance the goal of creating an interesting and attractive page against the need to keep the size of your page and its supporting files small and easy to retrieve. Each file format has its advantages and disadvantages, and you will probably use a combination of both formats in your Web page designs. First, let's look at the advantages and disadvantages of using GIF image files.

Working with GIF Images

GIF (Graphics Interchange Format), the most commonly used image format on the Web, is compatible with virtually all browsers. GIF files are limited to displaying 256 colors, so they are most often used for graphics requiring fewer colors, such as clip art images, line art, logos, and icons. Images that require more color depth, such as photographs, can appear grainy when saved as GIF files. There are actually two GIF file formats: GIF87 and GIF89a. The **GIF89a** format supports more features such as interlacing, transparent colors, and animation.

Interlacing refers to the way that graphics software saves a GIF file. In a **noninterlaced GIF**, which is the most common format, the image is saved one line at a time, starting from the top of the graphic and moving downward. Figure 3-29 shows the progress of a noninterlaced GIF as it opens in a Web browser. If a graphic is large, it might take a long time for the entire image to appear, which can frustrate visitors to your Web page.

Figure 3-29	Noninterlaced GIF

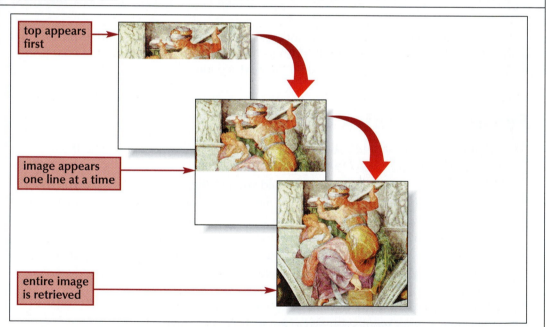

An **interlaced GIF**, by contrast, is saved and retrieved in stages. For example, every fifth line of the image might appear first, followed by every sixth line, and so forth through the remaining rows. As Figure 3-30 shows, an interlaced image starts out as a blurry representation of its final appearance, then gradually comes into focus. By contrast, a noninterlaced image is always a sharp image as it's being retrieved, but it is incomplete until it is fully loaded.

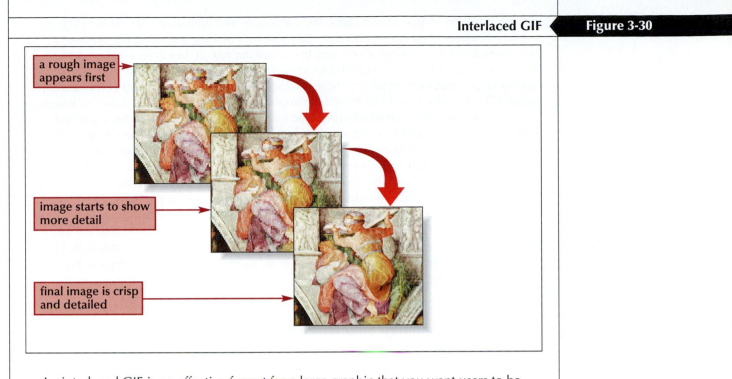

a rough image appears first

image starts to show more detail

final image is crisp and detailed

An interlaced GIF is an effective format for a large graphic that you want users to be able to see as it loads. Users with slower connections get an immediate idea of what the image looks like and can decide whether to wait for it to come into focus. On the down side, interlacing increases the size of a GIF file by anywhere from 3 to 20 kilobytes, depending on the image.

GIF image files can be large. One way to reduce the size of a GIF is to reduce the number of colors in its color palette. For example, if an image contains only 32 different colors, you can use an image editing program to reduce the palette to those 32 colors, resulting in a smaller image file that loads faster.

Working with Transparent Colors

Another feature of the GIF89a format is the ability to use transparent colors. A **transparent color** is a color that is not displayed when the image is viewed in an application. In place of the transparent color, a browser displays whatever is on the page background.

The process by which you create a transparent color depends on the graphics software you are using. Many applications include the option to designate a transparent color when saving an image, while other packages include a transparent color tool, which you use to select the color that you want to treat as transparent.

In the past, Web page designers used transparent GIFs as layout tools to help them place elements on a Web page. To accomplish this, a designer would create a GIF one pixel square in size, with the color of the pixel specified as transparent. This type of image was sometimes referred to as a **spacer**. A Web designer could then size the spacer in order to position objects in specific locations on the page. Because the spacer was transparent, users would see only the positioned object. With the advent of styles, there is little need for spacers anymore, but you may still see them in the code for older pages.

Using Animated GIFs

GIFs are also commonly used to create animated images. An **animated GIF** is composed of several images that are displayed one after the other. Some files play the frames in rapid succession, creating the illusion of motion, while other animated GIFs simply cycle slowly through multiple images or messages. You can easily find animated GIFs on the Web in online collections. You can also create your own by installing animated GIF software. Most animated GIF software allows you to control the rate at which an animation plays (as measured by frames per second) and to determine the number of times the animation repeats before stopping (or set it to repeat without stopping). You can also combine individual GIF files into a single animated file and create special transitions between images.

Animated GIFs are a mixed blessing. Because an animated GIF file is typically larger than a static GIF image file, using animated GIFs can greatly increase the size of a Web page. You should also be careful not to overwhelm users with animated images. Animated GIFs can quickly irritate users once the novelty wears off, especially because there is no way for users to turn them off! Like other GIF files, animated GIFs are limited to 256 colors. This makes them ideal for small icons and line art, but not for photographic images.

Recall that one of the pages in the Arcadium Web site is a splash screen. Tom wants to include some interesting visual effects on this page in order to draw users into the site. You decide to investigate whether this would be a good place for an animated GIF. One of the graphic designers at Arcadium has created an animated GIF of the company logo. You'll try adding that to the splash screen.

To insert the animated logo in the Web page:

1. Use your text editor to open the **indextxt.htm** file from the tutorial.03/tutorial folder of your Data Files. Enter **your name** and **the date** in the comments at the top of the file and save it as **index.htm**.

2. Replace the text "ARCADIUM" with the following tag, as shown in Figure 3-31.

```
<img src="logoanim.gif" alt="ARCADIUM" />
```

Figure 3-31 Inserting the animated logo

```
<body style="font-family: Arial, Helvetica, sans-serif">
<p style="text-align: center">
    <img src="logoanim.gif" alt="ARCADIUM" />
    <br />
    <span style="color: red; font-size: 18pt; font-weight: bold">
    Affordable Family Fun
    </span>
    <br /><br />
    <a href="about.htm">Enter Arcadium</a>
</p>
</body>
</html>
```

3. Save your changes to the file.

4. Open **index.htm** in your Web browser. Verify that the logo displays an animated set of cars racing down the track. See Figure 3-32

Figure 3-32 Animated logo

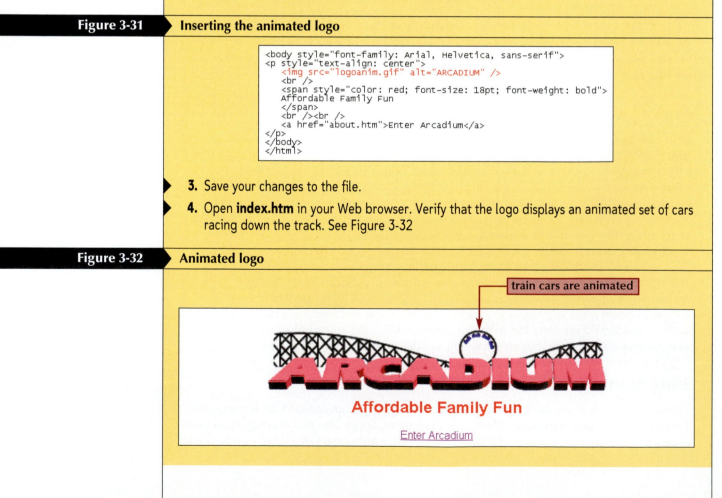

train cars are animated

Affordable Family Fun

Enter Arcadium

Working with JPEG Images

The other main image file format is the JPEG format. **JPEG** stands for **Joint Photographic Experts Group**. JPEGs differ from GIFs in several ways. In the JPEG format you can create images that use the full 16.7 million colors available in the color palette. Because of this, JPEG files are most often used for photographs and images that cover a wide spectrum of color.

In addition, the image compression algorithm used by JPEG files yields image files that are usually (though not always) smaller than their GIF counterparts. In some situations, though, the GIF format creates a smaller and better-looking image—for example, when an image contains large sections covered with a single color. As a general rule, you should use JPEGs for photos and GIFs for illustrations that involve only a few colors.

You can control the size of a JPEG by controlling the degree of image compression applied to the file. Increasing the compression reduces the file size, though often at the expense of image quality. Figure 3-33 shows the effect of compression on a JPEG file. As you can see, the increased compression cuts the file size to a fraction of the original, but the resulting image is more poorly defined than the image with low compression.

The effects of compression on JPEG quality and file size   **Figure 3-33**

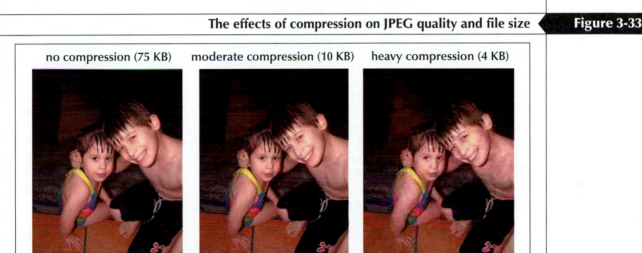

no compression (75 KB)   moderate compression (10 KB)   heavy compression (4 KB)

By testing different compression levels with image editing software, you can reduce the size of a JPEG file while maintaining an attractive image. Note that a smaller file size does not always mean that a Web page will load faster. Because a browser has to decompress a JPEG image when it retrieves it, opening a heavily compressed image can actually take more time than retrieving and displaying a less compressed file.

JPEGs do not support animation or transparent colors. However, a format called **progressive JPEG** does create an effect similar to interlacing, in which the JPEG image fades in from a low resolution to a high resolution. Like interlaced GIFs, progressive JPEG image files are larger than nonprogressive JPEGs.

Working with PNG Images

A third graphic format that is starting to gain wide acceptance is the **Portable Network Graphics** or **PNG** format. PNG files include most of the same features as GIFs (such as animation, interlacing, and transparency) but also provide the file compression available with JPEGs. In addition, like the JPEG format, PNG supports the full 16.7 million colors of the color palette. You can also designate several transparent colors in a PNG file, rather than the single color that GIFs support. The only problem with the PNG format is that older browsers do not support it. This is becoming less of a problem as time goes by, so you may find that using the PNG format is an acceptable choice for your Web site. Figure 3-34 summarizes the features of the three major graphics formats on the Web.

| Figure 3-34 | Comparison of image formats |

Feature	GIF	JPEG	PNG
Color Resolution	256	16.7 million	16.7 million
Useful for line art	Yes	No	Yes
Useful for photographs	No	Yes	Yes
Interlacing/Progressive Encoding	Yes	Yes	Yes
Compressible	Yes	Yes	Yes
Transparent colors	Yes (1)	No	Yes (multiple)
Supported by older browsers	Yes	Yes	No

Other Image Formats

Other image formats are available for your Web pages as well. The World Wide Web Consortium (W3C) is currently promoting the **Scalable Vector Graphics (SVG)** specification, which is a graphic format written with XML that you can use to create line art composed of straight lines and curves. The **Flash** software program from **Macromedia** is another popular way to add animated graphics to a Web site. You can use Flash to create interactive animations, scalable graphics, animated logos, and navigation controls for a Web site. To view a Flash animation, users must have the Flash player installed on their computers. Users can download and install the player for free, and are generally prompted to do this the first time they open a Web page that uses Flash.

Tom wants you to add a photo to the About page. The image has been saved as a JPEG file and you'll place the image in the first paragraph on the page.

To insert the photo in the About page:

1. Reopen the **about.htm** file in your text editor.

2. Directly above the line "Exciting adventures await you at", insert the following tag as shown in Figure 3-35.

   ```
   <img src="about.jpg" alt="" />
   ```

| Figure 3-35 | Inserting the about photo |

```
<p style="text-align: justify">
<img src="about.jpg" alt="" />
Exciting adventures await you at
<span style="font-weight: bold; font-family: Arial, Helvetica, sans-serif">Arcadium</span>,
your affordable family fun center. The park is located 5 miles northwest of
Derby - close to many of Georgia's scenic wonders. Arcadium offers over 50 rides,
including some of the state's most exciting roller coasters and water rides.
There's also plenty of fun for the younger kids, including two separate
kiddie pools and special rides for the kids.</p>
```

3. Save your changes to the file and reopen **about.htm** in your Web browser. The image appears inline with the rest of the paragraph text (see Figure 3-36).

Welcome

Exciting adventures await you at **Arcadium**, your affordable family fun center. The park is located 5 miles northwest of Derby - close to many of Georgia's scenic wonders. Arcadium offers over 50 rides, including some of the state's most exciting roller coasters and water rides. There's also plenty of fun for the younger kids, including two separate kiddie pools and special rides for the kids.

Aligning an Image

You show Tom the progress you've made on the Web page. Although he's pleased with the image of the kids, he doesn't like how the image is positioned on the page. The current layout includes a large blank space between the Welcome heading and the first paragraph. Tom wants you to wrap the paragraph text around the image.

Floating an Element

One way to achieve this is with the float style. The syntax of the float style is

```
float: position
```

where *position* is none (the default), left, or right. As shown in Figure 3-37, when a browser encounters the float style, it places the element on the specified margin and then wraps the subsequent content around the element.

Figure 3-37 **The float style**

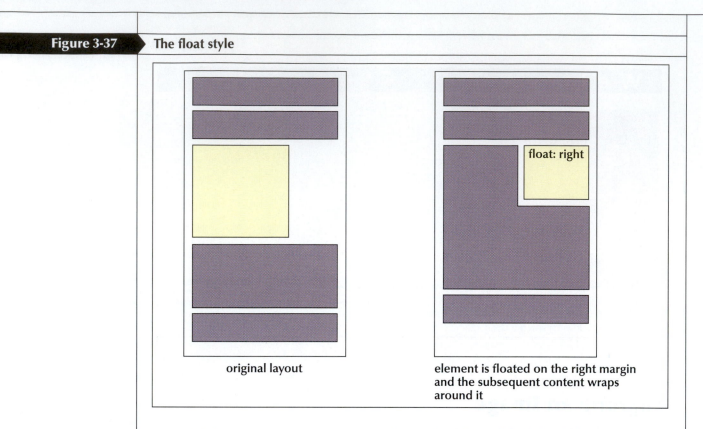

original layout

element is floated on the right margin
and the subsequent content wraps
around it

In addition to images, you can use the float style with any block-level element to create interesting layout effects, such as sidebars. We'll explore this layout technique in a future tutorial.

Clearing an Element

You can use the clear style to prevent other content from wrapping around a floating element. The clear style uses the syntax

```
clear: position
```

where *position* is none (the default), left, or right. For example, setting the clear value to "right" prevents an element from being displayed until the right margin is clear of floating elements (see Figure 3-38). You use the clear style when you want to ensure that an element, such as a page footer, is not moved up and wrapped around another element.

The clear style ◀ **Figure 3-38**

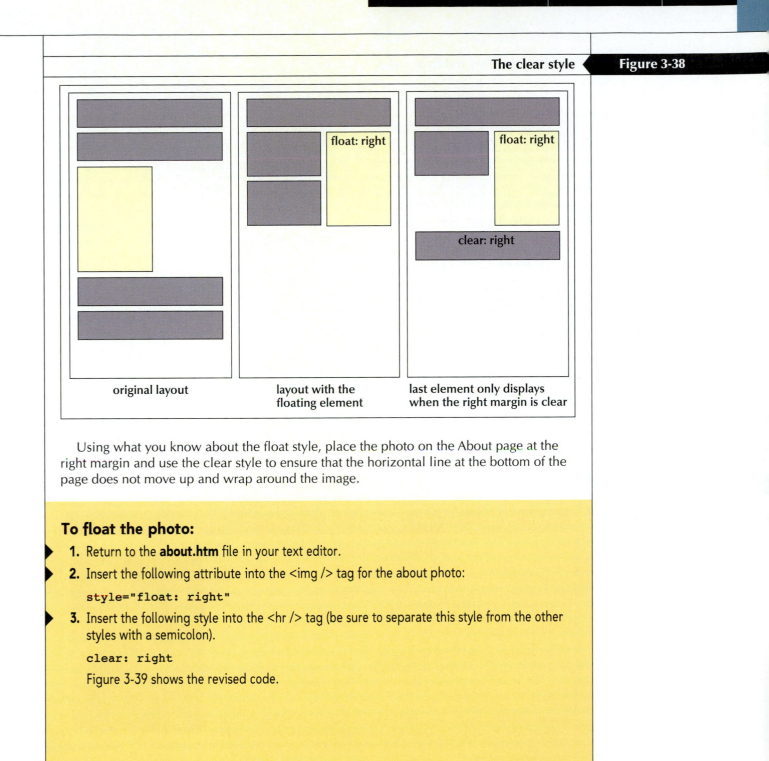

original layout   layout with the   last element only displays
                         floating element   when the right margin is clear

Using what you know about the float style, place the photo on the About page at the right margin and use the clear style to ensure that the horizontal line at the bottom of the page does not move up and wrap around the image.

To float the photo:

▶ **1.** Return to the **about.htm** file in your text editor.

▶ **2.** Insert the following attribute into the <img /> tag for the about photo:

```
style="float: right"
```

▶ **3.** Insert the following style into the <hr /> tag (be sure to separate this style from the other styles with a semicolon).

```
clear: right
```

Figure 3-39 shows the revised code.

Figure 3-39 | **Inserting the float and clear styles**

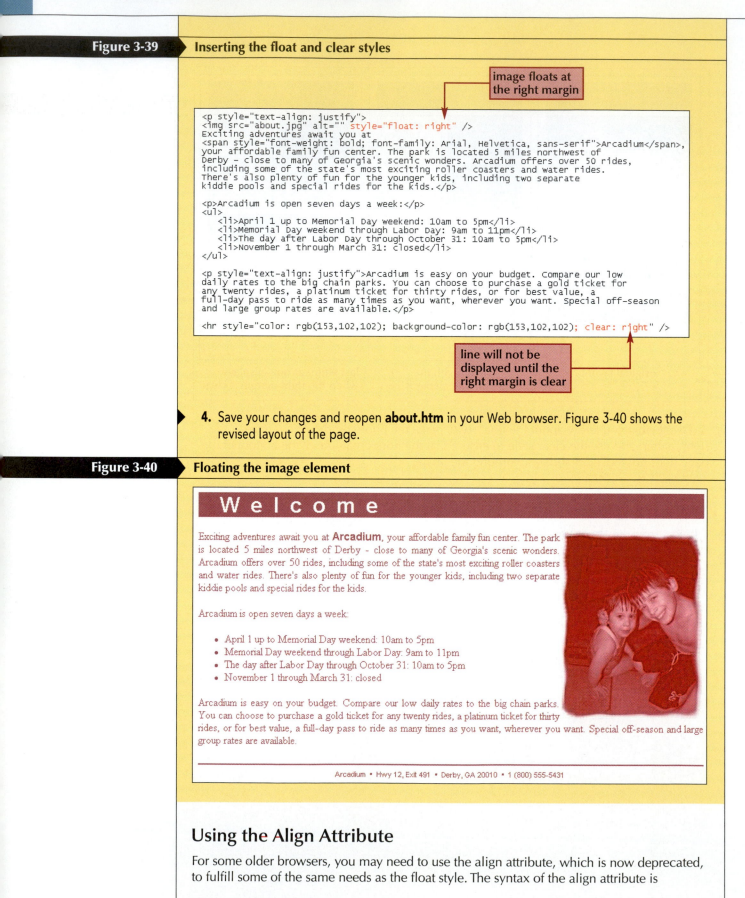

image floats at the right margin

```
<p style="text-align: justify">
<img src="about.jpg" alt="" style="float: right" />
Exciting adventures await you at
<span style="font-weight: bold; font-family: Arial, Helvetica, sans-serif">Arcadium</span>,
your affordable family fun center. The park is located 5 miles northwest of
Derby – close to many of Georgia's scenic wonders. Arcadium offers over 50 rides,
including some of the state's most exciting roller coasters and water rides.
There's also plenty of fun for the younger kids, including two separate
kiddie pools and special rides for the kids.</p>

<p>Arcadium is open seven days a week:</p>
<ul>
    <li>April 1 up to Memorial Day weekend: 10am to 5pm</li>
    <li>Memorial Day weekend through Labor Day: 9am to 11pm</li>
    <li>The day after Labor Day through October 31: 10am to 5pm</li>
    <li>November 1 through March 31: closed</li>
</ul>

<p style="text-align: justify">Arcadium is easy on your budget. Compare our low
daily rates to the big chain parks. You can choose to purchase a gold ticket for
any twenty rides, a platinum ticket for thirty rides, or for best value, a
full-day pass to ride as many times as you want, wherever you want. Special off-season
and large group rates are available.</p>

<hr style="color: rgb(153,102,102); background-color: rgb(153,102,102); clear: right" />
```

line will not be displayed until the right margin is clear

> **4.** Save your changes and reopen **about.htm** in your Web browser. Figure 3-40 shows the revised layout of the page.

Figure 3-40 | **Floating the image element**

Using the Align Attribute

For some older browsers, you may need to use the align attribute, which is now deprecated, to fulfill some of the same needs as the float style. The syntax of the align attribute is

```
<img align="position" />
```

where *position* indicates how you want the image aligned with the surrounding content. If you want the image placed on the left or right margin, use align values of "left" or "right". Figure 3-41 shows the other values of the align attribute.

Values of the align attribute ◄ **Figure 3-41**

align=	Description
absbottom	Aligns the bottom of the object with the absolute bottom of the surrounding text. The absolute bottom is equal to the baseline of the text minus the height of the largest descender in the text.
absmiddle	Aligns the middle of the object with the middle of the surrounding text. The absolute middle is the midpoint between the absolute bottom and text top of the surrounding text.
baseline	Aligns the bottom of the object with the baseline of the surrounding text.
bottom	Aligns the bottom of the object with the bottom of the surrounding text. The bottom is equal to the baseline minus the standard height of a descender in the text.
left	Aligns the object to the left of the surrounding text. All preceding and subsequent text flows to the right of the object.
middle	Aligns the middle of the object with the surrounding text.
right	Aligns the object to the right of the surrounding text. All subsequent text flows to the left of the object.
texttop	Aligns the top of the object with the absolute top of the surrounding text. The absolute top is the baseline plus the height of the largest ascender in the text.
top	Aligns the object to the right of the surrounding text. All subsequent text flows to the left of the object.

Note that you can duplicate the align values with styles. You can recreate the effects of the left and right values using the float style. You can duplicate the rest of the align values using the vertical-align style discussed in the previous session.

There is no general attribute to prevent an element from being displayed until a margin is clear. If you need to perform this task for older browsers, you can place the tag `<br clear="position" />` before the element you want cleared, where *position* is either "left" or "right", "all", or "none". This tag creates a line break only after the specified margin is clear. Note that like the align attribute, this attribute has been deprecated.

Floating and Clearing an Element

Reference Window

- To float an element on the left or right margin, use the style
    `float: position`
  where *position* is none (the default), left, or right.
- To display an element in the first available space where the specified margin is clear of floating elements, use the style
    `clear: position`

Deprecated

- To align an inline image with the left or right page margin, add the following attribute to the <img /> tag:
    `align="position"`
  where *position* is either left or right.
- To display an element in the first available space where the specified margin is clear of other elements, enter the following tag before the element:
    `<br clear="position" />`
  where *position* is left, right, all, or none.

Setting Margins

Wrapping the content around the image has solved the problem of the large white space in the middle of the About page. However, Tom feels that the text crowds the photo too much, and would like you to slightly increase the margin between the photo and the text. Four styles control the size of an element's top, right, bottom, and left margins:

```
margin-top: length
margin-right: length
margin-bottom: length
margin-left: length
```

where *length* is one of the units of length discussed in the previous session or a percentage of the width of the containing element. You can also use the keyword "auto", which enables the browser to determine the margin size. As with font sizes, the default unit is the pixel. To create a 2-pixel margin to the left and right of an element, and a 1-pixel margin above and below, you would use the style

```
margin-top: 1; margin-right: 2; margin-bottom: 1; margin-left: 2
```

A margin value can also be negative. Web page designers can use negative margins to create interesting overlay effects by forcing the browser to render one element on top of another. Note that some browsers do not support negative margins and using them may lead to unpredictable results.

The four margin styles can be combined into a single style using the format

```
margin: top right bottom left
```

where *top*, *right*, *bottom*, and *left* are the sizes of the top, right, bottom, and left margins. (If you have trouble remembering this order, just think of moving clockwise around the element, starting with the top margin.) If you include only three values in the margin style, they are applied to the top, right, and bottom margins. If you specify only two values, a browser applies the first value to both the top and bottom margins, and the second value to both the left and right margins. If you specify only a single value, a browser applies it to all four margins.

Tom suggests that you set the size of the left margin to 15 pixels and the size of the bottom margin to 5 pixels. The top and right margins can be set to 0 pixels.

To set the image margins:

1. Return to the **about.htm** file in your text editor.

2. Add the following style to the <img /> tag for the about photo (see Figure 3-42):

   ```
   margin: 0 0 5 15
   ```

   Be sure to separate this style from the other styles with a semicolon.

Figure 3-42 ▶ Setting the margin size

```
<p style="text-align: justify">
<img src="about.jpg" alt="" style="float: right; margin: 0 0 5 15" />
Exciting adventures await you at
<span style="font-weight: bold; font-family: Arial, Helvetica, sans-serif">Arcadium</span>,
your affordable family fun center. The park is located 5 miles northwest of
Derby - close to many of Georgia's scenic wonders. Arcadium offers over 50 rides,
including some of the state's most exciting roller coasters and water rides.
There's also plenty of fun for the younger kids, including two separate
kiddie pools and special rides for the kids.</p>
```

3. Save your changes to the file and reopen **about.htm** in your Web browser. Verify that there is now more space separating the photo from the surrounding content.

You can also set margins for elements other than inline images. You can use the margin styles to set margins for your entire Web page. Tom has looked at the splash screen and suggests that the animated logo might look better if it was further down the page. You can accomplish this by increasing the page's top margin.

To set the page margin:

1. Go to the **index.htm** file in your text editor.

2. Within the <body> tag at the top of the file, insert the following style, as shown In Figure 3-43:

   ```
   margin-top: 100
   ```

   Be sure to insert a semicolon, separating this style from the other style declarations.

Setting the top page margin for index.htm | **Figure 3-43**

```
<body style="font-family: Arial, Helvetica, sans-serif; margin-top: 100">
<p style="text-align: center">
    <img src="logoanim.gif" alt="ARCADIUM" />
    <br />
    <span style="color: red; font-size: 18pt; font-weight: bold">
    Affordable Family Fun
    </span>
    <br /><br />
    <a href="about.htm">Enter Arcadium</a>
</p>
</body>
</html>
```

3. Save your changes to the file and reopen **index.htm** in your Web browser. Verify that the contents have been shifted down the page.

For older browsers you can use the deprecated attributes vspace and hspace. The vspace attribute sets the vertical space above and below the inline image. The hspace attribute sets the horizontal space to the left and right of the image. There are no presentational attributes that allow you to specify the size of individual margins.

Setting the Margin Size

Reference Window

- To set the size of the margins around an element, use the styles
    ```
    margin-top: length
    margin-right: length
    margin-bottom: length
    margin-left: length
    ```
  where length is a unit of length, a percentage of the width of the containing element, or the keyword "auto" (the default), which enables the browser to set the margin size.
- To combine all margin styles in a single style, use
    ```
    margin: top right bottom left
    ```
  where top, right, bottom, and left are the margins of the top, right, bottom, and left edges. If you include only three values, the margins are applied to the top, right, and bottom. If you specify only two values, the first value is applied to the top and bottom edges, and the second value to the right and left edges. If you specify only one value, it is applied to all four edges.

Deprecated

- To set the margin around an inline image, add the following attributes to the <img /> tag:
    ```
    vspace="length" hspace="length"
    ```
  where the vspace attribute sets the margin size above and below the image, and the hspace attribute sets the margin size to the left and right of the image. All length values are measured in pixels.

Setting the Image Size

By default, browsers display an image at its saved size. You can specify a different size by adding the following attributes to the <img /> tag:

```
width="value" height="value"
```

where the width and height values represent the dimensions of the image in pixels.

Changing an image's dimensions within the browser does not affect the file size. If you want to decrease the size of an image, you should do so using an image editing application so that the image's file size is reduced in addition to its dimensions. Because of the way that browsers work with inline images, it is a good idea to specify the height and width of an image even if you're not trying to change its dimensions. When a browser encounters an inline image, it calculates the image size and then uses this information to lay out the page. If you include the dimensions of the image, the browser does not have to perform that calculation, reducing the time required to render the page. You can obtain the height and width of an image as measured in pixels using an image editing application such as Adobe Photoshop, or with Windows Explorer.

The logo images logo.gif and logoanim.gif are 517 pixels wide by 119 pixels high, and the photo about.jpg is 210 pixels wide by 280 pixels high. Add this information to each of the <img /> tags in the about.htm and index.htm files.

To set the image dimensions:

1. Return to the **about.htm** file in your text editor.

2. Within the <img /> tag for the logo.gif graphic, insert the attributes **width="517" height="119"**.

3. Within the <img /> tag for the about.jpg graphic, insert the attributes **width="210" height="280"**. You may want to place these attributes on a separate line to make your code more readable. Figure 3-44 shows the revised code.

Figure 3-44 | Setting the image size

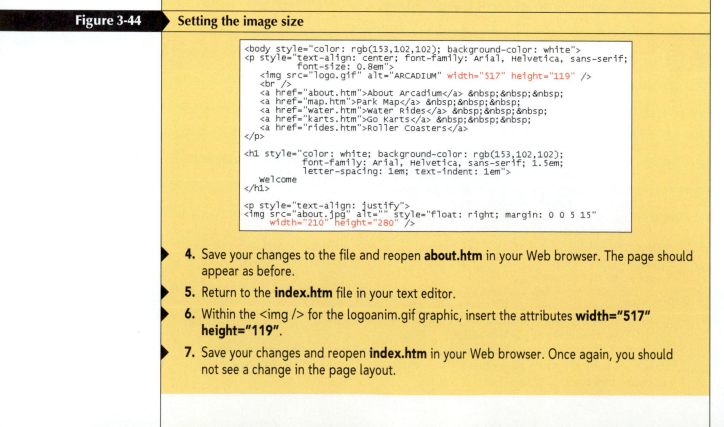

```
<body style="color: rgb(153,102,102); background-color: white">
<p style="text-align: center; font-family: Arial, Helvetica, sans-serif;
        font-size: 0.8em">
  <img src="logo.gif" alt="ARCADIUM" width="517" height="119" />
  <br />
  <a href="about.htm">About Arcadium</a>    
  <a href="map.htm">Park Map</a>    
  <a href="water.htm">Water Rides</a>    
  <a href="karts.htm">Go Karts</a>    
  <a href="rides.htm">Roller Coasters</a>
</p>

<h1 style="color: white; background-color: rgb(153,102,102);
        font-family: Arial, Helvetica, sans-serif; 1.5em;
        letter-spacing: 1em; text-indent: 1em">
  Welcome
</h1>

<p style="text-align: justify">
<img src="about.jpg" alt="" style="float: right; margin: 0 0 5 15"
        width="210" height="280" />
```

4. Save your changes to the file and reopen **about.htm** in your Web browser. The page should appear as before.

5. Return to the **index.htm** file in your text editor.

6. Within the <img /> for the logoanim.gif graphic, insert the attributes **width="517" height="119"**.

7. Save your changes and reopen **index.htm** in your Web browser. Once again, you should not see a change in the page layout.

Reference Window

Setting the Image Size

- To set the size of an inline image, add the following attributes to the <img /> tag:
  height="*length*" width="*length*"
  where *length* is the height and width of the image in pixels.

Inserting a Background Image

Tom has one more suggestion for the splash screen page. The art design department has created the image file displayed in Figure 3-45, which contains images of people enjoying themselves at Arcadium. He wants you to use this image file as a background for the splash screen page.

The background image file ◄ **Figure 3-45**

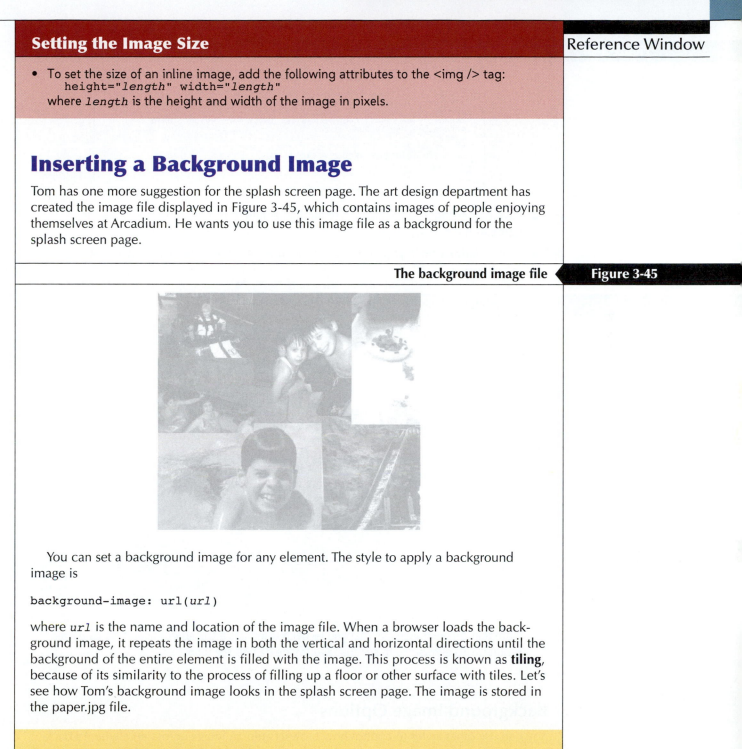

You can set a background image for any element. The style to apply a background image is

```
background-image: url(url)
```

where *url* is the name and location of the image file. When a browser loads the background image, it repeats the image in both the vertical and horizontal directions until the background of the entire element is filled with the image. This process is known as **tiling**, because of its similarity to the process of filling up a floor or other surface with tiles. Let's see how Tom's background image looks in the splash screen page. The image is stored in the paper.jpg file.

To insert a background image:

1. Return to the **index.htm** file in your text editor.

2. Add the following style to the <body> tag. Be sure to use a semicolon to separate this new style from the previous styles. You might want to place this style on a new line to make your code more readable. See Figure 3-46.

   ```
   background-image: url(paper.jpg)
   ```

Figure 3-46 | **Specifying a background image for the splash screen**

```
<body style="font-family: Arial, Helvetica, sans-serif; margin-top: 100;
              background-image: url(paper.jpg)">
<p style="text-align: center">
    <img src="logoanim.gif" alt="ARCADIUM" width="517" height="119" />
    <br />
    <span style="color: red; font-size: 18pt; font-weight: bold">
    Affordable Family Fun
    </span>
    <br /><br />
    <a href="about.htm">Enter Arcadium</a>
</p>
</body>
</html>
```

> **3.** Save your changes to the file. You're finished editing this file, so you may close the **index.htm** file now.

> **4.** Reopen **index.htm** in your Web browser. Figure 3-47 shows the final version of the splash screen.

Figure 3-47 | **The completed splash screen page**

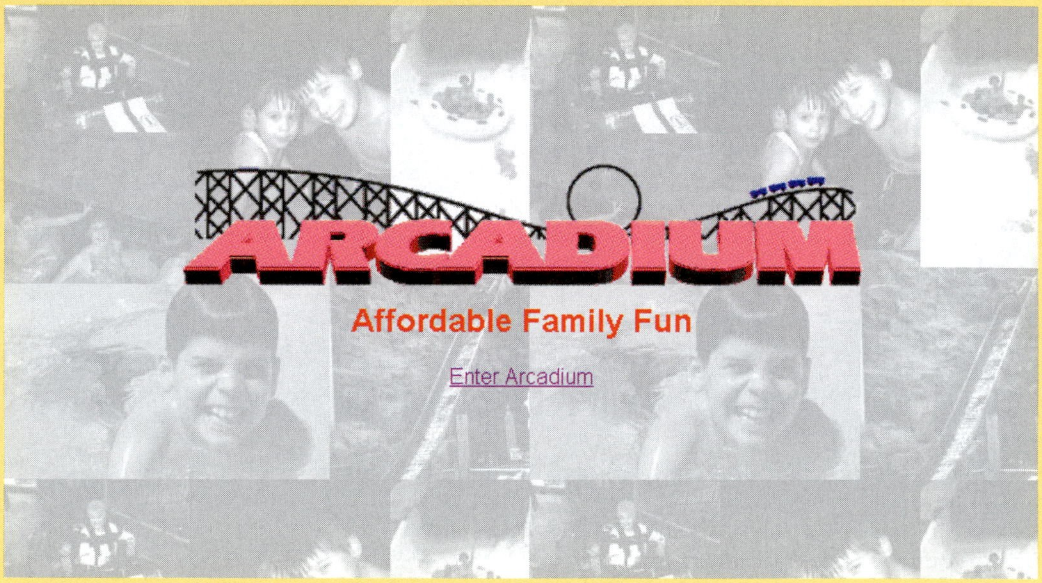

Note that the animated GIF that you've been using has a transparent color for its background. This allows you to see the tiled Image behind the logo.

Background Image Options

You can use other styles to control how browsers tile an image across an element's background. To specify the direction in which the tiling should take place, use the style

```
background-repeat: type
```

where *type* is repeat (the default), repeat-x, repeat-y, or no-repeat. Figure 3-48 describes each of the repeat types, and Figure 3-49 shows examples of the style values.

Values of the background-repeat style Figure 3-48

Background-Repeat	Description
repeat	The image is tiled both horizontally and vertically until the entire background of the element is covered.
repeat-x	The image is tiled only horizontally across the width of the element.
repeat-y	The image is tiled only vertically across the height of the element.
no-repeat	The image is not repeated at all.

Examples of the background-repeat style Figure 3-49

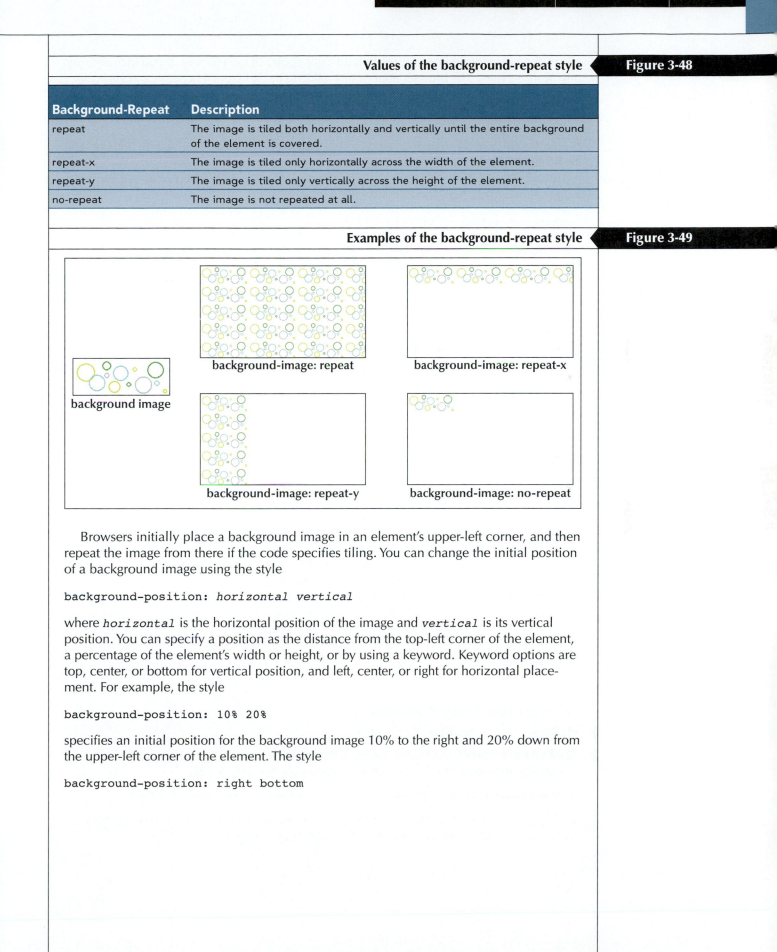

background image

background-image: repeat

background-image: repeat-x

background-image: repeat-y

background-image: no-repeat

Browsers initially place a background image in an element's upper-left corner, and then repeat the image from there if the code specifies tiling. You can change the initial position of a background image using the style

```
background-position: horizontal vertical
```

where `horizontal` is the horizontal position of the image and `vertical` is its vertical position. You can specify a position as the distance from the top-left corner of the element, a percentage of the element's width or height, or by using a keyword. Keyword options are top, center, or bottom for vertical position, and left, center, or right for horizontal placement. For example, the style

```
background-position: 10% 20%
```

specifies an initial position for the background image 10% to the right and 20% down from the upper-left corner of the element. The style

```
background-position: right bottom
```

places the background image at the bottom-right corner of the element. If you include only one position value, the browser applies that value to the horizontal position and vertically centers the image. Thus the style

```
background-position: 30px
```

places the background image 30 pixels to the right of the element's left margin and centers it vertically.

By default, a background image moves along with its element as a user scrolls through a page. You can change this using the style

```
background-attachment: type
```

where *type* is either scroll or fixed. "Scroll" (the default) scrolls the image along with the element. "Fixed" places the image in a fixed place in the browser's display window, preventing it from moving even if the user scrolls down through the Web page. Fixed background images are often used to create the effect of a **watermark**, which is a translucent graphic impressed into the very fabric of paper, often found in specialized stationery.

The Background Style

Like the font style discussed in the last session, you can combine the various background styles into the style

```
background: color image repeat attachment position
```

where *color*, *image*, and so on, are the values for the various background attributes. For example, the style

```
background: yellow url(logo.gif) no-repeat fixed center center
```

creates a yellow background on which the image file logo.gif is displayed . The image file is not tiled across the background, but is instead fixed in the horizontal and vertical center. As with the font style, you do not have to enter all of the values of the background style. However, those values that you do specify should follow the order indicated by the syntax in order to avoid unpredictable results in some browsers.

Standard procedure in the Web design team at Arcadium includes placing a watermark containing the word, "DRAFT" on any Web page that is still in the design stage. Because the About page is still undergoing review, Tom has asked you to change the background image to display the word "DRAFT". He supplies you with the appropriate image file for the watermark.

To insert the background image:

1. Return to the **about.htm** file in your text editor.

2. Replace the background-color style with the following style declaration. Be sure to use a semicolon to separate this style from the color style. See Figure 3-50.

   ```
   background: white url(draft.jpg) no-repeat fixed center center
   ```

Setting the background styles   **Figure 3-50**

```
<body style="color: rgb(153,102,102);
              background: white url(draft.jpg) no-repeat fixed center center">
<p style="text-align: center; font-family: Arial, Helvetica, sans-serif;
          font-size: 0.8em">
    <img src="logo.gif" alt="ARCADIUM" width="517" height="119" />
    <br />
    <a href="about.htm">About Arcadium</a>    
    <a href="map.htm">Park Map</a>    
    <a href="water.htm">Water Rides</a>    
    <a href="karts.htm">Go Karts</a>    
    <a href="rides.htm">Roller Coasters</a>
</p>
```

▶ **3.** Close the file, saving your changes.

▶ **4.** Reopen **about.htm** in your Web browser. Figure 3-51 shows the completed page. Note that as you scroll through the page, the watermark remains in the center of the browser window.

The completed About page   **Figure 3-51**

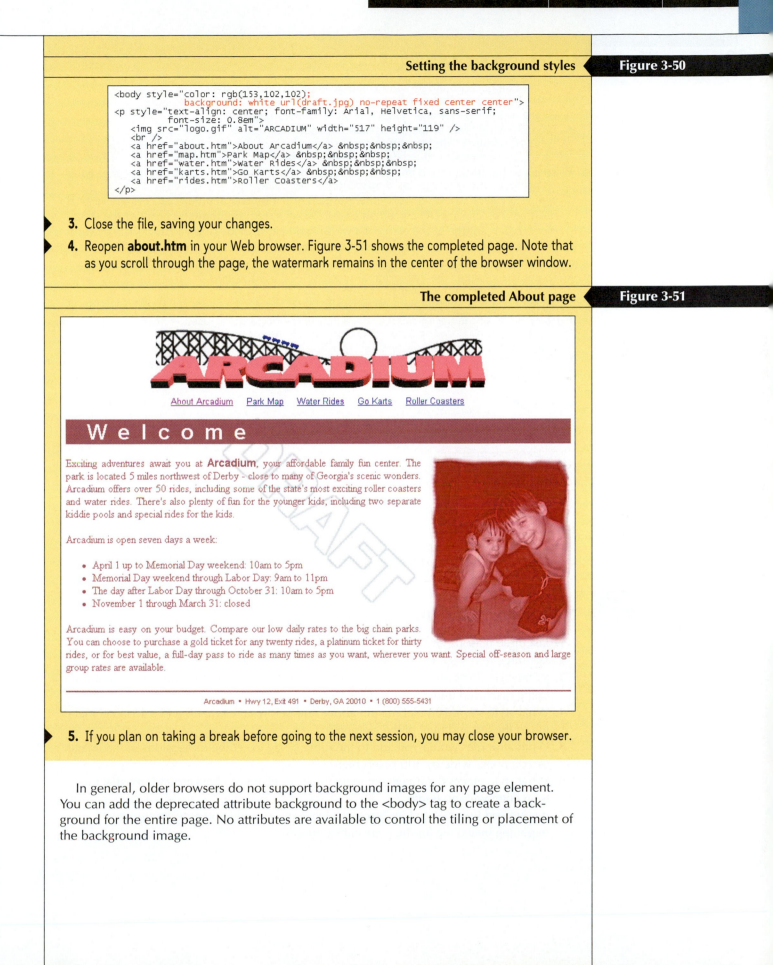

▶ **5.** If you plan on taking a break before going to the next session, you may close your browser.

In general, older browsers do not support background images for any page element. You can add the deprecated attribute background to the <body> tag to create a background for the entire page. No attributes are available to control the tiling or placement of the background image.

Reference Window

Inserting a Background Image

- To insert a background image behind an element, use the style
  ```
  background-image: url(url)
  ```
  where url is the filename and the location of the image file.
- To control the tiling of the background image, use the style
  ```
  background-repeat: type
  ```
  where type is repeat (the default), repeat-x, repeat-y, or no-repeat.
- To place the background image in a specific position behind the element, use the style
  ```
  background-position: horizontal vertical
  ```
  where horizontal is the horizontal position of the image, and vertical is the vertical position. You can specify a position as the distance from the top-left corner of the element, a percentage of the element's width and height, or by using a keyword. Keyword options are top, center, or bottom for vertical position, and left, center, or right for horizontal placement.
- To control whether the background image scrolls, use the style
  ```
  background-attachment: type
  ```
  where type is scroll (the default) or fixed.
- To place all of the background options in a single declaration, use the style
  ```
  background: color image repeat attachment position
  ```
  where color is the background color, image is the image file, repeat is the method of tiling the image, attachment defines whether the image scrolls or is fixed, and position defines the position of the image within the element.

Deprecated

- To specify a background image for the page body, add the following attribute to the <body> tag:
  ```
  background="url"
  ```
  where url is the filename and location of the image file.

You're finished working with the inline images on your Web page. You've learned about the different image formats supported by most browsers, and their advantages and disadvantages. You've also seen how to control the appearance and placement of images on your Web page. In the next session, you'll learn how to create image maps.

Review

Session 3.2 Quick Check

1. List three reasons for using the GIF image format instead of the JPEG format.
2. List three reasons for using the JPEG image format instead of the GIF format.
3. What style floats an element on the left margin? What style prevents an element from being displayed until that margin is clear?
4. What style sets a 10-pixel margin above and below an element, and a 15-pixel margin to the left and right of the element?
5. What attributes would you add to the <img /> tag to set the dimensions of the image to 200 pixels wide by 300 pixels high?
6. What style places the image file mark.jpg in an element's background, fixed at the top center with no tiling?
7. If you need to support older browsers, what code would you enter to use the paper.jpg image file for the page background?

Session 3.3

Understanding Image Maps

Tom has reviewed your Web site and is pleased with the progress you're making. His last task for you involves working with the park map on the Maps page. Tom wants the map to be interactive, so that when a user clicks on an area of the park, the browser opens a Web page describing the features of that area. Recall that the site includes three pages describing the different parts of the park: water.htm for the water rides, rides.htm for the roller coaster rides, and karts.htm for the go-karts. Figure 3-52 shows the relationships between the pages that Tom wants you to create.

Image map pointing to multiple pages ◄ **Figure 3-52**

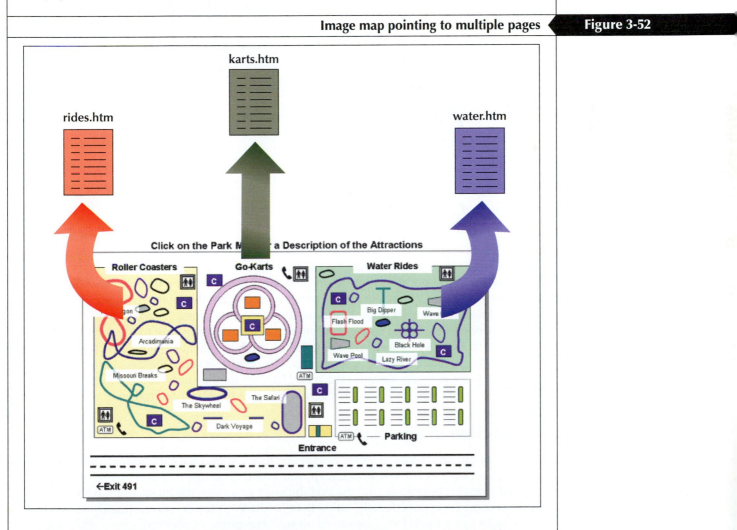

To link a single image to multiple destinations, you must set up hotspots within the image. A **hotspot** is a specific area of an image formatted with its own link. Any time a user clicks a hotspot, the user's browser opens the link target.

You define hotspots for an image by creating an **image map**, which lists the boundaries of all hotspots within a particular image. As a Web designer, you can use two types of image maps: server-side image maps and client-side image maps.

Server-Side Image Maps

In a **server-side image map**, the image map is stored on the Web server (see Figure 3-53). When a user clicks a hotspot, the coordinates where the user clicked are sent to a program running on the server. The program uses the coordinates to determine which hotspot was clicked and then activates the corresponding link.

Figure 3-53   **Server-side image map**

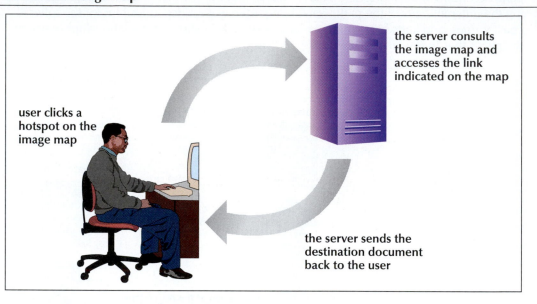

the server consults the image map and accesses the link indicated on the map

user clicks a hotspot on the image map

the server sends the destination document back to the user

The server-side image map was the original standard for image maps, and most graphical browsers still support server-side image maps. However, using them comes with some limitations. Because a program on the server must process the image map, you cannot test your HTML code using local files. Additionally, server-side image maps can be slow to operate, since every time a user clicks the image, the request is sent to the server for processing. With most Web browsers, the target of a link is indicated in the browser's status bar, providing valuable feedback to the user. However, this is not the case with hotspots in a server-side image map. Because the server handles the hotspots rather than the Web browser, users receive no feedback regarding hotspot locations and targets.

Client-Side Image Maps

Because of the limitations of server-side image maps, most maps are now handled by the client. To set up a **client-side image map**, you insert the image map into the same HTML file that contains the image, and the Web browser processes the image map. Because all of the processing is done locally, rather than on the Web server, you can easily test your Web pages using the HTML files stored on your computer. In addition, client-side image maps tend to respond to user interaction more quickly than server-side maps, because map coordinates and link information do not have to be sent over a network or Internet connection. Finally, when a user moves the pointer over a hotspot in a client-side image map, the browser's status bar displays the target URL. For the purposes of this tutorial, you'll concentrate solely on client-side image maps.

You create a client-side image map using the map element. The syntax of the map element is

```
<map name="map" id="map">
   hotspots
</map>
```

where *map* is the name of the map and *hotspots* are the locations of the hotspots within the map. If you need to create XHTML-compliant code, you should include both the name and id attributes within the map element, setting them to the same value; otherwise you can use only the name attribute. You can place a map element anywhere within the body of an HTML file, because the browser uses it for reference and does not actually render it. For the park map, we'll create an image map named "parkmap" directly below the inline image.

To create the map element:

1. Use your text editor to open the **maptxt.htm** file from the tutorial.03/tutorial folder of your Data Files. Enter **your name** and **the date** in the comment section at the top of the file. Save the file as **map.htm**.

2. Locate the <img /> tag for the parkmap.gif file, and directly below it, insert the following code (see Figure 3-54):

```
<map name="parkmap" id="parkmap">
</map>
```

Creating a map element ◀ **Figure 3-54**

```
<h1 style="color:white; font-family: Arial, Helvetica, sans-serif;
          font-size: 1.5em; background-color:black; letter-spacing: 1em;
          text-indent: 1em">
   Maps
</h1>

<p style="text-align: center">
   <img src="parkmap.gif" alt="Park Map" width="610" height="395" />
   <map name="parkmap" id="parkmap">
   </map>
</p>
```

3. Save your changes to the file.

   Next, create the three Web pages that this map will be linked to.

4. Use your text editor to open the **watertxt.htm**, **kartstxt.htm**, and **ridestxt.htm** files from the tutorial.03/tutorial folder. Enter **your name** and **the date** in the comment section of each file. Save the files as **water.htm**, **karts.htm**, and **rides.htm** respectively. You will not be editing these files, so you can close them.

Next, we'll enter the hotspots of the map.

Creating a Client-Side Image Map

Reference Window

- To create an image map, insert the code:
  ```
  <map name="map" id="map">
  hotspots
  </map>
  ```
  where *map* is the name of the image map and *hotspots* are the locations of the hotspots within the map.
- To access an image map, add the following attribute to the <img /> tag
  ```
  usemap="#map"
  ```

Defining Image Map Hotspots

You define a hotspot using two properties: its location in the image and its shape. The syntax of the hotspot element is:

```
<area shape="shape" coords="coordinates" href="url" alt="text" />
```

where *shape* is the shape of the hotspot, *coordinates* are the coordinates of the hotspot on the image, expressed in pixels, *url* is the URL of the link, and the alt attribute provides alternate text for nongraphical browsers. Note that the alt attribute is required for XHTML-compliant code.

If you want to test your coordinates but do not have a destination document ready, you can substitute the attribute "nohref" for the href attribute. The image map will then include the hotspot without a link. You can also include any of the attributes that you use with the <a> tag. Especially useful attributes for a hotspot include the target attribute, which allows you to open the destination document in a secondary browser window, and the title attribute, which creates a pop-up title describing the destination of the hotspot that appears as a user hovers the mouse pointer over the hotspot location.

One method of determining the locations and shapes of the hotspots is to open the image in an image editing application and record the coordinates of the points corresponding to the hotspot boundaries. However, this can be a time-consuming procedure if the image includes several hotspots. To make this process easier, Web designers instead often use image map software that allows you to specify hotspots by drawing over the image. Using your selections, the software generates <area /> tags that you can paste into your Web page. In this case, we'll assume that a colleague in the design department at Arcadium has given us the coordinates.

The shape attribute has three possible values: "rect" for a rectangular hotspot, "circle" for a circular hotspot, and "poly" for a polygon or an irregularly shaped hotspot. The values of the coords attribute depend on which shape you choose. You express the coordinates in terms of the distance of the top-left corner of the image. For example, the coordinate (123, 45) refers to a point that is 123 pixels from the left edge and 45 pixels down from the top.

There is no limit to the number of hotspots you can place on an image. An image's hotspots can also overlap. If this happens and a user clicks within the overlap, the browser opens the link of the first hotspot defined in the map. Thus, order can be important in entering the area elements.

Tom wants the image map to include three hotspots: a polygonal hotspot for the roller coaster rides, a circular hotspot for the go-kart track, and rectangular hotspot for the water park. You'll start with the water park hotspot.

Creating a Rectangular Hotspot

Two points define a rectangular hotspot: the upper-left corner and the lower-right corner. The syntax for entering the coordinate values is

```
shape="rect" coords="x1, y1, x2, y2"
```

where *x1* and *y1* are (x, y) coordinates for the upper-left corner and *x2, y2* are the coordinates of the lower-right corner. These points for the waterpark hotspot are located at (350, 38) and (582, 200). Thus the values for the shape and coords attributes are

```
shape="rect" coords="350, 38, 582, 200"
```

Add this hotspot to the parkmap image map. You'll link the hotspot to the water.htm file. The alternate text for this hotspot will be "Water Park".

To create the rectangular hotspot:

▶ **1.** Return to the **map.htm** file in your text editor and below the opening <map> tag you just added, insert the following area element (you can place this tag on two lines to make your code more readable):

```
<area shape="rect" coords="350,38,582,200" href="water.htm"
     alt="Water Park" />
```

▶ **2.** Save your changes to the file.

Creating a Circular Hotspot

A circular hotspot is defined by the location of its center and the size of the circle's radius. The attributes for creating a circular hotspot are

```
shape="circle" coords="x, y, r"
```

where x, y are the coordinates of the circle's center and r is the size of the radius in pixels. In the park map, the hotspot for the go-kart racetracks has the hotspot attributes

```
shape="circle" coords="255,133,74"
```

You'll link this hotspot to the water.htm file.

To create the circular hotspot:

▶ **1.** Below the area element you just created, insert the following tag:

```
<area shape="circle" coords="255,133,74" href="karts.htm"
     alt="Go-Karts" />
```

▶ **2.** Save your changes.

The final hotspot you need to define is for the roller coaster rides. Because of its irregular shape, you need to create a polygonal hotspot.

Creating a Polygonal Hotspot

The attributes for creating a polygonal hotspot are

```
shape="poly" coords="x1, y1, x2, y2, x3, y3, ..."
```

where $(x1, y1)$, $(x2, y2)$, $(x3, y3)$, and so on are the coordinates of each vertex in the shape. Figure 3-55 shows the coordinates for the vertices of the roller coaster hotspot.

Figure 3-55 Coordinates for the roller coaster hotspot

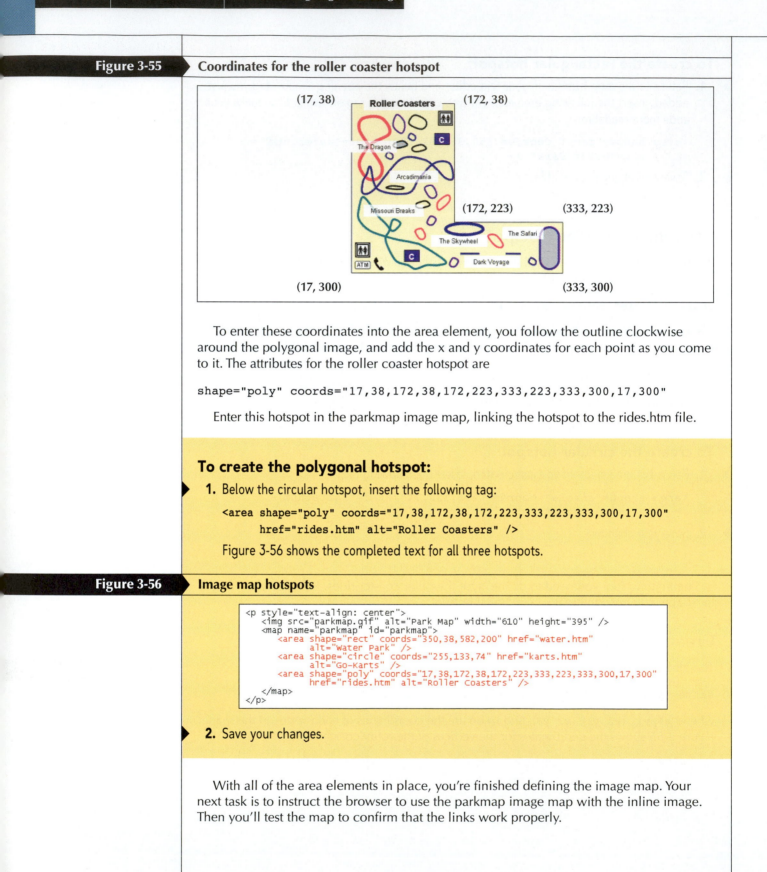

To enter these coordinates into the area element, you follow the outline clockwise around the polygonal image, and add the x and y coordinates for each point as you come to it. The attributes for the roller coaster hotspot are

```
shape="poly" coords="17,38,172,38,172,223,333,223,333,300,17,300"
```

Enter this hotspot in the parkmap image map, linking the hotspot to the rides.htm file.

To create the polygonal hotspot:

1. Below the circular hotspot, insert the following tag:

```
<area shape="poly" coords="17,38,172,38,172,223,333,223,333,300,17,300"
    href="rides.htm" alt="Roller Coasters" />
```

Figure 3-56 shows the completed text for all three hotspots.

Figure 3-56 Image map hotspots

```
<p style="text-align: center">
    <img src="parkmap.gif" alt="Park Map" width="610" height="395" />
    <map name="parkmap" id="parkmap">
        <area shape="rect" coords="350,38,582,200" href="water.htm"
            alt="Water Park" />
        <area shape="circle" coords="255,133,74" href="karts.htm"
            alt="Go-Karts" />
        <area shape="poly" coords="17,38,172,38,172,223,333,223,333,300,17,300"
            href="rides.htm" alt="Roller Coasters" />
    </map>
</p>
```

2. Save your changes.

With all of the area elements in place, you're finished defining the image map. Your next task is to instruct the browser to use the parkmap image map with the inline image. Then you'll test the map to confirm that the links work properly.

Creating Image Map Hotspots
Reference Window

- To create a rectangular hotspot, use the tag
  ```
  <area shape="rect" coords="x1, y1, x2, y2" href="url" alt="text"/>
  ```
  where the coordinates represent the upper-left and lower-right corners of the rectangle and *url* is the destination of the hotspot link.
- To create a circular hotspot, use the tag
  ```
  <area shape="circle" coords="x, y, r" href="url" alt="text"/>
  ```
  where *x* and *y* indicate the coordinates of the center of the circle and *r* specifies the radius of the circle, in pixels.
- To create a polygonal hotspot, use the tag
  ```
  <area shape="poly" coords="x1, y1, x2, y2, x3, y3, ..." href="url" alt="text"/>
  ```
  where the coordinates indicate the vertices of the polygon.

Using an Image Map

To apply an image map to an inline image you insert the following attribute into the `<img />` tag:

```
usemap="#map"
```

where *map* is the name or id of the image map. Note the similarity between the attribute and the href attribute used in the last tutorial to create links to locations within documents. Like those links, you can place your image map in a separate file, in which case the attribute has the form

```
usemap="file#map"
```

where *file* is the name of the HTML file containing the image map coordinates. You might see this format in a group project, for example, in which one employee is responsible for the creation and maintenance of graphics, including image maps, and others access the image maps for their own pages. Be aware, however, that this feature is not well supported in most browsers.

To assign the park map image map to the image:

1. Within the `<img />` tag for the parkmap graphic, insert the following attribute (see Figure 3-57):

   ```
   usemap="#parkmap"
   ```

Applying an image map to an inline image | **Figure 3-57**

```
<p style="text-align: center">
   <img src="parkmap.gif" alt="Park Map" width="610" height="395" usemap="#parkmap" />
   <map name="parkmap" id="parkmap">
      <area shape="rect" coords="350,38,582,200" href="water.htm"
         alt="Water Park" />
      <area shape="circle" coords="255,133,74" href="karts.htm"
         alt="Go-Karts" />
      <area shape="poly" coords="17,38,172,38,172,223,333,223,333,300,17,300"
         href="rides.htm" alt="Roller Coasters" />
   </map>
</p>
```

2. Save your changes to the file and open **map.htm** in your Web browser.
3. Click each hotspot to verify that it opens the correct page in the Arcadium Web site.

You may notice that the image map is surrounded by a colored border. Just as a browser underlines text links, it formats a linked image with a similarly colored border. In some cases, this border is distracting and can ruin the visual appearance of the image. You can remove the border by using the border-width style to set the width of the border to 0 pixels.

To remove the border from the image map:

▶ **1.** Return to **map.htm** in your text editor.

▶ **2.** Add the following style to the parkmap graphic, as shown in Figure 3-58:

   `style="border-width: 0"`

Figure 3-58	Removing the border around a linked image

```
<p style="text-align: center">
   <img src="parkmap.gif" alt="Park Map" width="610" height="395" usemap="#parkmap"
        style="border-width: 0" />
   <map name="parkmap" id="parkmap">
      <area shape="rect" coords="350,38,582,200" href="water.htm"
            alt="Water Park" />
      <area shape="circle" coords="255,133,74" href="karts.htm"
            alt="Go-Karts" />
      <area shape="poly" coords="17,38,172,38,172,223,333,223,333,300,17,300"
            href="rides.htm" alt="Roller Coasters" />
   </map>
</p>
```

▶ **3.** Close the file, saving your changes.

▶ **4.** Reopen **map.htm** in your Web browser and verify that no colored border appears around the image map. Figure 3-59 shows part of the completed page.

Figure 3-59	The completed Map page

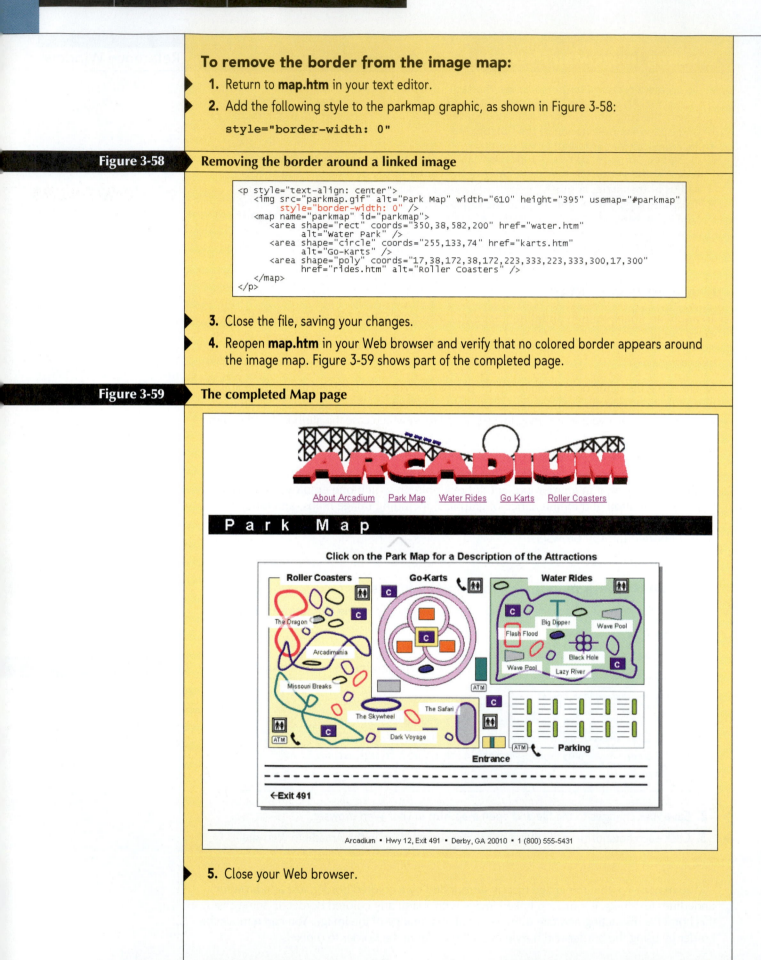

▶ **5.** Close your Web browser.

The border-width style is only one of the many styles that you can use to create and format borders around page elements. We'll explore the various border styles in greater detail in a future tutorial. Note that you can also add the attribute

```
border="0"
```

to the <img /> tag to achieve the same effect. However the border attribute has been deprecated in favor of styles.

Removing the Colored Border from a Linked Image

- To remove a border from linked image, apply the following style to the image:
  ```
  border-width: 0
  ```

Deprecated

- To remove the border, add the following attribute to the <img /> tag:
  ```
  border="0"
  ```

As you can see, an image map can be a useful addition to a Web page. However, you should always provide textual links in addition to an image map, so that users without graphical browsers can still navigate your site. You've done this in the Map page by providing the list of links at the top of the page.

Tips for Web Page Design

- View your color and images under different color resolutions. Use Web-safe colors to prevent dithering on browsers with 256-color palettes.
- Use foreground colors that contrast well with the background.
- When specifying a font face, list the specific and most desirable faces first, and conclude with the generic font.
- Keep your font choices simple. Too many font styles within a single page can distract users. In general, you should not use more than two font faces. Large blocks of bold or italicized text can be difficult to read. Keep your fonts to about 3 or 4 basic sizes.
- Use relative units (such as the em unit) when you want your fonts to be scalable under different monitor sizes and resolutions.
- Make your code easier to read and more compact by combining the various font styles into a single style.
- Use GIFs for illustrations and line art that involve a few basic colors. Use JPEGs for photographs and illustrations that involve more than 256 colors.
- Do not overload a Web page with images. The more images you include, the longer a page takes to load. Generally a Web page should contain no more than 40 to 50 kilobytes of inline images.
- Once a browser downloads an image, it keeps a copy of it on the user's computer; therefore, you can make a Web site load faster by reusing images whenever possible throughout the site. Use a single background image or logo on every page in order to give your Web site a consistent look and feel.
- Include the width and height attributes for each of your inline images to make the page load more quickly.

- Use miniature versions of images (known as thumbnails) to let users preview large image files. Link each thumbnail to the corresponding larger image so that interested users can view the image in greater detail. You should create thumbnails in a separate graphics program, rather than simply reducing the full-size image using the width and height attributes. Changing the width and height attributes decreases an image's dimensions, but not the file size.
- View your Web page in a browser without graphical capability (or with the graphic support turned off) to verify that users with non-graphical browsers can still effectively use your site.
- Avoid large areas of white space surrounded by page content. Use the float and margin styles to move white space to the outside margins of the page.
- If you use an image map, provide text link alternatives for users with non-graphical browsers.

Review

Session 3.3 Quick Check

1. What is a hotspot? What is an image map?
2. What are the two types of image maps?
3. What HTML tag would you use to define a rectangular hotspot with the upper-left edge of the rectangle at the point (5,20) and the lower-right edge located at (85,100) and with oregon.htm displayed when the hotspot is activated?
4. What HTML tag would you use for a circular hotspot centered at (44,81) with a radius of 23 pixels to be linked to la.htm?
5. What HTML tag would you use for a hotspot that connects the points (5,10), (5,35), (25,35), (30,20), and (15,10) and that you want linked to hawaii.htm?
6. What HTML tag would you use to assign an image map named States to westcoast.gif?

Review

Tutorial Summary

In this tutorial, you learned about the styles and HTML attributes available to modify the appearance of a Web site. You first learned how HTML handles color, and how to use color to format the foreground and background of your page elements. You then learned about the different styles for formatting the appearance of Web page text. You used these styles to specify different fonts, font sizes, weights, and spacing. In the second session, you learned about the different types of image formats supported by HTML and how to apply them. You saw how to wrap content around an element like an inline image, and you learned how to set margins around your elements. The session also showed how to create and format background images. The last session discussed the different types of image maps available to a Web designer, and showed how to create and use hotspots within an image map. The session concluded with a brief discussion of borders and how to remove them from linked images.

Key Terms

absolute unit	dithering	Flash
animated GIF	dpi	generic font
client-side image map	em unit	GIF
color value	ex unit	GIF89a

Graphics Interchange
   Format
hanging indent
hexadecimal
hotspot
image map
interlaced GIF
interlacing
Joint Photographic
   Experts Group
JPEG
kerning

leading
Macromedia
noninterlaced GIF
palette
pixel
PNG
Portable Network Graphics
progressive JPEG
relative unit
RGB triplet
safety palette
scalable

Scalable Vector Graphics
server-side image map
spacer
specific font
splash screen
SVG
tiling
tracking
transparent color
watermark
Web-safe colors

Practice

Practice the skills you learned in the tutorial using the same case scenario.

Review Assignments

Data files needed for this Review Assignment: about.jpg, abouttxt.htm, indextxt.htm, karts.jpg, kartstxt.htm, logo.gif, logoanim.gif, maptxt.htm, paper.jpg, parkmap.gif, review.jpg, rides.jpg, ridestxt.htm, toddler.jpg, toddtxt.htm, water.jpg, watertxt.htm

Tom has asked you to make some more changes and additions to the Arcadium Web site. The park has a new area called the Toddler Park, which is specifically designed for very young children. Tom needs you to revise the park map hotspots to accommodate the new park map, and he needs you to design a Web page for the toddler park. Figure 3-60 shows a preview of the toddler page you'll create.

Figure 3-60

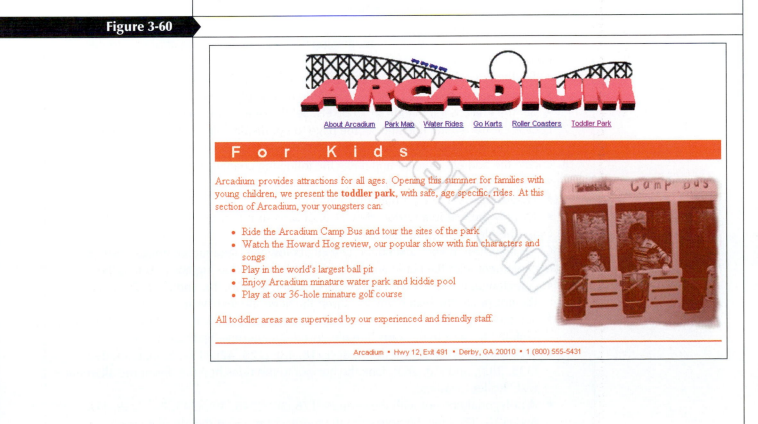

To complete this task:

1. Use your text editor to open the files **indextxt.htm**, **abouttxt.htm**, **maptxt.htm**, **kartstxt.htm**, **ridestxt.htm**, **toddtxt.htm**, and **watertxt.htm** from the tutorial.03/review folder of your Data Files. Enter *your name* and *the date* in the comment section of each file. Save the files as **index.htm**, **about.htm**, **map.htm**, **karts.htm**, **rides.htm**, **toddler.htm**, and **water.htm**, respectively.

2. Go to the **index.htm** file in your text editor. In the body section, enclose the text "Affordable Family Fun" in a span element and display the text in a blue 22pt bold font. Enclose the text, "Enter Arcadium" in another span element. Display this text in a 14pt italicized font. Close the file, saving your changes.

3. Go to the **toddler.htm** file in your text editor and make the following changes to the page:
   - Set the text color to the rgb color value (204, 102, 0).
   - Set the background color to white.
   - Display the review.jpg file as the background image, placed in the horizontal and vertical center of the page, without scrolling, and without tiling.

4. Locate the paragraph containing the list of links and set the font size of the paragraph to 0.7em and display the text in an Arial, Helvetica, or sans-serif font.

5. Locate the h1 heading containing the text, "For Kids" and make the following changes to the heading:
   - Set the text color to white.
   - Set the background color to the color value (204, 102, 0).
   - Display the text in an Arial, Helvetica, or sans-serif font.
   - Set the font size to 1.5 em.
   - Set the kerning value to 1.5em.
   - Set the indentation to 1em.

6. Locate the inline image for the toddler.jpg file. Add the following attributes to the inline image:
   - Set the image's width and height to 250 pixels by 239 pixels.
   - Float the image on the right margin of the paragraph.
   - Set the image's left margin to 15 pixels. Set the other three margin sizes to 0 pixels.

7. Locate the horizontal line and set the page to not display this line until the right margin is clear.

8. Locate the address element and make the following changes to it:
   - Display the address in a 8pt font.
   - Display the text in a normal (non-italic) font.
   - Display the text in an Arial, Helvetica, or sans-serif font.

9. Close the file, saving your changes.

10. Go to **map.htm** in your text editor. Directly below the parkmap.gif image, insert a map element with the name and id "park". Insert the following hotspots into the map:
    - A rectangular hotspot with the corners located at (350, 48) and (582, 293). Link the hotspot to the water.htm file. Insert the alternate text "Water Park".
    - A circular hotspot centered at the coordinate (256, 216) with a radius of 81 pixels. Link the hotspot to the karts.htm file. Insert the alternate text "Go-Karts".
    - A polygonal hotspot with the vertices (18, 48), (170, 48), (170, 293), (333, 293), (333, 383), and (18, 383). Link the hotspot to the rides.htm file. Insert the alternate text "Roller Coasters".
    - A polygonal hotspot with the vertices (176, 30), (345, 30), (345, 71), (259, 116), and (176, 72). Link the hotspot to the toddler.htm. Insert the alternate text "Toddler Park".

11. Apply the park image map to the parkmap.gif inline image.
12. Set the width of the border around the parkmap.gif inline image to 0 pixels.
14. Close the file, saving your changes.
15. Open the **index.htm** file in your Web browser. View the contents of the Arcadium Web site, verifying that all of the links work correctly and that the image map in the Map page is correctly linked to the attractions at the park. Verify that the layout of the Toddler page matches Figure 3-60 (there may be slight differences depending on your browser).
16. Submit the completed Web site to your instructor.

Case Problem 1

Data files needed for this Case Problem: back.gif, dc100.jpg, dc100txt.htm, dc250.jpg, dc250txt.htm, dc500.jpg, dc500txt.htm, indextxt.htm, logo.jpg, logoanim.gif, menu.gif, pixaltxt.htm

Pixal Digital Products, Inc. PDP, Inc. is a new local manufacturer and distributor of digital cameras. The Web site manager, Maria Sanchez, has hired you to work on the company's Web site. Someone has already created the basic text for the Web site, which encompasses five pages: a splash screen introduction, a home page, and three pages describing the features of individual cameras. Your task is to develop a design for those pages. Figure 3-61 shows a preview of one of the pages you'll create. The box of links along the left margin of the page is an inline image. To link the text entries in that box to their targets, you will have to create an image map.

Figure 3-61

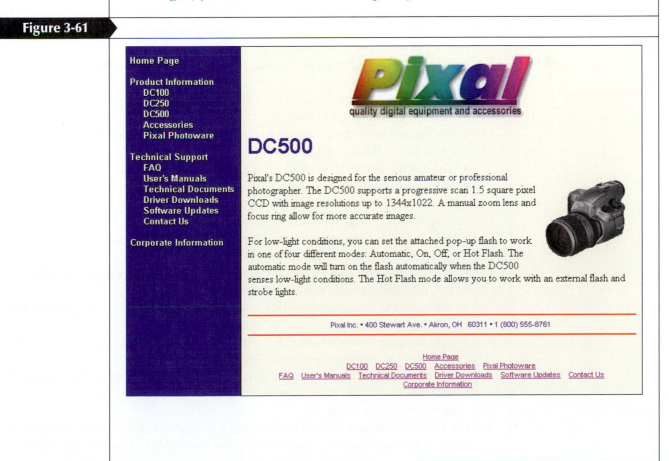

To complete this task:

1. Use your text editor to open the **indextxt.htm**, **pixaltxt.htm**, **dc100txt.htm**, **dc250txt.htm**, and **dc500txt.htm** files from the tutorial.03/case1 folder of your Data Files. Within each file, enter *your name* and *the date* in the comment section. Save the files as **index.htm**, **pixal.htm**, **dc100.htm**, **dc250.htm**, and **dc500.htm**, respectively.

2. Go to the **index.htm** file. Change the background color of the page to ivory and set the size of the top margin to 100 pixels. Locate the logoanim.gif inline image and set the dimensions of this image to 281 pixels wide by 140 pixels high. Set the border width of this inline image to 0 pixels. Save your changes to the file.

3. Go to the **pixal.htm** file. Make the following style changes to the page:
   - Set the background color to ivory and display the background image file back.gif. The image file should be tiled only in the y-direction and should scroll with the Web page.
   - Set the size of the left margin to 185 pixels.

4. Directly after the <body> tag, insert a paragraph containing the inline image menu.gif. This is the image that contains the list of links that will be displayed along the left margin of the page. Apply the following styles to this image:
   - Float the image on the left margin.
   - Set the border width to 0 pixels.
   - Set the size of the left margin to -185 pixels; this will have the effect of shifting the image to the left margin.
   - Set the dimensions of the image to 173 pixels wide by 295 pixels high.
   - Set the value of the alt attribute to an empty string, "".

5. Set the dimensions of the logo.jpg inline image to 281 pixels wide by 96 pixels high.

6. Change the color of the two horizontal lines in this page to red.

7. Apply the following style changes to the address element:
   - Display the address text in an Arial, Helvetica, or sans-serif font.
   - Set the font color to blue.
   - Set the font size to 0.7em.
   - Change the font style to normal.

8. Apply the following style changes to the paragraph containing the list of links (located below the address element):
   - Display the address text in an Arial, Helvetica, or sans-serif font.
   - Set the font size to 0.7em.

9. At the bottom of the file, above the closing </body> tag, insert an image map named "dcpages" containing the following hotspots:
   - A rectangular hotspot pointing to the pixal.htm file with coordinates (1, 1) and (81, 15). The alternate text is "Home".
   - A rectangular hotspot for the dc100.htm file with the coordinates (23, 50) and (64, 62). The alternate text is "DC100".
   - A rectangular hotspot for the dc250.htm file with the coordinates (23, 64) and (64, 79). The alternate text is "DC250".
   - A rectangular hotspot for the dc500.htm file with the coordinates (23, 81) and (64, 95). The alternate text is "DC500".

10. Apply the dcpages image map to the menu.gif inline image, located at the top of the page.

11. Save your changes to the file.

12. Go to the **dc100.htm** file and repeat Steps 3 through 11 above (you can use your text editor's copy and paste feature to transfer the code). Also, display the h1 heading,

"DC100" in a blue Arial, Helvetica, or sans-serif font. Align the inline image dc100.jpg with the page's right margin. Save your changes to the file.

13. Go to the **dc250.htm** file and apply the same style changes that you applied to the dc100.htm file. Save your changes.

14. Go to the **dc500.htm** file and match the style changes you made to the dc100.htm and dc250.htm files. Save your changes.

15. Open the **index.htm** file in your Web browser and then navigate through the Web site. Verify that the image maps work correctly in the three camera pages and in pixal.htm. Also verify that the design used in the three camera pages and in pixal.htm match.

16. Submit the completed Web site to your instructor.

Explore

Broaden your knowledge of the float style and inline images to create a page containing an irregular text wrap.

Case Problem 2

Data files needed for this Case Problem: back.jpg, king1.gif - king6.gif, kingtxt.htm

Midwest University Center for Diversity Stewart Findlay is the project coordinator for the Midwest University Center for Diversity. He is currently working on a Web site titled "The Voices of Civil Rights," containing Web pages with extended quotes from civil rights leaders of the past and present. He has asked you to help develop a design for the pages in the series. He has given you the text for one of the pages, which is about Martin Luther King, Jr.

Stewart has supplied a photo of Dr. King that he would like you to include in the page. He has seen how text can be made to wrap irregularly around a photo in graphic design software, and wonders if you can do the same thing in a Web page. While you cannot use this same technique with page elements, which are always a rectangular shape, you can break a single image into a series of rectangles of different sizes. When the text wraps around these stacked rectangles, they provide the appearance of a single image with an irregular line wrap. Stewart asks you to try this with his Dr. King photo. Figure 3-62 shows a preview of the page you'll create. Note how the right margin of the text seems to wrap around Dr. King's image along a diagonal line, rather than a vertical one.

Figure 3-62

Martin Luther King, Jr.

I have a dream that one day this nation will rise up and live out the true meaning of its creed: "We hold these truths to be self-evident: that all men are created equal." I have a dream that one day on the red hills of Georgia the sons of former slaves and the sons of former slaveowners will be able to sit down together at a table of brotherhood. I have a dream that one day even the state of Mississippi, a desert state, sweltering with the heat of injustice and oppression, will be transformed into an oasis of freedom and justice. I have a dream that my four children will one day live in a nation where they will not be judged by the color of their skin but by the content of their character. I have a dream today.

I have a dream that one day the state of Alabama, whose governor's lips are presently dripping with the words of interposition and nullification, will be transformed into a situation where little black boys and black girls will be able to join hands with little white boys and white girls and walk together as sisters and brothers. I have a dream today. I have a dream that one day every valley shall be exalted, every hill and mountain shall be made low, the rough places will be made plain, and the crooked places will be made straight, and the glory of the Lord shall be revealed, and all flesh shall see it together. This is our hope. This is the faith with which I return to the South. With this faith we will be able to hew out of the mountain of despair a stone of hope. With this faith we will be able to transform the jangling discords of our nation into a beautiful symphony of brotherhood. With this faith we will be able to work together, to pray together, to struggle together, to go to jail together, to stand up for freedom together, knowing that we will be free one day.

This will be the day when all of God's children will be able to sing with a new meaning, "My country, 'tis of thee, sweet land of liberty, of thee I sing. Land where my fathers died, land of the pilgrim's pride, from every mountainside, let freedom ring." And if America is to be a great nation, this must become true. So let freedom ring from the prodigious hilltops of New Hampshire. Let freedom ring from the mighty mountains of New York. Let freedom ring from the heightening Alleghenies of Pennsylvania! Let freedom ring from the snowcapped Rockies of Colorado! Let freedom ring from the curvaceous peaks of California! But not only that; let freedom ring from Stone Mountain of Georgia! Let freedom ring from Lookout Mountain of Tennessee! Let freedom ring from every hill and every molehill of Mississippi. From every mountainside, let freedom ring.

When we let freedom ring, when we let it ring from every village and every hamlet, from every state and every city, we will be able to speed up that day when all of God's children, black men and white men, Jews and Gentiles, Protestants and Catholics, will be able to join hands and sing in the words of the old Negro spiritual, Free at last! Free at last! Thank God Almighty, we are free at last!

The Voices of Civil Rights Series

CREATED BY THE MIDWEST UNIVERSITY CENTER FOR DIVERSITY

To complete this task:

1. Use your text editor to open the **kingtxt.htm** file from the tutorial.03/case2 folder of your Data Files. Enter *your name* and *the date* in the comment section of the file. Save the file as **king.htm**.
2. Make the following style changes to the entire page:
   - Set the foreground color to black.
   - Use a single style to set the background color to the value (204, 204, 153) and fix the background image, back.jpg, in the lower-left corner of the page. Make the image scrollable.
   - Set the default font size of the text on the page to 0.9em.
   - Set the left margin of the page to 60 pixels.
3. Go to the h1 heading and add the following styles:
   - Set the foreground color to the color value (204, 204, 153) and the background color to the value (102, 102, 204).
   - Display the text in an Arial, Helvetica, or sans-serif font.
   - Center the text of the heading.

Explore

4. Stewart wants to have a drop letter starting the quote from Dr. King. To create the drop letter:
   - Enclose the first word in Dr. King's speech, "I", in a span element.
   - Float the span element on the left margin of the paragraph.
   - Display the text in a bold font that is 3em in size. Set the font color to the value (102, 102, 204).
   - Set the line height of the span element to 1em.
   - Set the right margin of the element to 5 pixels. Set the size of the three other margins to 0 pixels.

Explore

5. To create an irregular line wrap around the image, you have to break the image into several files and then stack them on the left or right margin, displaying an image only when the margin is clear of the previous image. To remove the seams between the images, you have to set the top and bottom margins to 0. The Martin Luther King, Jr. graphic has been broken into six files for you. To stack them:
   - At the very end of the first paragraph (directly before the closing </p> tag), insert the king1.gif image, aligned with the right margin of the page. Set the left margin to 5 pixels and the other three margins to 0 pixels. For nongraphical browsers display an empty text string ("").
   - Below the king1.gif image, insert the king2.gif image, aligned with the right margin. Format this element to display only when the right margin is clear. As before, set the left margin to 5 pixels and set the other three margin sizes to 0 pixels. Set the alternate text string to the empty string, "".
   - Below the king2.gif, insert the king3.gif through king6.gif images, formatted in the same way you formatted the king2.gif image. Be sure to display each of these images only when the right margin is clear or they will not stack properly.
6. Enclose the phrase, "Free at last! Free at last! Thank God Almighty, we are free at last!" in a span element and make the following style changes:
   - Change the text color to the value (102, 102, 204).
   - Change the text to boldface.
   - Set the font size to 1.2em.
7. Change the color of the horizontal line at the bottom of the page to the value (102, 102, 204). Display the line only when the right margin is clear.
8. Make the following style changes to the address text at the bottom of the page:
   - Display the text in a normal font (not italic).
   - Set the font size to 0.7em and the font color to (102, 102, 204).
   - Display the text in an Arial, Helvetica, or sans-serif font.
   - Transform the text to uppercase letters using a style.
9. Save your changes to the file.
10. Open the **king.htm** file in your Web browser and verify that the layout matches that shown in Figure 3-62 (there may be small style differences depending on your browser).
11. Submit the completed Web page to your instructor.

Explore

Broaden your knowledge of Web page design by creating a Web page for the International Cryptographic Institute.

Case Problem 3

Data files needed for this Case Problem: back1.gif, back2.gif, crypttxt.htm, locks.jpg, logo.gif, scytale.gif

International Cryptographic Institute Sela Dawes is the media representative for the ICI, the International Cryptographic Institute. The ICI is an organization of cryptographers who study the science and mathematics of secret codes, encrypted messages, and code breaking. Part of the ICI's mission is to inform the public about cryptography and data security. Sela has asked you to work on a Web site containing information about cryptography for use by high school science and math teachers. She wants the design to be visually interesting in order to help draw students into the material. Figure 3-63 shows a preview of your design.

Figure 3-63

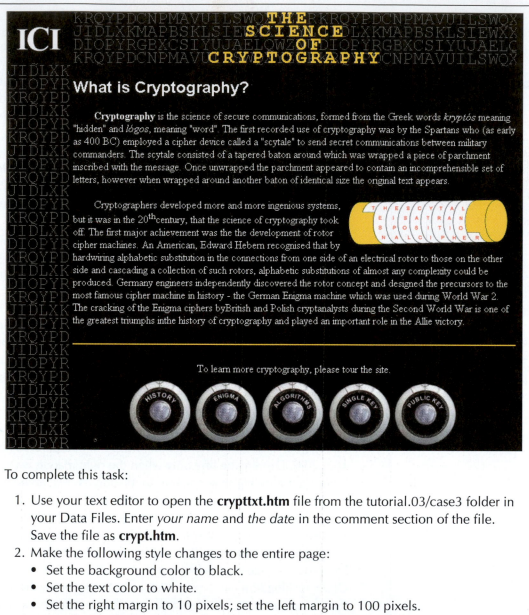

To complete this task:

1. Use your text editor to open the **crypttxt.htm** file from the tutorial.03/case3 folder in your Data Files. Enter *your name* and *the date* in the comment section of the file. Save the file as **crypt.htm**.
2. Make the following style changes to the entire page:
   - Set the background color to black.
   - Set the text color to white.
   - Set the right margin to 10 pixels; set the left margin to 100 pixels.
   - Display the back1.gif image in the page background. Tile this image in the y-direction.
3. Locate the logo.gif element and set the following styles and attributes:
   - Set the width and height of the image to 95 pixels wide by 78 pixels high.
   - Float the image on the left page margin.
   - Set the left margin of the image to -100 pixels (moving the image to the left).
4. Go to the h1 heading and make the following style changes:
   - Change the text to a Courier New or a monospace font.
   - Change the font size to 1.8em, the kerning to 0.3em, and the leading to 0.7em.
   - Display the text in a bold yellow font.
   - Add the back2.gif image to the background of the heading.

Explore

Explore

Explore

5. Display the h2 heading in an Arial, Helvetica, or sans-serif font.
6. Indent the first and second paragraphs to 2em.
7. Go to the scytale.gif element and make the following style and attribute changes:
   - Set the width and height of the image to 250 pixels by 69 pixels.
   - Float the image on the right margin of the page.
8. Change the color of the horizontal line after the second paragraph to yellow.
9. Go to the locks.jpg element and set the width and height of the image to 510 by 110 pixels.
10. Directly below the inline image locks.jpg, insert an image map with the name and id "locks". Insert the following hotspots (note that the targets of these links are not available):
    - A circular hotspot linked to history.htm centered at the coordinate (52, 52) with a radius of 43 pixels. The alternate text is "History".
    - A circular hotspot with a radius of 43 pixels located at the coordinate (155, 52). Link the hotspot to enigma.htm. The alternate text is "Enigma".
    - A circular hotspot with a radius of 43 pixels located at the coordinate (255, 52). Link the hotspot to algo.htm. The alternate text is "Algorithms".
    - A circular hotspot with a radius of 43 pixels located at the coordinate (355, 52). Link the hotspot to single.htm. The alternate text is "Single Key".
    - A circular hotspot with a radius of 43 pixels located at the coordinate (455, 52). Link the hotspot to public.htm. The alternate text is "Public Key".
11. Apply the locks image map to the locks.jpg inline image. Set the border width for this image to 0 pixels.
12. Save your changes to the file.
13. Open **crypt.htm** in your Web browser and verify that the design matches the page shown in Figure 3-63.
14. Submit your completed Web site to your instructor.

Create

Test your knowledge of HTML by creating a Web site for Midwest Homes.

Case Problem 4

Data files needed for this Case Problem: back.gif, logo.gif, logo.jpg, midwest,txt, r317081.jpg, r317082.jpg, r317083.jpg, r317084.jpg, thumb1.jpg, thumb2.jpg

Midwest Homes You've been hired by Midwest Homes to assist in developing their Web site. Dawn Upham, the site manager, has asked you to begin work on the new listings section. She's given you a text file containing information about Midwest Homes and the four new listings for the day. She's also provided you with two versions of the company logo (one in JPEG format, and one in GIF format with a transparent background), a background image, image files for the four new properties, and two image files containing thumbnail images of the four new properties—one oriented horizontally, and the other vertically. You are free to supplement this material with any additional resources available to you. Your job is to use this information to design a visually interesting Web site for the new listings.

To complete this task:

1. Locate the text files and image files in the tutorial.03/case4 folder of your Data Files. Review the content of the text files and view the image files. Note that there are four new properties with listing numbers: r317081, r317082, r317083, and r317084. The image files match up with the property descriptions in the midwest.txt file.

2. Once you become familiar with the contents of this proposed site, start designing the site. There should be five pages: a page introducing the new listings, and one page with details on each of the new homes. The name of the intro page should be new.htm, the names of the four listings pages should be r317081.htm, r317082.htm, r317083.htm, and r317084.htm. In your preparations for the site, create a storyboard of the site's contents and links. Make sure that you make your site easy to navigate.

3. Within each page, insert comments that include your name, the date, and a description of the page's content.

4. The design and layout of the site is up to you, but your pages should include at least one example of the following design elements:
   - A style that sets the foreground and background color for a page and an element within the page.
   - A style that sets a background image for either the entire page or an element within the page.
   - A style that changes the font family for at least one element.
   - A style that sets the font size for at least one element.
   - A style that sets the font weight and font style for at least one element.
   - An inline image that floats along the right or left border of its containing element.
   - A style that sets the margin size for an element or for the entire page.

5. Use one of the supplied thumbnail images to create an image map linking the introduction page to each of the pages describing the new listings. Use a graphics program to determine the coordinates of the hotspots in the image map.

6. Submit the completed Web site to your instructor.

Review

Quick Check Answers

Session 3.1

1. color: yellow; background-color: rgb(51,102,51)
2. Web-safe colors are colors that will not be dithered by a Web browser limited to a 256-color palette. You would use them when you want to ensure that your colors appear correctly without browser modification on monitors that display only 256 colors.
3. font-family: Courier New, monospace
4. font-size: 16pt
5. The em unit is a relative unit of length equal to the width of the capital letter "M" in the browser's default font. Because the size is expressed relative to the default font size, text that is sized with the em unit is scalable and will appear correct relative to other text, no matter what font size has been set on the user's browser.
6. Kerning refers to the amount of space between letters. To set the kerning to 2em, use the style letter-spacing: 2em.
7. line-height: 2
8. font-weight: bold; font-style: italic
9. The span element is a generic inline element used to contain or mark an inline content.

Session 3.2

1. Use GIF when you want to use a transparent color, when you want to create an animated image, and when your image is an illustration of 256 colors or less.
2. Use JPEG for photographic images, for images that contain more than 256 colors, or when you need to reduce the file size through compression.

3. float: left
   clear: left
4. margin: 10px 15px
5. width="200" height="300"
6. background: url(mark.jpg) no-repeat fixed center top
7. <body background="paper.jpg">

Session 3.3

1. A hotspot is a defined area of an image that acts as a link. An image map lists the coordinates of the hotspots within the image.
2. Server-side and client-side
3. <area shape="rect" coords="5,20,85,100" href="oregon.htm" />
4. <area shape="circle" coords="44,81,23" href="la.htm" />
5. <area shape="poly" coords="5,10,5,35,25,35,30,20,15,10" href="hawaii.htm" />
6. <img src="westcoast.gif" usemap="#States" />

Objectives

Session 4.1
- Work with preformatted text to create a basic text table
- Create the basic structure of a graphical table
- Organize table rows into row groups
- Add a caption to a table
- Describe how to add summary information to a table

Session 4.2
- Create table borders and gridlines
- Specify the width and height for different table elements
- Format the contents of table cells
- Apply a background image and color to a table
- Align a table and cell contents

Session 4.3
- Describe the different types of page layouts that you can achieve with tables
- Work with both fixed-width and fluid layouts
- Create a newspaper-style layout using tables

Designing a Web Page with Tables

Creating a News Page

Case

The *Park City Gazette*

Park City, Colorado, is a rural mountain community located near a popular national park. Visitors from around the world come to Park City to enjoy its natural beauty, hike and climb in the national park, and ski at the many area resorts. During the busy tourist season, the population of Park City can triple in size.

Kevin Webber is the editor of the weekly *Park City Gazette*. Kevin knows that the newspaper is a valuable source of information for tourists as well as year-round residents, and he would like to publish a Web edition.

He has approached you about designing a Web site for the paper. He would like the Web site to have the same look and feel as the printed *Gazette*, which has been published for over 100 years and maintains its classic, traditional design. The paper has a large and loyal readership.

In order to implement the design that Kevin is looking for, you'll need to learn how to use HTML to create and format tables.

Student Data Files

▼ **Tutorial.04**

▽ **Tutorial folder**
artcltxt.htm
page1txt.htm
racetxt1.htm
racetxt2.htm
+ 4 HTML files
+ 5 graphic files

▽ **Review folder**
art2txt.htm
page2txt.htm
sighttxt.htm
+ 1 HTML file
+ 5 graphic files

▽ **Case1 folder**
dhometxt.htm
introtxt.htm
+ 4 HTML files
+ 7 graphic files

▽ **Case2 folder**
dunsttxt.htm
welctxt.htm
+ 4 HTML files
+ 3 graphic files

▽ **Case3 folder**
febtxt.htm
+ 2 graphic files

▽ **Case4 folder**
luxair.txt
photo.txt
toronto.txt
twlinks.htm
twlinks2.htm
yosemite.txt
+ 4 graphic files

Session 4.1

Tables on the World Wide Web

The annual Front Range Marathon in Boulder has just been run, and a local woman, Laura Blake, won the women's open division. As your first assignment, Kevin wants you to place the marathon story on the Web. With the story, he would also like to see a table that lists the top three male and female finishers. Kevin presents you with a table of the race results, which is shown in Figure 4-1.

Figure 4-1 ▶ **Marathon results**

Group	Runner	Time	Origin
Men	1. Peter Teagan	2:12:34	San Antonio, Texas
Men	2. Kyle Wills	2:13:05	Billings, Montana
Men	3. Jason Wu	2:14:28	Cutler, Colorado
Women	1. Laura Blake	2:28:21	Park City, Colorado
Women	2. Kathy Lasker	2:30:11	Chicago, Illinois
Women	3. Lisa Peterson	2:31:14	Seattle, Washington

A table can be coded in HTML in either a text or a graphical format. A **text table**, like the one shown in Figure 4-2, contains only text, which is evenly spaced on the Web page to create rows and columns. Because text tables use only standard word processing characters, cell borders and lines must be created using characters such as hyphens or equal signs.

Figure 4-2 ▶ **A text table**

```
                        Computer Models

         Manufacturer          Model          Price
all table ================================================
elements  City Computers       P325+          $2500
are created MidWest CPU        586/Ultra       $2700
using a   CowCity Computers    P133/+         $2450
monospace CMF Computers        P150z          $2610
font
```

A **graphical table**, as shown in Figure 4-3, is rendered using graphical elements to distinguish the table components. In a graphical table, you can include design elements such as background colors and shaded borders. You can also control the size of individual table cells in a graphical table, and you can align text within those cells. A graphical table even allows you to create cells that span several rows or columns.

A graphical table   Figure 4-3

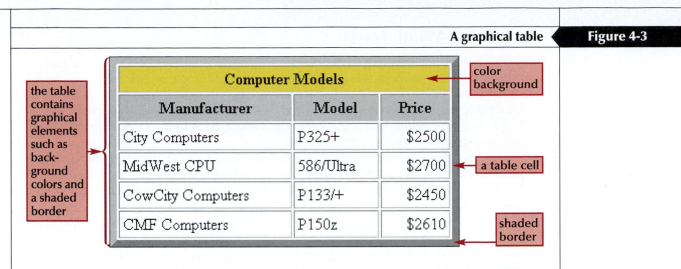

the table contains graphical elements such as background colors and a shaded border

color background

a table cell

shaded border

Although graphical tables are more flexible and attractive than text tables, it is quicker and easier to create a text table. You'll start on Kevin's project by creating a Web page that contains a text table; after finishing that page, you'll start working on a graphical version of the same table.

Creating a Text Table

The race results page has been created for you and is stored in your Data Files as racetxt1.htm. You will add a text table containing the race results to this page. To begin, you'll open this text file and save it with a new name.

To open racetxt1.htm and save it with a new name:

▶ 1. Using your text editor, open **racetxt1.htm** from the tutorial.04/tutorial folder. Enter *your name* and *the date* in the comment section of the file.

▶ 2. Save the file as **race1.htm** in the same folder.

Figure 4-4 shows a preview of the page as it is displayed in a browser.

The race1 page   Figure 4-4

Local Woman Wins Marathon

Park City native, **Laura Blake**, won the 27th Front Range Marathon over an elite field of the best long distance runners in the country. Laura's time of 2 hr. 28 min. 21 sec. was only 2 minutes off the women's course record set last year by Sarah Rawlings. Kathy Lasker and Lisa Peterson finished second and third, respectively. Laura's victory came on the heels of her performance at the NCAA Track and Field Championships, in which she placed second running for Colorado State.

In an exciting race, **Peter Teagan** of San Antonio, Texas, used a finishing kick to win the men's marathon for the second straight year, in a time of 2 hr. 12 min. 34 sec. Ahead for much of the race, Kyle Wills of Billings, Montana, finished second, when he could not match Teagan's finishing pace. Jason Wu of Cutler, Colorado, placed third in a very competitive field.

This year's race through downtown Boulder boasted the largest field in the marathon's history, with over 9500 men and 6700 women competing. Race conditions were perfect with low humidity and temperatures that never exceeded 85°.

The page consists of an article that Kevin has written about the marathon. You'll place the race results table between the first and second paragraphs.

Using Fixed-Width Fonts

A text table relies on the widths of the characters and spaces in each row to ensure that the column boundaries for different rows are aligned. For this reason, choosing the correct font is important when you create a text table. You can ensure that the column contents align properly by using a fixed-width font and including the same number of characters in each row. In a **fixed-width font**—also known as a **monospace font**—each character takes up the same amount of space.

Most typeset documents, including the one you're reading now, use proportional fonts. **Proportional fonts** assign a different amount of space for each character depending on the width of that character. For example, since the character "m" is wider than the character "l," a proportional font assigns it more space. Because of the variable spacing, proportional fonts are more visually attractive, and typically easier to read, than fixed-width fonts. However, proportional fonts are less suitable for text tables.

The distinction between fixed-width and proportional fonts is important. If you use a proportional font in a text table, the varying width of the characters and the spaces between characters can cause errors when the page is rendered in the user's browser. Figure 4-5 shows how a text table that uses a proportional font loses alignment when the font size is increased or decreased.

Figure 4-5	Alignment with proportional fonts

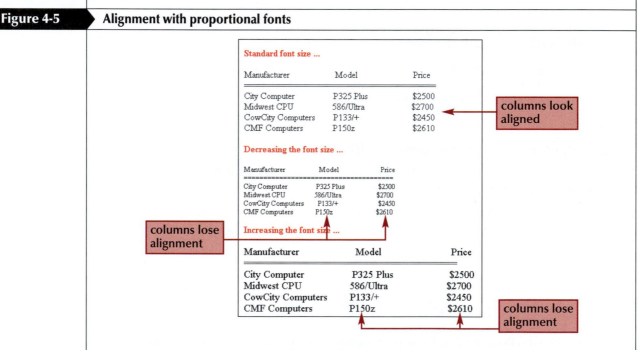

By contrast, the table shown in Figure 4-6 uses fixed-width fonts. Note that the columns remain aligned regardless of font size.

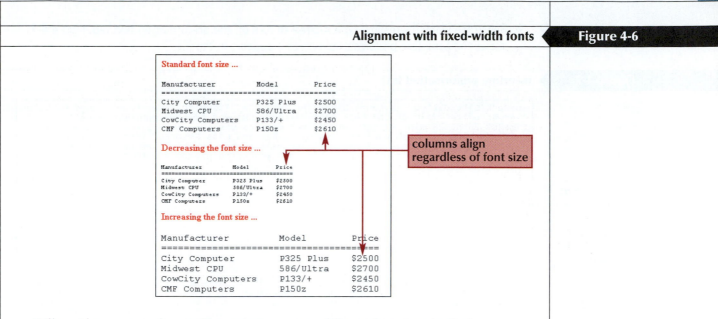

Different browsers and operating systems may use different font sizes to display your page's text, so you should always use a fixed-width font to ensure that the columns in your text tables remain in alignment.

Using Preformatted Text

To control the appearance of a text table, you need to insert extra spaces and other characters for alignment. However, HTML ignores extra occurrences of white space. One way to solve this problem is to mark the text as **preformatted text,** which retains the extra white space and causes the text to appear in the Web page as it appears in the HTML code. Preformatted text is created using the following syntax:

`<pre>content</pre>`

where `content` is text that will appear as preformatted text. Preformatted text is displayed by default in a monospace font, making it ideal for building text tables.

You'll use the <pre> tag to enter the table data from Figure 4-1 into race1.htm.

To create a text table using the <pre> tag:

1. Place the insertion point in the blank line located between the first and second paragraphs of Kevin's article.

2. Type **<pre>** and press **Enter** to create a blank line.

3. Type **Group** and press the spacebar **4** times.

4. Type **Runner** and press the spacebar **15** times.

5. Type **Time** and press the spacebar **10** times.

6. Type **Origin** and press the **Enter** key to create a blank line.

7. Underline each heading (Group, Runner, Time, Origin) using the equal sign symbol (see Figure 4-7) and press **Enter**.

8. Complete the table by entering the information from Figure 4-1 about the runners, their times, and their places of origin. Place a blank line between the men's and women's results, and align each entry with the left edge of the column headings.

9. Below the women's results, type **</pre>** to turn off the preformatted text tag. Figure 4-7 shows the complete preformatted text as it appears in the file.

Figure 4-7   **Inserting preformatted text**

table text will appear in the browser as it appears here

```
<p>Park City native, <b>Laura Blake</b>, won the 27<sup>th</sup> Front Range Marathon
over an elite field of the best long distance runners in the country. Laura's
time of 2 hr. 28 min. 21 sec. was only 2 minutes off the women's course record
set last year by Sarah Rawlings. Kathy Lasker and Lisa Peterson finished second
and third, respectively. Laura's victory came on the heels of her performance at
the NCAA Track and Field Championships, in which she placed second running for
Colorado State.</p>
<pre>
Group      Runner              Time           Origin
=====      ======              ====           ======
Men        1. Peter Teagan     2:12:34        San Antonio, Texas
Men        2. Kyle Wills       2:13:05        Billings, Montana
Men        3. Jason Wu         2:14:28        Cutler, Colorado

Women      1. Laura Blake      2:28:21        Park City, Colorado
Women      2. Kathy Lasker     2:30:11        Chicago, Illinois
Women      3. Lisa Peterson    2:31:14        Seattle, Washington
</pre>
<p>In an exciting race, <b>Peter Teagan</b> of San Antonio, Texas, used a finishing
kick to win the men's marathon for the second straight year, in a time of
2 hr. 12 min. 34 sec. Ahead for much of the race, Kyle Wills of Billings, Montana,
finished second, when he could not match Teagan's finishing pace. Jason Wu of
Cutler, Colorado, placed third in a very competitive field.</p>
```

10. Save your changes to **race1.htm** and close the file.

11. Using your Web browser, open **race1.htm**. Figure 4-8 displays the page as it appears in the browser.

Figure 4-8   **A text table in the race1 page**

Local Woman Wins Marathon

Park City native, **Laura Blake**, won the 27th Front Range Marathon over an elite field of the best long distance runners in the country. Laura's time of 2 hr. 28 min. 21 sec. was only 2 minutes off the women's course record set last year by Sarah Rawlings. Kathy Lasker and Lisa Peterson finished second and third, respectively. Laura's victory came on the heels of her performance at the NCAA Track and Field Championships, in which she placed second running for Colorado State.

```
Group      Runner              Time           Origin
=====      ======              ====           ======
Men        1. Peter Teagan     2:12:34        San Antonio, Texas
Men        2. Kyle Wills       2:13:05        Billings, Montana
Men        3. Jason Wu         2:14:28        Cutler, Colorado

Women      1. Laura Blake      2:28:21        Park City, Colorado
Women      2. Kathy Lasker     2:30:11        Chicago, Illinois
Women      3. Lisa Peterson    2:31:14        Seattle, Washington
```

In an exciting race, **Peter Teagan** of San Antonio, Texas, used a finishing kick to win the men's marathon for the second straight year, in a time of 2 hr. 12 min. 34 sec. Ahead for much of the race, Kyle Wills of Billings, Montana, finished second, when he could not match Teagan's finishing pace. Jason Wu of Cutler, Colorado, placed third in a very competitive field.

This year's race through downtown Boulder boasted the largest field in the marathon's history, with over 9500 men and 6700 women competing. Race conditions were perfect with low humidity and temperatures that never exceeded 85°.

By using preformatted text, you've created a text table that can be displayed by all browsers, and you've ensured that the columns will retain their alignment in any font size.

You show the completed table to Kevin. He's pleased with your work and would like you to create a similar page using a graphical table. Before creating the new table, you'll study how HTML defines table structures.

Creating Preformatted Text

- To create preformatted text, which retains any white space in the HTML file, use the tag
  `<pre>content</pre>`
  where `content` is the text you want displayed as preformatted text.

Defining a Table Structure

The first step in creating a graphical table is to specify the table structure, which includes the number of rows and columns, the locations of column headings, and the placement of a table caption. Once the table structure is in place, you can start entering data into the table.

The page that will contain the graphical table has been created for you and stored in the file racetxt2.htm in your Data Files. Open the file using your text editor and save it with a new name.

To open racetxt2.htm and save it with a new name:

1. Using your text editor, open **racetxt2.htm** from the tutorial.04/tutorial folder. Enter **your name** and **the date** in the comment section of the file.

2. Save the file as **race2.htm**.

   Figure 4-9 shows a preview of the page as it appears in the browser.

The race2 page | **Figure 4-9**

Local Woman Wins Marathon

Park City native, **Laura Blake**, won the 27th Front Range Marathon over an elite field of the best long distance runners in the country. Laura's time of 2 hr. 28 min. 21 sec. was only 2 minutes off the women's course record set last year by Sarah Rawlings. Kathy Lasker and Lisa Peterson finished second and third, respectively. Laura's victory came on the heels of her performance at the NCAA Track and Field Championships, in which she placed second running for Colorado State.

In an exciting race, **Peter Teagan** of San Antonio, Texas, used a finishing kick to win the men's marathon for the second straight year, in a time of 2 hr. 12 min. 34 sec. Ahead for much of the race, Kyle Wills of Billings, Montana, finished second, when he could not match Teagan's finishing pace. Jason Wu of Cutler, Colorado, placed third in a very competitive field.

This year's race through downtown Boulder boasted the largest field in the marathon's history, with over 9500 men and 6700 women competing. Race conditions were perfect with low humidity and temperatures that never exceeded 85°.

Marking a table, table row, and table cell

Tables are marked with a two-sided <table> tag that identifies the start and end of the table structure. Each row in a table is marked using a two-sided <tr> (for table row) tag. Finally, within each table row, the two-sided <td> (for table data) tag marks the content of individual table cells. The general syntax of a graphical table is therefore

```
<table>
   <tr>
      <td>First Cell</td>
      <td>Second Cell</td>
   </tr>
   <tr>
```

```
        <td>Third Cell</td>
        <td>Fourth Cell</td>
    </tr>
</table>
```

This example creates a table with two rows and two columns. Figure 4-10 shows the layout of a table with this HTML code.

Figure 4-10   **A simple table**

| First Cell | Second Cell |
| Third Cell | Fourth Cell |

two rows   two columns

HTML includes no tag for table columns because the number of columns is determined by the number of cells within a row. For example, if each table row includes four td elements, then the table has four columns.

The table that Kevin outlined in Figure 4-1 requires seven rows and four columns. The first row contains column headings, and the remaining six rows display the table's data. HTML provides a special tag for headings, which you'll learn about shortly. For now, you'll create the table structure for the table data.

To create the structure for the race results table:

1. Place the insertion point in the blank line between the first and second paragraphs of Kevin's article.

2. Type **<table>** to identify the beginning of the table structure, and then press the **Enter** key.

3. Type the entries for the first row of the table as follows:

```
<tr>
    <td></td>
    <td></td>
    <td></td>
    <td></td>
</tr>
```

Note that you do not need to indent the <tr> or <td> tags or place them on separate lines, but you may find it easier to interpret your code if you do so.

4. Press the **Enter** key and then repeat Step 3 five times to create the six rows of the table. You might want to use the copy and paste function of your text editor to save time.

5. Press the **Enter** key and then type **</table>** to complete the code for the table structure. See Figure 4-11.

```
<p><img src="blake.jpg" alt="" width="75" height="101" style="margin: 5; float: left" />
Park City native, <b>Laura Blake</b>, won the 27<sup>th</sup> Front Range Marathon
over an elite field of the best long distance runners in the country. Laura's
time of 2 hr. 28 min. 21 sec. was only 2 minutes off the women's course record
set last year by Sarah Rawlings. Kathy Lasker and Lisa Peterson finished second
and third, respectively. Laura's victory came on the heels of her performance at
the NCAA Track and Field Championships, in which she placed second running for
Colorado State.</p>

<table>
    <tr>
        <td></td>
        <td></td>
        <td></td>
        <td></td>
    </tr>
    <tr>
        <td></td>
        <td></td>
        <td></td>
        <td></td>
    </tr>
    <tr>
        <td></td>
        <td></td>
        <td></td>
        <td></td>
    </tr>
    <tr>
        <td></td>
        <td></td>
        <td></td>
        <td></td>
    </tr>
    <tr>
        <td></td>
        <td></td>
        <td></td>
        <td></td>
    </tr>
    <tr>
        <td></td>
        <td></td>
        <td></td>
        <td></td>
    </tr>
</table>
```

With the table structure in place, you're ready to add the text for each cell.

To insert the table text:

1. Locate the first <td> tag in the table structure and type **Men** between the opening and closing <td> tags.

2. Within the next three <td> tags, type the remaining entries for the first row of the table as follows:

```
<td>1. Peter Teagan</td>
<td>2:12:34</td>
<td>San Antonio, Texas</td>
```

3. Continue entering the text for the cells for the remaining five rows of the table. Figure 4-12 shows the completed text for the body of the table.

Figure 4-12 **Data for the table cells**

```
<table>
    <tr>
        <td>Men</td>
        <td>1. Peter Teagan</td>
        <td>2:12:34</td>
        <td>San Antonio, Texas</td>
    </tr>
    <tr>
        <td>Men</td>
        <td>2. Kyle Wills</td>
        <td>2:13:05</td>
        <td>Billings, Montana</td>
    </tr>
    <tr>
        <td>Men</td>
        <td>3. Jason Wu</td>
        <td>2:14:28</td>
        <td>Cutler, Colorado</td>
    </tr>
    <tr>
        <td>Women</td>
        <td>1. Laura Blake</td>
        <td>2:28:21</td>
        <td>Park City, Colorado</td>
    </tr>
    <tr>
        <td>Women</td>
        <td>2. Kathy Lasker</td>
        <td>2:30:11</td>
        <td>Chicago, Illinois</td>
    </tr>
    <tr>
        <td>Women</td>
        <td>3. Lisa Peterson</td>
        <td>2:31:14</td>
        <td>Seattle, Washington</td>
    </tr>
</table>
```

With the text for the body of the table entered, the next step is to add the column headings.

Creating Table Headings

Table headings are marked with the <th> tag. Table headings are like table cells, except that content marked with the <th> tag is centered within the cell and displayed in a bold-face font. The <th> tag is most often used for column headings.

In the race results table, Kevin has specified a single row of table headings. You'll mark this text using the <th> tag.

To insert the table headings:

1. Place the insertion point after the <table> tag and press the **Enter** key to create a blank line.
2. Type the following HTML code and content:

```
<tr>
    <th>Group</th>
    <th>Runner</th>
    <th>Time</th>
    <th>Origin</th>
</tr>
```

Figure 4-13 shows the code for the table headings as they appear in the file.

Inserting table headings ◄ **Figure 4-13**

row of table headings →

```
<table>
  <tr>
    <th>Group</th>
    <th>Runner</th>
    <th>Time</th>
    <th>Origin</th>
  </tr>
  <tr>
    <td>Men</td>
    <td>1. Peter Teagan</td>
    <td>2:12:34</td>
    <td>San Antonio, Texas</td>
  </tr>
```

▶ **3.** Save your changes to the file.

▶ **4.** Using your Web browser, open **race2.htm**. The table is shown in Figure 4-14.

Race results table data ◄ **Figure 4-14**

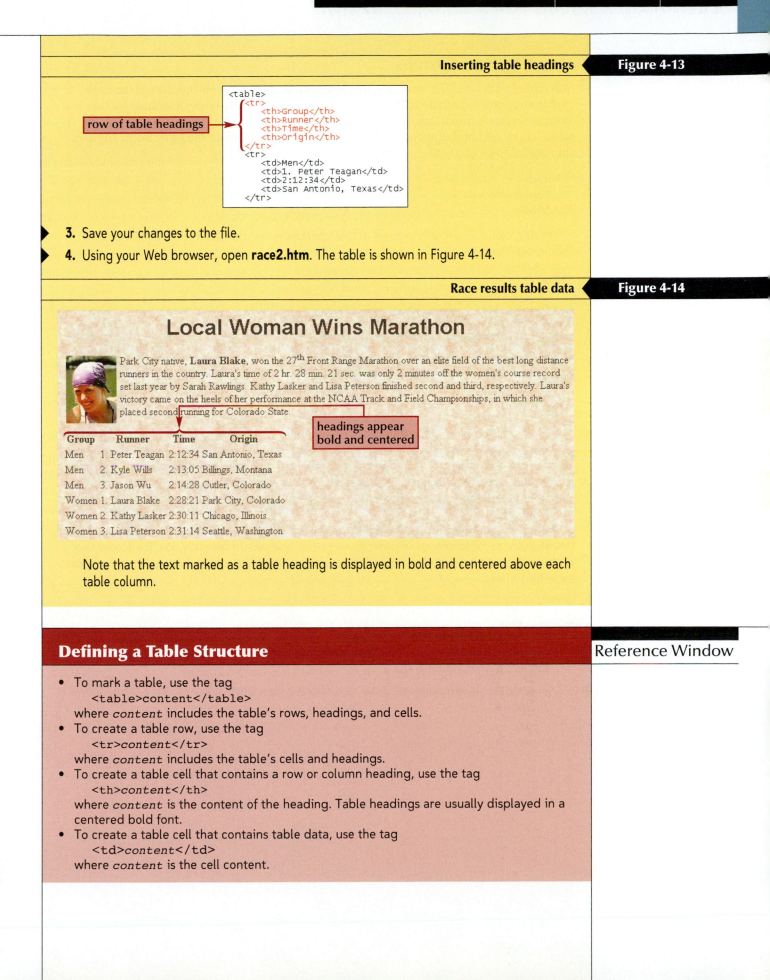

Local Woman Wins Marathon

Park City native, **Laura Blake**, won the 27th Front Range Marathon over an elite field of the best long distance runners in the country. Laura's time of 2 hr. 28 min. 21 sec. was only 2 minutes off the women's course record set last year by Sarah Rawlings. Kathy Lasker and Lisa Peterson finished second and third, respectively. Laura's victory came on the heels of her performance at the NCAA Track and Field Championships, in which she placed second running for Colorado State.

headings appear bold and centered

Group	Runner	Time	Origin
Men	1. Peter Teagan	2:12:34	San Antonio, Texas
Men	2. Kyle Wills	2:13:05	Billings, Montana
Men	3. Jason Wu	2:14:28	Cutler, Colorado
Women	1. Laura Blake	2:28:21	Park City, Colorado
Women	2. Kathy Lasker	2:30:11	Chicago, Illinois
Women	3. Lisa Peterson	2:31:14	Seattle, Washington

Note that the text marked as a table heading is displayed in bold and centered above each table column.

Defining a Table Structure

Reference Window

- To mark a table, use the tag
    `<table>`content`</table>`
  where *content* includes the table's rows, headings, and cells.
- To create a table row, use the tag
    `<tr>`content`</tr>`
  where *content* includes the table's cells and headings.
- To create a table cell that contains a row or column heading, use the tag
    `<th>`content`</th>`
  where *content* is the content of the heading. Table headings are usually displayed in a centered bold font.
- To create a table cell that contains table data, use the tag
    `<td>`content`</td>`
  where *content* is the cell content.

Creating Row Groups

You can classify a table's rows into **row groups** that indicate their purpose in the table. HTML supports three types of row groups: table header, table body, and table footer. Because order is important in an HTML file, the table header must be listed before the table footer, and both the header and footer must appear before the table body. To mark the header rows of a table, use the syntax

```
<thead>
    table rows
</thead>
```

A table can contain only one set of table header rows. To mark the rows of the table footer, use the syntax

```
<tfoot>
    table rows
</tfoot>
```

A table can contain only one footer. Finally, to mark the rows of the table body, use the syntax:

```
<tbody>
    table rows
</tbody>
```

A table can contain multiple table body sections.

Row groups are sometimes used for tables that draw their data from external sources such as databases or XML documents. In those cases, programs can be written in which the contents of a table body span across several different Web pages, with the contents of the table header and footer repeated on each page. Not all browsers support this capability, however.

Although creating row groups does not affect a table's appearance, you can apply different styles to table groups in order to make them appear differently. We'll explore this more in the next session. For now, we'll mark the table's header and body; this table contains no footer.

To mark the row groups:

1. Locate the row containing the table headings. Enclose this row within a two-sided <thead> tag as shown in Figure 4-15.

2. Enclose the six rows containing the race results within a two-sided <tbody> tag as shown in Figure 4-15.

Marking the row groups ◄ Figure 4-15

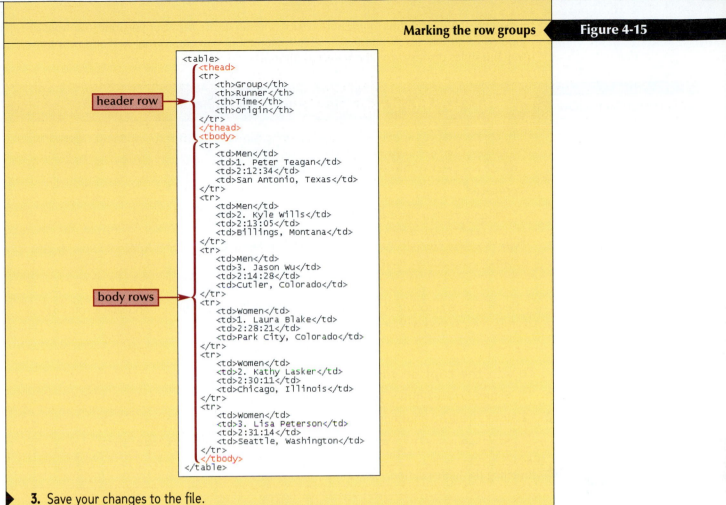

```
<table>
    <thead>
    <tr>
        <th>Group</th>
        <th>Runner</th>
        <th>Time</th>
        <th>Origin</th>
    </tr>
    </thead>
    <tbody>
    <tr>
        <td>Men</td>
        <td>1. Peter Teagan</td>
        <td>2:12:34</td>
        <td>San Antonio, Texas</td>
    </tr>
    <tr>
        <td>Men</td>
        <td>2. Kyle Wills</td>
        <td>2:13:05</td>
        <td>Billings, Montana</td>
    </tr>
    <tr>
        <td>Men</td>
        <td>3. Jason Wu</td>
        <td>2:14:28</td>
        <td>Cutler, Colorado</td>
    </tr>
    <tr>
        <td>Women</td>
        <td>1. Laura Blake</td>
        <td>2:28:21</td>
        <td>Park City, Colorado</td>
    </tr>
    <tr>
        <td>Women</td>
        <td>2. Kathy Lasker</td>
        <td>2:30:11</td>
        <td>Chicago, Illinois</td>
    </tr>
    <tr>
        <td>Women</td>
        <td>3. Lisa Peterson</td>
        <td>2:31:14</td>
        <td>Seattle, Washington</td>
    </tr>
    </tbody>
</table>
```

header row

body rows

3. Save your changes to the file.

Creating a Table Caption

You can add a caption to a table in order to provide descriptive information about the table's contents. The syntax for creating a caption is

`<caption>content</caption>`

where *content* is the content of the caption. The <caption> tag must appear directly after the opening <table> tag. By default, the caption appears centered above a table. However, you can change the placement of a caption using the align attribute:

`<caption align="position">content</caption>`

where *position* equals one of the following:

- "bottom" to place the caption centered below the table
- "top" to place the caption centered above the table
- "left" to place the caption above the table, aligned with the left table margin
- "right" to place the caption above the table, aligned with the right table margin

Internet Explorer also supports a value of "center" for the caption, which centers the caption above the table. Because HTML 3.2 specified only the "top" and "bottom" alignment options, older browsers support only those options. Note that the align attribute has been deprecated, and thus might not be supported in future browser versions. Captions are rendered as normal text without special formatting, but you can format and align captions using the styles discussed in the previous tutorial.

Reference Window	**Creating a Table Caption**

- To create a table caption, insert the following tag directly after the opening <table> tag:
  ```
  <caption>content</caption>
  ```
  where content is the content of the caption.

Deprecated

- To align a caption, add the following attribute to the <caption> tag:
  ```
  align="position"
  ```
  where position is either top (the default), bottom, left, or right. Internet Explorer also supports a position value of "center".

Kevin asks you to add the caption "Race Results" to the table in a boldface font. By default, the caption will be centered above the table.

To add the caption to the race results table:

1. Return to **race2.htm** in your text editor.

2. Insert the following code below the <table> tag (see Figure 4-16):
   ```
   <caption style="font-weight: bold">Race Results</caption>
   ```

Figure 4-16	Inserting the table caption

```
<table>
    <caption style="font-weight: bold">Race Results</caption>
    <thead>
    <tr>
        <th>Group</th>
        <th>Runner</th>
        <th>Time</th>
        <th>Origin</th>
    </tr>
    </thead>
```

3. Save your changes to the file.

4. Using your Web browser, reload or refresh **race2.htm**. Figure 4-17 shows the table with the newly added caption.

Figure 4-17	Viewing the table caption

caption ⟶ Race Results

Group	Runner	Time	Origin
Men	1. Peter Teagan	2:12:34	San Antonio, Texas
Men	2. Kyle Wills	2:13:05	Billings, Montana
Men	3. Jason Wu	2:14:28	Cutler, Colorado
Women	1. Laura Blake	2:28:21	Park City, Colorado
Women	2. Kathy Lasker	2:30:11	Chicago, Illinois
Women	3. Lisa Peterson	2:31:14	Seattle, Washington

Adding a Table Summary

For non-visual browsers (such as aural browsers that may be used by blind or visually impaired people) it is useful to include a summary of a table's contents. While a caption and the surrounding page text usually provide descriptive information about the table and its contents, you can use the summary attribute if you need to include a more detailed description. The syntax of the summary attribute is

```
<table summary="description"> ... </table>
```

where *description* is a description of the table's purpose and contents. For example, to summarize the race results table, you could add the following code to the HTML file:

```
<table summary="This table lists the top three male and female runners
in the recent Front Range Marathon, providing the name, time, and origin
of the runners.">
…
</table>
```

The information in the summary attribute does not affect a table's appearance in visual browsers.

You've completed your work with the initial structure of the race results table. Kevin is pleased with your progress, but he would like you to make some improvements in the table's appearance. In the next session, you'll learn how to format the table.

Session 4.1 Quick Check

Review

1. What are the two kinds of tables you can place in a Web page?
2. What is the difference between a proportional font and a fixed-width font? Which should you use in a text table, and why?
3. Which HTML tag would you use to create preformatted text?
4. Define the purpose of the following HTML tags in defining the structure of a table:

   ```
   <tr> ... </tr>
   <td> ... </td>
   <th> ... </th>
   ```

5. How do you specify the number of rows in a graphical table? How do you specify the number of columns?
6. What are three row groups and how do you create them?
7. What HTML code would you use to place the caption "Product Catalog" below a table? Where must this HTML code be placed in relation to the opening <table> tag?

Session 4.2

Working with the Table Border

After viewing the race results table in a browser, Kevin notes that the text is displayed with properly aligned columns, but the lack of gridlines and borders makes the table difficult to read. Kevin asks you to enhance the table's design by adding borders, gridlines, and a background color. He also wants you to control the placement and size of the table. HTML provides tags and attributes to do all of these things. You'll begin enhancing the race results table by adding a table border.

Adding a Table Border

By default, browsers display tables without table borders. You can create a table border by adding the border attribute to the <table> tag. The syntax for creating a table border is

```
<table border="value"> ... </table>
```

where *value* is the width of the border in pixels. Figure 4-18 shows the effect of different border sizes on a table's appearance. Note that unless you set the border size to 0 pixels, the size of the internal gridlines is not affected by the border attribute. You'll see how to change the size and appearance of these gridlines later in this session.

Figure 4-18 **Tables with different border sizes**

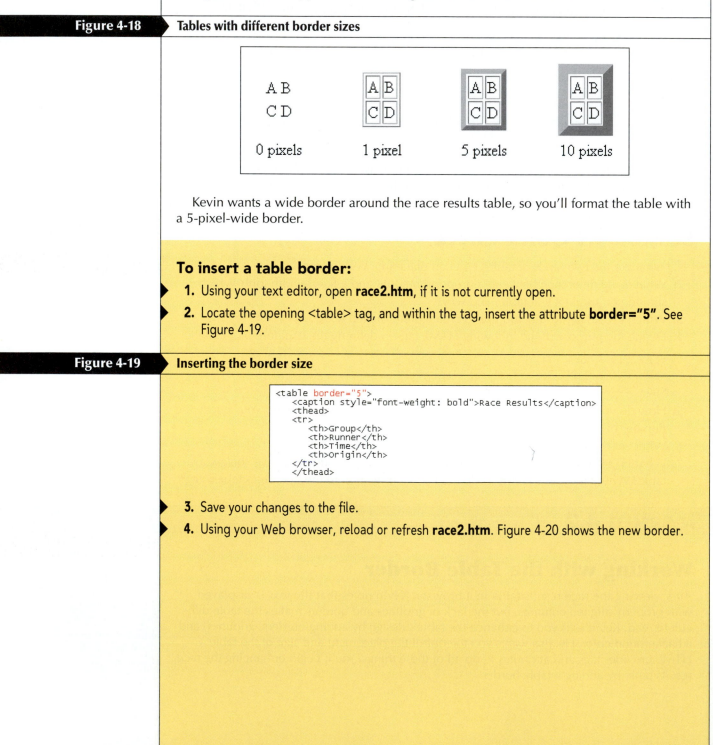

Kevin wants a wide border around the race results table, so you'll format the table with a 5-pixel-wide border.

To insert a table border:

1. Using your text editor, open **race2.htm**, if it is not currently open.
2. Locate the opening <table> tag, and within the tag, insert the attribute **border="5"**. See Figure 4-19.

Figure 4-19 **Inserting the border size**

```
<table border="5">
    <caption style="font-weight: bold">Race Results</caption>
    <thead>
    <tr>
        <th>Group</th>
        <th>Runner</th>
        <th>Time</th>
        <th>Origin</th>
    </tr>
    </thead>
```

3. Save your changes to the file.
4. Using your Web browser, reload or refresh **race2.htm**. Figure 4-20 shows the new border.

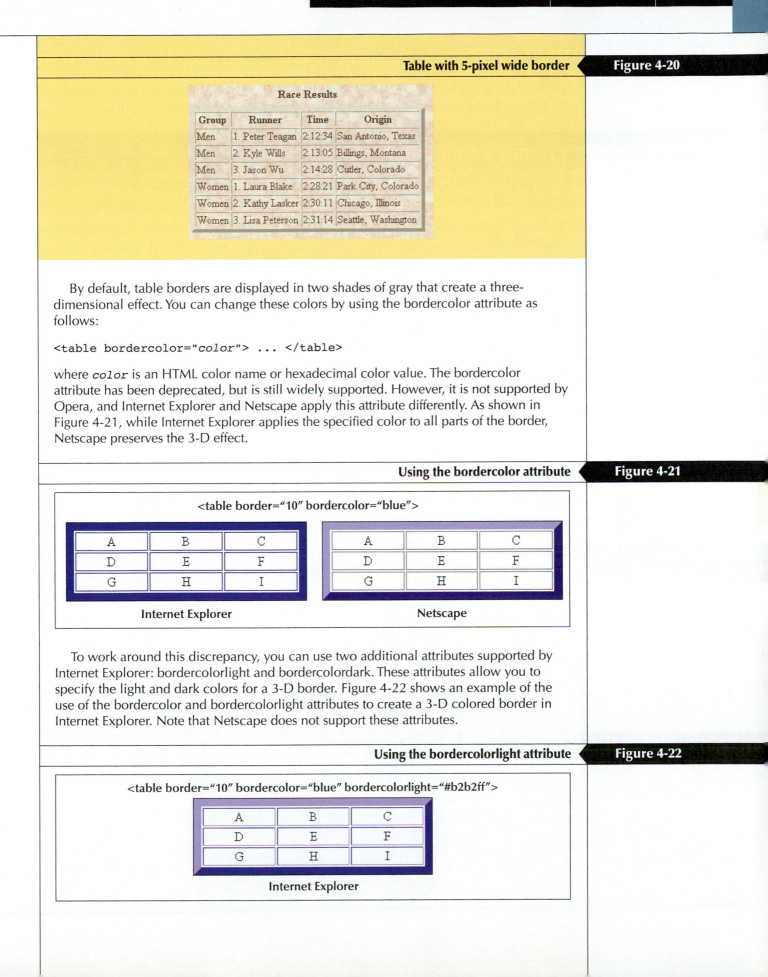

By default, table borders are displayed in two shades of gray that create a three-dimensional effect. You can change these colors by using the bordercolor attribute as follows:

```
<table bordercolor="color"> ... </table>
```

where *color* is an HTML color name or hexadecimal color value. The bordercolor attribute has been deprecated, but is still widely supported. However, it is not supported by Opera, and Internet Explorer and Netscape apply this attribute differently. As shown in Figure 4-21, while Internet Explorer applies the specified color to all parts of the border, Netscape preserves the 3-D effect.

Using the bordercolor attribute ◀ **Figure 4-21**

<table border="10" bordercolor="blue">

A	B	C
D	E	F
G	H	I

Internet Explorer

A	B	C
D	E	F
G	H	I

Netscape

To work around this discrepancy, you can use two additional attributes supported by Internet Explorer: bordercolorlight and bordercolordark. These attributes allow you to specify the light and dark colors for a 3-D border. Figure 4-22 shows an example of the use of the bordercolor and bordercolorlight attributes to create a 3-D colored border in Internet Explorer. Note that Netscape does not support these attributes.

Using the bordercolorlight attribute ◀ **Figure 4-22**

<table border="10" bordercolor="blue" bordercolorlight="#b2b2ff">

A	B	C
D	E	F
G	H	I

Internet Explorer

Another way to solve this problem is to use styles that create and format the border. The applicable styles will be explored in a future tutorial. For now, you'll use the bordercolor attribute to change the border color to brown. In order to maintain the 3-D border effect for Internet Explorer users, you'll also set the bordercolorlight attribute value to tan.

Reference Window

Creating a Table Border

- To create a table border, add the following attribute to the table element:
  `border="value"`
  where *value* is the width of the border in pixels.

Deprecated

- To change the border color, add the following attribute to the table element:
  `bordercolor="color"`
  where *color* is either a recognized color name or a hexadecimal color value.

Internet Explorer Only

- To break the border into separate dark and light bands, add the following attributes to the table element:
  `bordercolorlight="color" bordercolordark="color"`
  where *color* is either a recognized color name or a hexadecimal color value.

To change the color of the table border:

1. Return to **race2.htm** in your text editor.
2. Insert the attributes **bordercolor="brown"** and **bordercolorlight="tan"** within the <table> tag as shown in Figure 4-23.

Figure 4-23 **Changing the border color**

```
<table border="5" bordercolor="brown" bordercolorlight="tan">
   <caption style="font-weight: bold">Race Results</caption>
   <thead>
   <tr>
      <th>Group</th>
      <th>Runner</th>
      <th>Time</th>
      <th>Origin</th>
   </tr>
   </thead>
```

3. Save your changes to the file and reload it in your Web browser. Figure 4-24 shows the revised appearance of the table.

Figure 4-24 **Race results table with brown/tan border color**

Race Results

Group	Runner	Time	Origin
Men	1. Peter Teagan	2:12:34	San Antonio, Texas
Men	2. Kyle Wills	2:13:05	Billings, Montana
Men	3. Jason Wu	2:14:28	Cutler, Colorado
Women	1. Laura Blake	2:28:21	Park City, Colorado
Women	2. Kathy Lasker	2:30:11	Chicago, Illinois
Women	3. Lisa Peterson	2:31:14	Seattle, Washington

Trouble? Depending on your browser and browser version, your table border colors might not match the ones shown in Figure 4-24.

Creating Frames and Rules

By default a table border surrounds the entire table and each of the cells within the table. You can modify this by using the frame and rules attributes of the table element.

The frame attribute allows you to determine which sides of a table will have borders. The syntax is

```
<table frame="type"> ... </table>
```

where *type* is "box" (the default), "above", "border", "below", "hsides", "vsides", "lhs", "rhs", or "void". Figure 4-25 describes each of these options.

Values of the frame attribute ◄ **Figure 4-25**

Frame Value	Border Appearance
above	only above the table
below	only below the table
border	around all four sides of the table
box	around all four sides of the table
hsides	on the top and bottom sides of the table (the horizontal sides)
lhs	only on the left-hand side
rhs	only on the right-hand side
void	no border is drawn around the table
vsides	on the left and right sides of the table (the vertical sides)

Figure 4-26 shows the effect of each of these values on a table grid. The frame attribute was introduced in HTML 4.01 and thus might not be supported in older browsers.

Frame examples ◄ **Figure 4-26**

frame="above"   frame="below"   frame="border"

frame="box"   frame="hsides"   frame="lhs"

frame="rhs"   frame="vsides"   frame="void"

The rules attribute lets you control how gridlines are drawn within the table. The syntax of this attribute is

```
<table rules="type"> ... </table>
```

where *type* is "all" (the default), "cols", "groups", or "none". Figure 4-27 describes each of these attribute values.

Figure 4-27 **Values of the rules attribute**

Rules Value	Description of Rules
all	around cells
cols	around columns
groups	around row groups
none	no rules
rows	around rows

Figure 4-28 shows the effect of each of the attribute values on a table.

Figure 4-28 **Rules examples**

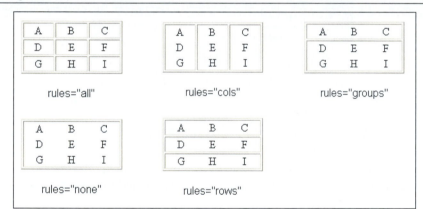

As with the frame attribute, the rules attribute was introduced in the specifications for HTML 4.01, and thus might not be supported in older browsers.

You're pleased with the current appearance of the table's border and gridlines, so you decide against making any changes to the frame or rules values.

Reference Window

Creating Frames and Rules

- To change the frame style of a table border, add the following attribute to the table element:
    frame="*type*"
  where *type* is "box" (the default), "above", "border", "below", "hsides", "vsides", "lhs", "rhs", or "void".
- To change the rules style of the internal gridlines, add the following attribute to the table element:
    rules="*type*"
  where *type* is "all" (the default), "cols", "groups", or "none".

Sizing a Table

While Kevin likes what you've done with the borders, he feels that the table still looks too crowded. He would like to see smaller internal borders, more space between the text and the borders, and would like the table to be slightly wider. Tables are sized automatically by the browser in order to create the smallest table that fits the largest amount of text into each column with the least amount of line wrapping. For the race results table, this results in cell borders that crowd the cell text. However, there are several attributes that you can use to override the size choices made by the browser.

Setting Cell Spacing

The first attribute we'll consider controls the amount of space between table cells, which is known as the **cell spacing**. By default, browsers set the cell spacing to 2 pixels. To set a different cell spacing value, use the cellspacing attribute as follows:

```
<table cellspacing="value"> ... </table>
```

where `value` is the size of the cell spacing in pixels. If you have applied a border to your table, changing this value also impacts the size of the interior borders. Figure 4-29 shows how different cell spacing values affect the appearance of these gridlines.

Different cell spacing values   **Figure 4-29**

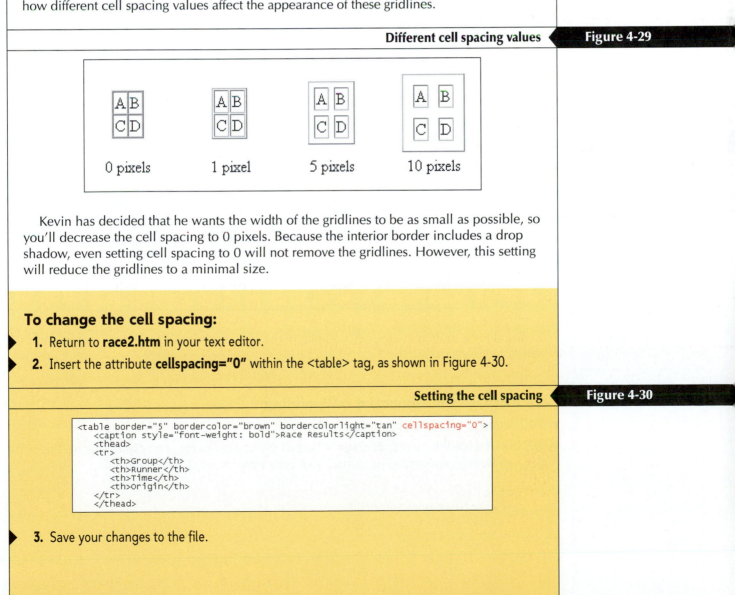

0 pixels   1 pixel   5 pixels   10 pixels

Kevin has decided that he wants the width of the gridlines to be as small as possible, so you'll decrease the cell spacing to 0 pixels. Because the interior border includes a drop shadow, even setting cell spacing to 0 will not remove the gridlines. However, this setting will reduce the gridlines to a minimal size.

To change the cell spacing:

1. Return to **race2.htm** in your text editor.
2. Insert the attribute **cellspacing="0"** within the <table> tag, as shown in Figure 4-30.

Setting the cell spacing   **Figure 4-30**

```
<table border="5" bordercolor="brown" bordercolorlight="tan" cellspacing="0">
    <caption style="font-weight: bold">Race Results</caption>
    <thead>
    <tr>
        <th>Group</th>
        <th>Runner</th>
        <th>Time</th>
        <th>Origin</th>
    </tr>
    </thead>
```

3. Save your changes to the file.

> **4.** Using your Web browser, reload or refresh **race2.htm**. Figure 4-31 shows the new cell spacing. Note that the line that separates the cells has been reduced, but not eliminated. Compare Figure 4-31 with Figure 4-24.

Figure 4-31 Table with a cell spacing of 0 pixels

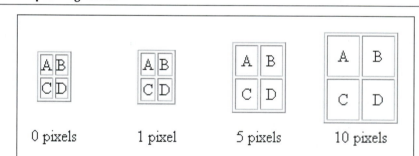

Setting Cell Padding

Next, we want to set the space between the cell text and the cell border. This distance is known as the **cell padding**. The default cell padding value is 1 pixel, which to Kevin's eyes is too little. To set a different cell padding value, use the following attribute:

```
<table cellpadding="value"> ... </table>
```

where `value` is the size of the cell padding in pixels. Figure 4-32 shows how different cell padding values affect the appearance of the text within a table.

Figure 4-32 Different cell padding values

You decide to increase the cell padding of the race results table to 4 pixels in order to satisfy Kevin's request.

To increase the amount of cell padding:

> **1.** Return to **race2.htm** in your text editor.
>
> **2.** Insert the attribute **cellpadding="4"** within the <table> tag (you may want to place this attribute on a separate line to make your code easier to read). See Figure 4-33.

Setting the cell padding ◄ **Figure 4-33**

```
<table border="5" bordercolor="brown" bordercolorlight="tan" cellspacing="0"
     cellpadding="4">
   <caption style="font-weight: bold">Race Results</caption>
   <thead>
   <tr>
       <th>Group</th>
       <th>Runner</th>
       <th>Time</th>
       <th>Origin</th>
   </tr>
   </thead>
```

► **3.** Save your changes to the file, and then reload **race2.htm** in your Web browser. Figure 4-34 shows the table with the increased amount of cell padding.

Table with a cell padding of 4 pixels ◄ **Figure 4-34**

Group	Runner	Time	Origin
Men	1. Peter Teagan	2:12:34	San Antonio, Texas
Men	2. Kyle Wills	2:13:05	Billings, Montana
Men	3. Jason Wu	2:14:28	Cutler, Colorado
Women	1. Laura Blake	2:28:21	Park City, Colorado
Women	2. Kathy Lasker	2:30:11	Chicago, Illinois
Women	3. Lisa Peterson	2:31:14	Seattle, Washington

Race Results

Setting the Table Width

Kevin likes the extra cell padding, but still feels that the table would look better if it was larger. Recall that the overall size of the table is largely determined by its content. The table expands in width to match the contents of the cells. If you want to specify the overall width, use the following attribute:

```
<table width="value"> ... </table>
```

where *value* is the width in either pixels or as a percentage of the width of the containing element. If the containing element is the page itself, you can set the table to fill the entire page width by specifying a width value of "100%". You can also set the table width to a fixed value—for example, you can specify a width of 600 pixels, by changing the width value to "600". If you specify an absolute size, the table size remains constant, regardless of a user's monitor size. On the other hand, specifying a percentage allows your table to match each monitor's dimensions. For example, a table that is 600 pixels wide fills a monitor at 640 × 480 resolution, but leaves a lot of blank space if the monitor size is 1280 × 760. We'll explore this issue more in the next session as we look at tables as tools for layout. Note that a browser will never display a table with a width smaller than that required to display the content. If table content requires a width of 100 pixels, for example, then a browser ignores a width value of 50 pixels.

Many browsers, including Internet Explorer and Netscape, support the attribute

```
<table height="value"> ... </table>
```

where *value* is the height of the table either in pixels or as a percentage of the height of the containing element. However, the height attribute is not part of the HTML specifications and is not supported by XHTML. Like the width attribute, the height attribute only indicates the minimum height of the table, assuming that the content fits. If the table content cannot fit into the specified height, the table height increases to match the contents.

Kevin suggests that you set the width of the table to 70% of the page width.

To set the width of the race results table:

1. Return to **race2.htm** in your text editor.

2. Insert the attribute, **width="70%"** within the <table> tag, as shown in Figure 4-35.

Figure 4-35	Setting the table width

```
<table border="5" bordercolor="brown" bordercolorlight="tan" cellspacing="0"
       cellpadding="4" width="70%">
   <caption style="font-weight: bold">Race Results</caption>
   <thead>
   <tr>
      <th>Group</th>
      <th>Runner</th>
      <th>Time</th>
      <th>Origin</th>
   </tr>
   </thead>
```

3. Save your changes to the file and then reload it in your Web browser. Figure 4-36 shows the revised page with the table width set to 70% of the page width.

Figure 4-36	Table with a width of 70% of the page width

Trouble? Depending on your browser and browser version, your page might appear differently from the one shown in Figure 4-36.

Setting Cell and Column Width

The width attribute can also be applied to individual cells within the table, using the form

```
<td width="value"> … </td>
```

or

```
<th width="value"> ... </th>
```

where *value* is the cell's width either in pixels or as a percentage of the width of the entire table. You can set the width of a column by setting the width of the first cell in the column; the remaining cells in the column will adopt that width. If the content of one of the other cells exceeds that width, however, the browser expands the size of all cells in the column to match the width required to display that content. If you set different widths for two cells in the same column, a browser applies the larger value to the column.

You can also set the height of a cell using the attribute

```
<td height="value"> ... </td>
```

or

```
<th height="value"> ... </th>
```

where *value* is the height either in pixels or as a percentage of the height of the table. The height attribute has been deprecated and might not be supported in future browsers.

Sizing a Table

Reference Window

- To set the size of a table, add the following attributes to the table element:
    ```
    width="value" height="value"
    ```
    where *value* is the size either in pixels or as a percentage of the containing element.
- To set cell spacing, add the following attribute to the table element:
    ```
    cellspacing="value"
    ```
    where *value* is the gap between adjacent cells in pixels. The default spacing is 2 pixels.
- To set cell padding, add the following attribute to the table element:
    ```
    cellpadding="value"
    ```
    where *value* is the size of the gap between the cell content and the cell border. The default padding is 1 pixel.

Deprecated

- To set the size of a table cell, add the following attributes to the td or th element:
    ```
    width="value" height="value"
    ```
or
    ```
    width="value" height="value"
    ```
    where *value* is the size either in pixels or as a percentage of the table's width or height.

Preventing Line Wrap

If you change the widths of the table and the table cells, you might want to ensure that the contents of certain cells do not wrap. For example, if a cell contains a date or name, you might want to ensure that the name always appears on a single line. To prevent line wrapping, add the following attribute to the appropriate cell:

```
<td nowrap="nowrap"> ... </td>
```

or

```
<th nowrap="nowrap"> ... </th>
```

Some browsers also accept the nowrap attribute with no attribute value; however this form is not supported in XHTML since XHTML requires values for all attributes.

Kevin is pleased with the width and height that the browser has chosen for the cells in the race results table, so you do not need to modify these attributes.

Spanning Rows and Columns

Kevin has reviewed your table and would like to make a few more changes. He feels that repeating the group information for each row in the table is redundant and wonders if you can merge several cells into a single cell. He draws a proposed layout for the table, which is displayed in Figure 4-37.

Figure 4-37 ▸ **Kevin's proposed table layout**

	Runner	Time	Origin
Men	1. Peter Teagan	2:12:34	San Antonio, Texas
	2. Kyle Wills	2:13:05	Billings, Montana
	3. Jason Wu	2:14:28	Cutler, Colorado
Women	1. Laura Blake	2:28:21	Park City, Colorado
	2. Kathy Lasker	2:30:11	Chicago, Illinois
	3. Lisa Peterson	2:31:14	Seattle, Washington

To merge several cells into one, you need to create a **spanning cell**, which is a cell that occupies more than one row or column in a table. Figure 4-38 shows a table of opinion poll data in which some of the cells span several rows and/or columns.

Figure 4-38 ▸ **Spanning cells**

this cell spans two columns and two rows

this cell spans three columns

this cell spans three rows

Today's Opinion Poll Question		Political Party		
		Democrat	Republican	Independent
"Do you favor or oppose increasing the minimum wage?"	Favor	70%	35%	55%
	Oppose	25%	60%	30%
	Unsure	5%	5%	15%

Spanning cells are created by inserting the rowspan attribute, the colspan attribute, or both attributes in a <td> or <th> tag. The syntax for these attributes is:

```
<td rowspan="value" colspan="value"> ... </td>
```

or

```
<th rowspan="value" colspan="value"> ... </th>
```

where *value* is the number of rows or columns that the cell spans in the table. The direction of the spanning is downward and to the right of the cell containing the rowspan and colspan attributes. For example, to create a cell that spans two columns in the table, you enter the <td> tag as

```
<td colspan="2"> ... </td>
```

For a cell that spans two rows, the tag is

```
<td rowspan="2"> ... </td>
```

and to span two rows and two columns at the same time, the tag is

```
<td rowspan="2" colspan="2"> ... </td>
```

It's important to remember that when a table includes a cell that spans multiple rows or columns, you must adjust the number of cell tags used in one or more table rows. For example, if a row contains five columns, but one of the cells in the row spans three columns, you only need three <td> tags within the row: two <td> tags for each of the cells that occupy a single column, and a third for the cell spanning three rows.

When a cell spans several rows, you need to adjust the number of cell tags in the rows below the spanning cell. Consider the table shown in Figure 4-39, which contains three rows and four columns. The first cell in the first row is a spanning cell that spans three rows. You need four <td> tags for the first row, but only three <td> tags for rows two and three. This is because the spanning cell from row one occupies the cells that would normally appear in those rows.

A row-spanning cell — **Figure 4-39**

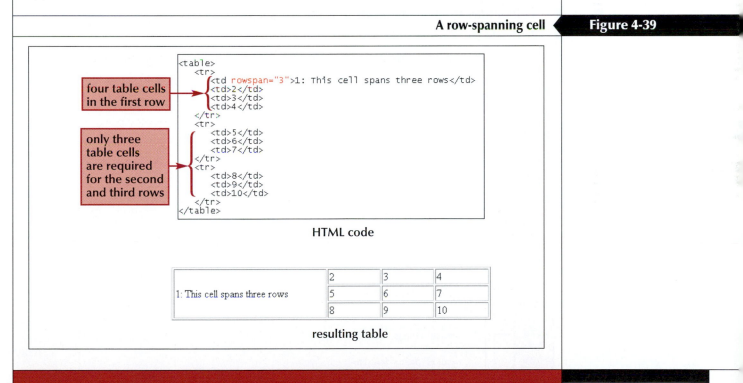

HTML code

resulting table

To make the changes that Kevin has requested, start by deleting the table heading for the Group column, and then spanning the Runner table heading across two columns.

To create a cell that spans two columns:

1. Return to **race2.htm** in your text editor.

2. Delete the Group table heading, including both the opening and closing <th> tags.

3. Insert the attribute **colspan="2"** within the opening <th> tag for the Runner table heading.

Next, you'll delete the second and third occurrences of the "Men" and "Women" cells in the table, keeping only the first occurrences. You'll also span those two cells over three rows of the table.

To span two cells over three rows:

1. Insert the attribute **rowspan="3"** in the first <td> tag that contains the text "Men".

2. Delete the next two <td> tags that contain the text "Men".

3. Insert the attribute **rowspan="3"** in the first <td> tag that contains the text "Women".

4. Delete the next two <td> tags that contain the text "Women". Figure 4-40 shows the revised table code.

Figure 4-40 | **Adding spanning cells to the race results table**

```
<table border="5" bordercolor="brown" bordercolorlight="tan" cellspacing="0"
      cellpadding="4" width="70%">
   <caption style="font-weight: bold">Race Results</caption>
   <thead>
   <tr>
      <th colspan="2">Runner</th>
      <th>Time</th>
      <th>Origin</th>
   </tr>
   </thead>
   <tbody>
   <tr>
      <td rowspan="3">Men</td>
      <td>1. Peter Teagan</td>
      <td>2:12:34</td>
      <td>San Antonio, Texas</td>
   </tr>
   <tr>
      <td>2. Kyle Wills</td>
      <td>2:13:05</td>
      <td>Billings, Montana</td>
   </tr>
   <tr>
      <td>3. Jason Wu</td>
      <td>2:14:28</td>
      <td>Cutler, Colorado</td>
   </tr>
   <tr>
      <td rowspan="3">Women</td>
      <td>1. Laura Blake</td>
      <td>2:28:21</td>
      <td>Park City, Colorado</td>
   </tr>
   <tr>
      <td>2. Kathy Lasker</td>
      <td>2:30:11</td>
      <td>Chicago, Illinois</td>
   </tr>
   <tr>
      <td>3. Lisa Peterson</td>
      <td>2:31:14</td>
      <td>Seattle, Washington</td>
   </tr>
   </tbody>
</table>
```

this cell spans two columns

these cells span three rows

5. Save your changes to **race2.htm** and reload it in your Web browser. Figure 4-41 shows the revised table.

Table with spanning cells   Figure 4-41

Race Results			
	Runner	Time	Origin
Men	1. Peter Teagan	2:12:34	San Antonio, Texas
	2. Kyle Wills	2:13:05	Billings, Montana
	3. Jason Wu	2:14:28	Cutler, Colorado
Women	1. Laura Blake	2:28:21	Park City, Colorado
	2. Kathy Lasker	2:30:11	Chicago, Illinois
	3. Lisa Peterson	2:31:14	Seattle, Washington

Formatting Table Contents

Kevin has a few final suggestions for the appearance of the table content. He would like the group names, Men and Women, aligned with the tops of their cells and he wants to see the race times right-aligned within the Time column. He would like the table text displayed in a sans-serif font on a colored background in order to stand out better on the page. Finally, he wants the table aligned with the page's right margin, with the article text flowing around it.

Aligning the Contents of a Cell

By default, cell text is placed in the middle of a cell, aligned with the cell's left edge. You can specify a different horizontal alignment for a td or th element using the attribute

```
align="position"
```

where *position* is either left (the default for a td element), center (the default for a th element), right, justify, or char. You may recall the align attribute from the first tutorial, when it was introduced as a deprecated attribute for aligning the text of headings and paragraphs. This align attribute is similar, except that it is not deprecated. However, you can use the text-align style here as well if you wish to use styles for all of your formatting tasks.

A value of "char" for the align attribute tells the browser to align the values in a cell based on the position of a particular character, such as a decimal point. This value is primarily used for columns containing currency data or other numeric values. The default character is assumed to be a decimal point, which is determined by the language of the browser. In English this would be a period ("."), while in French it would be a comma (","). You can specify a different character using the char attribute. Thus to align the value within a cell based on the position of the comma character, you would use the following attributes:

```
<td align="char" char=","> ... </td>
```

The char attribute value and char attributes are not currently well supported by browsers. To specify a different vertical alignment of cell content, use the attribute

```
valign="position"
```

where *position* is top, middle (the default), bottom, or baseline. Figure 4-42 shows how different combinations of the align and valign attributes can affect the position of cell content in relation to cell borders.

Figure 4-42 | **Values of the align and valign attributes**

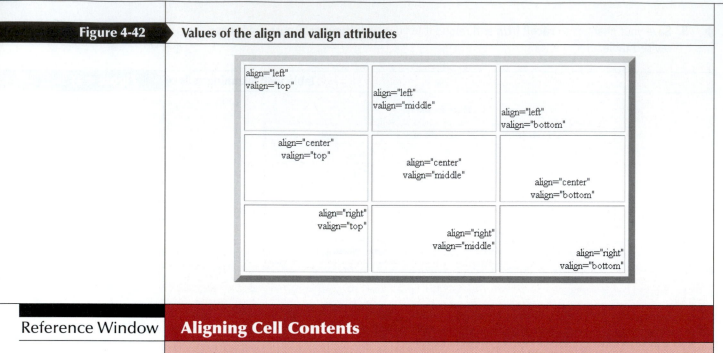

Reference Window | **Aligning Cell Contents**

- To horizontally align the contents of a cell, use the following attribute for a td or th element:
    `align="position"`
 where *position* is left (the default for the td element), center (the default for the th element), right, or char.
- To vertically align the contents of a cell, use the following attribute for a td or th element:
    `valign="position"`
 where *position* is top, middle (the default), bottom, or baseline.

Kevin wants you to right-align each time value in the race results table, and align the group names with the tops of their cells.

To align the time and group values:

1. Return to **race2.htm** in your text editor.

2. Insert the attribute **align="right"** within each <td> tag in the Time column.

3. Locate the <td> tag containing the Men group name and insert the attribute **valign="top"**.

4. Locate the <td> tag containing the Women group name and insert the attribute **valign="top"**. Figure 4-43 shows the revised HTML code for the table.

```
<table border="5" bordercolor="brown" bordercolorlight="tan" cellspacing="0"
       cellpadding="4" width="70%">
   <caption style="font-weight: bold">Race Results</caption>
   <thead>
   <tr>
      <th colspan="2">Runner</th>
      <th>Time</th>
      <th>Origin</th>
   </tr>
   </thead>
   <tbody>
   <tr>
      <td rowspan="3" valign="top">Men</td>
      <td>1. Peter Teagan</td>
      <td align="right">2:12:34</td>
      <td>San Antonio, Texas</td>
   </tr>
   <tr>
      <td>2. Kyle Wills</td>
      <td align="right">2:13:05</td>
      <td>Billings, Montana</td>
   </tr>
   <tr>
      <td>3. Jason Wu</td>
      <td align="right">2:14:28</td>
      <td>Cutler, Colorado</td>
   </tr>
   <tr>
      <td rowspan="3" valign="top">Women</td>
      <td>1. Laura Blake</td>
      <td align="right">2:28:21</td>
      <td>Park City, Colorado</td>
   </tr>
   <tr>
      <td>2. Kathy Lasker</td>
      <td align="right">2:30:11</td>
      <td>Chicago, Illinois</td>
   </tr>
   <tr>
      <td>3. Lisa Peterson</td>
      <td align="right">2:31:14</td>
      <td>Seattle, Washington</td>
   </tr>
   </tbody>
</table>
```

5. Save your changes to the file and reload it in your Web browser. Figure 4-44 shows the revised alignment of the table contents.

Formatting Table Text

You can apply the same text and font styles that were introduced in the last tutorial to table text. The styles cascade down through the table structure, from the table element, through the row groups and table rows, and down to individual cells. For example, if you want to change the font style of all of the text in a table, you can apply a style to the table element; to change the font style of the table body, apply the style to the tbody element.

Kevin suggests that you display all of the table text in a sans-serif font. He wants the default font size for the table text to be 1em, but he wants the body text to be 80% of that size. You'll make these changes by applying the font-family and font-size styles to the table and tbody elements.

To format the table text:

► 1. Return to **race2.htm** in your text editor.

► 2. Insert the attribute **style="font-family: Arial, Helvetica, sans-serif; font-size: 1em"** in the <table> tag (you may want to insert this attribute on a separate line to make your code easier to read).

► 3. Insert the attribute **style="font-size: 80%"** in the <tbody> tag. This sets the table body text to 80% of the font size of the rest of the table text. Figure 4-45 shows the revised HTML code.

Figure 4-45	Setting font styles in the table

```
<table border="5" bordercolor="brown" bordercolorlight="tan" cellspacing="0"
       cellpadding="4" width="70%"
       style="font-family: Arial, Helvetica, sans-serif; font-size: 1em">
<caption style="font-weight: bold">Race Results</caption>
<thead>
<tr>
    <th colspan="2">Runner</th>
    <th>Time</th>
    <th>Origin</th>
</tr>
</thead>
<tbody style="font-size: 80%">
<tr>
    <td rowspan="3" valign="top">Men</td>
    <td>1. Peter Teagan</td>
    <td align="right">2:12:34</td>
    <td>San Antonio, Texas</td>
</tr>
```

► 4. Save your changes to the file and reload it in your Web browser. Figure 4-46 shows the revised table text format.

Figure 4-46	Revised font styles in the race results table

If you need to support older browsers that don't recognize styles, you must enclose the content of each cell within a <font> tag in order to format the cell text.

Setting the Background Color

Table elements support the same background-color style that you used in the last tutorial. As with font styles, color styles cascade down through the table structure from the table itself down to individual cells. Kevin would like the header row to be displayed with a yellow background, the group names with backgrounds of light blue and light green, and the rest of the table with a white background.

To set the background color:

1. Return to **race2.htm** in your text editor.

2. Add the style **background-color: white** to the inline style of the table element (be sure to insert a semicolon to separate this style from the other style declarations).

3. Insert the attribute **style="background-color: yellow"** in the <tr> tag for the heading row.

4. Insert the attribute **style="background-color: lightblue"** in the <td> tag for the cell containing the Men group name.

5. Insert the attribute **style="background-color: lightgreen"** in the <td> tag for the cell containing the Women group name. Figure 4-47 shows the revised HTML code.

Setting background colors in the table ◄ **Figure 4-47**

```
<table border="5" bordercolor="brown" bordercolorlight="tan" cellspacing="0"
    cellpadding="4" width="70%"
    style="font-family: Arial, Helvetica, sans-serif; font-size: 1em;
    background-color: white">
<caption style="font-weight: bold">Race Results</caption>
<thead>
<tr style="background-color: yellow">
    <th colspan="2">Runner</th>
    <th>Time</th>
    <th>Origin</th>
</tr>
</thead>
<tbody style="font-size: 80%">
<tr>
    <td rowspan="3" valign="top" style="background-color: lightblue">Men</td>
    <td>1. Peter Teagan</td>
    <td align="right">2:12:34</td>
    <td>San Antonio, Texas</td>
</tr>
<tr>
    <td>2. Kyle Wills</td>
    <td align="right">2:13:05</td>
    <td>Billings, Montana</td>
</tr>
<tr>
    <td>3. Jason Wu</td>
    <td align="right">2:14:28</td>
    <td>Cutler, Colorado</td>
</tr>
<tr>
    <td rowspan="3" valign="top" style="background-color: lightgreen">Women</td>
    <td>1. Laura Blake</td>
    <td align="right">2:28:21</td>
    <td>Park City, Colorado</td>
</tr>
```

6. Save your changes to the file and reload it in your Web browser. Figure 4-48 shows the new color scheme for the race results table.

Revised color scheme in the race results table ◄ **Figure 4-48**

Race Results			
	Runner	Time	Origin
Men	1. Peter Teagan	2:12:34	San Antonio, Texas
	2. Kyle Wills	2:13:05	Billings, Montana
	3. Jason Wu	2:14:28	Cutler, Colorado
Women	1. Laura Blake	2:28:21	Park City, Colorado
	2. Kathy Lasker	2:30:11	Chicago, Illinois
	3. Lisa Peterson	2:31:14	Seattle, Washington

For older browsers that don't recognize styles, you can use the deprecated bgcolor attribute. The syntax of this attribute is

```
bgcolor="color"
```

where *color* is either a recognized color name or a hexadecimal color value. The bgcolor attribute can be applied to <table>, <tr>, <th>, and <td> tags.

Setting the Background Image

Though not needed for the race results table, you can add a background image to a table using the same background-image style you learned about in the last tutorial. A background can be applied to the entire table, to a row group, a row, or an individual cell. For older browsers that don't recognize styles, you can use the deprecated background attribute, which uses the syntax

```
background="url"
```

where *url* is the name and location of the graphic image file. This attribute can be added to the <table>, <tr>, <th>, and <td> tags.

Reference Window

Formatting the Table Background

- To change the background color of any table element, apply the following style:
  ```
  background-color: color
  ```
  where *color* is a color name or color value.
- To change the background image of any table element, apply the following style:
  ```
  background-image: url(url)
  ```
  where *url* is the URL of the graphic image file.

Deprecated

- To change the background color of any table element, add the following attribute to the tag:
  ```
  bgcolor="color"
  ```
  where *color* is either a color name or a hexadecimal color value. This attribute can be applied to <table>, <tr>, <th>, and <td> tags.
- To change the background image of any table element, add the following attribute to the tag:
  ```
  background="file"
  ```
  where *file* is the filename of the graphic image file. This attribute can be added to <table>, <tr>, <th>, and <td> tags.

Aligning a Table on a Web Page

Kevin's final task for you is to align the table with the right margin of the page, with the rest of the article text wrapping around the table. You can align the entire table using the same style used to float an inline image on a page. To float the table, you would use the following style for the table element:

```
float: position
```

where *position* is either left or right. As with inline images, you can use the margin style to set the margin space around the floating table. Kevin would like a 5pixel space on the top, left, and bottom of the table and a 0 pixel margin on the table's right margin.

To float the race results table:

1. Return to **race2.htm** in your text editor.

2. Add the styles **float: right; margin: 5 0 5 5** to the table element (be sure to separate these styles from the other declarations with a semicolon). Figure 4-49 shows the revised HTML code.

Floating the race results table ◀ **Figure 4-49**

```
<table border="5" bordercolor="brown" bordercolorlight="tan" cellspacing="0"
      cellpadding="4" width="70%"
      style="font-family: Arial, Helvetica, sans-serif; font-size: 1em;
            background-color: white; float: right; margin: 5 0 5 5">
  <caption style="font-weight: bold">Race Results</caption>
  <thead>
  <tr style="background-color: yellow">
    <th colspan="2">Runner</th>
    <th>Time</th>
    <th>Origin</th>
  </tr>
  </thead>
```

3. Save your changes to the file, then close it.

4. Reopen **race2.htm** in your Web browser. Figure 4-50 shows the final appearance of the page.

Final race2 page ◀ **Figure 4-50**

Local Woman Wins Marathon

Park City native, **Laura Blake**, won the 27th Front Range Marathon over an elite field of the best long distance runners in the country. Laura's time of 2 hr. 28 min. 21 sec. was only 2 minutes off the women's course record set last year by Sarah Rawlings. Kathy Lasker and Lisa Peterson finished second and third, respectively. Laura's victory came on the heels of her performance at the NCAA Track and Field Championships, in which she placed second running for Colorado State.

In an exciting race, **Peter Teagan** of San Antonio, Texas, used a finishing kick to win the men's marathon for the second straight year, in a time of 2 hr. 12 min. 34 sec. Ahead for much of the race, Kyle Wills of Billings, Montana, finished second, when he could not match Teagan's finishing pace. Jason Wu of Cutler, Colorado, placed third in a very competitive field.

This year's race through downtown Boulder boasted the largest field in the marathon's history, with over 9500 men and 6700 women competing. Race conditions were perfect with low humidity and temperatures that never exceeded 85°.

Race Results

Runner		Time	Origin
Men	1. Peter Teagan	2:12:34	San Antonio, Texas
	2. Kyle Wills	2:13:05	Billings, Montana
	3. Jason Wu	2:14:28	Cutler, Colorado
Women	1. Laura Blake	2:28:21	Park City, Colorado
	2. Kathy Lasker	2:30:11	Chicago, Illinois
	3. Lisa Peterson	2:31:14	Seattle, Washington

If you need to support older browsers that do not recognize styles, you can use the deprecated align attribute

```
align="position"
```

where *position* equals "left" (the default), "right", or "center". As with the float style, using left or right alignment places the table on the margin of the Web page and wraps surrounding text to the side. Center alignment places the table in the horizontal center of the page, but does not allow text to wrap around it.

Floating a Table

- To float the entire table, apply the following style to the table element:
  ```
  float: position
  ```
  where *position* is none (the default), left, or right.

Deprecated

- To align the table on the margins of the containing element, add the following attribute to the <table> tag:
  ```
  align="position"
  ```
  where *position* equals "left" (the default), "right", or "center".

Working with Column Groups

In this session, you've formatted the content of the table columns by modifying the attributes of individual cells within a column. You can also organize the columns into **column groups** and format one or more entire columns with a single style declaration or attribute. To define a column group, insert the following element into the table structure:

```
<colgroup span="value" />
```

where *value* is the number of columns in the group. The colgroup element should be placed directly after the opening <table> tag. However, for a table that includes a caption, it should be placed directly after the <caption> tag. For example, a table with five columns could be organized into two groups: one group for the first three columns and a second group for the last two:

```
<colgroup span="3" />
<colgroup span="2" />
```

If you want to display the first three columns with a white background and the last two columns with a yellow background, the HTML code would be:

```
<colgroup span="4" style="background-color: white" />
<colgroup span="2" style="background-color: yellow" />
```

The colgroup element can also be expressed as a two-sided element, using the syntax:

```
<colgroup>
    columns
</colgroup>
```

where *columns* are elements that define the properties for individual columns within the group. To define a single column within the group, use the one-sided col element. The col element is useful when individual columns within a group need to have slightly different formats. For example, if you want to define a different text color for each column, you might use the following HTML code:

```
<colgroup span="3" style="background-color: white">
    <col style="color: black" />
    <col style="color: red" />
    <col style="color: blue" />
</colgroup>
```

In this case, each column in the group has a white background; however the first column has a black font, the second column has a red font, and the third column has a blue font. The col element can also be used along with the span attribute to format several columns within a group, as in the following example:

```
<colgroup span="5" style="background-color: white">
     <col style="color: black" span="2" />
     <col style="color: red" />
     <col style="color: blue" span="2" />
</colgroup>
```

In this case the column group consists of five columns: the first two columns contain black text on a white background, the middle column contains red text on a white background, and the last two columns contain blue text on a white background.

Currently, browser support for the colgroup and col elements is uneven. Thus, you may still have to format individual cells within a column if you want your table to be supported across all browsers.

You've completed your work on the race results table and the story that Kevin wanted you to work on. In the next session, you'll use tables to create a layout for this story and other features of the *Park City Gazette*.

Session 4.2 Quick Check

Review

1. What attributes would you use to create a table with a 5-pixel-wide outside border, a 3-pixel-wide space between table cells, and 4 pixels of padding between the cell content and the cell border?
2. What attributes would you use to vertically align a cell's contents with the top of the cell?
3. What attribute would you add to center the contents of a table cell?
4. What HTML code would you use to size a table to half the width of the browser window area, regardless of the resolution of a user's monitor?
5. Under what conditions will a table cell exceed the size specified by the width attribute?
6. What attribute creates a cell that spans three rows and two columns?
7. What HTML code would you enter to create a column group spanning three columns that sets the background color of the columns to yellow?

Session 4.3

Using Tables for Layout

The table element was originally introduced simply to display tabular data, such as the race results table. However, table cells can contain any page element including inline images, headings, paragraphs, lists, and other tables. It became immediately obvious to Web designers that tables could also be used for page layout by enclosing the entire contents of a page within a collection of table cells and nested tables. Let's examine some of the classic layouts that can be achieved through the use of tables.

Layout Designs

One of the most basic layouts, which is shown in Figure 4-51, consists of placing the entire contents of the page within a table that is centered on the page. By specifying different backgrounds for the page and the table, this layout gives the effect of a printed page displayed against a colored background.

Figure 4-51 | **Pseudo page**

In another popular layout, the **columnar layout**, the page content is placed in columns. Figure 4-52 shows a layout consisting of two columns. The page heading is placed in a separate table cell, spanning the two columns. This type of layout is popularly used to create a vertical column of links on the left margin of the page, while another column contains the main text of the page. Note that the text does not flow from one column to another as it would in a desktop publishing program. Instead, you have to specify the text for each column. If you want the lengths of the text in the columns to match, you have to work with the column widths or the amount of text in each column. The layout in Figure 4-52 achieves an approximate balance between the two columns by making the first column slightly narrower than the second. Also, for a columnar layout you have to vertically align the text in each column with the top of the table cell.

Figure 4-52 | **Two column layout**

In a **sectional layout**, such as the one shown in Figure 4-53, you break the page content into sections, placing each section in its own table cell. You can label the sections in an accompanying table cell. Notice that in this example, the section names in the first column are right-aligned in order to better line up with the content in the second column.

Sectional layout | **Figure 4-53**

table grid

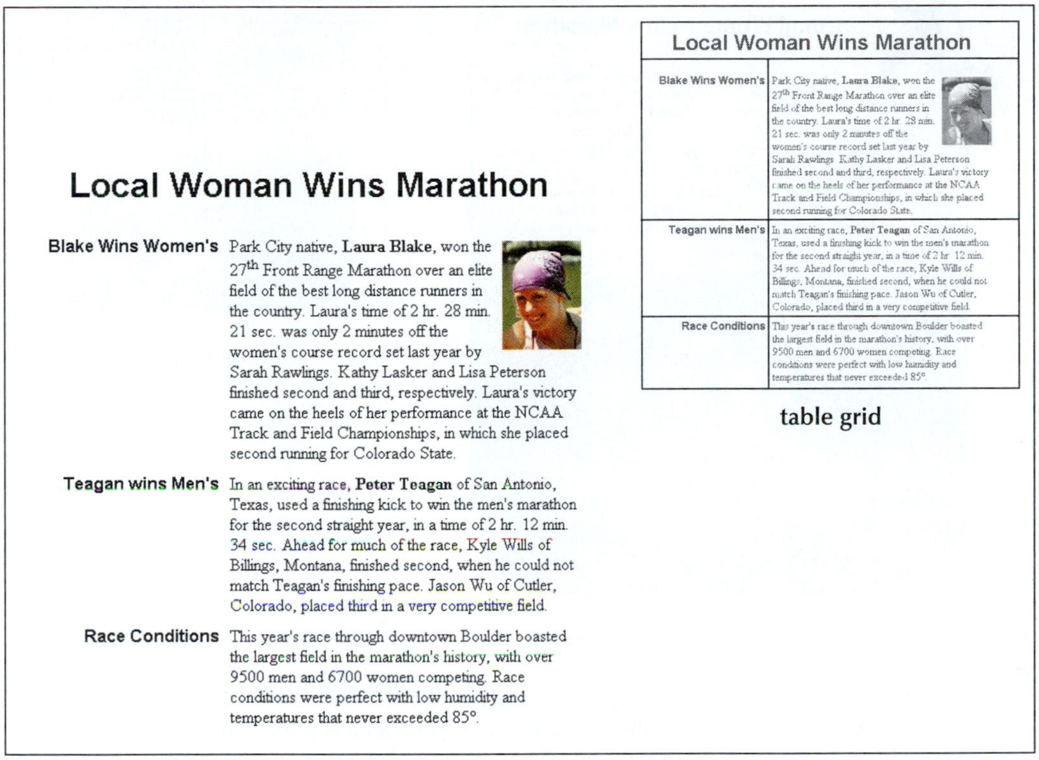

By breaking up page content into separate pieces, you can create almost any type of layout. This technique is sometimes referred to as a **jigsaw table** or **jigsaw layout**, because the page is broken up into a number of pieces that are meticulously assembled to create the layout. Figure 4-54 shows an example of a jigsaw layout in which layout is broken into fourteen table cells, including an image file that has been sliced into nine distinct pieces. Page content can be placed within those cells and the pieces can be reassembled into the complete table. After removing the borders, it appears that the page content flows naturally alongside and within the graphic images or other features of the page.

Figure 4-54 ▶ **Jigsaw layout**

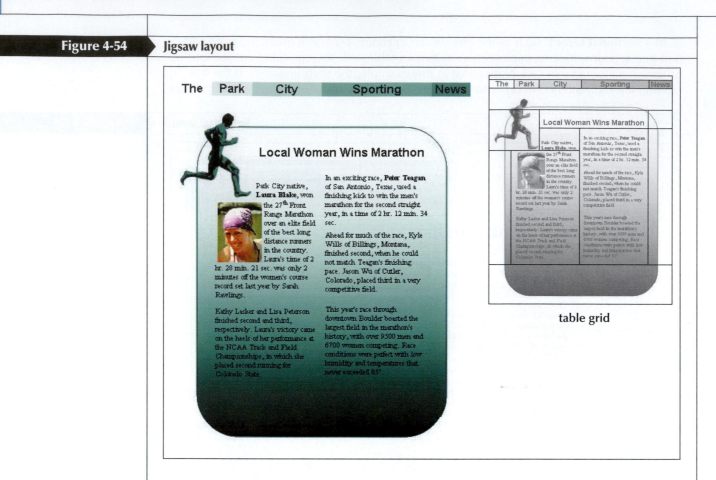

table grid

To create a jigsaw layout containing an image, you first have to cut your background image into the appropriately sized slices, saving each slice as a separate image file. Several graphics packages are available that will perform this task automatically for you. Each slice can act as either a background image in a table cell (if you intend to display text in front of the image) or as the complete cell content. To ensure that the table cells are the correct size, you should define the width and height of each cell (usually in pixels) and set the border, cellspacing, and cellpadding values to 0 pixels. You must also ensure that the cell content fits within the specified dimensions; if the content is too large, browsers increase the cell size, potentially ruining the layout. Empty cells can be another source of trouble. Some browsers reduce the size of an empty cell, even if you've specified the cell's width and height. To avoid this, all cells should have some content—either an inline image sized to match the cell's dimensions, or a nonbreaking space (which you create with the   character entity). Because jigsaw layouts often need to be precisely measured and browsers can differ in how they render tables, you should definitely test such a layout on a variety of browsers.

Fixed-width and Fluid Layouts

Table layouts generally fall into two classes: fixed-width and fluid. In a **fixed-width layout**, the Web designer defines the exact size of every table element in absolute units such as pixels. This layout has the advantage of giving the Web designer precise control over the appearance of the page. One drawback to a fixed-width layout is that it does not take into account the size of the browser window. This can result in unused blank areas for users whose browser windows are wider than the defined table width. Figure 4-55 shows a layout that has been sized for a width of 610 pixels. As the size of the browser window increases, the table width remains the same size, resulting in larger areas of unused space. This problem can be allevi-ated somewhat either by centering the table to cut the blank areas into two sections, or by providing background images or effects that make the unused areas more interesting.

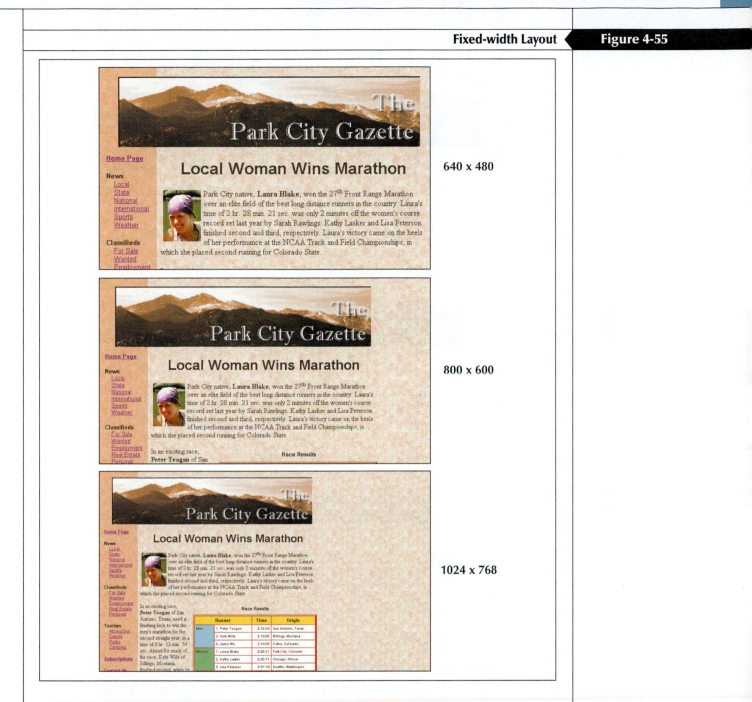

640 x 480

800 x 600

1024 x 768

Determining the correct width is another problem with fixed-width layouts. Although larger screens are being constantly introduced, screen resolutions usually vary from 640 × 480 pixels up to 1600 × 1200, with 800 × 600 being perhaps the most common. However, if you choose a width of 770 pixels for your page, users with smaller monitors may need to scroll horizontally as well as vertically through your page, which can be a source of irritation for those users.

In a **fluid layout**, one or more of the table elements is sized as a percentage of the page width. This enables the page content to flow into those blank areas as the size of the browser window increases (see Figure 4-56). One drawback of a fluid layout is that it can result in long lines of text, which can be difficult to view since the reader needs to use the muscles of the eye or neck to track from the end of one line to the beginning of the next. Fluid layouts can also be difficult to design. A layout that looks fine at a smaller resolution may not look as good as the content flows into a larger browser window.

Figure 4-56 | **Fluid Layout**

Many page layouts contain combinations of fluid and fixed-width elements. For example, a column of links placed on the left margin of the page can be fixed, while the content of the page can be fluid. As with all layouts, the best approach is to examine your page under a variety of conditions, incorporating several browsers and window sizes to verify that the page always conveys a positive impression.

Challenges of Table Layouts

Not all Web designers support using tables for layout. Many now prefer to use styles to perform various layout tasks previously reserved for tables, arguing that tables should be reserved for strictly tabular information (such as the data in the race results table). Some of the challenges often associated with tables include:

- **Tables can slow down page rendering.** Unless the size of every element in the table is specified, the browser needs to first load the table content, then run an algorithm to determine how to size each element of the table. This can be time consuming for a large, complex table that involves several cells and nested elements.
- **Tables can be inflexible.** If you try to speed up page rendering by specifying the size of each table element, you're essentially creating a fixed-width layout, which may not be the best way to display your page for all users.
- **Tables can be code-heavy.** To create a visually striking table layout may require several table cells, rows, and columns, and some nested tables. This is particularly true if you create a jigsaw layout. Thus, the ratio of HTML code to actual page content becomes more heavily weighted toward the HTML code, resulting in a longer file that takes longer to load and can be difficult to interpret for people who need to edit the underlying code.
- **Tables can be inaccessible.** People with disabilities who access a table layout with an aural or Braille browser can experience difficulty with tables. The problem is that screen readers and speech output browsers read the HTML source code line-by-line in a linear direction, but a table can sometimes convey information in a non-linear direction. Figure 4-57 shows how a table whose content is quite clear visually could become jumbled when presented aurally. While this example shows the problems associated with a simple 2 × 2 table, a truly complex table layout could present even more severe difficulties.

Aural browsers and tables ◄ **Figure 4-57**

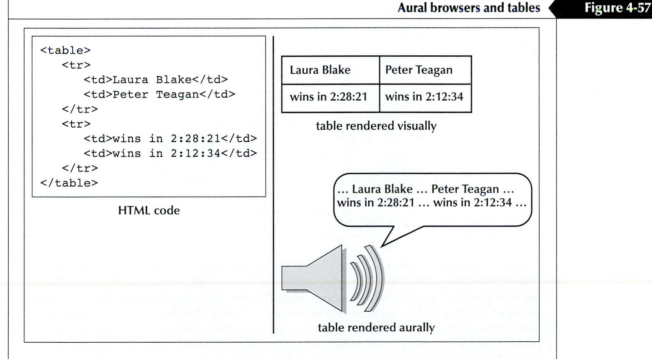

```
<table>
    <tr>
        <td>Laura Blake</td>
        <td>Peter Teagan</td>
    </tr>
    <tr>
        <td>wins in 2:28:21</td>
        <td>wins in 2:12:34</td>
    </tr>
</table>
```

HTML code

Laura Blake	Peter Teagan
wins in 2:28:21	wins in 2:12:34

table rendered visually

... Laura Blake ... Peter Teagan ... wins in 2:28:21 ... wins in 2:12:34 ...

table rendered aurally

Despite these challenges, most Web page layout is still done using tables. In the future, many of the layout tasks currently done with tables will be done using styles (and we'll explore how that is done in a later tutorial). For now, however, the layout techniques that are best suited to the widest variety of browsers and operating environments involve tables.

Creating a Newspaper-Style Layout

Kevin is satisfied with your work on the results of the Front Range Marathon. He now wants you to use that article as part of a newspaper-style Web page for the entire *Gazette*. The Web page will contain the *Gazette* logo, a list of links to other pages, and a few articles, one of which is the race results article you've been working on. Figure 4-58 displays the page layout that Kevin has in mind.

Figure 4-58 **Design sketch for the *Gazette* home page**

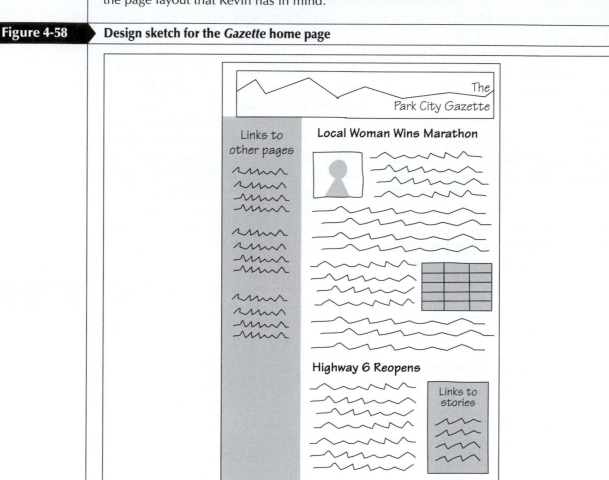

One way to lay out the page specified in Kevin's sketch is to create two tables, one nested inside the other. The outer table, shown in Figure 4-59, consists of four cells that are contained in two columns and three rows. The first cell, containing the *Gazette* logo, occupies the first row of the table and spans two columns. The second cell, displaying the list of links, occupies one column and spans the remaining two rows. The articles and newspaper address are placed in the remaining two cells, each occupying a single row and column.

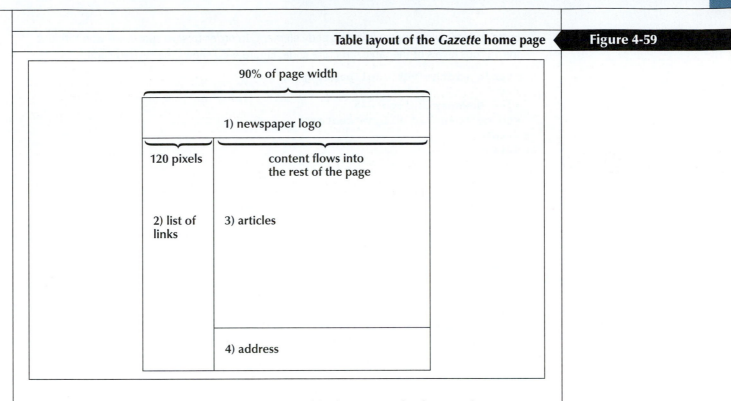

You'll use a combination of fluid and fixed-width elements in this layout. The entire layout will occupy 90% of the width of the browser window. Kevin has chosen this value in order to reduce the amount of unused space for large monitors, without making the lines too long to read comfortably. The first column, containing the list of links, will be set to 120 pixels wide, and the second column, containing the articles and the paper's address, will flow into the rest of the page.

Creating the Outer Table

Kevin has created the initial part of the file for the front page, setting the page background and text color. Your first job is to create the table structure displayed in Figure 4-59. As you add more text to this file, it will become long and unwieldy. To make it easier to navigate the code, you'll insert comments describing the different sections.

To create the outer table and comments:

► **1.** Use your text editor to open **page1txt.htm** located in the tutorial.04/tutorial folder. Insert *your name* and *the date* in the comment section at the top of the file. Save the file as **page1.htm**.

2. Enter the following code within the body element. In order to save space, we won't indent the various levels of the table structure code. Figure 4-60 shows the revised code.

```
<table width="90%" cellpadding="5">
<tr>
<!-- Newspaper logo -->
<td colspan="2" align="center">
</td>
</tr>

<tr>
<!-- List of links -->
<td width="120" rowspan="2" valign="top">
</td>
<!-- Articles -->
<td valign="top">
</td>
</tr>

<tr>
<!-- Address -->
<td valign="top" align="center">
</td>
</tr>
</table>
```

Figure 4-60	Inserting the table structure for page1.htm

```
<body style="color: rgb(82,64,32); background: white url(parch2.jpg) repeat-y">
<table width="90%" cellpadding="5">
<tr>
<!-- Newspaper logo -->
<td colspan="2" align="center">
</td>
</tr>

<tr>
<!-- List of links -->
<td width="120" rowspan="2" valign="top">
</td>
<!-- Articles -->
<td valign="top">
</td>
</tr>

<tr>
<!-- Address -->
<td valign="top" align="center">
</td>
</tr>
</table>
</body>
```

Note that in three of the cells of this outer table, you've set the vertical alignment to top, rather than using the default value of middle. This is because the cells in this table act as a framework for newspaper columns. The tables in this layout don't display any borders.

Now you place the *Gazette* logo, pcglogo.jpg, in the Web page.

To insert the logo in a table cell:

▶ **1.** Within the first table cell insert the following img element:

```
<img src="pcglogo.jpg" alt="The Park City Gazette" width="600"
height="140" />
```

▶ **2.** Save your changes to **page1.htm** and open the file in your Web browser. Your page should appear as shown in Figure 4-61.

Initial view of Page1 ◀ **Figure 4-61**

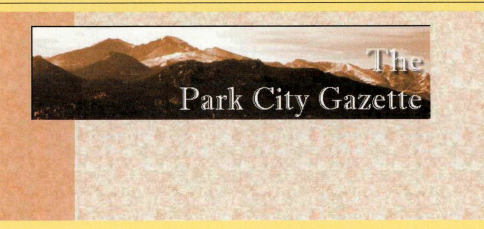

Next, you'll add the list of links to the second table cell. The contents of this cell have been created for you and stored in a file named links.htm. You'll copy the information from that document and paste it into the table cell. If you don't know how to copy and paste with your text editor, ask your instructor or technical support person for assistance.

To insert the contents of the links.htm file:

▶ **1.** Using your text editor, open **links.htm** from the tutorial.04/tutorial folder.

▶ **2.** Copy the HTML code within the <body> tags of links.htm, but do not include the opening and closing <body> tags.

▶ **3.** Close the file and return to **page1.htm** in your text editor.

▶ **4.** Paste the HTML code you copied from links.htm with the table cell for the list of links as shown in Figure 4-62.

Figure 4-62 **Inserting the list of links**

```
<!-- List of links -->
<td width="120" rowspan="2" valign="top">
  <h5 style="font-family: sans-serif"><a href="#">Home Page</a></h5>
  <h5 style="margin-bottom: 0; font-family: sans-serif">News</h5>
    <p style="margin: 0 0 0 15; font-size: 0.8em">
    <a href="#">Local</a><br />
    <a href="#">State</a><br />
    <a href="#">National</a><br />
    <a href="#">International</a><br />
    <a href="#">Sports</a><br />
    <a href="#">Weather</a>
    </p>
  <h5 style="margin-bottom: 0; font-family: sans-serif">Classifieds</h5>
    <p style="margin: 0 0 0 15; font-size: 0.8em">
    <a href="#">For Sale</a><br />
    <a href="#">Wanted</a><br />
    <a href="#">Employment</a><br />
    <a href="#">Real Estate</a><br />
    <a href="#">Personal</a>
    </p>
  <h5 style="margin-bottom: 0; font-family: sans-serif">Tourism</h5>
    <p style="margin: 0 0 0 15; font-size: 0.8em">
    <a href="#">Attractions</a><br />
    <a href="#">Events</a><br />
    <a href="#">Parks</a><br />
    <a href="#">Camping</a>
    </p>
  <h5 style="font-family: sans-serif"><a href="#">Subscriptions</a></h5>
  <h5 style="font-family: sans-serif"><a href="#">Contact Us</a></h5>
</td>
```

insert
list of
links
here

5. Save your changes to the file and reload **page1.htm** in your Web browser. Figure 4-63 shows the current state of the home page of the *Park City Gazette*.

Figure 4-63 **Page1 with link list**

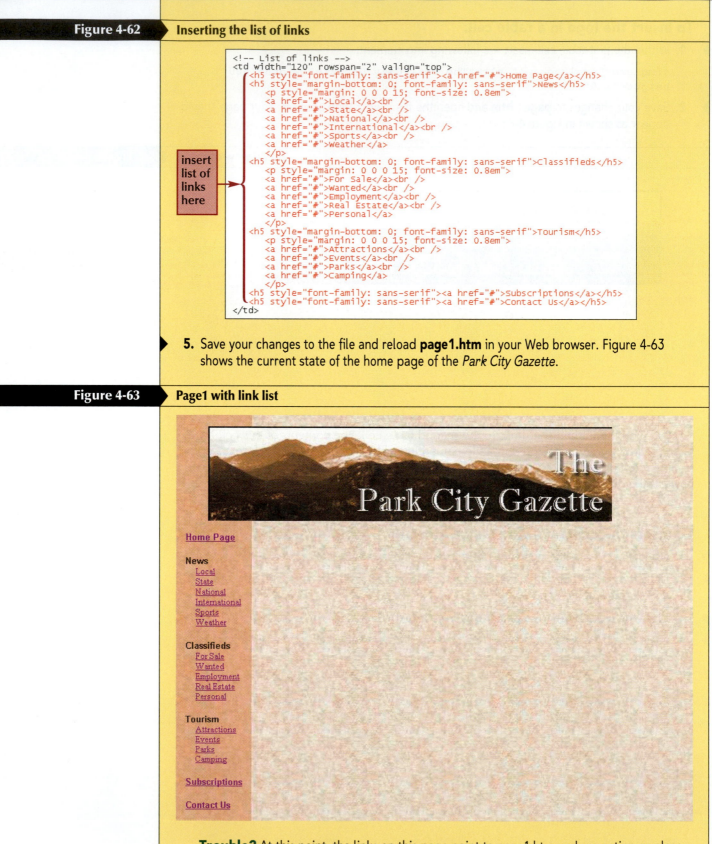

Trouble? At this point, the links on this page point to page1.htm and are acting as place-holders. Kevin will add the actual links as more work is done on the *Gazette*'s Web site.

The next part of the outer table that you'll add is the newspaper address and phone number, which will be located at the bottom of the page. The content for this cell has been created for you and saved in the file address.htm.

To insert the contents of address.htm into a table:

1. Using your text editor, open **address.htm** from the tutorial.04/tutorial folder.

2. Copy the HTML code within the <body> tags of address.htm, not including the opening and closing <body> tags.

3. Close the file and return to page1.htm in your text editor.

4. Paste the HTML code you copied from address.htm directly within the fourth table cell as shown in Figure 4-64.

Inserting the address　　**Figure 4-64**

insert address here

```
<!-- Address -->
<td valign="top" align="center">
   <hr style="color: tan; background-color: tan; width: 90%" />
   <address style="font-style: normal; font-size: 0.7em; font-family: sans-serif">
      Park City Gazette &#183;
      801 Elkhart Avenue &#183;
      Park City, CO  80511 &#183;
      1 (800) 555-2918
   </address>
</td>
```

5. Save your changes to **page1.htm**.

At this point, you've populated all of the table cells with information except for the articles cell. The articles cell is the only cell with content that changes on a weekly basis. When Kevin wants to update this Web page, he only needs to edit the contents of a single cell.

Creating a Nested Table

Kevin has decided on the stories he wants you to use for the current front-page articles. The main story is the results of the marathon, and another story concerns the reopening of Highway 6 (one of Park City's main roads over the Continental Divide). He also wants the Web page to include a sidebar with links to some of the other current important stories and features. Figure 4-65 shows a layout that Kevin has sketched to assist you with the design of the Web page.

Figure 4-65 | **Design sketch for the articles section**

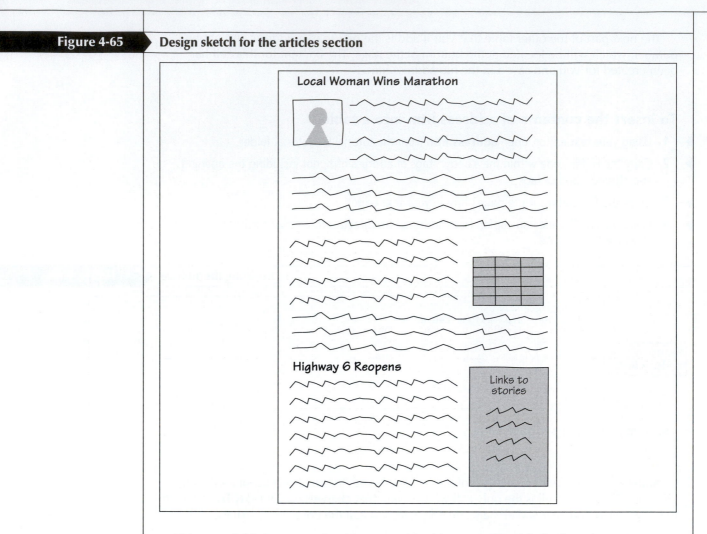

This material is best organized in a second table, an outline of which is shown in Figure 4-66. The first cell contains the marathon story and spans two columns. The second cell, 60% of the width of the table, contains the Highway 6 story. The third cell contains a list of links to other stories and occupies the remaining 40% of the table's width. For this third cell, you'll use the parch3.jpg graphic for a background image.

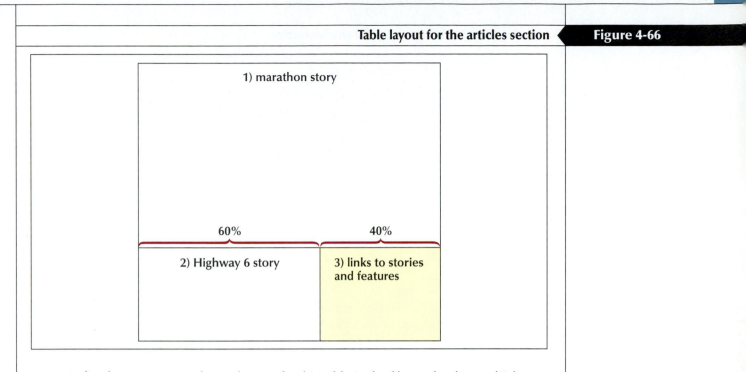

Kevin has begun creating the Web page for this table in the file artcltxt.htm, which you'll open now.

To create the outer table and comments:

1. Using your text editor, open **artcltxt.htm** located in the tutorial.04/tutorial folder. Enter **your name** and **the date** into the comment section of the file. Save the file as **articles.htm**.

2. Insert the following table structure within the body element:

```
<table cellpadding="5" cellspacing="5">
<tr>
   <!-- Marathon story -->
   <td colspan="2" valign="top">
   </td>
</tr>

<tr>
   <!-- Highway story -->
   <td width="60%" valign="top">
   </td>

   <!-- Features -->
   <td width="40%" valign="top"
   style="background-image: url(parch3.jpg)">
   </td>
</tr>
</table>
```

Figure 4-67 displays the revised HTML code.

Figure 4-67 | **Inserting the table structure for the articles section**

```
<body>
<table cellpadding="5" cellspacing="5">
<tr>
   <!-- Marathon story -->
   <td colspan="2" valign="top">
   </td>
</tr>

<tr>
   <!-- Highway story -->
   <td width="60%" valign="top">
   </td>

   <!-- Features -->
   <td width="40%" valign="top" style="background-image: url(parch3.jpg)">
   </td>
</tr>
</table>
</body>
```

▶ **3.** Save your changes to the file.

The next step is to copy the code for the marathon article that you created in race2.htm and paste it in the first cell of the table. You will also have to edit some of the contents of this material to fit the size of the cell.

To insert the contents of race2.htm into the first cell:

▶ **1.** Using your text editor, open **race2.htm** from the tutorial.04/tutorial folder.

▶ **2.** Copy the HTML code within the <body> tags of race2.htm, but do not include the <body> tags themselves.

▶ **3.** Close the file and return to **articles.htm** in your text editor.

▶ **4.** Paste the HTML code you copied from race2.htm within the first table cell.

One problem with the race results table is that when we're finished with the front page, it will be placed within a smaller area than it originally occupied in the race2.htm file. To make the text in the race results table look better, we'll reduce the font size of the text in that table.

▶ **5.** Locate the inline style for the race results table and change the value of the font-size style from 1em to **0.8em**. Figure 4-68 shows part of the revised code for the articles.htm file.

Inserting the contents of race2.htm ◄ **Figure 4-68**

paste the contents
copied from race2.htm here

```
<body>
<table cellpadding="5" cellspacing="5">
<tr>
   <!-- Marathon story -->
   <td colspan="2" valign="top">
<h1 style="text-align: center; font-family: Arial, Helvetica, sans-serif">
  Local Woman Wins Marathon
</h1>

<p><img src="blake.jpg" alt="" width="75" height="101" style="margin: 5; float: left" />
Park City native, <b>Laura Blake</b>, won the 27<sup>th</sup> Front Range Marathon
over an elite field of the best long distance runners in the country. Laura's
time of 2 hr. 28 min. 21 sec. was only 2 minutes off the women's course record
set last year by Sarah Rawlings. Kathy Lasker and Lisa Peterson finished second
and third, respectively. Laura's victory came on the heels of her performance at
the NCAA Track and Field Championships, in which she placed second running for
Colorado State.</p>

<table border="5" bordercolor="brown" bordercolorlight="tan" cellspacing="0"
      cellpadding="4" width="70%"
      style="font-family: Arial, Helvetica, sans-serif; font-size: 0.8em;
           background-color: white; float: right; margin: 5 0 5 5">
```

change the font-size
value from 1em to 0.8em

6. Save your changes to the file.

Next, you need to insert the article about the reopening of Highway 6 in the second table cell. The text for this file has been created for you and stored in the highway.htm file.

To insert the contents of highway.htm in the second table cell:

1. Open **highway.htm** from the tutorial.04/tutorial folder in your text editor.

2. Copy the HTML code contained between the <body> tags of highway.htm.

3. Close the file and open **articles.htm** with your text editor if it is not currently open.

4. Paste the copied HTML code into articles.htm within the second table cell as shown in Figure 4-69.

Inserting the contents of highway.htm ◄ **Figure 4-69**

```
   <!-- Highway story -->
   <td width="60%" valign="top">
<h3 style="text-align: center; font-family: sans-serif">Highway 6 Reopens</h3>

<p>Highway 6 will reopen this Friday, May 3<sup>rd</sup>, after a final safety
inspection. A late blizzard delayed road crews, marking this as one of the
latest dates for the highway's reopening on record.</p>

<p>Rising to an elevation of 12,351 feet at Grace Pass, Highway 6 is a main link
between Park City and Lake Elton. The reopening of the road is one of the annual signs
that summer is near and the tourist season will soon be upon us!</p>
</td>

   <!-- Features -->
   <td width="40%" valign="top" style="background-image: url(parch3.jpg)">
</td>
```

5. Save your changes to **articles.htm** and open it in your Web browser (see Figure 4-70).

Figure 4-70 | Articles page with the highway story

Local Woman Wins Marathon

Park City native, **Laura Blake**, won the 27th Front Range Marathon over an elite field of the best long distance runners in the country. Laura's time of 2 hr. 28 min. 21 sec. was only 2 minutes off the women's course record set last year by Sarah Rawlings. Kathy Lasker and Lisa Peterson finished second and third, respectively. Laura's victory came on the heels of her performance at the NCAA Track and Field Championships, in which she placed second running for Colorado State.

In an exciting race, **Peter Teagan** of San Antonio, Texas, used a finishing kick to win the men's marathon for the second straight year, in a time of 2 hr. 12 min. 34 sec. Ahead for much of the race, Kyle Wills of Billings, Montana, finished second, when he could not match Teagan's finishing pace. Jason Wu of Cutler, Colorado, placed third in a very competitive field.

Race Results

	Runner	Time	Origin
Men	1. Peter Teagan	2:12:34	San Antonio, Texas
	2. Kyle Wills	2:13:05	Billings, Montana
	3. Jason Wu	2:14:28	Cutler, Colorado
Women	1. Laura Blake	2:28:21	Park City, Colorado
	2. Kathy Lasker	2:30:11	Chicago, Illinois
	3. Lisa Peterson	2:31:14	Seattle, Washington

This year's race through downtown Boulder boasted the largest field in the marathon's history, with over 9500 men and 6700 women competing. Race conditions were perfect with low humidity and temperatures that never exceeded 85°.

Highway 6 Reopens

Highway 6 will reopen this Friday, May 3rd, after a final safety inspection. A late blizzard delayed road crews, marking this as one of the latest dates for the highway's reopening on record.

Rising to an elevation of 12,351 feet at Grace Pass, Highway 6 is a main link between Park City and Lake Elton. The reopening of the road is one of the annual signs that summer is near and the tourist season will soon be upon us!

The final piece you'll add to articles.htm is the code for the links to stories and features. The code for this cell is stored in the features.htm file.

To insert the contents of features.htm in a table cell:

1. Using your text editor, open **features.htm** from the tutorial.04/tutorial folder.
2. Copy the HTML code located between the <body> tags of the file.
3. Close the file and return to **articles.htm** in your text editor.
4. Paste the copied HTML code within the third table cell as shown in Figure 4-71.

Inserting the contents of features.htm ◄ **Figure 4-71**

```
<!-- Features -->
<td width="40%" valign="top" style="background-image: url(parch3.jpg)">
<h3 style="text-align: center; font-family: sans-serif;
        color: ivory; background-color: rgb(82,64,32)">
   Stories Inside
</h3>
<ul style="font-family: sans-serif; font-size: 0.75em; list-style-type: square">
   <li><a href="#">Complete Marathon Results</a></li>
   <li><a href="#">National Park Acquires Land</a></li>
   <li><a href="#">School Board Election Results</a></li>
   <li><a href="#">Spending Referendum Defeated</a></li>
   <li><a href="#">Graduation Awards</a></li>
   <li><a href="#">New Highway Proposed</a></li>
   <li><a href="#">Camping Tips</a></li>
   <li><a href="#">Cougar Sightings Increase</a></li>
   <li><a href="#">Editorials</a></li>
   <li><a href="#">Park City Profile</a></li>
</ul>
</td>
```

▶ **5.** Save your changes to **articles.htm** and reload the file in your Web browser. The completed page appears in Figure 4-72.

Completed articles page ◄ **Figure 4-72**

Combining the Outer and Inner Tables

It's now time to place the code from articles.htm into page1.htm. You'll use the same copy and paste techniques that you've used to populate the other table cells.

To insert the contents of articles.htm in page1.htm:

1. Return to **articles.htm** in your text editor.

2. Copy the HTML code between the <body> tags.

3. Close the file and reopen **page1.htm** using your text editor if it is not currently open.

4. Paste the copied HTML code from Step 2 within the third table cell as shown in Figure 4-73.

Figure 4-73 | **Inserting the contents of articles.htm**

paste the contents of articles.htm here →

```
<!-- Articles -->
<td valign="top">
<table cellpadding="5" cellspacing="5">
<tr>
   <!-- Marathon story -->
   <td colspan="2" valign="top">
<h1 style="text-align: center; font-family: Arial, Helvetica, sans-serif">
   Local Woman Wins Marathon
</h1>

<p><img src="blake.jpg" alt="" width="75" height="101" style="margin: 5; float: left" />
Park City native, <b>Laura Blake</b>, won the 27<sup>th</sup> Front Range Marathon
over an elite field of the best long distance runners in the country. Laura's
time of 2 hr. 28 min. 21 sec. was only 2 minutes off the women's course record
set last year by Sarah Rawlings. Kathy Lasker and Lisa Peterson finished second
and third, respectively. Laura's victory came on the heels of her performance at
the NCAA Track and Field Championships, in which she placed second running for
Colorado State.</p>
```

5. Save your changes to the file and reload it in your Web browser. Figure 4-74 shows the final appearance of the front page of the *Park City Gazette*.

The Park City Gazette

Home Page

News
Local
State
National
International
Sports
Weather

Classifieds
For Sale
Wanted
Employment
Real Estate
Personal

Tourism
Attractions
Events
Parks
Camping

Subscriptions

Contact Us

Local Woman Wins Marathon

Park City native, **Laura Blake**, won the 27th Front Range Marathon over an elite field of the best long distance runners in the country. Laura's time of 2 hr. 28 min. 21 sec. was only 2 minutes off the women's course record set last year by Sarah Rawlings. Kathy Lasker and Lisa Peterson finished second and third, respectively. Laura's victory came on the heels of her performance at the NCAA Track and Field Championships, in which she placed second running for Colorado State.

In an exciting race, **Peter Teagan** of San Antonio, Texas, used a finishing kick to win the men's marathon for the second straight year, in a time of 2 hr. 12 min. 34 sec. Ahead for much of the race, Kyle Wills of Billings, Montana, finished second, when he could not match Teagan's finishing pace. Jason Wu of Cutler, Colorado, placed third in a very competitive field.

Race Results

	Runner	Time	Origin
Men	1. Peter Teagan	2:12:34	San Antonio, Texas
	2. Kyle Wills	2:13:05	Billings, Montana
	3. Jason Wu	2:14:28	Cutler, Colorado
Women	1. Laura Blake	2:28:21	Park City, Colorado
	2. Kathy Lasker	2:30:11	Chicago, Illinois
	3. Lisa Peterson	2:31:14	Seattle, Washington

This year's race through downtown Boulder boasted the largest field in the marathon's history, with over 9500 men and 6700 women competing. Race conditions were perfect with low humidity and temperatures that never exceeded 85°.

Highway 6 Reopens

Highway 6 will reopen this Friday, May 3rd, after a final safety inspection. A late blizzard delayed road crews, marking this as one of the latest dates for the highway's reopening on record.

Rising to an elevation of 12,351 feet at Grace Pass, Highway 6 is a main link between Park City and Lake Elton. The reopening of the road is one of the annual signs that summer is near and the tourist season will soon be upon us!

Stories Inside

- Complete Marathon Results
- National Park Acquires Land
- School Board Election Results
- Spending Referendum Defeated
- Graduation Awards
- New Highway Proposed
- Camping Tips
- Cougar Sightings Increase
- Editorials
- Park City Profile

Park City Gazette · 801 Elkhart Avenue · Park City, CO 80511 · 1 (800) 555-2918

6. Close your text editor and browser.

You show the final version of the Web page to Kevin. He's pleased that you were able to create a Web page that closely resembles his original design sketch, and decides to use this layout for future issues of the *Gazette*. As he compiles new articles, he may look for your help in providing design assistance.

Tips for Effective Use of Tables

- Diagram the table layout before you start writing your HTML code.
- First create a table structure with minimal content. Once the layout appears correct, start formatting the content within the table cells and add more content.
- Insert comment tags throughout the table layout to document each section.
- Indent the code for the various levels of nested tables to make your code easier to interpret.
- Enter opening and closing table tags at the same time in order to avoid the error of either omitting or misplacing the closing tag.
- Test and preview your layout as you proceed in order to catch errors early in the design process.
- Limit the number and extent of nested tables, since they can increase the amount of time required to render a page and cause accessibility problems for non-visual browsers.
- Use cell padding and cell spacing to keep the table content from appearing too crowded.
- Use row spanning to vary the size and starting point of articles within a columnar layout. Side-by-side articles that start and end at the same location are often visually boring and can be difficult to read.
- Avoid using more than three columns of text. Too many columns can result in column widths that are too narrow.
- Use fluid elements to reduce the amount of unused space in the browser window. Use fixed-width elements when you need to precisely place elements on the page.

Review

Session 4.3 Quick Check

1. What is a columnar layout? Can text flow from one column to another in such a layout?
2. What is a jigsaw layout? What cell spacing value should you use in this layout?
3. What is a fixed-width layout?
4. What is a fluid layout?
5. Why can tables be difficult for aural (non-visual) browsers?
6. What HTML code would you use to create a 2 × 2 table nested inside the upper-left cell of another 2 × 2 table?

Review

Tutorial Summary

In this tutorial, you learned how to create and use tables, both to display tabular data and as a layout tool. You first learned how to create simple text tables using preformatted text. Then you learned how to create similar tables using HTML's table elements. You learned about the different parts of a table, including table rows, table cells, and the table heading, body, and footer. You also learned how to create a table caption. In the second session, you learned how to format a table's appearance by modifying the table size, alignment, and background colors. You also learned how to create row and column spanning cells, and how to work with column groups. The third session discussed the different types of page layouts that can be created using tables. In this session, you employed some of those techniques to create a newspaper-style columnar layout.

Key Terms

cell padding	fluid layout	proportional font
cell spacing	graphical table	row group
column group	jigsaw layout	sectional layout
columnar layout	jigsaw table	spanning cell
fixed-width font	monospace font	text table
fixed-width layout	preformatted text	

Practice

Practice the skills you learned in the tutorial using the same case scenario.

Review Assignments

Data files needed for this Review Assignment: art2txt.htm, cougar.jpg, page2txt.htm, parch2.jpg, parch3.jpg, parch.jpg, pcglogo.jpg, sighttxt.htm, tips.htm

Kevin would like to place another page of the *Park City Gazette* on the Web site. Cougar sightings have recently increased in the Park City area, causing great concern for both local residents and tourists. Kevin has written an article describing the sightings and providing safety tips for effectively handling a cougar encounter. Kevin has also created a table, shown in Figure 4-75, that lists local cougar sightings for the last six months. Kevin would like you to include this table with his article.

Figure 4-75

Location	April	May	June	July	August	Total
Park City	0	2	1	3	4	10
Riley	2	1	1	3	2	9
Dixon	0	2	3	1	4	10
TOTAL	2	5	5	7	10	29

The articles should employ the same layout you designed for the paper's front page. Figure 4-76 shows a preview of the Web page you'll create for Kevin.

Figure 4-76

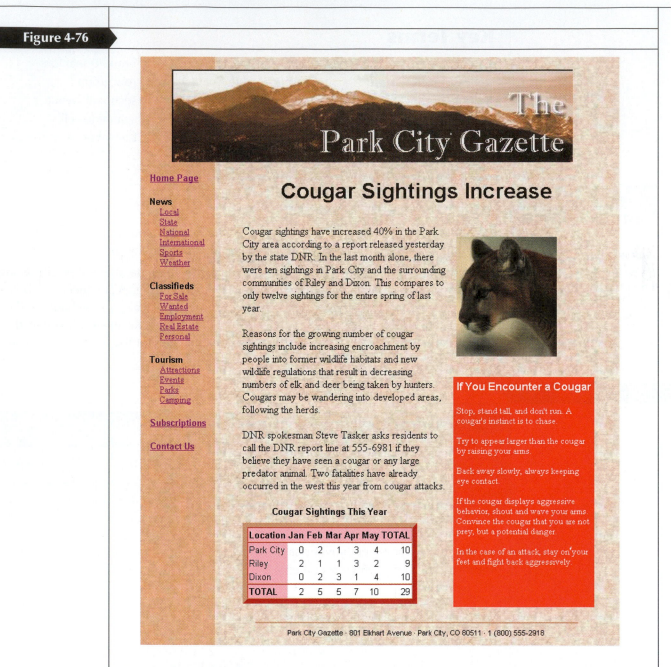

To complete this task:

1. Use your text editor to open the files **sightxt.htm**, **art2txt.htm**, and **page2txt.htm** from the tutorial.04/review folder. Enter *your name* and *the date* in the comment section of each file. Save the files as **sighting.htm**, **article2.htm**, and **page2.htm** respectively.

2. Go to the **sighting.htm** file in your text editor. Below the last paragraph in the story, insert a table with the following features:
   - The table should contain row groups for the header, table body, and footer.
   - The table should have a 7-pixel-wide brown border. The light border color should be tan.
   - Table rules should be set to "groups".
   - The default font for the table text should be sans-serif with a font size of 0.8em.
   - The cell spacing should be set to 0 pixels. The cell padding should be set to 2 pixels.

3. Insert the caption "Cougar Sightings This Year" in a bold font above the table.
4. Insert the table entries shown in Figure 4-75. The first row should be placed in the header row group and marked as table headings. Set the background color of this row to pink.
5. Below the table heading row group, insert the table footer row group. This row contains the total cougar sightings from all of the communities for each month and for the year so far. The first cell should have a pink background and the text should be displayed in a bold font. Right-align the numeric values in the row. (Note that even though this is a table footer and will appear as the last row in the rendered table, it precedes the table body in the HTML code.)
6. The next three rows should be placed in the table body group. The table body row group contains the cougar sightings for each city. Change the background color of the first cells in each row to pink and right align the numeric values in each row.
7. Save your changes to **sighting.htm**.
8. Go to the **article2.htm** file in your text editor.
9. In the body section, create a table with a cell spacing value of 3 and a cell padding value of 5.
10. Create a cell in the first row of the table that spans two columns, and identify this cell with the comment "Cougar headline". Within this cell, insert a centered h1 heading that contains the text "Cougar Sightings Increase". Display the headline in a sans-serif font.
11. In the second row of the table, insert a cell that is 60% wide and spans two rows. Vertically align the text of this cell with the cell's top border. Identify this cell with the comment "Cougar story". Insert the page contents of the **sighting.htm** file (excluding the <body> tags) into this cell.
12. Also in the table's second row, insert a cell that is 40% wide. Identify this cell with the comment "Cougar photo". Display the image, **cougar.jpg**, with an empty text string for the alternate text. The size of the photo is 150 pixels wide by 178 pixels high.
13. In the table's third row, insert a cell that is 40% wide, has a red background, and align the cell text with the cell's top border. Insert the comment "Cougar tips" for this cell. Insert the contents of the **tips.htm** file (excluding the <body> tags) into this cell.
14. Save your changes to **article2.htm**.
15. Go to the **page2.htm** file in your text editor.
16. Locate the Articles cell in the main table of this file (it will be the third cell). Insert the page contents of **article2.htm**. Save your changes to the file and view its contents with your Web browser.
17. Submit your completed Web site to your instructor.

Apply

Use the skills you've learned in this tutorial to design a Web page for a company that creates geodesic domes for businesses and homes.

Case Problem 1

Data files needed for this Case Problem: address.htm, back.jpg-back5.jpg, dhome.jpg, dhometxt.htm, footer.htm, introtxt.htm, links.jpg, textbox.htm, uses.htm

dHome, Inc.   dHome is one of the nation's leading manufacturers of geodesic dome houses. Olivia Moore, the director of advertising for dHome, has hired you to work on the company's Web site. She has provided you with all of the text you need for the Web page, and your job is to design the page's layout. Olivia would like each page in the Web site to display the company logo, a column of links, a footer displaying additional links, and another footer displaying the company's address and phone number. She would like you to place the appropriate text for the topic of each Web page in the center. Olivia wants you to use a fixed-width layout. Figure 4-77 shows a preview of the completed Web page.

Figure 4-77

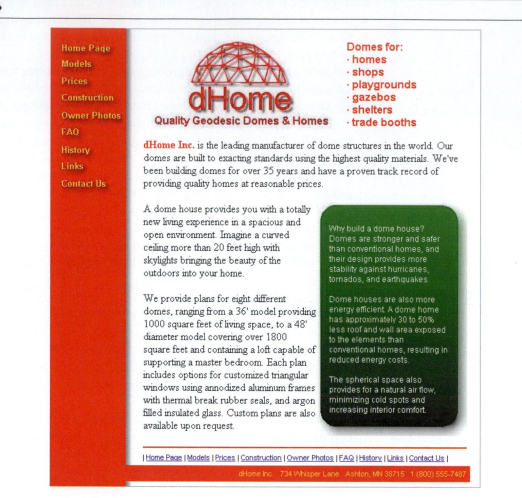

To create the dHome Web page:

1. Open **introtxt.htm** and **dhometxt.htm** from the tutorial.04/case1 folder. Enter *your name* and *the date* in the comment section of each file. Save the files as **intro.htm** and **dhome.htm** respectively.

2. Go to **intro.htm** in your text editor. Between the first and second paragraphs, create a table 224 pixels wide and 348 pixels high. Set the border, cell padding, and cell spacing values to zero. Float the table with the right margin of the Web page.

3. The table should have a single row with three columns. The first cell should be 20 pixels wide, using the **back3.jpg** file for its background. There is no content for this cell, so insert a non-breaking space into the cell.

4. The second cell should be 200 pixels wide, using the **back4.jpg** file as a background. Insert the contents of the **uses.htm** file into this cell.

5. The third cell should be 30 pixels wide and use the **back5.jpg** file as its background. There is no content for this cell, so insert a non-breaking space.

6. Save your changes to **intro.htm**.

7. Return to the file **dhome.htm** in your text editor.

8. Within the body section, create a table 620 pixels wide with a cell padding of 5 and a cell spacing of 0.

9. The first row of the table should contain three cells. The first cell should be 120 pixels wide and span three rows. Within this cell, insert the **links.jpg** image, aligning it with

the cell's top border. Set the alternate text for this image to an empty text string. The size of the image is 94 pixels wide by 232 pixels high. Identify this cell with the comment tag "List of links".

10. The second cell should be 300 pixels wide. Within this cell, insert the company's logo, found in the **dhome.jpg** file. Align the logo with the cell's top border. For non-graphical browsers, provide the alternate text "dHome Quality Geodesic Domes & Homes". The size of the inline image is 270 pixels wide by 134 pixels high. Identify this cell with the comment tag "Company logo".

11. The third cell should be 200 pixels wide. Insert the contents of the **textbox.htm** file into this cell. Align the text of the cell with the cell's top border. Change the text color of the cell content to the color value (182,29,23) and display the text in bold sans-serif font. Identify the cell with the comment "Text box".

12. In the table's second row, create a single cell 500 pixels wide that spans two columns. Insert the contents of the **intro.htm** file into this cell. Align the text with the top of the cell. Identify the cell with the comment "Intro text".

13. In the table's third row, create another cell 500 pixels wide that spans two columns. Within this cell, insert the contents of the **footer.htm** file, aligning the contents with the top of the cell. The text of this cell should be displayed in a sans-serif font that is 0.7em in size. Identify the contents of this cell with the comment "Footer".

14. In the fourth and last row of the table, create a cell 620 pixels wide and 15 pixels high, that spans three columns. Use **back2.jpg** as the background image for the cell. Insert the contents of the **address.htm** file into the cell, aligned with the cell's right border. The cell content should be displayed in yellow sans-serif font with a size of 0.7em. Identify the cell with the comment "Address".

15. Save your changes to the file.

16. Submit the completed Web site to your instructor.

Use the skills you've learned in this tutorial to design a Web page for a retreat center.

Case Problem 2

Data files needed for this Case Problem: adams.jpg, address.htm, back.jpg, dlogo.jpg, dunsttxt.htm, events.htm, letter.htm, next.htm, welctxt.htm

Dunston Retreat Center The Dunston Retreat Center, located in northern Wisconsin, offers weekends of quiet and solitude for all who visit. The center, started by a group of Trappist monks, has grown in popularity over the last few years as more people have become aware of its services. The director of the center, Benjamin Adams, wants to advertise the center on the Internet and has asked you to create a Web site for the center. He wants the Web site to include a welcome message from him, a list of upcoming events, a letter from one of the center's guests, and a description of the current week's events. The Web page you'll create is shown in Figure 4-78.

Figure 4-78

Upcoming

June 11-13
Marriage
Encounter

June 18-20
Recovering
Alcoholics

June 25-27
Spirituality
Workshop

July 2-4
Lutheran
Brotherhood

July 9-11
Recovering
Alcoholics

July 16-18
Duluth
Fellowship

July 23-25
Special Needs
Children

August 6-8
St. James
Men's Group

August 13-15
St. James
Women's Group

August 20-22
Recovering
Alcoholics

August 27-29
Knights of
Columbus

Welcome. Whether you are planning to attend one of our many conferences or embarking on a private retreat, we're sure that you will enjoy your stay.

Located in the northern woods of Wisconsin, the Dunston Retreat Center provides comfortable and attractive accommodations while you enjoy the rustic setting available just outside your door. The Retreat Center has 32 beds, large meeting rooms, a chapel, and kitchen facilities. If you want to get out, there are ample opportunities for hiking, canoeing and horseback riding in the surrounding area.

Throughout the year the center staff conducts retreats to accommodate the needs of various groups. We offer retreats for men, for women, and for couples. Please call about special needs retreats.

If you prefer, an individually directed retreat is possible. The retreat includes a time of daily sharing and guidance by a retreat director to supplement your private time of solitude and meditation.

At the Dunston Retreat Center we make everything as easy as possible, providing meals, towels, bedding - everything you need. Just bring yourself.

Benjamin Adams
Director

I'm writing to tell you how much I enjoyed my retreat at Dunston. I came to your center haggard and worn out from a long illness and job difficulties. I left totally refreshed.

I've enthusiastically told all of my friends about the wonderful place you have. Some of us are hoping to organize a group retreat. Rest assured that you'll see me again. Going to Dunston will become a yearly event for me.

- P. Davis, Paulson, MN

Next week at the Dunston Retreat Center

The annual meeting of the Midwest Marriage Encounter, June 11-13. Registration is $50 and includes room and board. A boating trip on Lake Superior is planned for Saturday night ($10 fee).

Contact Maury Taylor at 555-2381 for reservation information.

Dunston Retreat Center   1415 Sugar River Lane   Dunston, WI 57817   1 (800) 555-8812

To create the Dunston Retreat Center Web page:

1. Use your text editor to open **welctxt.htm** and **dunsttxt.htm** from the tutorial.04/case2 folder. Enter *your name* and *the date* in the comment sections. Save the files as **welcome.htm** and **dunston.htm** respectively.

2. Go to the **welcome.htm** file in your text editor. Between the second and third paragraphs, insert a table with the following attributes:
   - The table floats on the right page margin.
   - The table should have a 1-pixel-wide border and a cell padding value of 5 pixels. The table should be 40% of the page width.
   - The border color should be white. The table background should be equal to the color value (125,178,116).

3. Within the table insert a single cell containing the body contents of the **letter.htm** file. The content should be aligned with the top of the cell, and the text should appear in a white sans-serif font with a font size of 0.8em.
4. Save your changes to **welcome.htm**.
5. Go to the **dunston.htm** file in your text editor.
6. Create a table that is 90% of the width of the page with cell spacing and padding equal to 5 pixels.
7. In the first row of the table, insert a single cell two columns wide containing the image **dlogo.jpg**. The alternate text for this image is "The Dunston Retreat Center". The size of the image is 626 pixels wide by 148 pixels high. Align the contents with the left edge of the table.
8. The second row of the table should contain two cells. The first cell should be 100 pixels wide, spanning three rows. It should contain the contents of the **events.htm** file, aligned with the cell's top border. Display the contents of this cell in a sans-serif font.
9. The second cell should contain the contents of **welcome.htm**, aligned with the top border of the cell.
10. In the third row of the table, insert a single cell containing the contents of **next.htm**, aligned with the top of the cell.
11. The table's fourth row contains a single cell containing the contents of **address.htm**, centered horizontally within the cell.
12. Save your changes to the file. Open the file in your Web browser and verify that the layout displays correctly.
13. Submit the completed Web site to your instructor.

Explore

Broaden your knowledge of table design by creating a calendar table for a civic center.

Case Problem 3

Data files needed for this Case Problem: back.jpg, ccc.gif, febtxt.htm

Chamberlain Civic Center The Chamberlain Civic Center of Chamberlain, Iowa, is in the process of designing a Web page to advertise its events and activities. Stacy Dawes, the director of publicity, has asked you to create a Web page describing the events in February, which are shown in the following list. Ticket prices are provided in parentheses.

- Every Sunday, the Carson Quartet plays at 1 p.m. ($8)
- February 1, 8 p.m.: Taiwan Acrobats ($16/$24/$36)
- February 5, 8 p.m.: Joey Gallway ($16/$24/$36)
- February 7-8, 7 p.m.: West Side Story ($24/$36/$64)
- February 10, 8 p.m.: Jazz Masters ($18/$24/$32)
- February 13, 8 p.m.: Harlem Choir ($18/$24/$32)
- February 14, 8 p.m.: Chamberlain Symphony ($18/$24/$32)
- February 15, 8 p.m.: Edwin Drood ($24/$36/$44)
- February 19, 8 p.m.: The Yearling ($8/$14/$18)
- February 21, 8 p.m.: An Ellington Tribute ($24/$32/$48)
- February 22, 8 p.m.: Othello ($18/$28/$42)
- February 25, 8 p.m.: Madtown Jugglers ($12/$16/$20)
- February 28, 8 p.m.: Robin Williams ($32/$48/$64)

Figure 4-79 shows a preview of the Web page you'll create for Stacy.

Figure 4-79

To create the CCC calendar:

1. Using your text editor, open **febtxt.htm** from the tutorial.04/case3 folder. Enter *your name* and *the date* in the comment section of the file. Save the file as **feb.htm**.

2. At the top of the page, create a table with the following attributes:
   - The border size should be 5 pixels with a width of 100% of the page and a cell padding value of 10 pixels. The table should have a red border.
   - The rules value should be set to "none" and the frame value to "below".
   - The content of this table should be displayed in a red sans-serif font with a font size of 18 pixels. The bottom margin size of the table should be set to 20 pixels. (Note: Some browsers may not support the rules or frame attributes).

3. The first table cell should contain the inline image **ccc.gif**. The alternate text for this image should be "The Chamberlain Civic Center". The size of the image is 322 pixels wide by 144 pixels high.

4. The next four cells in the row should contain the text strings, "Home Page", "Tickets", "Events", and "Facilities". Vertically align the contents of these cells with the bottom border of the cell. Horizontally align the contents with the cell's right border.

5. Below the table you just created, insert another table with the following attributes:
   - The table should float on the right margin of the Web page with a left margin of 5 pixels.

- The table border should be 5 pixels wide. The color of the table border should be red and pink. The cell padding value should be set to 3 pixels. The cell spacing value should be set to 0 pixels.
- The contents of the table should be displayed in a sans-serif font at a font size of 0.7em on a white background.

Explore

6. Within the table, create a column group spanning seven columns. These columns represent the seven days of the week in the calendar table. Set the width of the columns to 60 pixels and align the text in the column group with the top of each cell. (*Hint:* To set the width for each column in a column group, add the width attribute to the <colgroup> tag.)

Explore

7. Within the column group, assign the first column a background color of pink. Assign a background color of white to the next four columns, and assign a background color of pink to the last two columns.

8. In the table's first row, create a heading that spans seven columns. Insert the text "Events in February" centered horizontally within the cell.

9. In the table's second row, insert the following table headings: "Sun", "Mon", "Tue", "Wed", "Thu", "Fri", and "Sat".

10. Enclose the first two rows of the table in a table head row group. Change the background color of this row group to black and the font color to white.

11. The next five rows contain the individual days from the calendar, each placed in a separate table cell. Format the dates as follows:
    - Display the day of the month on its own line, formatted with a boldface font.
    - If there is an event for that date, display the name of the event on one line, the time the event takes place on the second line, and the ticket price on a third line. Separate one line from another using the <br /> tag.
    - If the date is not in the month of February, use the **back.jpg** image as the cell's background.

12. Save your changes to the file. Using your Web browser, verify that the table displays correctly. Note that some browsers do not support column groups, so the page rendered by those browsers may not resemble the one in Figure 4-79.

13. Submit your completed Web page to your instructor.

Create

Test your knowledge of HTML by creating a Web site for the TravelWeb E-Zine.

Case Problem 4

Data files needed for this Case Problem: luxair.txt, photo.txt, ppoint2.jpg, ppoint.jpg, toronto.txt, twlinks2.htm, twlinks.htm, twlogo.jpg, yosemite.jpg, yosemite.txt

TravelWeb E-Zine Magazine   You have joined the staff of TravelWeb, which provides travel information and tips to online subscribers. You have been asked to work on the layout for the E-Zine Magazine Web page. Figure 4-80 describes the files that you have been given to use in creating the page.

Figure 4-80

File	Description
luxair.txt	Article about LuxAir reducing airfares to Europe
photo.txt	Article about the Photo of the Week
ppoint.jpg	Large version of the Photo of the Week (320 x 228)
ppoint2.jpg	Small version of the Photo of the Week (180 x 128)
toronto.txt	Article about traveling to Toronto
twlinks.htm	Links to other TravelWeb pages (list version)
twlinks2.htm	Links to other TravelWeb pages (table version)
twlogo.jpg	Image file of the TravelWeb logo (425 x 105)
yosemite.txt	Article about limiting access to Yosemite National Park
yosemite.jpg	Image file of Yosemite National Park (112 x 158)

To create a Web page for TravelWeb:

1. Use the files listed in Figure 4-80 to create a newspaper-style page. All of these files are stored in the tutorial.04/case4 folder. The page should include several columns, but the number, size, and layout of the columns is up to you.
2. Use all of the files on the page, with the following exceptions: use only one of the two files **twlinks.htm** or **twlinks2.htm**, and use only one of the two image files **ppoint.jpg** or **ppoint2.jpg**. Note that not all of the links in the content files point to existing files.
3. Use background colors to give the Web page an attractive and interesting appearance.
4. Include comment tags to describe the different parts of your page layout.
5. Save your page as tw.htm in the tutorial.04/case4 folder.
6. Submit the completed Web page to your instructor.

Review

Quick Check Answers

Session 4.1

1. Text tables and graphical tables. Text tables are supported by all browsers and are easier to create. The graphical table is more difficult to create but provides the user with a wealth of formatting options.
2. A proportional font assigns a different amount of space to each character depending on each character's width. A fixed-width font assigns the same space to each character regardless of width. You should use a fixed-width font in a text table in order to keep columns aligned under all font sizes.
3. The <pre> tag
4. The <tr> tag identifies a table row. The <td> tag identifies individual table cells, and the <th> tag identifies table cells that act as table headings.
5. The number of rows in a table is determined by the number of <tr> tags. The number of columns is equal to the largest number of <td> and <th> tags within a single table row.
6. The three row groups are the table head, created by enclosing tables within the <thead> tag, the table body created with the <tbody> tag, and the table footer, created with the <tfoot> tag.
7. <caption align="bottom">Product Catalog</caption>
This caption must be placed directly after the opening <table> tag.

Session 4.2

1. `<table border="5" cellspacing="3" cellpadding="4"> ... </table>`
2. `<td valign="top"> ... </td>`
   or
   `<th valign="top"> ... </th>`
3. `<td align="center"> ... </td>`
   or
   `<th align="center"> ... </th>`
4. `<table width="50%">`
5. When the contents of the table do not fit within the cell dimensions or when another cell in the same column has been set to a larger width.
6. `<td rowspan="3" colspan="2"> ... </td>`
   or
   `<th rowspan="3" colspan="2"> ... </th>`
7. `<colgroup span="3" style="background-color: yellow" />`

Session 4.3

1. A columnar layout is a layout in which the page content has been laid out in columns. Text cannot flow from one column to another.
2. A jigsaw layout breaks the page into separate pieces like the pieces of a jigsaw puzzle. The cell spacing value should be set to 0 pixels.
3. A fixed-width layout sets the absolute size of the page elements, regardless of the size of the browser window.
4. In a fluid layout, one or more of the table elements is sized as a percentage of the page width. The effect of a fluid layout is to set the sizes of page elements based on the size of the browser window.
5. Aural browsers often render the content of the table in the order in which the content appears in the HTML code. If the content is not intelligible when reproduced in that order, the table will be difficult to interpret.
6.

```
<table>
   <tr>
      <td>
      <table><tr><td></td><td></td></tr>
            <tr><td></td><td></td></tr>
      </table>
      </td>
      <td></td>
   </tr>
   <tr>
      <td></td>
      <td></td>
   </tr>
</table>
```

Objectives

Session 5.1
- Describe the uses of frames in a Web site
- Lay out frames within a browser window
- Display a document within a frame
- Format the appearance of frames by setting the margin widths, removing scrollbars, and specifying whether users can resize frames

Session 5.2
- Direct a link target to a specific frame
- Direct a link target outside of a frame layout
- Add page content for browsers that don't support frames
- Format the color and size of frame borders
- Incorporate an inline frame in a page

Designing a Web Site with Frames

Using Frames to Display Multiple Web Pages

Case

The Yale Climbing School

One of the most popular climbing schools and touring agencies in Colorado is the Yale Climbing School (YCS). Located in Vale Park, outside Rocky Mountain National Park, YCS specializes in teaching beginning and advanced climbing techniques. The school also sponsors several tours, leading individuals on some of the most exciting, challenging, and picturesque climbs in North America. The school has been in business for 15 years, and in that time it has helped thousands of people experience the mountains in ways they never thought possible.

Yale Climbing School has a lot of competition from other climbing schools and touring groups in the area. Debbie Chen is the owner of the school and is always looking for ways to market her programs and improve the visibility of the school. Early on, she decided to use the Internet and the World Wide Web as a means of promoting the school, and she has already created many Web pages.

Debbie has seen other Web sites use frames to display several Web pages in a single browser window. She feels that frames would allow the school to more effectively present its offerings to potential students. She asks you to help develop a frame-based Web site for YCS.

Student Data Files

▼Tutorial.05

▽ **Tutorial folder**
  linkstxt.htm
  tourstxt.htm
  yaletxt.htm
  + 22 HTML files
  + 24 graphic files

▽ **Review folder**
  headtxt.htm
  slisttxt.htm
  sltxt.htm
  stafftxt.htm
  tlisttxt.htm
  tltxt.htm
  tourstxt.htm
  yale2txt.htm
  + 16 HTML files
  + 24 graphic files

▽ **Case1 folder**
  dcctxt.htm
  headtxt.htm
  maptxt.htm
  + 5 HTML files
  + 6 graphic files

▽ Case2 folder

listtxt.htm
+ 17 graphic files

▽ Case3 folder

messtxt.htm
mxxtxt.htm
+ 9 HTML files
+ 15 graphic files

▽ Case4 folder

drive15l.htm
drive15l.jpg
drive20m.htm
drive20m.jpg
drive33m.htm
drive33m.jpg
drive60s.htm
drive60s.jpg
tape800.htm
tape800.jpg
tape3200.htm
tape3200.jpg
tape9600.htm
tape9600.jpg
wlogo.gif
wlogo.htm

Session 5.1

Introducing Frames

Typically, as a Web site grows in size and complexity, each page is dedicated to a particular topic or group of topics. One page might contain a list of links, another page might display contact information for the company or organization, and another page might describe the business philosophy. As more pages are added to the site, the designer might wish for a way to display information from several pages at the same time.

One solution is to duplicate that information across the Web site, but this strategy presents problems. It requires a great deal of time and effort to repeat (or copy and paste) the same information over and over again. Also, each time a change is required, you need to repeat your edit for each page in the site—a process that could easily result in errors.

Such considerations contributed to the creation of frames. A **frame** is a section of the browser window capable of displaying the contents of an entire Web page. Figure 5-1 shows an example of a browser window containing two frames. The frame on the left displays the contents of a Web page containing a list of links. The frame on the right displays an old version of the NEC Web site that utilized frames.

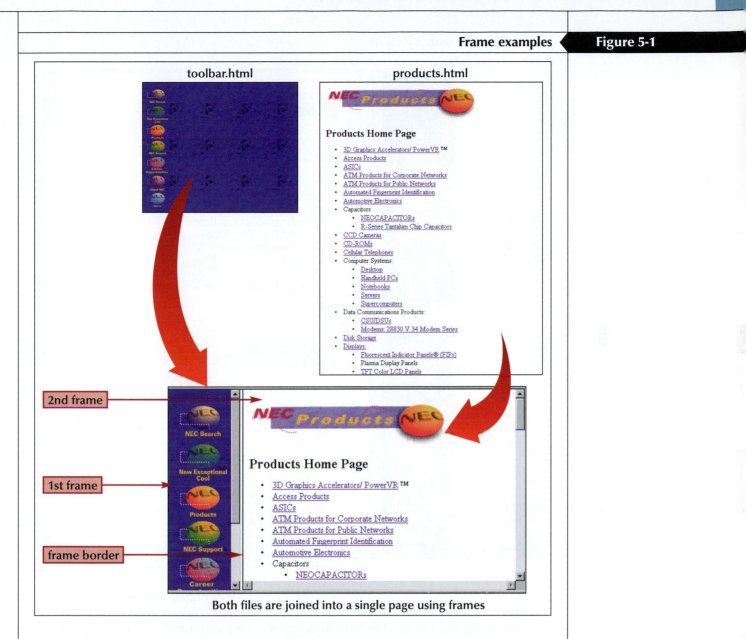

Both files are joined into a single page using frames

This example illustrates a common use of frames: displaying a table of contents in one frame, while showing individual pages from the site in another. Figure 5-2 illustrates how a list of links can remain on the screen while the user navigates through the contents of the site. Using this layout, a designer can easily update the list of links because it is stored on only one page.

Figure 5-2 ▶ **Activating a link within a frame**

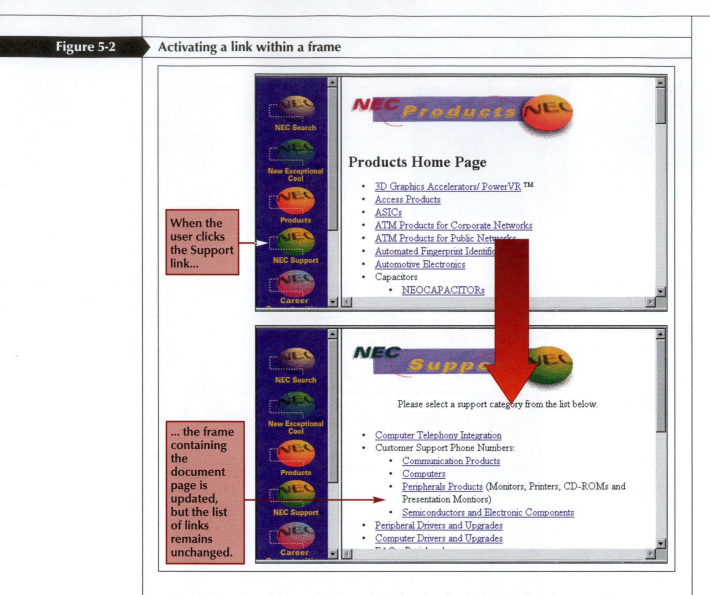

Frame-based Web sites also have their drawbacks. For example, when opening a page that uses frames, a browser has to load multiple HTML files before a user can view the contents of the site. This can result in increased waiting time for potential customers. It is also very difficult for users to bookmark pages within a Web site that uses frames. In addition, Internet search engines that create content-based catalogs can have problems adding framed pages to their listings—meaning that if you want your content to be easily found by the world, it's wise not to use frames. Some browsers also have difficulty printing the pages within individual frames, though this is less of a problem than it once was. Finally, some users simply prefer Web page designs in which the entire browser window is devoted to a single page. For these reasons, many Web designers suggest that if you still want to use frames, you should create both framed and non-framed versions for a Web site and give users the option of which one to use.

Planning Your Frames

Before you start creating your frames, it is a good idea to plan their appearance and determine how you want to use them. There are several issues to consider:

- What information will be displayed in each frame?
- How do you want the frames placed on the Web page? What is the size of each frame?
- Which frames will be static—that is, always showing the same content?
- Which frames will change in response to links being clicked?
- What Web pages will users first see when they access the site?
- Should users be permitted to resize the frames to suit their needs?

As you progress with your design for the Web site for the Yale Climbing School, you'll consider each of these questions. Debbie has already created the Web pages for the YCS Web site. Figure 5-3 describes the different Web pages you'll work with in this project.

Documents at the YCS Web site | **Figure 5-3**

Topic	Filename	Content
Biographies	staff.htm	Links to biographical pages of the YCS staff
Home page	home.htm	The YCS home page
Lessons	lessons.htm	Climbing lessons offered by the YCS
Logo	head.htm	A page containing the company logo
Philosophy	philosoph.htm	Statement of the YCS's business philosophy
Table of contents	links.htm	Links to the YCS pages
Tours	diamond.htm	Description of the Diamond climbing tour
Tours	eldorado.htm	Description of the Eldorado Canyon tour
Tours	grepon.htm	Description of the Petit Grepon climbing tour
Tours	kieners.htm	Description of the Kiener's Route climbing tour
Tours	lumpy.htm	Description of the Lumpy Ridge climbing tour
Tours	nface.htm	Description of the North Face climbing tour

Debbie has organized the pages by topic, such as tour descriptions, climbing lessons, and company philosophy. Two of the files, links.htm and staff.htm, do not focus on a particular topic, but contain links to other YCS Web pages.

Debbie has carefully considered how this material should be organized on the Web site, and what information the user should see first. She has sketched a layout that illustrates how she would like the frames to be organized. See Figure 5-4.

Figure 5-4 **Design sketch for the frames at the YCS Web site**

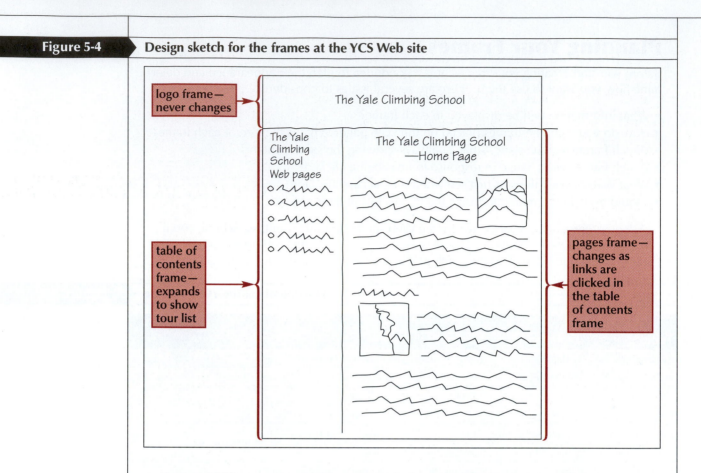

She would like you to create three frames. The top frame displays the school's logo and address. The frame on the left displays a list of the Web pages at the YCS Web site. Finally, the frame on the lower right displays the contents of those pages.

Your first task is to enter the HTML code for the frame layout that Debbie has described.

Creating a Frameset

Two elements are involved in creating frames. The **frameset** element describes how the frames are organized and displayed within the browser window. The **frame** element defines which document is displayed within a frame. The general syntax for using the frameset element is

```
<html>
<head>
<title>title</title>
</head>
<frameset>
    frames
</frameset>
</html>
```

where *frames* are the individual frames within the frameset. We'll explore how to create these frames shortly.

Note that the frameset element replaces the body element in this HTML document. Because this HTML file displays the contents of other Web pages, it is not technically a Web page and thus does not include a page body. Later in the tutorial, we'll explore situations in which you would include a body element in order to support browsers that do not display frames. For now, we'll concentrate on defining the appearance and content of the frames.

Specifying Frame Size and Orientation

Frames are placed within a frameset in either rows or columns, but not both. Figure 5-5 shows two framesets, one in which the frames are laid out in three columns, and the other in which they are placed in three rows.

Frame layouts in rows and columns ◄ **Figure 5-5**

Frames laid out in columns

| The first frame | The second frame | The third frame |

Frames laid out in rows

The first frame

The second frame

The third frame

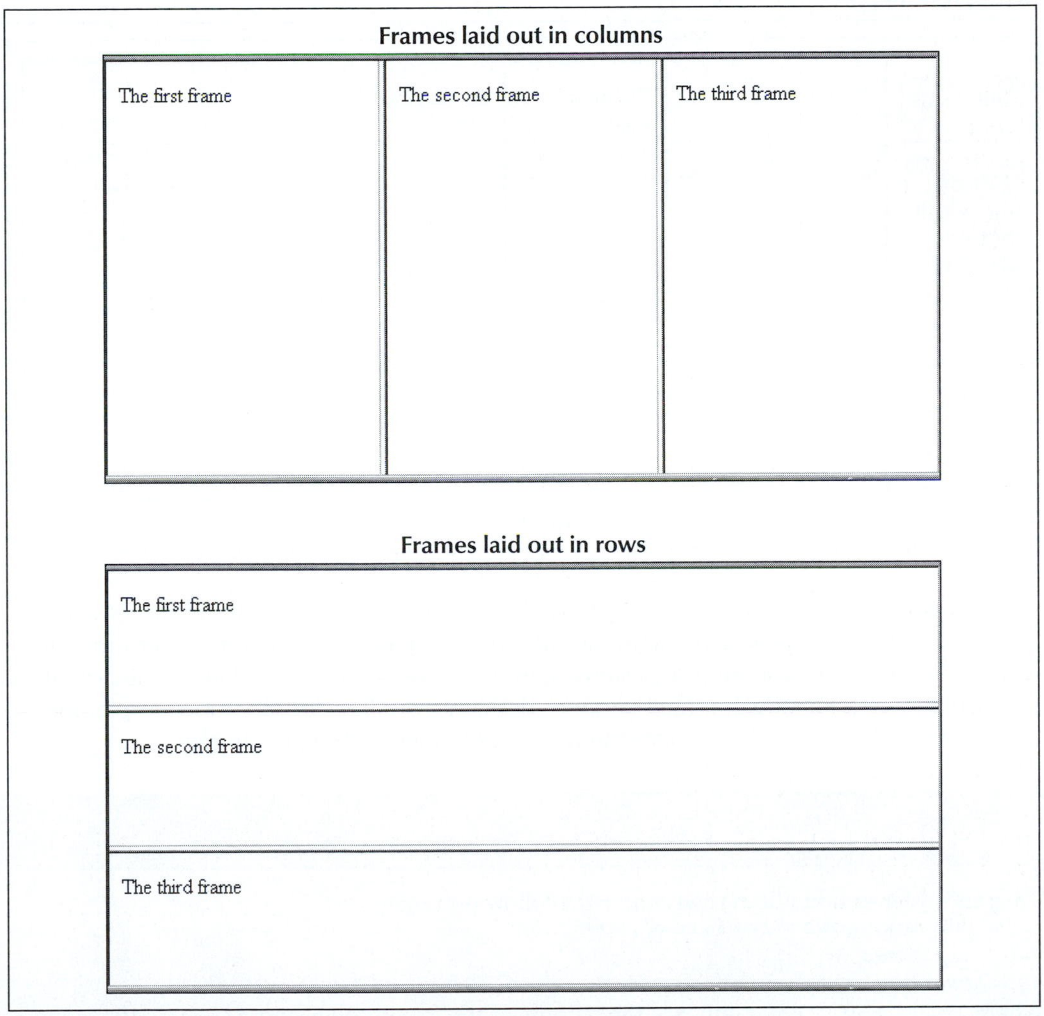

The syntax for creating a row or column frame layout is:

```
<frameset rows="row1,row2,row3,…"> … </frameset>
```

or

```
<frameset cols="column1,column2,column3,…"> … </frameset>
```

where *row1*, *row2*, *row3*, and so on is the height of each frame row, and *column1*, *column2*, *column3*, and so forth is the width of each frame column. There is no limit to the number of rows or columns you can specify for a frameset.

Row and column sizes can be specified in three ways: in pixels, as a percentage of the total size of the frameset, or by an asterisk (*). The asterisk instructs the browser to allocate any unclaimed space in the frameset to the given row or column. For example, the tag <frameset rows="160,*"> creates two rows of frames. The first row has a height of 160 pixels, and the height of the second row is equal to whatever space remains in the display area. You can combine the three methods. The tag <frameset cols="160,25%,*"> lays out the frames in the columns shown in Figure 5-6. The first column is 160 pixels wide, the second column is 25% of the width of the display area, and the third column covers whatever space is left.

Figure 5-6   **Sizing frames**

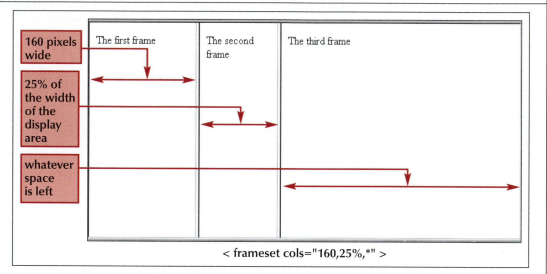

< frameset cols="160,25%,*" >

It is a good idea to specify at least one of the rows or columns of your frameset with an asterisk, in order to ensure that the frames fill up the screen regardless of a user's monitor settings. You can also use multiple asterisks. In that case, the browser divides the remaining display space equally among the frames designated with asterisks. For example, the tag <frameset rows="*,*,*"> creates three rows of frames with equal heights.

Reference Window

Creating a Frameset

To create frames laid out in rows, enter the following tags:
```
<frameset rows="row1,row2,row3,…">
    frames
</frameset>
```
where *row1*, *row2*, *row3*, etc. are the heights of the frame rows, and *frames* defines the frames within the frameset.

To create frames laid out in columns, enter the following tags:
```
<frameset cols="column1,column2,column3,…">
    frames
</frameset>
```
where *column1*, *column2*, *column3*, etc. are the widths of the frame columns.

The first frameset you'll create for the Yale Climbing School page has two rows. The top row is used for the company logo, and the second row is used for the remaining content of the Web page. A frame that is 85 pixels high should provide enough space to display the logo. The second row will occupy the rest of the display area.

To create the first set of frames:

1. Use your text editor to open **yaletxt.htm** from the tutorial.05/tutorial folder. Enter **your name** and **the date** in the comment section of the file. Save the file as **yale.htm**.

2. Insert the following HTML code after the closing </head> tag:

```
<frameset rows="85,*">
</frameset>
```

This code specifies a height of 85 pixels for the top row and allocates the remaining space to the second row. Figure 5-7 shows the revised yale.htm file.

Creating the initial frameset   Figure 5-7

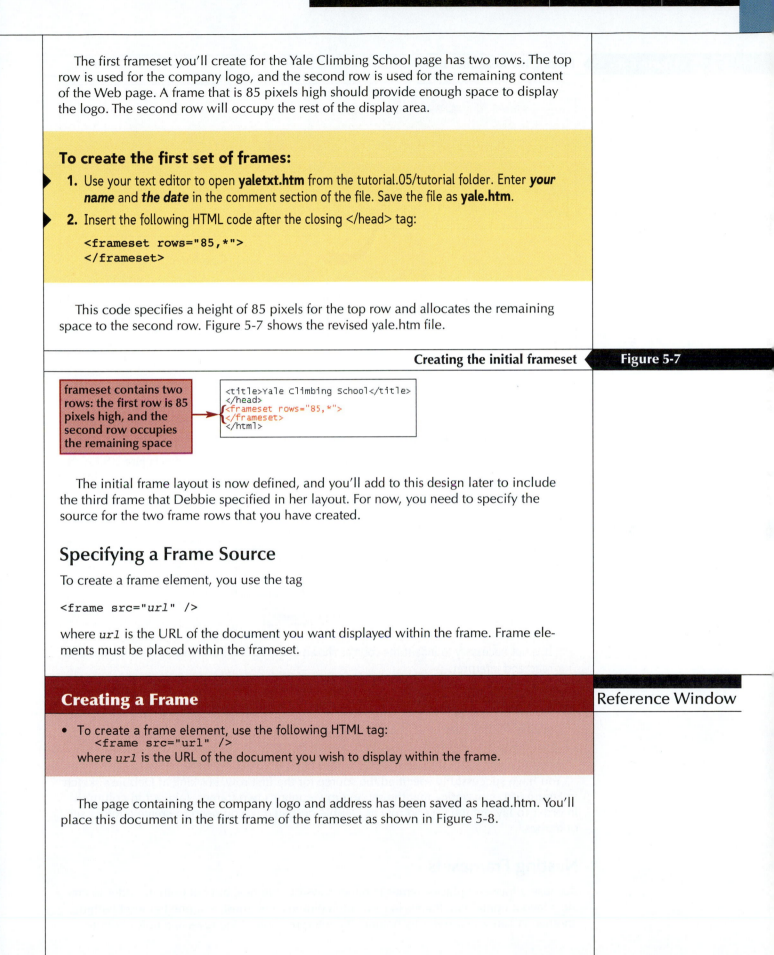

frameset contains two rows: the first row is 85 pixels high, and the second row occupies the remaining space

```
<title>Yale Climbing School</title>
</head>
<frameset rows="85,*">
</frameset>
</html>
```

The initial frame layout is now defined, and you'll add to this design later to include the third frame that Debbie specified in her layout. For now, you need to specify the source for the two frame rows that you have created.

Specifying a Frame Source

To create a frame element, you use the tag

```
<frame src="url" />
```

where *url* is the URL of the document you want displayed within the frame. Frame elements must be placed within the frameset.

Creating a Frame   Reference Window

- To create a frame element, use the following HTML tag:
  ```
  <frame src="url" />
  ```
  where *url* is the URL of the document you wish to display within the frame.

The page containing the company logo and address has been saved as head.htm. You'll place this document in the first frame of the frameset as shown in Figure 5-8.

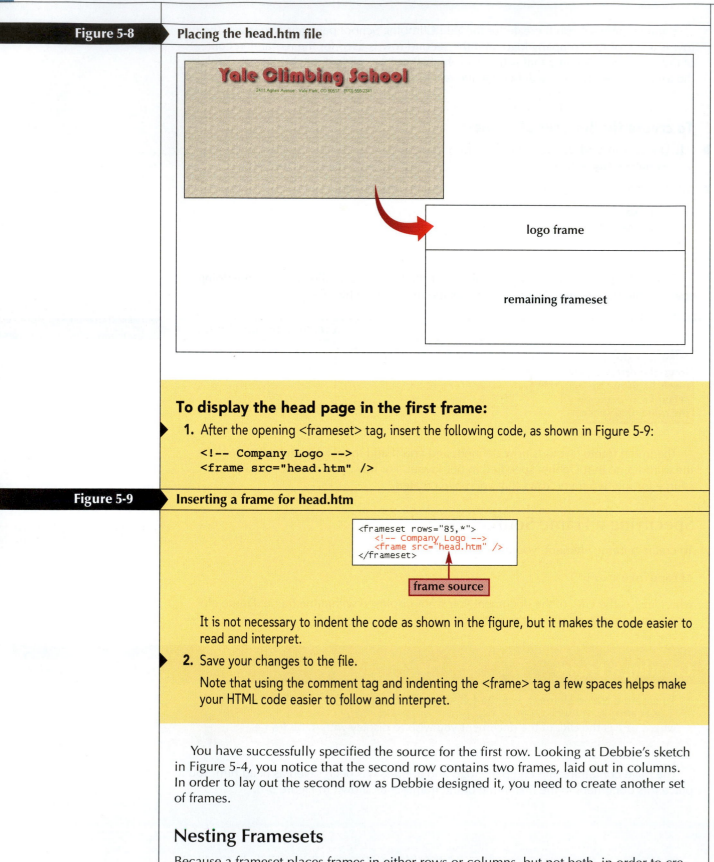

Figure 5-8 Placing the head.htm file

To display the head page in the first frame:

1. After the opening <frameset> tag, insert the following code, as shown in Figure 5-9:

```
<!-- Company Logo -->
<frame src="head.htm" />
```

Figure 5-9 Inserting a frame for head.htm

```
<frameset rows="85,*">
    <!-- Company Logo -->
    <frame src="head.htm" />
</frameset>
```

frame source

It is not necessary to indent the code as shown in the figure, but it makes the code easier to read and interpret.

2. Save your changes to the file.

Note that using the comment tag and indenting the <frame> tag a few spaces helps make your HTML code easier to follow and interpret.

You have successfully specified the source for the first row. Looking at Debbie's sketch in Figure 5-4, you notice that the second row contains two frames, laid out in columns. In order to lay out the second row as Debbie designed it, you need to create another set of frames.

Nesting Framesets

Because a frameset places frames in either rows or columns, but not both, in order to create a layout containing frames in rows *and* columns, you must nest one frameset within another. When you use this technique, the interpretation of the rows and cols attributes changes slightly. For example, a row height of 25% does not mean 25% of the display area, but rather 25% of the height of the frame in which that row is located.

Debbie wants the second row of the current frame layout to contain two columns: the first column will display a table of contents, and the second column will display a variety of YCS documents. You'll specify a width of 140 pixels for the first column, and whatever remains in the display area will be allotted to the second column.

To create the second set of frames:

1. Add a blank line immediately below the <frame> tag line that you just inserted.

2. Insert the following HTML code:

```
<!-- Nested Frames -->
<frameset cols="140,*">
</frameset>
```

Your file should appear as shown in Figure 5-10.

Creating a nested frameset ◄ **Figure 5-10**

```
<frameset rows="85,*">
    <!-- Company Logo -->
    <frame src="head.htm" />
    <!-- Nested Frames -->
    <frameset cols="140,*">
    </frameset>
</frameset>
```

nested frameset of two frame columns →

Next, you'll specify the sources for the two frames in the frameset. The frame in the first column displays the contents of links.htm. The Yale Climbing School home page, home.htm, is displayed in the second frame. Figure 5-11 shows the contents of these two pages and their locations in the frameset.

Placing links.htm and home.htm ◄ **Figure 5-11**

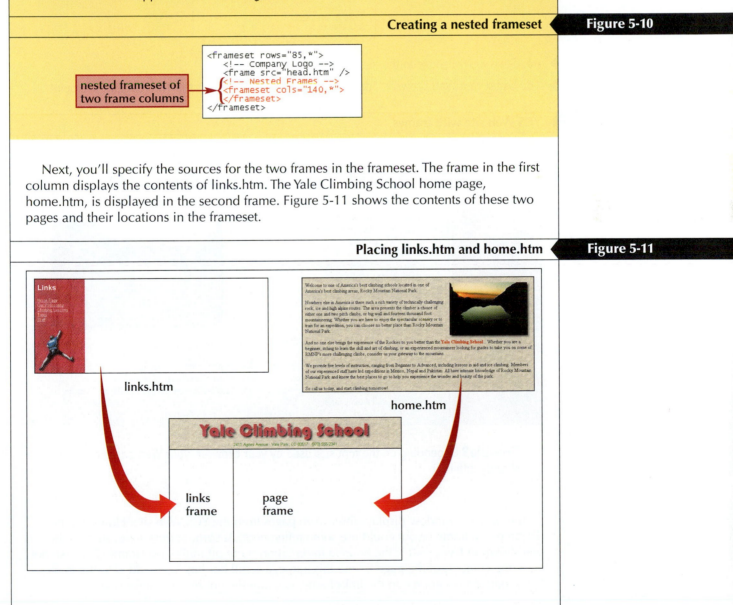

links.htm

home.htm

links frame

page frame

To insert the sources for the two frames:

1. Add a blank line immediately below the nested <frameset> tag you just inserted.

2. Type the following HTML code:

```
<!-- List of Links -->
<frame src="links.htm" />
<!-- YCS Home Page -->
<frame src="home.htm" />
```

Figure 5-12 shows the code for the two new frames.

Figure 5-12   Inserting frame columns

```
<frameset rows="85,*">
    <!-- Company Logo -->
    <frame src="head.htm" />
    <!-- Nested Frames -->
    <frameset cols="140,*">
        <!-- List of Links -->
        <frame src="links.htm" />
        <!-- YCS Home Page -->
        <frame src="home.htm" />
    </frameset>
</frameset>
```

3. Save your changes to the file.

4. Using your Web browser, open **yale.htm**. Figure 5-13 shows the Web page at this point.

Figure 5-13   YCS Web site with frames

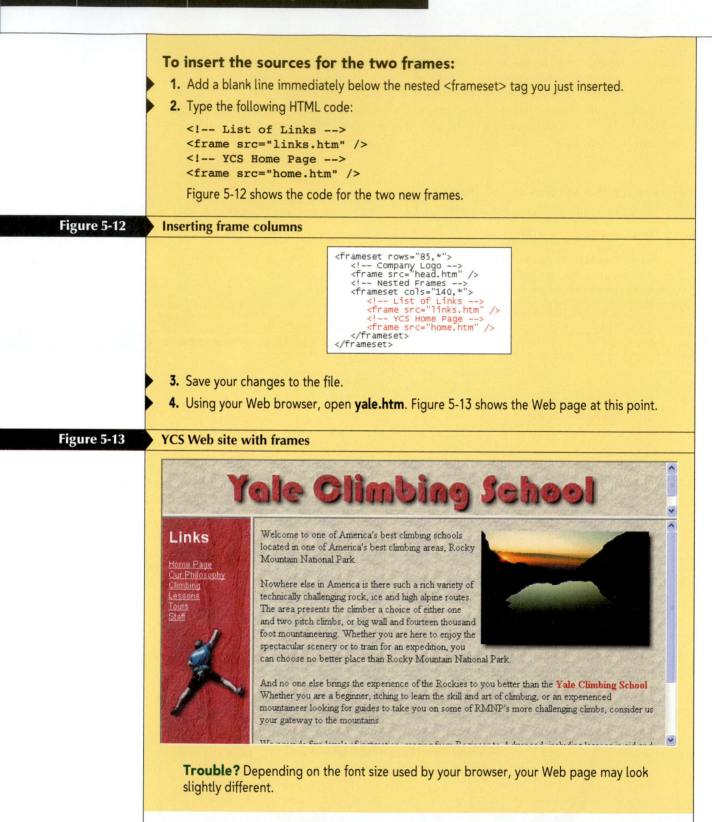

Trouble? Depending on the font size used by your browser, your Web page may look slightly different.

The browser window displays three Web pages from the YCS Web site. However, the design of the frame layout could use some refinement. At some screen sizes, such as the one shown in Figure 5-13, the address information is cut off in the logo frame. Because not all of the contents of the page fit into this frame, a scroll bar has been added to the frame. Scroll bars do not appear in the links frame, because the entire list of links is visible.

Debbie doesn't mind the appearance of a scroll bar for the school's home page—she realizes that the entire page won't necessarily fit into the frame—but she doesn't want a scroll bar for the frame containing the school's logo and address.

Formatting a Frame

You can control three attributes of a frame: the appearance of scroll bars, the size of the margin between the source document and the frame border, and whether or not users are allowed to change the frame size.

The first attribute you'll work with is the scrolling attribute.

Hiding and Displaying Scroll Bars

By default, a scroll bar is displayed when the content of the source page does not fit within a frame. You can override this setting using the scrolling attribute. The syntax for this attribute is

```
scrolling="type"
```

where *type* can be either "yes" (to always display a scroll bar) or "no" (to never display a scroll bar). If you don't specify a setting for the scrolling attribute, the browser displays a scroll bar when necessary.

Debbie feels that a scroll bar is inappropriate for the logo frame, and she wants to ensure that a scroll bar is never displayed for that frame. Therefore, you need to add the scrolling="no" attribute to the frame element. However, Debbie does want scroll bars for the other two frames, as needed, so the default value for those frames is sufficient. Note that for some browsers you need to close and then open the file for changes to the frames to take effect. If you simply reload the page, your changes may not be displayed. With other browsers, however, reloading the page does allow you to view changes to the page.

To remove the scroll bar from the logo frame:

1. Return to **yale.htm** in your text editor.

2. Within the frame element for the logo frame, insert the attribute **scrolling="no"**, as shown in Figure 5-14.

Figure 5-14 ▶ **Removing the scroll bars from the logo frame**

```
<frameset rows="85,*">
    <!-- Company Logo -->
    <frame src="head.htm" scrolling="no" />
    <!-- Nested Frames -->
    <frameset cols="140,*">
        <!-- List of Links -->
        <frame src="links.htm" />
        <!-- YCS Home Page -->
        <frame src="home.htm" />
    </frameset>
</frameset>
```

3. Save your changes to the file and reload it in your Web browser. Note that for some browsers you might have to close and then open yale.htm for the changes to take effect.

Although the scroll bar for the logo frame has been removed, depending on your screen size you may still not be able to see all of the text contained in head.htm. You can correct this problem by modifying the frame margins.

When working with frames, keep in mind that you should remove scroll bars from a frame only when you are convinced that the entire Web page will be visible in the frame. To do this, you should view your Web page using several different monitor settings. Few things are more irritating to Web site visitors than to discover that some content is missing from a frame with no scroll bars available to reveal the missing content.

With that in mind, your next task is to solve the problem of the missing text from the logo frame. To do so, you need to modify the internal margins of the frame.

Setting Frame Margins

When your browser retrieves a frame's Web page, it determines the amount of space between the content of the page and the frame border. Occasionally, the browser sets the margin between the border and the content too large. Generally, you want the margin to be big enough to keep the source's text or images from running into the frame's borders. However, you do not want the margin to take up too much space, because you typically want to display as much of the source as possible.

You've already noted that the margin height for the logo frame is too large, and this has shifted some of the text beyond the border of the frame. To fix this problem, you need to specify a smaller margin for the frame so that the logo can move up and allow all of the text to be displayed in the frame.

The attribute for specifying margin sizes for a frame is

```
marginheight="value" marginwidth="value"
```

where the marginheight value specifies the amount of space, in pixels, above and below the frame source, and the marginwidth value specifies the amount of space to the left and right of the frame source. You do not have to specify both the margin height and width. However, if you specify only one, the browser assumes that you want to use the same value for both. Setting margin values is a process of trial and error as you determine what combination of margin sizes looks best.

To correct the problem with the logo frame, you'll decrease its margin size to 0 pixels. This setting will allow the entire page to be displayed within the frame. Also, to keep the home page from running into the borders of its frame, you'll set the frame's margin width to 10 pixels. Debbie also wants you to decrease the margin height to 0 pixels. The links frame margin does not require any changes.

To set the margin sizes for the frames:

1. Return to the **yale.htm** file in your text editor.

2. Within the frame element for the logo frame, insert the attribute **marginheight="0"**. This sets both the margin height and the margin width to 0 by default.

3. Within the frame element for the home page frame, insert the attributes **marginheight="0" marginwidth="10"**.

   Figure 5-15 shows the revised HTML code for yale.htm.

Setting the frame margin sizes | Figure 5-15

```
<frameset rows="85,*">
    <!-- Company Logo -->
    <frame src="head.htm" scrolling="no" marginheight="0" />
    <!-- Nested Frames -->
    <frameset cols="140,*">
        <!-- List of Links -->
        <frame src="links.htm" />
        <!-- YCS Home Page -->
        <frame src="home.htm" marginheight="0" marginwidth="10" />
    </frameset>
</frameset>
```

4. Save your changes to the file and reload or refresh it in your Web browser. The revised frames are shown in Figure 5-16.

YCS Web site with resized frame margins | Figure 5-16

Debbie is satisfied with the changes you've made to the Web page. Your next task is to lock in the sizes and margins for each frame on the page to prevent users from resizing the frames.

Controlling Frame Resizing

By default, users can resize frame borders in the browser by simply dragging a frame border. However, some Web designers prefer to freeze, or lock, frames so that users cannot resize them. This insures that the Web site displays as the designer intended. Debbie would like you to do this for the YCS Web site. The attribute for controlling frame resizing is

```
noresize="noresize"
```

HTML also allows you to insert this attribute as

```
noresize
```

without an attribute value. However this form is not supported by XHTML, because XHTML requires all attributes to have attribute values. We'll follow this principle in the code we create for Debbie's Web site.

To prevent the frames in the YCS Web site from being resized:

1. Return to **yale.htm** in your text editor.
2. Within each of the three <frame> tags in the file, add the attribute **noresize="noresize"**
3. Save your changes to the file and reload it in your Web browser.
4. Try to drag one of the frame borders to verify that the frames are now "locked in" and cannot be resized by the user.

You're ready to take a break from working on the YCS Web site. Debbie is pleased with the progress you've made on the site. She still wants you to accomplish a few more things before your work is complete, such as specifying where the targets of the site's links should be displayed. You'll deal with this question and others in the next session.

Review

Session 5.1 Quick Check

1. What are frames, and why are they useful in displaying and designing a Web site?
2. Why is the <body> tag unnecessary for pages that contain frames?
3. What HTML code do you use to create three rows of frames with the height of the first row set to 200 pixels, the height of the second row set to 50% of the display area, and the height of the third row set to occupy the remaining space?
4. What HTML code do you use to specify home.htm as a source for a frame?
5. What HTML code do you use to remove the scroll bars from the frame for home.htm?
6. What HTML code do you use to set the size of the margin above and below the contents of the home.htm frame to 3 pixels?
7. What is the size of the margins to the right and left of the frame in Question 6?
8. What code would you use to prevent users from moving the frame borders in home.htm?

Session 5.2

Working with Frames and Links

Now that you've created frames for the Yale Climbing School Web site, you're ready to work on formatting the links for the Web page. The links page contains five links (see Figure 5-17):

- The Home Page link points to home.htm
- The Our Philosophy link points to philosph.htm
- The Climbing Lessons link points to lessons.htm
- The Tours link points to tours.htm
- The Staff link points to staff.htm

Links in the links.htm file ◀ **Figure 5-17**

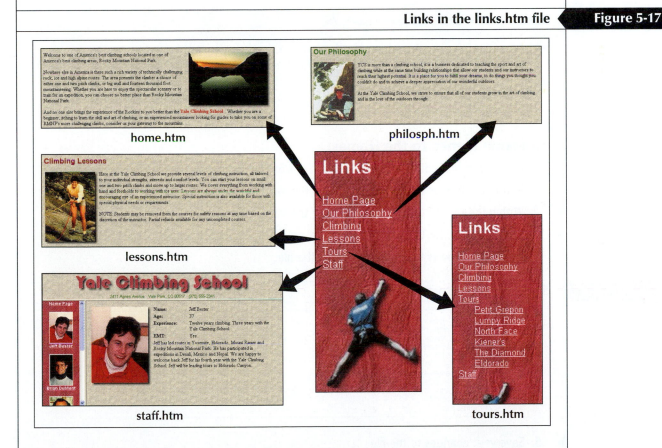

home.htm

philosph.htm

lessons.htm

staff.htm

tours.htm

By default, clicking a link within a frame opens the linked file inside the same frame. However, this is not the way Debbie wants each of the links to work. She wants the links to work as follows:

- The Home, Our Philosophy, and Climbing Lessons pages should display in the bottom-right frame
- The Tours page should display in the table of contents frame
- The Staff page should occupy the entire browser window

Controlling the behavior of links in a framed page requires two steps: you need to give each frame on the page a name, and then point each link to one of the named frames.

Reference Window

Directing a Link to a Frame

- To assign a name to a frame, insert the following attribute:
  `<frame name="name" />`
  where *name* is of the frame.
- To point the target of a link to a named frame, use the target attribute:
  `target="name"`
  where *name* is the name you assigned to the frame.
- To use the same target for all links, add the target attribute to the base element in the document head.

Assigning a Name to a Frame

To assign a name to a frame, add the name attribute to the frame tag. The syntax for this attribute is

`<frame src="url" name="name" />`

where *name* is the name assigned to the frame. Case is important in assigning names: "information" is considered a different name than "INFORMATION". Frame names cannot include spaces.

You'll name the three frames in the YCS Web site "logo," "links," and "pages."

To assign names to the frames:

1. Using your text editor, open **yale.htm** if it is not currently open.

2. Within the tag for the logo frame, enter the attribute **name="logo"**.

3. Within the tag for the links frame, enter the attribute **name="links"**.

4. Within the tag for the home page frame, enter the attribute **name="pages"**.

   Figure 5-18 shows the revised code for the file.

Figure 5-18 Setting the frame names

```
<frameset rows="85,*">
   <!-- Company Logo -->
   <frame src="head.htm" scrolling="no" marginheight="0" name="logo" />
   <!-- Nested Frames -->
   <frameset cols="140,*">
      <!-- List of Links -->
      <frame src="links.htm" name="links" />
      <!-- YCS Home Page -->
      <frame src="home.htm" marginheight="0" marginwidth="10" name="pages" />
   </frameset>
</frameset>
```

5. Save your changes to the file.

Now that you've named the frames, the next task is to specify the "pages" frame as the target for the Home Page, Our Philosophy, and Climbing Lessons links, so that clicking each of these links opens the corresponding file in the home page frame.

Specifying a Link Target

Previously, you may have used the target attribute to open a linked document in a new browser window. You can also use the target attribute to open a linked target in a frame. To point the link to a specific frame, add the following attribute to the link:

```
target="name"
```

where *name* is the name you've assigned to a frame in your Web page. In this case, the target name for the frame you need to specify is "pages". To change the targets for the links, edit the <a> tags in links.htm. You'll start by editing only the <a> tags pointing to the Home Page, Our Philosophy, and Climbing Lessons pages. These are the links to be displayed in the "pages" frame of yale.htm. You'll work with the other links later.

To specify the targets for the links:

1. Using your text editor, open **links.htm** from the tutorial.05/tutorial folder. Enter *your name* and *the date* in the comment section of the file.

2. Within the <a> tags for the Home Page, Our Philosophy, and Climbing Lessons links, enter the attribute **target="pages"**. The revised code is shown in Figure 5-19.

Assigning a target to a link ◀ **Figure 5-19**

```
<h2>Links</h2>
<p style="font-size: 0.8em">
<a href="home.htm" target="pages">Home Page</a><br />
<a href="philosph.htm" target="pages">Our Philosophy</a><br />
<a href="lessons.htm" target="pages">Climbing Lessons</a><br />
<a href="tours.htm">Tours</a><br />
<a href="staff.htm">Staff</a>
</p>
```

3. Save your changes to the file.

   Trouble? If you need to return to the original version of the file, you can open linkstxt.htm in the tutorial.05/tutorial folder in your Data Files.

   Now test the first three links in the list.

4. Using your Web browser, open **yale.htm**.

5. Click the **Our Philosophy** link in the Links frame. The Our Philosophy Web page should display in the lower-right frame. See Figure 5-20.

Figure 5-20 | **Viewing the philosophy page**

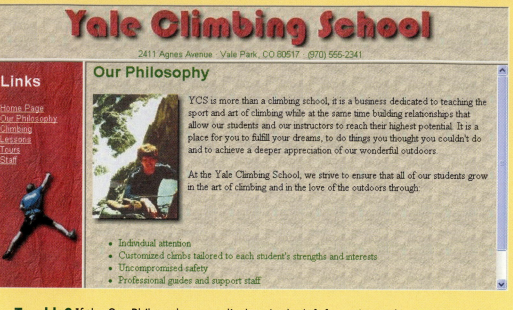

Trouble? If the Our Philosophy page displays in the left frame instead, you may need to close and open yale.htm for your changes to take effect.

▶ 6. Click the **Home Page** and **Climbing Lessons** links, and verify that the links are working properly and the pages are displaying in the "pages" frame.

Sometimes pages can contains dozens of links that should all open in the same frame. Instead of repetitively inserting target attributes for each link, you can instead specify the target in the base element within the document head. See Tutorial 2 for a discussion of the base element. Note that the target attribute is not supported in strictly compliant XHTML code.

Using Reserved Target Names

The remaining two tags in the list of links point to a list of the tours offered by the Yale Climbing School (tours.htm) and to a staff information page (staff.htm), respectively. The tours.htm file does not contain information about individual tours; instead, it is an expanded table of contents of YCS Web pages, some of which are devoted to individual tours. Each tour has its own Web page, as shown in Figure 5-21.

Tour pages | **Figure 5-21**

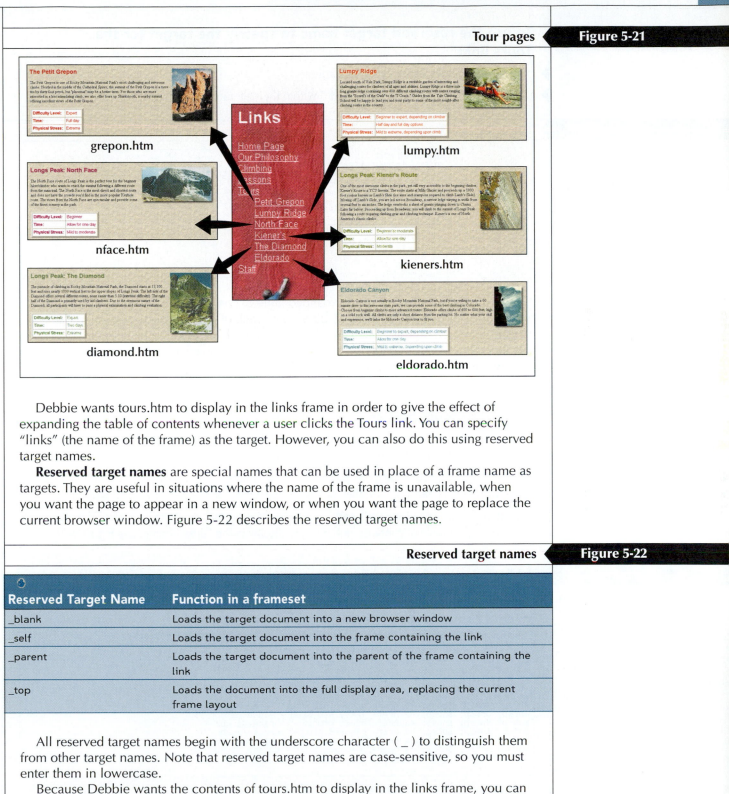

Debbie wants tours.htm to display in the links frame in order to give the effect of expanding the table of contents whenever a user clicks the Tours link. You can specify "links" (the name of the frame) as the target. However, you can also do this using reserved target names.

Reserved target names are special names that can be used in place of a frame name as targets. They are useful in situations where the name of the frame is unavailable, when you want the page to appear in a new window, or when you want the page to replace the current browser window. Figure 5-22 describes the reserved target names.

Reserved target names | **Figure 5-22**

Reserved Target Name	Function in a frameset
_blank	Loads the target document into a new browser window
_self	Loads the target document into the frame containing the link
_parent	Loads the target document into the parent of the frame containing the link
_top	Loads the document into the full display area, replacing the current frame layout

All reserved target names begin with the underscore character (_) to distinguish them from other target names. Note that reserved target names are case-sensitive, so you must enter them in lowercase.

Because Debbie wants the contents of tours.htm to display in the links frame, you can use the reserved target name, _self, which overrides the target specified in the <base> tag and instructs the browser to open the page in the same frame that contains the link.

To use the reserved target name to specify the target for the Tours link:

▶ 1. Return to **links.htm** in your text editor.

▶ 2. Enter the attribute **target="_self "** within the <a> tag for the Tours link. See Figure 5-23.

Figure 5-23	Using the _self target

```
<h2>Links</h2>
<p style="font-size: 0.8em">
<a href="home.htm" target="pages">Home Page</a><br />
<a href="philosph.htm" target="pages">Our Philosophy</a><br />
<a href="lessons.htm" target="pages">Climbing Lessons</a><br />
<a href="tours.htm" target="_self">Tours</a><br />
<a href="staff.htm">Staff</a>
</p>
```

▶ 3. Save your changes to **links.htm**.

The tours.htm Web page is an expanded table of contents for Web pages containing information about specific tours. Debbie wants each of these pages to display in the "pages" frame. To do this, specify the "pages" frame as the default link target in tours.htm. The tours.htm file also contains a link that takes the user back to links.htm. You should specify _self as the target for this link.

To modify tours.htm as you did links.htm:

▶ 1. Using your text editor, open **tours.htm** from the tutorial.05/tutorial folder. Enter **your name** and **the date** in the comment section of the file.

▶ 2. Insert the tag **<base target="pages" />** directly above the </head> tag. This code displays the individual tour pages in the "pages" frame when a user clicks any of the tour links.

▶ 3. Enter the attribute **target="_self"** within the <a> tag that points to links.htm. This will cause the original table of contents, links.htm, to display in the "links" frame. See Figure 5-24.

Figure 5-24	Adding targets to the tours page

```
<title>List of links</title>
<base target="pages" />
</head>

<body style="background-image: url(wall3.jpg); background-repeat: repeat-y;
            font-family: sans-serif; color: white" link="white" alink="white" vlink="white">
<h2>Links</h2>
<p style="font-size: 0.8em">
<a href="home.htm">Home Page</a><br />
<a href="philosph.htm">Our Philosophy</a><br />
<a href="lessons.htm">Climbing Lessons</a><br />
<a href="links.htm" target="_self">Tours</a><br />
      <a href="grepon.htm">Petit Grepon</a><br />
      <a href="lumpy.htm">Lumpy Ridge</a><br />
      <a href="nface.htm">North Face</a><br />
      <a href="kieners.htm">Kiener's</a><br />
      <a href="diamond.htm">The Diamond</a><br />
      <a href="eldorado.htm">Eldorado</a><br />
<a href="staff.htm">Staff</a>
</p>
```

▶ 4. Save your changes to the file.

Trouble? If you need to revert back to the original version of tours.htm for any reason, it is saved in the tutorial.05/tutorial folder as tourstxt.htm

▶ 5. Reload **yale.htm** in your Web browser.

6. Verify that the Tours link works as you intended. As you click on the link, the table of contents list should alternately collapse and expand. In addition, click on the links to the individual tour pages to verify that they display correctly in the "pages" frame. See Figure 5-25.

Viewing a tour page | Figure 5-25

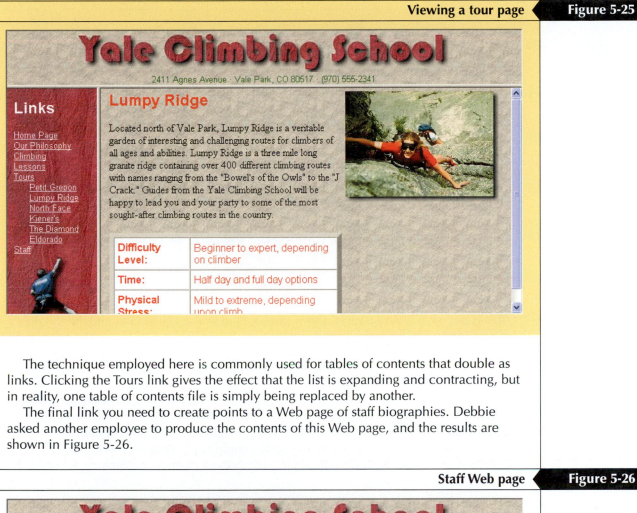

The technique employed here is commonly used for tables of contents that double as links. Clicking the Tours link gives the effect that the list is expanding and contracting, but in reality, one table of contents file is simply being replaced by another.

The final link you need to create points to a Web page of staff biographies. Debbie asked another employee to produce the contents of this Web page, and the results are shown in Figure 5-26.

Staff Web page | Figure 5-26

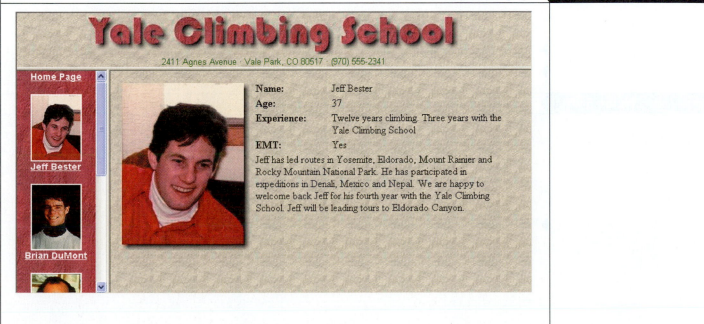

As you can see, this Web page also uses frames. If you specify the "pages" frame as the target, the result is a series of nested frame images, as shown in Figure 5-27.

Figure 5-27 **Nested frame layout**

This is not what Debbie wants. She wants the Staff Web page to load into the full display area, replacing the frame layout with its own layout. To target a link to the full display area, you use the _top reserved target name. The _top target is often used when one framed page is accessed from another. It's also used when you are linking to pages that lie outside your Web site altogether.

For example, a link to the Colorado Tourism Board Web site should not display within a frame on the YCS Web site for two reasons. First, once you go outside your Web site, you lose control of the frame layout, and you could easily end up with nested frame images. The second reason is that such a design could easily confuse users, making it appear as if the Colorado Tourism Board is a component of the Yale Climbing School.

To specify the target for the Staff link:

1. Return to **links.htm** in your text editor.

2. Enter the attribute **target="_top"** within the <a> tag for the Staff link. See Figure 5-28.

Figure 5-28 **Revised links.htm**

```
<h2>Links</h2>
<p style="font-size: 0.8em">
<a href="home.htm" target="pages">Home Page</a><br />
<a href="philosph.htm" target="pages">Our Philosophy</a><br />
<a href="lessons.htm" target="pages">Climbing Lessons</a><br />
<a href="tours.htm" target="_self">Tours</a><br />
<a href="staff.htm" target="_top">Staff</a>
</p>
```

3. Save your changes to the file.

Because tours.htm also acts as a detailed table of contents, you should edit the link to the Staff page in that file. That way, a user can click the Staff link from either the table of contents with the expanded list of tours, or the original table of contents.

To edit tours.htm:

▶ 1. Return to **tours.htm** in your text editor.

▶ 2. Enter the attribute **target="_top"** within the <a> tag for the Staff link.

▶ 3. Save your changes to the file.

▶ 4. Using your Web browser, reload **yale.htm**. Verify that the Staff link now opens the Staff page and replaces the existing frame layout with its own. Be sure to test the Staff link from both the original table of contents and the table of contents with the expanded list of tours.

Trouble? If the Staff link does not work properly, verify that you used lowercase letters for the reserved target name.

Debbie has viewed all the links on the YCS Web site and is quite satisfied with the results. However, she wonders what would happen if a user with an older browser encountered the page. If possible, she wants to be able to accommodate browsers that don't support frames.

Using the noframes Element

You can use the noframes element to make your Web site viewable with browsers that do not support frames (known as frame-blind browsers) as well as by those that do. The noframes element marks a section of your HTML file as code that browsers incapable of displaying frames can use. The noframes element is nested within the frameset element and uses the following syntax:

```
<html>
<head>
<title>title</title>
</head>
<frameset>
    frames
    <noframes>
        <body>
            page content
        </body>
    </noframes>
</frameset>
</html>
```

where *page content* is the content that you want the browser to display in place of the frames. There can be only one noframes element in the document. When a browser that supports frames processes this code, it ignores everything within the <noframes> tag and concentrates solely on the code to create the frames. When a browser that doesn't support frames processes this HTML code, however, it doesn't know what to do with the <frameset> and <noframes> tags, so it ignores them. It does know how to render whatever appears within the <body> tags, though. Using this setup, both types of browsers are supported within a single HTML file. Note that when you use the <noframes> tag, you must include <body> tags to specify the extent of the page content.

Reference Window

Supporting Frame-Blind Browsers

- Create a version of your page that does not use frames.
- In the frames document, insert the following tags within the frameset element:
  ```
  <noframes>
    <body>
     page content
    </body>
  </noframes>
  ```
  where *page content* is the content of the page you want displayed in place of the frames.

The Yale Climbing School has been using the nonframed Web site displayed in Figure 5-29 for several years.

Figure 5-29 | **Frameless version of the YCS home page**

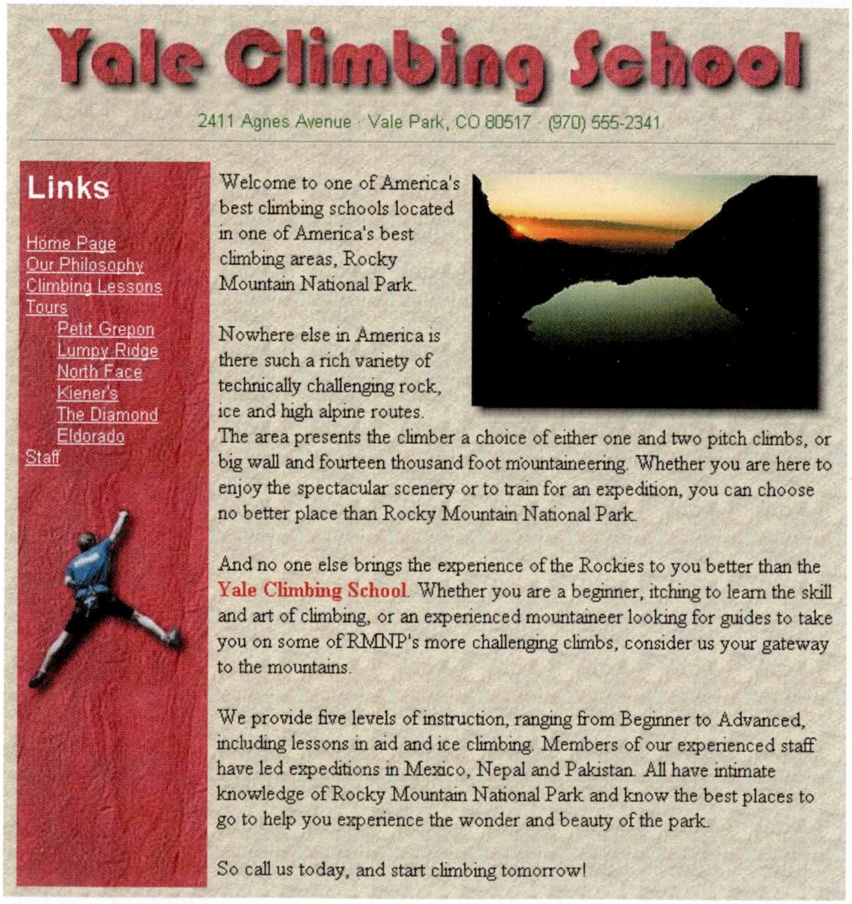

If you want this Web page to display for frame-blind browsers, while still making your framed version available as the default, copy the HTML code, including the <body> tags, from the source code of the nonframed Web page and place it within a pair of <noframes> tags in the framed Web document yale.htm.

To insert support for frame-blind browsers:

1. Using your text editor, return to **yale.htm**.

2. Create a blank line immediately above the </html> tag.

3. Enter the following HTML code directly before the closing </frameset> tag at the bottom of the file:

   ```
   <!-- Noframes version of this page -->
   <noframes>
   </noframes>
   ```

4. Save your changes to the file.

   Next, copy the code from the noframe page into **yale.htm**.

5. Using your text editor, open **noframes.htm** from the tutorial.05/tutorial folder.

6. Copy the HTML code for the page content. Be sure to include both the opening and closing <body> tags in your copy selection.

7. Return to **yale.htm** in your text editor.

8. Create a blank line immediately below the <noframes> tag.

9. Paste the text you copied from noframes.htm in the blank line you created below the <noframes> tag. Figure 5-30 shows the beginning and end of the revised code.

Inserting the noframes page version ◀ **Figure 5-30**

```
<frameset rows="85,*">
    <!-- Company Logo -->
    <frame src="head.htm" scrolling="no" marginheight="0" name="logo" />
    <!-- Nested Frames -->
    <frameset cols="140,*">
        <!-- List of Links -->
        <frame src="links.htm" name="links" />
        <!-- YCS Home Page -->
        <frame src="home.htm" marginheight="0" marginwidth="10" name="pages" />
    </frameset>

<!-- Noframes version of this page -->
<noframes>
<body style="background-image: url(wall.jpg)" link="white" vlink="white" alink="white">
<table width="620" cellpadding="5">
<tr>
```

```
        <p>We provide five levels of instruction, ranging from Beginner to
        Advanced, including lessons in aid and ice climbing. Members of our
        experienced staff have led expeditions in Mexico, Nepal and Pakistan.
        All have intimate knowledge of Rocky Mountain National Park and know the
        best places to go to help you experience the wonder and beauty of the
        park.</p>
        <p>So call us today, and start climbing tomorrow!</p>
    </td>
</tr>
</table>
</body>
</noframes>

</frameset>
</html>
```

10. Save your changes to **yale.htm**.

Another way of supporting browsers that do not display frames is to create a Web page that contains links to the framed and nonframed versions of your Web site. A user with an older browser can thereby avoid the frames. This technique also provides users with the option of not viewing frames, even though their browsers have the ability to. Some people just don't like frames.

Working with Frame Borders

Some browsers support additional attributes that you can use to change border size and appearance. For example, you can remove borders from your frames to free up more space for text and images, or you can change the color of the frame borders so that they match or complement the color scheme for your Web site.

Modifying Frame Borders

- To specify whether a frame border is displayed, insert the following attribute:
  `<frame frameborder="value" />`
  where a value of "0" hides the border, and a value of "1" displays it.

Internet Explorer and Netscape

- To define the width of frame borders, add the following attribute to the frameset element:
  `<frameset border="value"> … <frameset>`
  where *value* is the size of the border in pixels. Adding this attribute to a frameset applies the border width to all frames in the frameset. Note that you can also change border width in Internet Explorer using the framespacing attribute.
- To define a color for your frame borders, add the following attribute to either the frameset or frame element:
  `bordercolor="color"`
  where *color* is a color name or a hexadecimal color value.

Setting the Frame Border Color

To change the color of a frame's border, both Internet Explorer and Netscape support the bordercolor attribute. The attribute can be applied either to an entire set of frames, using the <frameset> tag, or to individual frames, using the <frame> tag. The syntax for this attribute is

`bordercolor="color"`

where *color* is either a color name or a hexadecimal color value. Applying the bordercolor attribute to the <frameset> tag affects all of the frames and nested frames within the set. If you apply the bordercolor attribute to a single <frame> tag, the border color for that particular frame changes in Internet Explorer, but in Netscape, all of the frame borders change. It is important to remember that when you apply these types of tags and attributes to your Web page, you should always view the page using different browsers and, if possible, browser versions. Note that this attribute is not part of the official specifications for HTML, nor is it supported by XHTML.

Debbie asks you to test the bordercolor attribute on the YCS Web site by changing the color of the frame borders to brown.

To change the frame border color:

1. Return to **yale.htm** in your text editor.
2. Enter the attribute **bordercolor="brown"** within the opening <frameset> tag.
3. Save your changes to the file, and then reload it in your Web browser. Figure 5-31 shows the frames with a brown border.

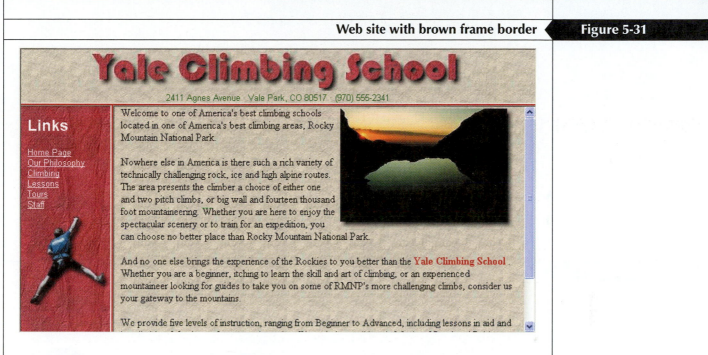

Setting the Frame Border Width

You can also remove the frame borders entirely. The attribute for specifying whether a frame border appears is

```
<frame frameborder="value" />
```

where a frameborder value of "0" removes the frame border and a value of "1" displays the border. Different browsers respond in different ways to this attribute, and some browsers do not support the attribute at all. Internet Explorer and Netscape also support the border attribute, which has the syntax:

```
<frameset border="value"> … </frame>
```

where *value* is the size of the border in pixels. Note that the border attribute is applied to the frameset element, while the frameborder attribute is applied only the frame element. Like bordercolor, the border attribute is not part of the specifications for HTML, and is not supported by XHTML.

Debbie has asked you to remove the frame borders from the document. In order to ensure capability with the greatest number of browsers, you'll use both the frameborder and the border attributes in your HTML code.

To change the size of the frame borders:

1. Return to **yale.htm** in your text editor.
2. Delete the bordercolor attribute that you entered in the previous set of steps. You don't need this attribute because you're going to remove the frame borders entirely.
3. Insert the attribute **border="0"** within the <frameset> tag.
4. Insert the attribute **frameborder="0"** within each of the <frame> tags. Figure 5-32 shows the revised code.

Figure 5-32 | **Removing the frame borders**

```
<frameset rows="85,*" border="0">
  <!-- Company Logo -->
  <frame src="head.htm" scrolling="no" marginheight="0" name="logo"
         frameborder="0" />
  <!-- Nested Frames -->
  <frameset cols="140,*">
    <!-- List of Links -->
    <frame src="links.htm" name="links" frameborder="0" />
    <!-- YCS Home Page -->
    <frame src="home.htm" marginheight="0" marginwidth="10" name="pages"
           frameborder="0" />
  </frameset>
</frameset>
```

▶ **5.** Save your changes to **yale.htm** and close the file.

▶ **6.** Reload **yale.htm** in your Web browser. As shown in Figure 5-33, the frame borders are removed from the page.

Figure 5-33 | **The YCS Web site without frame borders**

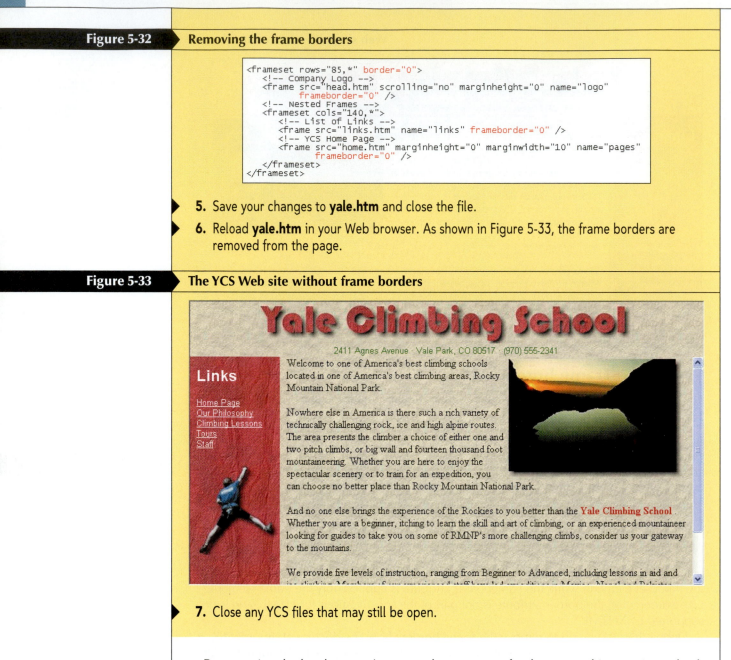

▶ **7.** Close any YCS files that may still be open.

By removing the borders, you've created more space for the text and images in each of the Web pages. You've also created the impression of a "seamless" Web page. Some Web designers prefer not to show frame borders in order to give the illusion of a single Web page rather than three separate ones. However, other Web designers believe that hiding frame borders can confuse users as they navigate the Web site.

Creating Inline Frames

Another way of using frames is to create a floating frame. Introduced by Internet Explorer 3.0 and added to the HTML 4.0 specifications, a **floating frame**, or **inline frame**, is displayed as a separate box or window within a Web page. The frame can be placed within a Web page in much the same way as an inline image. The syntax for a floating frame is

```
<iframe src="url">
   alternate content
</iframe>
```

where *url* is the URL of the document you want displayed in the inline frame and *alternate content* is the content you want displayed by browsers that don't support inline frames. For example, the following code displays the contents of the jobs.htm file within an inline frame; for browsers that don't support inline frames, it displays a paragraph containing a link to the file:

```
<iframe src="jobs.htm">
     <p>
     View the online <a href="jobs.htm">jobs listing</a>
     </p>
</iframe>
```

Inline frames support many of the same features as inline images. You can resize them, float them on the page margins, and specify the size of the margin around the frame. You can also use many of the attributes associated with frame elements. Figure 5-34 summarizes some of the attributes associated with inline frames. Note that the iframe element is not supported in strictly compliant XHTML code.

Attributes of inline frames ◄ **Figure 5-34**

Attribute	Description
align="*position*"	Places the frame in relationship to the surrounding content. **Deprecated**
border="*value*"	The size of the border around the frame, in pixels. **Deprecated**
frameborder="*value*"	Specifies whether to display a frame border (1) or not (0)
height="*value*" width="*value*"	The height and width of the frame, in pixels
hspace="*value*" vspace="*value*"	The horizontal and vertical space around the frame, in pixels. **Deprecated**
marginheight="*value*" marginwidth="*value*	The size of the internal margins of the frame, in pixels
name="*text*"	The name of the frame
scrolling="*type*"	Specifies whether the frame can be scrolled ("yes") or not ("no")
src="*url*"	The URL of the document displayed in the inline frame
style="*styles*"	Styles applied to the inline frame

Debbie is interested in working with inline frames, and she would like you to create a staff page that employs this feature.

To create an inline frame:

1. Using your text editor, open **iftxt.htm** from the tutorial.05/tutorial folder. Enter *your name* and *the date* in the comment section of the file. Save the document as **iframe.htm**.

2. Immediately following the horizontal line, insert the following HTML code. See Figure 5-35.

```
<p>
<iframe src="bios.htm" width="400" height="250"
style="float: right; margin: 0 0 0 5">
    Frames not supported.<br />
    Click to view detailed <a href="bios.htm">biographies</a>
of our staff.
</iframe>
</p>
```

Figure 5-35	Inserting an inline frame

```
<hr />
<p>
<iframe src="bios.htm" width="400" height="250" style="float: right; margin: 0 0 0 5">
   Frames not supported.<br />
   Click to view detailed <a href="bios.htm">biographies</a> of our staff.
</iframe>
</p>
<h1 style="color: brown; font-family: sans-serif">Staff</h1>
<p>The staff at the Yale Climbing School is here to help with all of your climbing needs.
All of our instructors are fully qualified with years of climbing and teaching experience.
Scroll through the biographies at the right for more information.</p>
```

3. Save your changes to **iframe.htm** and close the file.

4. Open **iframe.htm** in your Web browser. Figure 5-36 shows the resulting Web page.

   Trouble? If you're running Netscape version 4.7 or earlier, you will not see the floating frame displayed in Figure 5-36.

Figure 5-36	Viewing an inline frame

Yale Climbing School · 2411 Agnes Avenue · Vale Park, CO 80517 · (970) 555-2341

Staff

The staff at the Yale Climbing School is here to help with all of your climbing needs. All of our instructors are fully qualified with years of climbing and teaching experience. Scroll through the biographies at the right for more information.

Name: Jeff Bester
Age: 37
Experience: Twelve years climbing. Three years with the YCS
EMT: Yes

Jeff has led routes in Yosemite, Eldorado, Mount Rainier and Rocky Mountain National Park. He has participated in expeditions in Denali, Mexico and Nepal. We are happy to welcome back Jeff for his fourth year with the YCS. Jeff will be leading tours to Eldorado Canyon

5. Use the scroll bars in the floating frame to view the entire list of staff biographies.

6. Close your Web browser.

You've completed your work for Debbie and the Yale Climbing School. Using frames, you've created an interesting presentation that is both attractive and easy to navigate. Debbie is pleased and will get back to you if she needs any additional work done.

Tips for Using Frames

- Create framed and frameless versions of your Web site to accommodate different browsers and to offer a choice to users who don't like frames.
- Do not turn off vertical and horizontal scrolling unless you are certain that the page content will fit within the specified frame size.
- Assign names to all frames, in order to make your code easier to read and interpret and to direct links to the correct target.
- Simplify your HTML code by using the base element when most of the links in your frame document point to the same target.
- NEVER display pages that lie outside of your Web site within your frames. Use the "_top" target to open external sites in the full browser window.

Session 5.2 Quick Check

Review

1. When you click a link inside a frame, in what frame does the target Web page appear by default?
2. What attribute would you use to assign the name "Address" to a frame?
3. What attribute would you add to a link to direct it to a frame named "News"?
4. What attribute would you use to point a link to the document "sales.htm" with the result that the sales.htm file is displayed in the entire browser window?
5. What tag would you use to direct all links in a document to the "News" target?
6. Describe what you would do to make your Web page readable by browsers that support frames and by those that do not.
7. What attribute would you use to set the frame border color of every frame on the page to red?
8. How would you set the frame border width to 5 pixels?

Tutorial Summary

Review

In this tutorial, you learned how to create and use frames. In the first session, you learned how to create a frameset and arrange the frames in rows or columns within a set. You also learned how to specify which document appears within each frame. The first session concluded with a discussion of some of the frame attributes used to control the frame's appearance. The second session explored how to direct a link's target to a specific frame. In addition, you learned some of the other attributes that can be used to format the frame's appearance. The session also showed how to support browsers that don't recognize frames. The tutorial concluded by demonstrating how to create inline frames.

Key Terms

floating frame   frameset   reserved target name

frame   inline frame

Practice

Practice the skills you learned in the tutorial using the same case scenario.

Review Assignments

Data files needed for this Review Assignment: headtxt.htm, slisttxt.htm, sltxt.htm, stafftxt.htm, tlisttxt.htm, tltxt.htm, tourstxt.htm, yale2txt.htm, + 16 HTML files, + 24 JPEG files

Debbie has asked you to revise the layout for the YCS Web site. She would like links for all of the Web pages to display in separate frames so that users can always click a link for a specific page or collection of pages no matter where they are in the Web site. Figure 5-37 shows a preview of the frames you'll create for the Yale Climbing School Web site.

Figure 5-37

This is a large Web site containing 48 files; however you'll only have to create the following files in order to complete the site:

- tlist.htm—contains a list of links to the tour pages (data file: tlisttxt.htm)

- slist.htm—contains a list of links to staff bios (data file: slisttxt.htm)

- tours2.htm—a frame layout displaying YCS tours (data file: tourstxt.htm)

- staff2.htm—a frame layout displaying YCS staff bios (data file: stafftxt.htm)
- tourlink.htm—a Web page containing a link to tours2.htm (data file: tltxt.htm)
- staflink.htm—a Web page containing a link to staff2.htm (data file: sltxt.htm)
- head2.htm—a Web page containing the company logo and links to three pages (data file: headtxt.htm)
- yale2.htm—a frame layout displaying all of the YCS Web pages (data file: yale2txt.htm)

To create the YCS Web site:

1. Using your text editor, open the **tlisttxt.htm**, **slisttxt.htm**, **tourstxt.htm**, **stafftxt.htm**, **tltxt.htm**, **sltxt.htm**, **headtxt.htm**, and **yale2txt.htm** files from the tutorial.05/review folder. Enter *your name* and *the date* in each file. Save the files as **tlist.htm**, **slist.htm**, **tours2.htm**, **staff2.htm**, **tourlink.htm**, **staflink.htm**, **head2.htm**, and **yale2.htm**, respectively.

2. Go to the **tlist.htm** file in your text editor. This file contains a list of links to the tours pages. Define "Tours" as the default target for links in this file and close the file, saving your changes.

3. Go to the **slist.htm** file in your text editor. This file contains a list of links to the staff bios. Set "Bios" as the default target for links on this page. Save your changes and close the file.

4. Go to the **tours2.htm** file in your text editor. This file will display a frame layout showing the list of tour links and the individual tour pages. To complete this document, do the following:

   - Create a frameset consisting of two columns of frames. The first frame should be 140 pixels wide; the second frame should occupy the remaining space.
   - Make the frame borders 5 pixels wide and brown in color.
   - The source for the first frame should be the **tlist.htm** file.
   - The source for the second frame should be the **grepon.htm** file. Assign the frame the name "Tours".
   - Do not allow users to resize either frame in the frameset.

5. Save your changes and close the file.

6. Open the **staff2.htm** in your text editor. This file will display a frame layout showing the list of staff links and the individual staff bio pages. To complete the frame layout, do the following:

   - Create a frameset containing two columns. Make the first frame 140 pixels wide; the second frame should occupy the remaining space.
   - Make the frame borders 5 pixels wide and brown in color.

- The first frame should have a margin height of 1 pixel and a margin width of 10 pixels. The source for this frame should be the **slist.htm** file.

- Display the contents of the **bester.htm** file in the second frame. Name the frame "Bios". You do not have to specify a margin height or width.

- Do not allow users to resize either frame.

7. Save your changes and close the file.

8. Open **tourlink.htm** in your text editor. This page contains a link to the frameset in the tours2.htm file. To complete this page, set the target of the link in this file to the name "docs". Save your changes and close the file.

9. Open **staflink.htm** in your text editor. This page contains a link to the frameset in the staff2.htm file. To complete this page, set the target of the link in this file to the name "docs". Close the file, saving your changes.

10. Open **head2.htm** in your text editor. This file contains links for the home, philosophy, and lessons pages. Once again, point the target of these links to the name "docs". Close the file, saving your changes.

11. Open **yale2.htm** in your text editor. This document contains the frameset for the entire Web site. To complete the frameset, do the following:

- Create a frameset containing three rows of frames. The first frame should be 85 pixels high, the third frame should be 30 pixels high, and the middle frame should occupy the remaining space. The first frame will contain the Web site header, the second frame will contain informational documents, and the third frame will contain the Web site footer. Note that the second frame will either display the Web pages stored in the home.htm, philosph.htm, and lessons.htm files, or it will display the frame lay-outs stored in the staff2.htm and tours2.htm files.

- Make the frame borders brown, 5 pixels in width. Do not allow users to resize the frames.

- Display **head2.htm** in the first frame. Set the margin height to 0 pixels and remove the scrollbars.

- Display the contents of the **home.htm** file in the second frame and name the frame "docs". Set the second frame's margin height to 0 pixels and the margin width to 10 pixels.

- Insert a frameset containing three columns into the third frame. The first and third columns of the nested frameset should be 100 pixels wide; the second column should occupy the remaining space. Use **staflink.htm** as the source for the first frame, **footer.htm** as the source for the second frame, and **tourlink.htm** as the source for the third frame. Set the margin width and height of each frame to 5 pix-els. Make the frame borders brown and 5 pixels wide. Do not allow users to resize the frames and remove the scrollbars from these three frames.

12. For browsers that don't support frames, insert the contents of **noframes.htm** into **yale2.htm** within a noframes element just before the closing </frameset> tag.

13. Save your changes and close the file.

14. Open **yale2.htm** in your Web browser, and verify that you can view all of the Web pages in the YCS Web site in the appropriate frames.

15. Submit the completed Web site to your instructor.

Apply

Use the skills you've learned in this tutorial to create a frameset for a financial report at a shareholders' convention.

Case Problem 1

Data files needed for this Case Problem: dcclogo.jpg, dccmw.htm, dccne.htm, dccs.htm, dcctxt.htm, dccw.htm, headtxt.htm, map.jpg, maptxt.htm, mwchart.jpg, nechart.jpg, report.htm, schart.jpg, wchart.jpg

Doc-Centric Copiers Located in Salt Lake City, Doc-Centric is one of the nation's leading manufacturers of personal and business copiers. The annual shareholders' convention in Chicago is approaching, and the general manager, David Edgars, wants you to create an online report for the convention participants. The report will be posted on the company Web site before the convention so that shareholders can review the company's financial data. Most of the Web pages have been created for you. Your job is to display that information using frames. A preview of the layout you'll create is shown in Figure 5-38.

Figure 5-38

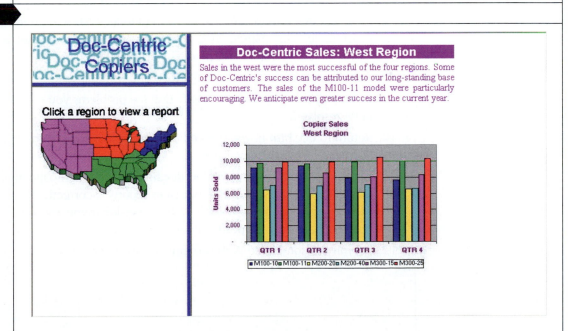

To create the Doc-Centric Copiers sales presentation:

1. Use your text editor to open the **dcctxt.htm**, **headtxt.htm**, and **maptxt.htm** files from the tutorial.05/case1 folder. Enter *your name* and *the date* in the comment section of each file. Save the files as **dcc.htm**, **head.htm**, and **map.htm**, respectively.

2. Go to the **dcc.htm** file in your text editor. This documents the frameset for the entire Web site. To complete this document, do the following:

   - Create a frameset containing two columns with a blue frame border, 10 pixels in width. The first frame should be 240 pixels wide. The second frame should occupy the remaining space in the design window.

   - Create two rows of nested frames in the first frame. The first row should be 75 pixels high; the second row should fill up the remaining space. Display the contents of the **head.htm** file in the first row. Display the contents of the **map.htm** file in the second row. Name the first frame "logo", the second frame "usmap".

   - In the second frame, display the contents of the **report.htm** file. Name the frame "reports".

3. Save your changes to the file.

4. Go to the **map.htm** file in your text editor. This page contains an image map of the sales regions. Direct each link in the map.htm file to the reports target, so that the pages will appear in the reports frame. Save your changes and close the file.

5. Go to the **head.htm** file in your text editor. This page contains the company logo, formatted as a link to the title page. Direct this link to the reports target. Close the file, saving your changes.

6. Use your Web browser to view dcc.htm. Think about what improvements could be made to the page, and what should be removed.

7. Return to **dcc.htm** in your text editor and reduce the margin for the logo frame to 1 pixel. Reduce the margin width for the usmap frame to 1 pixel, and change that frame's margin height to 30 pixels.

8. Remove scroll bars from both the logo and usmap frames.

9. View the Web page again to verify that the problems you identified in Step 6 have been resolved.

10. Return to **dcc.htm** in your text editor, and lock the size of the frames to prevent users from changing the frame sizes.

11. Using your Web browser, reload **dcc.htm** and test the image map in the usmap frame. Verify that each of the four sales reports is correctly displayed in the reports frame. Click the company logo in the upper-left frame and verify that it redisplays the opening page in the reports frame.

12. Submit the completed Web site to your instructor.

Explore

Broaden your knowledge of inline frames by creating an inline frame that shows different photos of a real estate property.

Case Problem 2

Data files needed for this Case Problem: back.jpg, brlogo.jpg, img01.jpg–img13.jpg, l20481.jpg, listtxt.htm, pback.jpg

Browyer Realty   Linda Browyer is the owner of Browyer Realty, a real estate company in Minnesota. She's asked you to help her design a Web page for her current listings. Linda envisions a Web page that displays basic information about a listing, including the owner's description. She would like to have several photos of the listing on the page, but rather than cluttering up the layout with several images, she would like users to be able to view different images by clicking a link on the page. Linda wants the images to open within the listing page, not in a separate Web page. Figure 5-39 shows a preview of the page you'll create for Linda.

Figure 5-39

To create the Browyer Realty listing:

1. Using your text editor, open **listtxt.htm** from the tutorial.05/case2 folder. Enter *your name* and *the date* in the comment section and save the file as **listing.htm**.

Explore

2. Locate the inline image for the img01.jpg file (it's floated off the left side of the second paragraph). Use this image as the alternate content for an inline frame, enclosing the image within an inline frame with the following attributes:
   - The source of the frame is the **img01.jpg** file.
   - The name of the frame is "images".

- The frame is 310 pixels wide and 240 pixels high.
- The width of the frame border is 0.
- The frame's internal margin width and height are 0 pixels.
- The frame is floated on the left.
- The margin size around the frame is 5 pixels to the left and right and 0 pixels to the top and bottom.

3. Insert a comment above the floating frame indicating its purpose in the Web page.

4. Change each of the 13 entries in the list of photos to a link. Direct the first entry to **img01.jpg**, the second entry to **img02.jpg**, and so forth.

5. Direct the 13 links you created in the previous step to the "images" floating frame.

6. Save your changes to the file.

7. Using your Web browser, open listing.htm. Verify that each link displays a different photo in the Web page and that the rest of the page remains unchanged.

8. Submit the completed Web site to your instructor.

Explore

Expand your skill with inline frames by using nested frames to create an interactive slide show.

Case Problem 3

Data files needed for this Case Problem: messtxt.htm, mxxtxt.htm, + 9 HTML files, + 15 JPEG files

SkyWeb Astronomy   Dr. Andrew Weiss of Central Ohio University maintains an astronomy page called SkyWeb for his students. On his Web site he discusses many aspects of astronomy and observing. One of the pages he wants your help with involves the Messier catalog, which is a list of deep sky objects of particular interest to astronomers and amateur observers.

Dr. Weiss wants his page to contain a slide show of various Messier objects, displaying both a photo of the object and a text box describing the object's history and features. He wants his users to be able to click a forward or backward button to move through the slide show, and wants the rest of the Web page to remain unchanged as users view the presentation. Figure 5-40 shows a preview of the page that Dr. Weiss wants to create.

Figure 5-40

The Messier Objects

Messier objects are stellar objects, classified by astronomer **Charles Messier** in the 18th century, ranging from distant galaxies to star clusters to stellar nebula. The catalog was a major milestone in the history of astronomy, as it was the first comprehensive list of deep sky objects. Ironically, Charles Messier wasn't all that interested in the objects in his list. He made the catalog in order to *avoid* mistaking those objects for comets, which were his true passion.

Messier objects are identified by **Messier Numbers**. The first object in Messier's catalog, the Crab Nebula, is labelled **M1**. The last object, **M110** is a satellite galaxy located in the constellation Andromeda. There is no systematic ordering in the Messier Catalog. Messier entered objects into the list as he found them. Sometimes he made mistakes and once he entered the same stellar object twice. The catalog has undergone some slight revisions since Messier's time, correcting the mistakes in the original.

One of the great pursuits for amateur astronomers is to do a **Messier Marathon,** trying to view all of the objects in Messier's catalog in one night. Unfortunately, if you want to see all of them, you have to start looking right after sunset and continue until just before sunrise — hence the term, "marathon." March is the only month in the year in which an astronomer can run the complete marathon.

Use the buttons to view some of the more popular objects in Messier's catalog.

M16: The Eagle Nebula

M16, better known as the Eagle Nebula, is located in the distant constellation, Serpens. The source of light for M16 is the high-energy radiation of the massive young stars being formed in its core. By studying M16, astronomers hope to learn more about the early years

| Home Page | The Night Sky | The Moon | The Planets | The Messier Objects | Stars |

To create a presentation like this, you can nest one inline frame inside of another. Dr. Weiss has created the text you need for the Web site. Your job is to create the frames needed to complete the Web page.

To create the SkyWeb Web page:

1. Using your text editor, open **mxxtxt.htm** from the tutorial.05/case3 folder. This file will act as a model for pages that display descriptions and images of the Messier objects. You'll start by using this file to create the page for Messier object, M01. Enter *your name* and *the date* in the comment section of this file and save the file as **m01.htm**.

Explore

2. Replace the text of the page title and the first table cell with the text, "M1: The Crab Nebula".

3. Replace the inline image mxx.jpg with the image **m01.jpg**.

4. Replace the inline image mxxdesc.jpg with an inline frame of the same dimensions and attributes, displaying the contents of the file **m01desc.htm**. Copy the page content of the **m01desc.htm** file (excluding the <body> tags) and paste that content within the inline frame to provide alternate text for browsers that don't support inline frames.

5. Target the link for the Previous button located at the bottom of the page to the file **m57.htm**. Note that you'll create this file later.

6. Direct the link for the Next button to the file **m13.htm**—another file you'll create shortly.

7. Save your changes to **m01.htm**.

8. With your work on m01.htm as a guide, use your text editor with the **mxxtxt.htm** file to create similar Web pages for the other eight Messier objects. Save the files as **m13.htm**, **m16.htm**, **m20.htm**, **m27.htm**, **m31.htm**, **m42.htm**, **m51.htm**, and **m57.htm**. Be sure to enter *your name* and *the date* in the comment section of each file. The titles for these pages are:

   • M13: Hercules Globular Cluster

   • M16: The Eagle Nebula

   • M20: The Trifid Nebula

   • M27: The Dumbbell Nebula

   • M31: The Andromeda Galaxy

   • M42: The Orion Nebula

   • M51: The Whirlpool Galaxy

   • M57: The Ring Nebula

The inline frame for each page should point to the file containing descriptive text on the Messier object. For example, the floating frame for the m13.htm file should display the m13desc.htm file, and so forth.

The Previous and Next buttons in each page should point to the previous and next Messier object files. For example, the buttons in m27.htm should point to m20.htm and m31.htm. The Next button for m57.htm should point to m01.htm. Save your changes to all the files, and then close them.

Explore

9. Using your text editor, open **messtxt.htm** and save it as **messier.htm**.

10. At the beginning of the fourth paragraph, insert an inline frame with the following properties:
    - Make the source of the floating frame **m01.htm**.
    - Make the frame 460 pixels wide by 240 pixels high.
    - Make the internal margin width and height 0 pixels.
    - There should be no border around the frame.
    - Float the frame on the right margin of the page.
    - Make a 5-pixel margin around the frame.
    - For browsers that don't support inline frames, display a text message that contains a link to the **m01.htm** file.

11. Save your changes to **messier.htm** and close the file.

12. Open **messier.htm** in your Web browser. Click the Previous and Next buttons and verify that you can navigate through the list of Messier objects without disturbing the rest of the Web page. Verify that you can use the scroll bars around the description box to view descriptions of each object.

13. Submit the completed Web site to your instructor.

Create

Test your knowledge of frames by creating a frameset for a computer supply store.

Case Problem 4

Data files needed for this Case Problem: drive15l.htm, drive15l.jpg, drive20m.htm, drive20m.jpg, drive33m.htm, drive33m.jpg, drive60s.htm, drive60s.jpg, tape800.htm, tape800.jpg, tape3200.htm, tape3200.jpg, tape9600.htm, tape9600.jpg, wlogo.gif, wlogo.htm

Warner Peripherals, Inc. Warner Peripherals, a company located in Tucson, Arizona, makes high-quality peripherals for computers. The company is an industry leader and has been delivering innovative technical solutions to consumers for more than 20 years. Part of its line of legacy products directed toward older computer systems are the SureSave line of tape drives and the SureRite line of disk drives. You've been asked to consolidate several Web pages describing these products into a single Web presentation using frames. The files shown in Figure 5-41 are available for your use. You are free to supplement this material with any other resources available to you.

Figure 5-41

File	Contents
drive15l.htm	Description of the 15L SureRite hard drive
drive20m.htm	Description of the 20M SureRite hard drive
drive33m.htm	Description of the 33M SureRite hard drive
drive60s.htm	Description of the 60S SureRite hard drive
tape800.htm	Description of the 800 SureSave tape backup drive
tape3200.htm	Description of the 3200 SureSave tape backup drive
tape9600.htm	Description of the 9600 SureSave tape backup drive
wlogo.htm	Warner Peripherals logo

To create the Warner Peripherals Web site:

1. Create a table of contents page that includes links to the files listed in Figure 5-41. The design of this Web page is up to you. Save this page as **wtoc.htm** in the tutorial.05/case4 folder.

2. In the same folder, create a file named **warner.htm** that consolidates the logo page, table of contents page, and product description pages into a single page, using frames. Include comment tags in the file describing each element of the page.

3. Test your Web page and verify that each link works properly and appears in the correct frame.

4. Submit your completed Web site to your instructor.

Review

Quick Check Answers

Session 5.1

1. A frame is a section of a browser window capable of displaying the contents of an entire Web page. Frames do not require the same information (such as a list of links) to be repeated on multiple pages of a Web site. They also allow a Web designer to update content in one place in order to affect an entire Web site.

2. Because there is no page body in a frame document. The frame document displays the content of other pages.

3. `<frameset rows="200,50%,*"> … </frameset>`

4. `<frame src="home.htm" />`

5. `<frame src="home.htm" scrolling="no" />`

6. `<frame src="home.htm" marginheight="3" />`

7. 3 pixels

8. `<frame src="home.htm" noresize="noresize" />`

Session 5.2

1. The frame containing the link

2. `name="Address"`

3. `target="News"`

4. `target="_top"`

5. Place the tag `<base target="News" />` in the head element of the document.

6. Create a section starting with the `<noframes>` tag. After the `<noframes>` tag enter a `<body>` tag to identify the text and images you want frame-blind browsers to display. Complete this section with a `</body>` tag followed by a `</noframes>` tag.

7. `<frameset bordercolor="red">`

8. `<frameset border="5">`

Color Names and Color Values

Both HTML and XHTML allow you to define colors using either color names or color values. HTML and XHTML support a list of 16 basic color names. Most browsers also support an extended list of color names, which are listed in the following table along with their RGB and hexadecimal values. The sixteen color names supported by HTML and XHTML appear highlighted in the table. Web-safe colors appear in a bold font.

If you want to use only Web-safe colors, limit your RGB values to 0, 51, 153, 204, and 255 (or limit your hexadecimal values to 00, 33, 66, 99, CC, and FF). For example, an RGB color value of (255, 51, 204) would be Web safe, while an RGB color value of (255, 192, 128) would not.

Color Name	RGB Value	Hexadecimal Value
aliceblue	(240,248,255)	#F0F8FF
antiquewhite	(250,235,215)	#FAEBD7
aqua	**(0,255,255)**	**#00FFFF**
aquamarine	(127,255,212)	#7FFFD4
azure	(240,255,255)	#F0FFFF
beige	(245,245,220)	#F5F5DC
bisque	(255,228,196)	#FFE4C4
black	**(0,0,0)**	**#000000**
blanchedalmond	(255,235,205)	#FFEBCD
blue	**(0,0,255)**	**#0000FF**
blueviolet	(138,43,226)	#8A2BE2
brown	(165,42,42)	#A52A2A
burlywood	(222,184,135)	#DEB887
cadetblue	(95,158,160)	#5F9EA0
chartreuse	(127,255,0)	#7FFF00
chocolate	(210,105,30)	#D2691E
coral	(255,127,80)	#FF7F50
cornflowerblue	(100,149,237)	#6495ED
cornsilk	(255,248,220)	#FFF8DC
crimson	(220,20,54)	#DC1436
cyan	**(0,255,255)**	**#00FFFF**
darkblue	(0,0,139)	#00008B
darkcyan	(0,139,139)	#008B8B
darkgoldenrod	(184,134,11)	#B8860B
darkgray	(169,169,169)	#A9A9A9
darkgreen	(0,100,0)	#006400

Color Name	RGB Value	Hexadecimal Value
darkkhaki	(189,183,107)	#BDB76B
darkmagenta	(139,0,139)	#8B008B
darkolivegreen	(85,107,47)	#556B2F
darkorange	(255,140,0)	#FF8C00
darkorchid	(153,50,204)	#9932CC
darkred	(139,0,0)	#8B0000
darksalmon	(233,150,122)	#E9967A
darkseagreen	(143,188,143)	#8FBC8F
darkslateblue	(72,61,139)	#483D8B
darkslategray	(47,79,79)	#2F4F4F
darkturquoise	(0,206,209)	#00CED1
darkviolet	(148,0,211)	#9400D3
deeppink	(255,20,147)	#FF1493
deepskyblue	(0,191,255)	#00BFFF
dimgray	(105,105,105)	#696969
dodgerblue	(30,144,255)	#1E90FF
firebrick	(178,34,34)	#B22222
floralwhite	(255,250,240)	#FFFAF0
forestgreen	(34,139,34)	#228B22
fuchsia	**(255,0,255)**	**#FF00FF**
gainsboro	(220,220,220)	#DCDCDC
ghostwhite	(248,248,255)	#F8F8FF
gold	(255,215,0)	#FFD700
goldenrod	(218,165,32)	#DAA520
gray	(128,128,128)	#808080
green	(0,128,0)	#008000
greenyellow	(173,255,47)	#ADFF2F
honeydew	(240,255,240)	#F0FFF0
hotpink	(255,105,180)	#FF69B4

Color Name	RGB Value	Hexadecimal Value
indianred	(205,92,92)	#CD5C5C
indigo	(75,0,130)	#4B0082
ivory	(255,255,240)	#FFFFF0
khaki	(240,230,140)	#F0E68C
lavender	(230,230,250)	#E6E6FA
lavenderblush	(255,240,245)	#FFF0F5
lawngreen	(124,252,0)	#7CFC00
lemonchiffon	(255,250,205)	#FFFACD
lightblue	(173,216,230)	#ADD8E6
lightcoral	(240,128,128)	#F08080
lightcyan	(224,255,255)	#E0FFFF
lightgoldenrodyellow	(250,250,210)	#FAFAD2
lightgreen	(144,238,144)	#90EE90
lightgrey	(211,211,211)	#D3D3D3
lightpink	(255,182,193)	#FFB6C1
lightsalmon	(255,160,122)	#FFA07A
lightseagreen	(32,178,170)	#20B2AA
lightskyblue	(135,206,250)	#87CEFA
lightslategray	(119,136,153)	#778899
lightsteelblue	(176,196,222)	#B0C4DE
lightyellow	(255,255,224)	#FFFFE0
lime	**(0,255,0)**	**#00FF00**
limegreen	(50,205,50)	#32CD32
linen	(250,240,230)	#FAF0E6
magenta	**(255,0,255)**	**#FF00FF**
maroon	(128,0,0)	#800000
mediumaquamarine	(102,205,170)	#66CDAA
mediumblue	(0,0,205)	#0000CD
mediumorchid	(186,85,211)	#BA55D3

Color Name	RGB Value	Hexadecimal Value
mediumpurple	(147,112,219)	#9370DB
mediumseagreen	(60,179,113)	#3CB371
mediumslateblue	(123,104,238)	#7B68EE
mediumspringgreen	(0,250,154)	#00FA9A
mediumturquoise	(72,209,204)	#48D1CC
mediumvioletred	(199,21,133)	#C71585
midnightblue	(25,25,112)	#191970
mintcream	(245,255,250)	#F5FFFA
mistyrose	(255,228,225)	#FFE4E1
moccasin	(255,228,181)	#FFE4B5
navajowhite	(255,222,173)	#FFDEAD
navy	**(0,0,128)**	#000080
oldlace	(253,245,230)	#FDF5E6
olive	(128,128,0)	#808000
olivedrab	(107,142,35)	#6B8E23
orange	(255,165,0)	#FFA500
orangered	(255,69,0)	#FF4500
orchid	(218,112,214)	#DA70D6
palegoldenrod	(238,232,170)	#EEE8AA
palegreen	(152,251,152)	#98FB98
paleturquoise	(175,238,238)	#AFEEEE
palevioletred	(219,112,147)	#DB7093
papayawhip	(255,239,213)	#FFEFD5
peachpuff	(255,218,185)	#FFDAB9
peru	(205,133,63)	#CD853F
pink	(255,192,203)	#FFC0CB
plum	(221,160,221)	#DDA0DD
powderblue	(176,224,230)	#B0E0E6
purple	**(128,0,128)**	#808080

Color Name	RGB Value	Hexadecimal Value
red	**(255,0,0)**	**#FF0000**
rosybrown	(188,143,143)	#BC8F8F
royalblue	(65,105,0)	#4169E1
saddlebrown	(139,69,19)	#8B4513
salmon	(250,128,114)	#FA8072
sandybrown	(244,164,96)	#F4A460
seagreen	(46,139,87)	#2E8B57
seashell	(255,245,238)	#FFF5EE
sienna	(160,82,45)	#A0522D
silver	(192,192,192)	#C0C0C0
skyblue	(135,206,235)	#87CEEB
slateblue	(106,90,205)	#6A5ACD
slategray	(112,128,144)	#708090
snow	(255,250,250)	#FFFAFA
springgreen	(0,255,127)	#00FF7F
steelblue	(70,130,180)	#4682B4
tan	(210,180,140)	#D2B48C
teal	(0,128,128)	#008080
thistle	(216,191,216)	#D8BFD8
tomato	(255,99,71)	#FF6347
turquoise	(64,224,208)	#40E0D0
violet	(238,130,238)	#EE82EE
wheat	(245,222,179)	#F5DEB3
white	**(255,255,255)**	**#FFFFFF**
whitesmoke	(245,245,245)	#F5F5F5
yellow	**(255,255,0)**	**#FFFF00**
yellowgreen	(154,205,50)	#9ACD32

HTML Character Entities

The following table lists the extended character set for HTML, also known as the ISO Latin-1 Character Set. You can specify characters by name or by numeric value. For example, you can use either ® or ® to specify the registered trademark symbol, ®.

Not all browsers recognize all code names. Some older browsers that support only the HTML 2.0 standard do not recognize × as a code name, for instance. Code names that older browsers may not recognize are marked with an asterisk in the following table.

CHARACTER	CODE	CODE NAME	DESCRIPTION
	&#09;		Tab
	&#10;		Line feed
	&#32;		Space
!	&#33;		Exclamation mark
"	&#34;	&quot;	Double quotation mark
#	&#35;		Pound sign
$	&#36;		Dollar sign
%	&#37;		Percent sign
&	&#38;	&amp;	Ampersand
'	&#39;		Apostrophe
(	&#40;		Left parenthesis
)	&#41;		Right parenthesis
*	&#42;		Asterisk
+	&#43;		Plus sign
,	&#44;		Comma
-	&#45;		Hyphen
.	&#46;		Period
/	&#47;		Forward slash
0 - 9	0–9		Numbers 0–9
:	&#58;		Colon
;	&#59;		Semicolon
<	&#60;	&lt;	Less than sign

CHARACTER	CODE	CODE NAME	DESCRIPTION
=	&#61;		Equal sign
>	&#62;	&gt;	Greater than sign
?	&#63;		Question mark
@	&#64;		Commercial at sign
A – Z	A–Z		Letters A–Z
[	&#91;		Left square bracket
\	&#92;		Back slash
]	&#93;		Right square bracket
^	&#94;		Caret
_	&#95;		Horizontal bar (underscore)
`	&#96;		Grave accent
a – z	a–z		Letters a–z
{	&#123;		Left curly brace
|	|		Vertical bar
}	&#125;		Right curly brace
~	&#126;		Tilde
,	&#130;		Comma
ƒ	&#131;		Function sign (florin)
"	&#132;		Double quotation mark
…	&#133;		Ellipsis
†	&#134;		Dagger
‡	&#135;		Double dagger
ˆ	&#136;		Circumflex

CHARACTER	CODE	CODE NAME	DESCRIPTION
‰	&#137;		Permil
A	&#138;		Capital S with hacek
‹	&#139;		Left single angle
Œ	&#140;		Capital OE ligature
	–		Unused
'	&#145;		Single beginning quotation mark
'	&#146;		Single ending quotation mark
"	&#147;		Double beginning quotation mark
"	&#148;		Double ending quotation mark
•	&#149;		Bullet
–	&#150;		En dash
—	&#151;		Em dash
~	&#152;		Tilde
™	&#153;	™*	Trademark symbol
B	&#154;		Small s with hacek
›	&#155;		Right single angle
œ	&#156;		Lowercase oe ligature
Ÿ	&#159;		Capital Y with umlaut
		*	Non-breaking space
¡	&#161;	¡*	Inverted exclamation mark
¢	&#162;	¢*	Cent sign
£	&#163;	£*	Pound sterling
C	&#164;	¤*	General currency symbol

CHARACTER	CODE	CODE NAME	DESCRIPTION
¥	&#165;	¥*	Yen sign
¦	&#166;	¦*	Broken vertical bar
§	&#167;	§*	Section sign
¨	&#168;	¨*	Umlaut
©	&#169;	©*	Copyright symbol
ª	&#170;	ª*	Feminine ordinal
«	&#171;	«*	Left angle quotation mark
¬	&#172;	¬*	Not sign
	&#173;	­*	Soft hyphen
®	&#174;	®*	Registered trademark
¯	&#175;	¯*	Macron
°	&#176;	°*	Degree sign
±	&#177;	±*	Plus/minus symbol
²	&#178;	²*	Superscript 2
³	&#179;	³*	Superscript 3
´	&#180;	´*	Acute accent
µ	&#181;	µ*	Micro sign
¶	&#182;	¶*	Paragraph sign
·	&#183;	·*	Middle dot
ç	&#184;	¸*	Cedilla
¹	&#185;	¹*	Superscript 1
º	&#186;	º*	Masculine ordinal
»	&#187;	»*	Right angle quotation mark

CHARACTER	CODE	CODE NAME	DESCRIPTION
¼	&#188;	¼*	Fraction one-quarter
½	&#189;	½*	Fraction one-half
¾	&#190;	¾*	Fraction three-quarters
¿	&#191;	¿*	Inverted question mark
À	&#192;	&Agrave;	Capital A, grave accent
Á	&#193;	&Aacute;	Capital A, acute accent
Â	&#194;	&Acirc;	Capital A, circumflex accent
Ã	&#195;	&Atilde;	Capital A, tilde
Ä	&#196;	&Auml;	Capital A, umlaut
Å	&#197;	&Aring;	Capital A, ring
Æ	&#198;	&Aelig;	Capital AE ligature
Ç	&#199;	&Ccedil;	Capital C, cedilla
È	&#200;	&Egrave;	Capital E, grave accent
É	&#201;	&Eacute;	Capital E, acute accent
Ê	&#202;	&Ecirc;	Capital E, circumflex accent
Ë	&#203;	&Euml;	Capital E, umlaut
Ì	&#204;	&Igrave;	Capital I, grave accent
Í	&#205;	&Iacute;	Capital I, acute accent
Î	&#206;	&Icirc;	Capital I, circumflex accent
Ï	&#207;	&Iuml;	Capital I, umlaut
Ð	&#208;	Ð*	Capital ETH, Icelandic
Ñ	&#209;	&Ntilde;	Capital N, tilde
Ò	&#210;	&Ograve;	Capital O, grave accent

CHARACTER	CODE	CODE NAME	DESCRIPTION
Ó	&#211;	&Oacute;	Capital O, acute accent
Ô	&#212;	&Ocirc;	Capital O, circumflex accent
Õ	&#213;	&Otilde;	Capital O, tilde
Ö	&#214;	&Ouml;	Capital O, umlaut
×	&#215;	×*	Multiplication sign
Ø	&#216;	&Oslash;	Capital O slash
Ù	&#217;	&Ugrave;	Capital U, grave accent
Ú	&#218;	&Uacute;	Capital U, acute accent
Û	&#219;	&Ucirc;	Capital U, circumflex accent
Ü	&#220;	&Uuml;	Capital U, umlaut
Ý	&#221;	&Yacute;	Capital Y, acute accent
Þ	&#222;	&THORN;	Capital THORN, Icelandic
ß	&#223;	&szlig;	Small sz ligature
à	&#224;	&agrave;	Small a, grave accent
á	&#225;	&aacute;	Small a, acute accent
â	&#226;	&acirc;	Small a, circumflex accent
ã	&#227;	&atilde;	Small a, tilde
ä	&#228;	&auml;	Small a, umlaut
å	&#229;	&aring;	Small a, ring
æ	&#230;	&aelig;	Small ae ligature
ç	&#231;	&ccedil;	Small c, cedilla
è	&#232;	&egrave;	Small e, grave accent
é	&#233;	&eacute;	Small e, acute accent

CHARACTER	CODE	CODE NAME	DESCRIPTION
ê	&#234;	&ecirc;	Small e, circumflex accent
ë	&#235;	&euml;	Small e, umlaut
ì	&#236;	&igrave;	Small i, grave accent
í	&#237;	&iacute;	Small i, acute accent
î	&#238;	&icirc;	Small i, circumflex accent
ï	&#239;	&iuml;	Small i, umlaut
ð	&#240;	&eth;	Small eth, Icelandic
ñ	&#241;	&ntilde;	Small n, tilde
ò	&#242;	&ograve;	Small o, grave accent
ó	&#243;	&oacute;	Small o, acute accent
ô	&#244;	&ocirc;	Small o, circumflex accent
õ	&#245;	&otilde;	Small o, tilde
ö	&#246;	&ouml;	Small o, umlaut
÷	&#247;	÷*	Division sign
ø	&#248;	&oslash;	Small o slash
ù	&#249;	&ugrave;	Small u, grave accent
ú	&#250;	&uacute;	Small u, acute accent
û	&#251;	&ucirc;	Small u, circumflex accent
ü	&#252;	&uuml;	Small u, umlaut
ý	&#253;	&yacute;	Small y, acute accent
þ	&#254;	&thorn;	Small thorn, Icelandic
ÿ	&#255;	&yuml;	Small y, umlaut

Putting a Document on the World Wide Web

Once you complete work on a Web page, you're probably ready to place it on the World Wide Web for others to see. To make a file available on the World Wide Web, it must be located on a computer connected to the Web called a **Web server**.

Your **Internet Service Provider (ISP)**—the company or institution through which you have Internet access—probably has a Web server available for your use. Because each Internet Service Provider has a different procedure for storing Web pages, you should contact your ISP to learn its policies and procedures. Generally you should be prepared to do the following:

- Extensively test your files with a variety of browsers and under different display conditions. Eliminate any errors and design problems before you place the page on the Web.
- Check the links and inline objects in each of your documents to verify that they point to the correct filenames. Verify your filename capitalization—some Web servers distinguish between a file named "Image.gif" and one named "image.gif." To be safe, use only lowercase letters in all your filenames.
- If your links use absolute pathnames, change them to relative pathnames.
- Find out from your ISP the name of the folder into which you'll be placing your HTML documents. You may also need a special user name and password to access this folder.
- Use FTP, an Internet protocol for transferring files, or e-mail to place your pages in the appropriate folder on your Internet Service Provider's Web server. This capability is built in to some Web browsers, including Internet Explorer and Netscape, allowing you to easily transfer files to your Web server.
- Decide on a name for your Web site (such as "http://www.jackson_electronics.com"). Choose a name that will be easy for customers and interested parties to remember and return to.
- If you select a special name for your Web site, you may have to register it. Registration information can be found at http://www.internic.net. Your ISP may also provide this service for a fee. Registration is necessary to ensure that any name you give to your site is unique and not already in use. Usually you will have to pay a yearly fee to use a special name for your Web site.

Once you've completed these steps, your work will be available on the World Wide Web in a form that is easy for users to access.

Making the Web More Accessible

Accessibility and the Web

Studies indicate that about 20% of the population has some type of disability. Many of these disabilities do not impact an individual's ability to interact with the World Wide Web. For example, a person who is paralyzed below the waist can generally still navigate the Web without difficulty. Likewise, a person with a heart condition can still use most of the features of the Web.

However, other disabilities can severely affect an individual's ability to participate in the Web community. For example, on a news Web site, a blind user could not see the latest headlines. A deaf user would not be able to hear a news clip embedded in the site's main page. A user with motor disabilities might not be able to move a mouse pointer to activate important links featured on the site's home page.

Disabilities that inhibit an individual's ability to use the Web fall into four main categories:

- **Visual disability:** A visual disability can include complete blindness, colorblindness, or an untreatable visual impairment.
- **Hearing disability:** A hearing disability can include complete deafness or the inability to distinguish sounds of certain frequencies.
- **Motor disability:** A motor disability can include the inability to use a mouse, to exhibit fine motor control, or to respond in a timely manner to computer prompts and queries.
- **Cognitive disability:** A cognitive disability can include a learning disability, attention deficit disorder, or the inability to focus on large amounts of information.

While the Web includes some significant obstacles to full use by disabled people, it also offers the potential for contact with a great amount of information that is not otherwise cheaply or easily accessible. For example, before the Web, in order to read a newspaper, a blind person was constrained by the expense of Braille printouts and audio tapes, as well as the limited availability of sighted people willing to read the news out loud. As a result, blind people would often only be able to read newspapers after the news was no longer new. The Web, however, makes news available in an electronic format and in real-time. A blind user can use a browser that converts electronic text into speech, known as a **screen reader**, to read a newspaper Web site. Combined with the Web, screen readers provide access to a broader array of information than was possible through Braille publications alone.

In addition to screen readers, many other programs and devices—known collectively as **assistive technology** or **adaptive technology**—are available to enable people with different disabilities to use the Web. The challenge for the Web designer, then, is to create Web pages that are accessible to everyone, including (and perhaps especially) to people with disabilities. In addition to being a design challenge, for some designers, Web accessibility is the law.

Working with Section 508 Guidelines

In 1973, Congress passed the Rehabilitation Act, which aimed to foster economic independence for people with disabilities. Congress amended the act in 1998 to reflect the latest changes in information technology. Part of the amendment, **Section 508**, requires that any electronic information developed, procured, maintained, or used by the federal government be accessible to people with disabilities. Because the Web is one of the main sources of electronic information, Section 508 has had a profound impact on how Web pages are designed and how Web code is written. Note that the standards apply to federal Web sites, but not to private sector Web sites; however, if a site is provided under contract to a federal agency, the Web site or portion covered by the contract has to comply. Required or not, though, you should follow the Section 508 guidelines not only to make your Web site more accessible, but also to make your HTML code more consistent and reliable. Thus, the Section 508 guidelines are of interest not just to Web designers who work for the federal government, but to all Web designers.

The Section 508 guidelines encompass a wide range of topics, covering several types of disabilities. The part of Section 508 that impacts Web design is sub-section 1194.22, titled

§ 1194.22   Web-based intranet and internet information and applications.

Within this section are 15 paragraphs, numbered (a) through (p), which describe how each facet of a Web site should be designed so as to maximize accessibility. Let's examine each of these paragraphs in detail.

Graphics and Images

The first paragraph in sub-section 1194.22 deals with graphic images. The standard for the use of graphic images is that

§1194.22 (a)   A text equivalent for every non-text element shall be provided (e.g., via "alt", "longdesc", or in element content).

In other words, any graphic image that contains page content needs to include a text alternative to make the page accessible to visually impaired people. One of the simplest ways to do this is to use the alt attribute with every inline image that displays page content. For example, in Figure D-1, the alt attribute provides the text of a graphical logo for users who can't see the graphic.

Figure D-1	Using the alt attribute

```
<img src="jkson.jpg" alt="Jackson Electronics" />
```

Not every graphic image requires a text alternative. For example, a decorative image such as a bullet does not need a text equivalent. In those cases, you should include the alt attribute, but set its value to an empty text string. You should never neglect to include the alt attribute. If you are writing XHTML-compliant code, use of the alt attribute is required. In other cases, screen readers and other non-visual browsers will recite the filename of a graphic image file if no value is specified for the alt attribute. Since the filename is usually of no interest to the end-user, this results in needless irritation.

The alt attribute is best used for short descriptions that involve five words or less. It is less effective for images that require long descriptive text. You can instead link these images to a document containing a more detailed description. One way to do this is with the longdesc attribute, which uses the syntax

```
<img src="url" longdesc="url" />
```

where `url` for the longdesc attribute points to a document containing a detailed description of the image. Figure D-2 shows an example that uses the longdesc attribute to point to a Web page containing a detailed description of a sales chart.

Using the alt attribute | **Figure D-2**

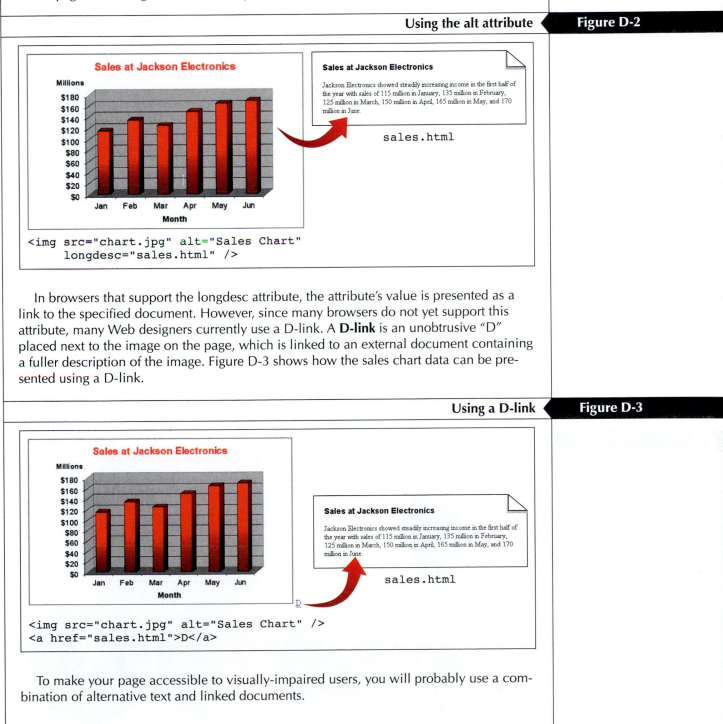

```
<img src="chart.jpg" alt="Sales Chart"
     longdesc="sales.html" />
```

In browsers that support the longdesc attribute, the attribute's value is presented as a link to the specified document. However, since many browsers do not yet support this attribute, many Web designers currently use a D-link. A **D-link** is an unobtrusive "D" placed next to the image on the page, which is linked to an external document containing a fuller description of the image. Figure D-3 shows how the sales chart data can be presented using a D-link.

Using a D-link | **Figure D-3**

```
<img src="chart.jpg" alt="Sales Chart" />
<a href="sales.html">D</a>
```

To make your page accessible to visually-impaired users, you will probably use a combination of alternative text and linked documents.

Multimedia

Audio and video have become important ways of conveying information on the Web. However, creators of multimedia presentations should also consider the needs of deaf users and users who are hard of hearing. The standard for multimedia accessibility is

§1194.22 (b)   Equivalent alternatives for any multimedia presentation shall be synchro-nized with the presentation.

This means that any audio clip needs to be accompanied by a transcript of the audio's content, and any video clip needs to include closed captioning. Refer to your multimedia software's documentation on creating closed captioning and transcripts for your video and audio clips.

Color

Color is useful for emphasis and conveying information, but when color becomes an essential part of the site's content, you run the risk of shutting out people who are color blind. For this reason the third Section 508 standard states that

§1194.22 (c)   Web pages shall be designed so that all information conveyed with color is also available without color, for example from context or markup.

About 8% of men and 0.5% of women are afflicted with some type of color blindness. The most serious forms of color blindness are:

- **deuteranopia**: an absence of green sensitivity; deuteranopia is one example of red-green color blindness, in which the colors red and green cannot be easily distinguished.
- **protanopia**: an absence of red sensitivity; protanopia is another example of red-green color blindness.
- **tritanopia**: an absence of blue sensitivity. People with tritanopia have much less loss of color sensitivity than other types of color blindess.
- **achromatopsia**: absence of any color sensitivity.

The most common form of serious color blindness is red-green color blindness. Figure D-4 shows how each type of serious color blindness would affect a person's view of a basic color wheel.

Figure D-4 **Types of color blindness**

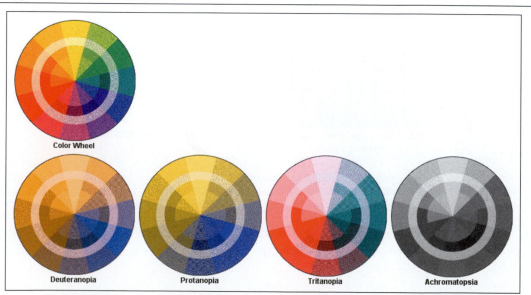

Color Wheel

Deuteranopia   Protanopia   Tritanopia   Achromatopsia

Color combinations that are easily readable for most people may be totally unreadable for users with certain types of color blindness. Figure D-5 demonstrates the accessibility problems that can occur with a graphical logo that contains green text on a red background. For people who have deuteranopia, protanopia, or achromatopsia, the logo is much more difficult to read.

The effect of color blindness on graphical content | **Figure D-5**

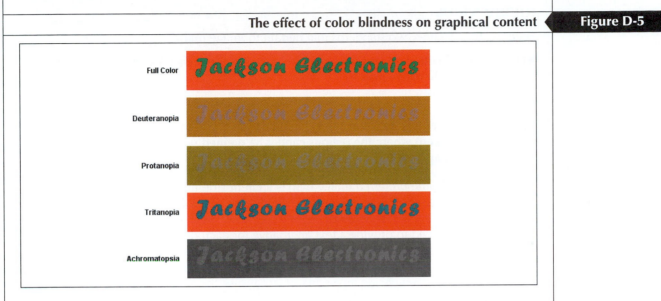

To make your page more accessible to people with color blindness, you can do the following:

- Provide non-color clues to access your page's content. For example, some Web forms indicate required entry fields by displaying the field names in a red font. You can supplement this for color blind users by marking required fields with a red font *and* with an asterisk or other special symbol.
- Avoid explicit references to color. Don't instruct your users to click a red button in a Web form when some users are unable to distinguish red from other colors.
- Avoid known areas of color difficulty. Since most color blindness involves red-green color blindness, you should avoid red and green text combinations.
- Use bright colors, which are the easiest for color blind users to distinguish.
- Provide a grayscale or black and white alternative for your color blind users, and be sure that your link to that page is easily viewable.

Several sites on the Web include tools you can use to test your Web site for color blind accessibility. You can also load color palettes into your graphics software to see how your images will appear to users with different types of color blindness.

Style Sheets

By controlling how a page is rendered in a browser, style sheets play an important role in making the Web accessible to users with disabilities. Many browsers, such as Internet Explorer, allow a user to apply their own customized style sheet in place of the style sheet specified by a Web page's designer. This is particular useful for visually impaired users who need to display text in extra large fonts with a high contrast between the text and the background color (yellow text on a black background is a common color scheme for such users). In order to make your pages accessible to those users, Section 508 guidelines state that

§1194.22 (d) **Documents shall be organized so they are readable without requiring an associated style sheet.**

To test whether your site fulfills this guideline, you should view the site without the style sheet. Some browsers allow you to turn off style sheets; alternately, you can redirect a page to an empty style sheet. You should modify any page that is unreadable without its style sheet to conform with this guideline.

Image Maps

Section 508 provides two standards that pertain to image maps:

§1194.22 (e)   Redundant text links shall be provided for each active region of a server-side image map.

and

§1194.22 (f)   Client-side image maps shall be provided instead of server-side image maps except where the regions cannot be defined with an available geometric shape.

In other words, the *preferred* image map is a client-side image map, unless the map uses a shape that cannot be defined on the client side. Since client-side image maps allow for polygonal shapes, this should not be an issue; however if you must use a server-side image map, you need to provide a text alternative for each of the map's links. Because server-side image maps provide only map coordinates to the server, this text is necessary in order to provide link information that is accessible to blind or visually impaired users. Figure D-6 shows a server-side image map that satisfies the Section 508 guidelines by repeating the graphical links in the image map with text links placed below the image.

Figure D-6   **Making a server-side image map accessible**

Client-side image maps do not have the same limitations as server-side maps because they allow you to specify alternate text for each hotspot within the map. For example, if the image map shown in Figure D-6 were a client-side map, you could make it accessible using the following HTML code:

```
<img src="servermap.jpg" alt="Jackson Electronics"
usemap="#links" />
<map name="links">
<area shape="rect" href="home.html" alt="home"
coords="21,69,123,117" />
<area shape="rect" href="products.html" alt="products"
coords="156,69,258,117" />
<area shape="rect" href="stores.html" alt="stores"
coords="302,69,404,117" />
<area shape="rect" href="support.html" alt="support"
coords="445,69,547,117" />
</map>
```

Screen readers or other non-visual browsers use the value of the alt attribute within each <area /> tag to give users access to each area. However, because some older browsers cannot work with the alt attribute in this way, you should also include the text alternative used for server-side image maps.

Tables

Tables can present a challenge for disabled users, particular those who employ screen readers or other non-visual browsers. To render a Web page, these browsers employ a technique called **linearizing**, which processes Web page content using a few general rules:

1. Convert all images to their alternative text.
2. Present the contents of each table one cell at a time, working from left to right across each row before moving down to the next row.
3. If a cell contains a nested table, that table is linearized before proceeding to the next cell.

Figure D-7 shows how a non-visual browser might linearize a sample table.

Linearizing a table   **Figure D-7**

table	linearized content
(table image below)	Desktop PCs Model Processor Memory DVD Burner Modem Network Adapter Paragon 2.4 Intel 2.4 GHz 256MB No Yes No Paragon 3.7 Intel 3.7GHz 512MB Yes Yes No Paragon 5.9 Intel 5.9GHz 1024MB Yes Yes Yes

Desktop PCs

Model	Processor	Memory	DVD Burner	Modem	Network Adapter
Paragon 2.4	Intel 2.4GHz	256MB	No	Yes	No
Paragon 3.7	Intel 3.7GHz	512MB	Yes	Yes	No
Paragon 5.9	Intel 5.9GHz	1024MB	Yes	Yes	Yes

One way of dealing with the challenge of linearizing is to structure your tables so that they are easily interpreted even when linearized. However, this is not always possible, especially for tables that have several rows and columns or may contain several levels of nested tables. The Section 508 guidelines for table creation state that

§1194.22 (g)   Row and column headers shall be identified for data tables.

and

§1194.22 (h)   Markup shall be used to associate data cells and header cells for data tables that have two or more logical levels of row or column headers.

To fulfill the 1194.22 (g) guideline, you should use the <th> tag for any table cell that contains a row or column header. By default, header text appears in a bold centered font; however, you can override this format using a style sheet. Many non-visual browsers can search for header cells. Also, as a user moves from cell to cell in a table, these browsers can announce the row and column headers associated with each cell. Thus, using the <th> tag can significantly reduce some of the problems associated with linearizing.

You can also use the scope attribute to explicitly associate a header with a row, column, row group, or column group. The syntax of the scope attribute is

```
<th scope="type"> … </th>
```

where *type* is either row, column, rowgroup, or colgroup. Figure D-8 shows how to use the scope attribute to associate the headers with the rows and columns of a table.

Figure D-8 | **Using the scope attribute**

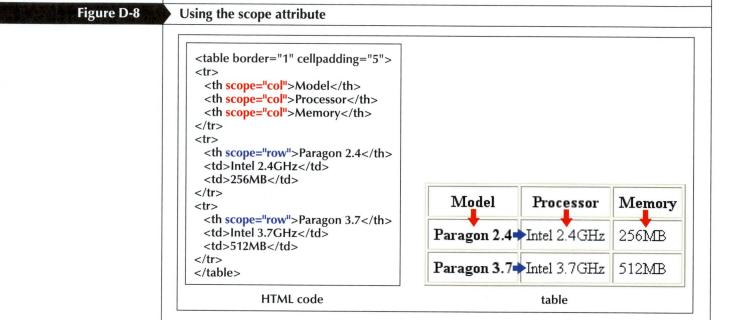

	HTML code		table

A non-visual browser that encounters the table in Figure D-8 can indicate to users which rows and columns are associated with each data cell. For example, the browser could indicate that the cell value, "512MB" is associated with the Memory column and the Paragon 3.7 row.

For more explicit references, HTML also supports the headers attribute, which specifies the cell or cells that contain header information for a particular cell. The syntax of the headers attribute is

```
<td headers="ids"> … </td>
```

where *ids* is a list of id values associated with header cells in the table. Figure D-9 demonstrates how to use the headers attribute.

```
<table>
<tr>
  <th id="c1">Model</th>
  <th id="c2">Processor</th>
  <th id="c3">Memory</th>
</tr>
<tr>
  <th id="r1" headers="c1">Paragon 2.4</th>
  <td headers="r1 c2">Intel 2.4GHz</td>
  <td headers="r1 c3">256MB</td>
</tr>
<tr>
  <th id="r2" headers="c1">Paragon 3.7</th>
  <td headers="r2 c2">Intel 3.7GHz</td>
  <td headers="r2 c3">512MB</td>
</tr>
</table>
```

Model	Processor	Memory
Paragon 2.4	Intel 2.4GHz	256MB
Paragon 3.7	Intel 3.7GHz	512MB

HTML code   table

Note that some older browsers do not support the scope and headers attributes. For this reason, it can be useful to supplement your tables with caption and summary attributes in order to provide even more information to blind and visually impaired users. See Tutorial 4 for a more detailed discussion of these elements and attributes.

Frame Sites

When a non-visual browser opens a frame site, it can render the contents of only one frame at a time. Users are given a choice of which frame to open. Thus, it's important that the name given to a frame indicate the frame's content. For this reason, the Section 508 guideline for frames states that

§1194.22 (i)   Frames shall be titled with text that facilitates frame identification and navigation.

Frames can be identified using either the title attribute or the name attribute, and different non-visual browsers use different attributes. For example, the Lynx browser uses the name attribute, while the IBM Home Page Reader uses the title attribute. For this reason, you should use both attributes in your framed sites. If you don't include a title or name attribute in the frame element, some non-visual browsers retrieve the document specified as the frame's source and then use that page's title as the name for the frame.

The following code demonstrates how to make a frame site accessible to users with disabilities.

```
<frameset cols="25%, *">
   <frame src="title.htm" title="banner" name="banner" />
   <frameset rows="100, *">
      <frame src="links.htm" title="links" name="links" />
      <frame src="home.htm" title="documents" name="documents" />
   </frameset>
</frameset>
```

Naturally, you should make sure that any document displayed in a frame follows the Section 508 guidelines.

Animation and Scrolling Text

Animated GIFs, scrolling marquees, and other special features can be a source of irritation for any Web user; however, they can cause serious problems for certain users. For example, people with photosensitive epilepsy can experience seizures when exposed to a screen or portion of a screen that flickers or flashes within the range of 2 to 55 flashes per second (2 to 55 Hertz). For this reason, the Section 508 guidelines state that

§1194.22 (j) Pages shall be designed to avoid causing the screen to flicker with a frequency greater than 2 Hz and lower than 55 Hz.

In addition to problems associated with photosensitive epilepsy, users with cognitive or visual disabilities may find it difficult to read moving text, and most screen readers are unable to read moving text. Thus, if you decide to use animated elements, you must ensure that each element's flickering and flashing is outside of the prohibited range, and you should not place essential page content within these elements.

Scripts, Applets and Plug-ins

Scripts, applets, and plug-ins are widely used to make Web pages more dynamic and interesting. The Section 508 guidelines for scripts state that

§1194.22 (l) When pages utilize scripting languages to display content, or to create interface elements, the information provided by the script shall be identified with functional text that can be read by adaptive technology.

Scripts are used for a wide variety of purposes. The following list describes some of the more popular uses of scripts and how to modify them for accessibility:

- **Pull-down menus**: Many Web designers use scripts to save screen space by inserting pull-down menus containing links to other pages in the site. Pull-down menus are usually accessed with a mouse. To assist users who cannot manipulate a mouse, include keyboard shortcuts to all pull-down menus. In addition, the links in a pull-down menu should be repeated elsewhere on the page or on the site in a text format.
- **Image rollovers**: Image rollovers are used to highlight linked elements. However, since image rollovers rely on the ability to use a mouse, pages should be designed so that rollover effects are not essential for navigating a site or for understanding a page's content.
- **Dynamic content**: Scripts can be used to insert new text and page content. Because some browsers designed for users with disabilities have scripting turned off by default, you should either not include any crucial content in dynamic text, or you should provide an alternate method for users with disabilities to access that information.

Applets and plug-ins are programs external to a Web page or browser that add special features to a Web site. The Section 508 guideline for applets and plug-ins is

§1194.22 (m) When a Web page requires that an applet, plug-in or other application be present on the client system to interpret page content, the page must provide a link to a plug-in or applet that complies with §1994.21(a) through (i).

This guideline means that any applet or plug-in used with your Web site must be compliant with sections §1994.21(a) through (i) of the Section 508 accessibility law, which deal with accessibility issues for software applications and operating systems. If the default applet or plug-in does not comply with Section 508, you need to provide a link to a version of that applet or plug-in which does. For example, a Web page containing a Real Audio clip should have a link to a source for the necessary player. This places the responsibility on the Web page designer to know that a compliant application is available before requiring the clip to work with the page.

Web Forms

The Section 508 standard for Web page forms states that

§1194.22 (n) **When electronic forms are designed to be completed on-line, the form shall allow people using assistive technology to access the information, field elements, and functionality required for completion and submission of the form, including all directions and cues.**

This is a general statement that instructs designers to make forms accessible, but it doesn't supply any specific instructions. The following techniques can help you make Web forms that comply with Section 508:

- **Push buttons** should always include value attributes. The value attribute contains the text displayed on a button, and is rendered by different types of assistive technology.
- **Image buttons** should always include alternate text that can be rendered by non-visual browsers.
- **Labels** should be associated with any input box, text area box, option button, checkbox, or selection list. The labels should be placed in close proximity to the input field and should be linked to the field using the label element.
- **Input boxes** and **text area boxes** should, when appropriate, include either default text or a prompt that indicates to the user what text to enter into the input box.
- **Interactive form elements** should be triggered by either the mouse or the keyboard.

The other parts of a Web form should comply with other Section 508 standards. For example, if you use a table to lay out the elements of a form, make sure that the form still makes sense when the table is linearized.

Links

It is common for Web designers to place links at the top, bottom, and sides of every page in their Web sites. This is generally a good idea, because those links enable users to move quickly and easily through a site. However, this technique can make it difficult to navigate a page using a screen reader, because screen readers move through a page from the top to bottom, reading each line of text. Users of screen readers may have to wait several minutes before they even get to the main body of a page, and the use of repetitive links forces such users to reread the same links on each page as they move through a site. To address this problem, the Section 508 guidelines state that

§1194.22 (o) **A method shall be provided that permits users to skip repetitive navigation links.**

One way of complying with this rule is to place a link at the very top of each page that allows users to jump to the page's main content. In order to make the link unobtrusive, it can be attached to a transparent image that is one pixel wide by one pixel high. For example, the following code lets users of screen readers jump to the main content of the page without needing to go through the content navigation links on the page; however, the image itself is invisible to other users and thus does not affect the page's layout or appearance.

```
<a href="#main">
   <img src="spacer.gif" height="1" width="1" alt="Skip to main
content" />
</a>


...


<a name="main"> </a>
page content goes here …
```

One advantage to this approach is that a template can be easily written to add this code to each page of the Web site.

Timed Responses

For security reasons, the login pages of some Web sites automatically log users out after a period of inactivity, or if users are unable to log in quickly. Because disabilities may prevent some users from being able to complete a login procedure within the prescribed time limit, the Section 508 guidelines state that

§1194.22 (p) **When a timed response is required, the user shall be alerted and given sufficient time to indicate that more time is required.**

The guideline does not suggest a time interval. To satisfy Section 508, your page should notify users when a process is about to time out and prompt users whether additional time is needed before proceeding.

Providing a Text-Only Equivalent

If you cannot modify a page to match the previous accessibility guidelines, as a last resort you can create a text-only page:

§1194.22 (k) **A text-only page, with equivalent information or functionality, shall be provided to make a Web site comply with the provisions of this part, when compliance cannot be accomplished in any other way. The content of the text-only pages shall be updated whenever the primary page changes.**

To satisfy this requirement, you should

- Provide an easily accessible link to the text-only page.
- Make sure that the text-only page satisfies the Section 508 guidelines.
- Duplicate the essential content of the original page.
- Update the alternate page when you update the original page.

By using the Section 508 guidelines, you can work towards making your Web site accessible to everyone, regardless of disabilities.

Understanding the Web Accessibility Initiative

In 1999, the World Wide Web Consortium (W3C) developed its own set of guidelines for Web accessibility called the **Web Accessibility Initiative (WAI)**. The WAI covers many of the same points as the Section 508 rules, and expands on them to cover basic Web site design issues. The overall goal of the WAI is to facilitate the creation of Web sites that are accessible to all, and to encourage designers to implement HTML in a consistent way.

The WAI sets forth 14 guidelines for Web designers. Within each guideline is a collection of checkpoints indicating how to apply the guideline to specific features of a Web site. Each checkpoint is also given a priority score that indicates how important the guideline is for proper Web design:

- **Priority 1:** A Web content developer **must** satisfy this checkpoint. Otherwise, one or more groups will find it impossible to access information in the document. Satisfying this checkpoint is a basic requirement for some groups to be able to use Web documents.
- **Priority 2:** A Web content developer **should** satisfy this checkpoint. Otherwise, one or more groups will find it difficult to access information in the document. Satisfying this checkpoint will remove significant barriers to accessing Web documents.

- **Priority 3:** A Web content developer **may** address this checkpoint. Otherwise, one or more groups will find it somewhat difficult to access information in the document. Satisfying this checkpoint will improve access to Web documents.

The following table lists WAI guidelines with each checkpoint and its corresponding priority value.

WAI Guidelines	Priority
1. Provide equivalent alternatives to auditory and visual content	
1.1 Provide a text equivalent for every non-text element (e.g., via "alt", "longdesc", or in element content). *This includes:* images, graphical representations of text (including symbols), image map regions, animations (e.g., animated GIFs), applets and programmatic objects, ascii art, frames, scripts, images used as list bullets, spacers, graphical buttons, sounds (played with or without user interaction), stand-alone audio files, audio tracks of video, and video.	1
1.2 Provide redundant text links for each active region of a server-side image map.	1
1.3 Until user agents can automatically read aloud the text equivalent of a visual track, provide an auditory description of the important information of the visual track of a multimedia presentation.	1
1.4 For any time-based multimedia presentation (e.g., a movie or animation), synchronize equivalent alternatives (e.g., captions or auditory descriptions of the visual track) with the presentation.	1
1.5 Until user agents render text equivalents for client-side image map links, provide redundant text links for each active region of a client-side image map.	3
2. Don't rely on color alone	
2.1 Ensure that all information conveyed with color is also available without color, for example from context or markup.	1
2.2 Ensure that foreground and background color combinations provide sufficient contrast when viewed by someone having color deficits or when viewed on a black and white screen. [Priority 2 for images, Priority 3 for text].	2
3. Use markup and style sheets and do so properly	
3.1 When an appropriate markup language exists, use markup rather than images to convey information.	2
3.2 Create documents that validate to published formal grammars.	2
3.3 Use style sheets to control layout and presentation.	2
3.4 Use relative rather than absolute units in markup language attribute values and style sheet property values.	2
3.5 Use header elements to convey document structure and use them according to specification.	2
3.6 Mark up lists and list items properly.	2
3.7 Mark up quotations. Do not use quotation markup for formatting effects such as indentation.	2
4. Clarify natural language usage	
4.1 Clearly identify changes in the natural language of a document's text and any text equivalents (e.g., captions).	1
4.2 Specify the expansion of each abbreviation or acronym in a document where it first occurs.	3
4.3 Identify the primary natural language of a document.	3
5. Create tables that transform gracefully	
5.1 For data tables, identify row and column headers.	1
5.2 For data tables that have two or more logical levels of row or column headers, use markup to associate data cells and header cells.	1
5.3 Do not use a table for layout unless the table makes sense when linearized. If a table does not make sense, provide an alternative equivalent (which may be a linearized version).	2
5.4 If a table is used for layout, do not use any structural markup for the purpose of visual formatting.	2

WAI Guidelines	Priority
5.5 Provide summaries for tables.	3
5.6 Provide abbreviations for header labels.	3
6. Ensure that pages featuring new technologies transform gracefully	
6.1 Organize documents so they may be read without style sheets. For example, when an HTML document is rendered without associated style sheets, it must still be possible to read the document.	1
6.2 Ensure that equivalents for dynamic content are updated when the dynamic content changes.	1
6.3 Ensure that pages are usable when scripts, applets, or other programmatic objects are turned off or not supported. If this is not possible, then provide equivalent information on an alternative accessible page.	1
6.4 For scripts and applets, ensure that event handlers are input device-independent.	2
6.5 Ensure that dynamic content is accessible or provide an alternative presentation or page.	2
7. Ensure user control of time-sensitive content changes	
7.1 Until user agents allow users to control flickering, avoid causing the screen to flicker.	1
7.2 Until user agents allow users to control blinking, avoid causing content to blink (i.e., change presentation at a regular rate, such as turning on and off).	2
7.3 Until user agents allow users to freeze moving content, avoid movement in pages.	2
7.4 Until user agents provide the ability to stop the refresh, do not create periodically auto-refreshing pages.	2
7.5 Until user agents provide the ability to stop auto-redirect, do not use markup to redirect pages automatically. Instead, configure the server to perform redirects.	2
8. Ensure direct accessibility of embedded user interfaces	
8.1 Make programmatic elements such as scripts and applets directly accessible or compatible with assistive technologies [Priority 1 if functionality is important and not presented elsewhere, otherwise Priority 2.]	2
9. Design for device-independence	
9.1 Provide client-side image maps instead of server-side image maps except where the regions cannot be defined with an available geometric shape.	1
9.2 Ensure that any element with its own interface can be operated in a device-independent manner.	2
9.3 For scripts, specify logical event handlers rather than device-dependent event handlers.	2
9.4 Create a logical tab order through links, form controls, and objects.	3
9.5 Provide keyboard shortcuts to important links (including those in client-side image maps), form controls, and groups of form controls.	3
10. Use interim solutions	
10.1 Until user agents allow users to turn off spawned windows, do not cause pop-ups or other windows to appear and do not change the current window without informing the user.	2
10.2 Until user agents support explicit associations between labels and form controls, ensure that labels are properly positioned for all form controls with implicitly associated labels.	2
10.3 Until user agents (including assistive technologies) render side-by-side text correctly, provide a linear text alternative (on the current page or some other) for *all* tables that lay out text in parallel, word-wrapped columns.	3
10.4 Until user agents handle empty controls correctly, include default, place-holding characters in edit boxes and text areas.	3
10.5 Until user agents (including assistive technologies) render adjacent links distinctly, include non-link, printable characters (surrounded by spaces) between adjacent links.	3
11. Use W3C technologies and guidelines	
11.1 Use W3C technologies when they are available and appropriate for a task and use the latest versions when supported.	2
11.2 Avoid deprecated features of W3C technologies.	2

WAI Guidelines	Priority
11.3 Provide information so that users may receive documents according to their preferences (e.g., language, content type, etc.)	3
11.4 If, after best efforts, you cannot create an accessible page, provide a link to an alternative page that uses W3C technologies, is accessible, has equivalent information (or functionality), and is updated as often as the inaccessible (original) page.	1
12. Provide context and orientation information	
12.1 Title each frame to facilitate frame identification and navigation.	1
12.2 Describe the purpose of frames and how frames relate to each other if this is not obvious from frame titles alone.	2
12.3 Divide large blocks of information into more manageable groups where natural and appropriate.	2
12.4 Associate labels explicitly with their controls.	2
13. Provide clear navigation mechanisms	
13.1 Clearly identify the target of each link.	2
13.2 Provide metadata to add semantic information to pages and sites.	2
13.3 Provide information about the general layout of a site (e.g., a site map or table of contents).	2
13.4 Use navigation mechanisms in a consistent manner.	2
13.5 Provide navigation bars to highlight and give access to the navigation mechanism.	3
13.6 Group related links, identify the group (for user agents), and, until user agents do so, provide a way to bypass the group.	3
13.7 If search functions are provided, enable different types of searches for different skill levels and preferences.	3
13.8 Place distinguishing information at the beginning of headings, paragraphs, lists, etc.	3
13.9 Provide information about document collections (i.e., documents comprising multiple pages.).	3
13.10 Provide a means to skip over multi-line ASCII art.	3
14. Ensure that documents are clear and simple	
14.1 Use the clearest and simplest language appropriate for a site's content.	1
14.2 Supplement text with graphic or auditory presentations where they will facilitate comprehension of the page.	3
14.3 Create a style of presentation that is consistent across pages.	3

You can learn more about the WAI guidelines and how to implement them by going to the World Wide Web Consortium Web site at http://www.w3.org.

Checking your Web Site for Accessibility

As you develop your Web site, you should periodically check it for accessibility. In addition to reviewing the Section 508 and WAI guidelines, you can do several things to verify that your site is accessible to everyone:

- Set up your browser to suppress the display of images. Does each page still convey all of the necessary information?
- Set your browser to display pages in extra large fonts and with a different color scheme. Are your pages still readable under these conditions?
- Try to navigate your pages using only your keyboard. Can you access all of the links and form elements?
- View your page in a text-only browser. (You can use the Lynx browser for this task, located at http://www.lynx.browser.org.)

- Open your page in a screen reader or other non-visual browser. (The W3C Web site contains links to several alternative browsers that you can download as freeware or on a short-term trial basis in order to evaluate your site.)
- Use tools that test your site for accessibility. (The WAI pages at the W3C Web site contains links to a wide variety of tools that report on how well your site complies with the WAI and Section 508 guidelines.)

Following the accessibility guidelines laid out by Section 508 and the WAI will result in a Web site that is not only more accessible to a wider audience, but whose design is also cleaner, easier to work with, and easier to maintain.

"The power of the Web is in its universality. Access by everyone regardless of disability is an essential aspect."
— Tim Berners-Lee, W3C Director and inventor of the World Wide Web

HTML and XHTML Elements and Attributes

This appendix provides descriptions of the major elements and attributes of HTML and XHTML. It also indicates the level of browser support for the Windows version of three major browsers: Internet Explorer (IE), Netscape (NS), and Opera (OP). Browser support is indicated in the columns on the right of each of the following tables. For example, a value of 4.0 in the Internet Explorer column indicates that the element or attribute is supported by the Windows version of Internet Explorer 4.0 and above. A version number with an asterisk indicates that the browser support is not extended to the more recent browser versions. For example, the entry "4.0*" in the Netscape column means that the feature is supported only in the 4.0 version of the Netscape browser and not in any other version (including later versions). In each of the tables that follow, values in the first column indicate the page number in the text in which the element or attribute is introduced and discussed.

Be aware that browsers are constantly being modified, so you should check a browser's documentation for the most current information. Also, the level of browser support can vary between operating systems.

The following data types are used throughout this appendix:

- *char* — A single text character
- *char code* — A character encoding
- *color* — An HTML color name or hexadecimal color value
- *date* — A date and time in the format: *yyyy-mm-dd*T*hh: mm:ss*TIMEZONE
- *integer* — An integer value
- *mime-type* — A MIME data type, such as "text/css", "audio/wav", or "video/x-msvideo"
- *mime-type list* — A comma-separated list of mime-types
- **option1**|option2| ... — The value is limited to the specified list of *options*. A default value, if it exists, is displayed in **bold**.
- *script* — A script or a reference to a script
- *styles* — A list of style declarations
- *text* — A text string
- *text list* — A comma-separated list of text strings
- *url* — The URL for a Web page or file
- *value* — A numeric value
- *value list* — A comma-separated list of numeric values

General Attributes

Several attributes are common to many page elements. Rather than repeating this information each time it occurs, the following tables summarize these attributes.

Core Attributes

The following five attributes, which are laid out in the specifications for HTML and XHTML, apply to all page elements and are supported by most browser versions.

PAGE	ATTRIBUTE	DESCRIPTION	HTML	XHTML	IE	NS	OP
	class="text"	Specifies the class or group to which an element belongs	4.0	1.0	3.0	4.0	3.5
58	id="text"	Specifies a unique identifier to be associated with the element	4.0	1.0	3.0	4.0	3.5
18	style="styles"	Defines an inline style for the element	4.0	1.0	3.0	4.0	3.5
	title="text"	Provides an advisory title for the element	2.0	1.0	4.0	6.0	3.0

Language Attributes

The Web is designed to be universal and has to be adaptable to languages other than English. Thus, another set of attributes provides language support. This set of attributes is not as widely supported by browsers as the core attributes are. As with the core attributes, they can be applied to most page elements.

PAGE	ATTRIBUTE	DESCRIPTION	HTML	XHTML	IE	NS	OP
	dir="ltr | rtl"	Indicates the text direction as related to the lang attribute. A value of ltr displays text from left to right. A value rtl displays text from right to left.	4.0	1.0	5.5	6.0	7.1
	lang="text"	Identifies the language used in the page content	4.0	1.0	4.0		

Form Attributes

The following attributes can be applied to most form elements or to a Web form itself, but not to other page elements.

PAGE	ATTRIBUTE	DESCRIPTION	HTML	XHTML	IE	NS	OP
	accesskey="*char*"	Indicates the keyboard character that can be pressed along with the accelerator key to access a form element	4.0	1.0	4.0	6.0	7.0
	disabled="disabled"	Disables a form field for input	4.0	1.0	4.0	6.0	7.0
	tabindex="*integer*"	Specifies a form element's position in a document's tabbing order	4.0	1.0	4.0	6.0	7.0

Internet Explorer Attributes

Internet Explorer supports a collection of attributes that can be applied to almost all page elements. Other browsers do not support these attributes, or support them only for a more limited collection of elements.

PAGE	ATTRIBUTE	DESCRIPTION	HTML	XHTML	IE	NS	OP
	accesskey="*char*"	Indicates the keyboard character that can be pressed along with the accelerator key to access the page element			5.0		
	contenteditable= "true | false | **inherit**"	Specifies whether the element's content can be modified online by the user			5.5		
	disabled="disabled"	Disables the page element for input			5.0		
	hidefocus= "true | **false**"	Controls whether the element provides a visual indication of whether the element is in focus			5.5		
	tabindex="*integer*"	Specifies the position of the page element in the tabbing order of the document			5.0		
	unselectable= "on | **off**"	Specifies whether the element can be selected by the user			5.5		

Event Attributes

To make Web pages more dynamic, HTML and XHTML support event attributes that identify scripts to be run in response to an event occurring within an element. For example, clicking a main heading with a mouse can cause a browser to run a program that hides or expands a table of contents. Each event attribute has the form

```
event = "script"
```

where *event* is the name of the event attribute and *script* is the name of the script or command to be run by the browser in response to the occurrence of the event within the element.

Core Events

The general event attributes are part of the specifications for HTML and XHTML. They apply to almost all page elements.

PAGE	ATTRIBUTE	DESCRIPTION	HTML	XHTML	IE	NS	OP
	onclick	The mouse button is clicked.	4.0	1.0	3.0	2.0	3.0
	ondblclick	The mouse button is double-clicked.	4.0	1.0	4.0	6.0	7.0
	onkeydown	A key is pressed down.	4.0	1.0	4.0	4.0	5.0
	onkeypress	A key is initially pressed.	4.0	1.0	4.0	4.0	5.0
	onkeyup	A key is released.	4.0	1.0	4.0	4.0	5.0
	onmousedown	The mouse button is pressed down.	4.0	1.0	4.0	4.0	5.0
	onmousemove	The mouse pointer is moved within the element's boundaries.	4.0	1.0	4.0	6.0	5.0
	onmouseout	The mouse pointer is moved out of the element's boundaries.	4.0	1.0	4.0	3.0	3.0
	onmouseover	The mouse pointer hovers over the element.	4.0	1.0	3.0	2.0	3.0
	onmouseup	The mouse button is released.	4.0	1.0	4.0	4.0	5.0

Document Events

The following list of event attributes applies not to individual elements within the page, but to the entire document as it displayed within the browser window or frame.

PAGE	ATTRIBUTE	DESCRIPTION	HTML	XHTML	IE	NS	OP
	onafterprint	The document has finished printing.			5.0		
	onbeforeprint	The document is about to be printed.			5.0		
	onload	The page is finished being loaded.	4.0	1.0	3.0	2.0	3.0
	onunload	The page is finished unloading.	4.0	1.0	3.0	2.0	3.0

Form Events

The following list of event attributes applies either to the entire Web form or fields within the form.

PAGE	ATTRIBUTE	DESCRIPTION	HTML	XHTML	IE	NS	OP
	onblur	The form field has lost the focus.	4.0	1.0	3.0	2.0	3.0
	onchange	The value of the form field has been changed.	4.0	1.0	3.0	2.0	3.0
	onfocus	The form field has received the focus.	4.0	1.0	3.0	2.0	3.0
	onreset	The form has been reset.	4.0	1.0	4.0	3.0	3.0
	onselect	Text content has been selected in the form field.	4.0	1.0	4.0	6.0	
	onsubmit	The form has been submitted for processing.	4.0	1.0	3.0	2.0	3.0

Data Events

The following list of event attributes applies to elements within the Web page capable of data binding. Note that these events are supported only by the Internet Explorer browser.

PAGE	ATTRIBUTE	DESCRIPTION	HTML	XHTML	IE	NS	OP
	oncellchange	Data has changed in the data source.			5.0		
	ondataavailable	Data has arrived from the data source.			4.0		
	ondatasetchange	The data in the data source has changed.			4.0		
	ondatasetcomplete	All data from the data source has been loaded.			4.0		
	onrowenter	The current row in the data source has changed.			5.0		
	onrowexit	The current row is about to be changed in the data source.			5.0		
	onrowsdelete	Rows have been deleted from the data source.			5.0		
	onrowsinserted	Rows have been inserted into the data source.			5.0		

Internet Explorer Events

The Internet Explorer browser supports a wide collection of customized event attributes. Unless otherwise noted, these event attributes can be applied to any page element and are not supported by other browsers or included in the HTML or XHTML specifications.

PAGE	ATTRIBUTE	DESCRIPTION	HTML	XHTML	IE	NS	OP
	onactive	The element is set to an "active" state.			5.5		
	onafterupdate	Data has been transferred from the element to a data source.			4.0		
	onbeforeactivate	The element is about to be set to an "active" state.			6.0		
	onbeforecopy	A selection from the element is about to be copied to the clipboard.			5.0		
	onbeforecut	A selection from the element is about to be cut to the clipboard.			5.0		
	onbeforedeactivate	The element is about to be "deactivated".			5.5		
	onbeforeeditfocus	The element is about to become "active".			5.0		
	onbeforepaste	Data from the clipboard is about to be pasted into the element.			5.0		
	onbeforeunload	The page is about to be unloaded.			4.0		
	onbeforeupdate	The element's data is about to be updated.			5.0		
	onblur	The element has lost the focus.			5.0		
	oncontextmenu	The right mouse button is activated.			5.0	6.0	
	oncontrolselect	Selection using a modifier key (Ctrl for Windows, Command for Macintosh) has begun within the element.			5.5		
	oncopy	Data from the element has been copied to the clipboard.			5.0		
	oncut	Data from the element has been cut to the clipboard.			5.0		
	ondrag	The element is being dragged.			5.0		
	ondragdrop	The element has been dropped into the window or frame.			5.0		
	ondragend	The element is no longer being dragged.			5.0		

PAGE	ATTRIBUTE	DESCRIPTION	HTML	XHTML	IE	NS	OP
	ondragenter	The dragged element has entered a target area.			5.0		
	ondragleave	The dragged element has left a target area.			5.0		
	ondragover	The dragged element is over a target area.			5.0		
	ondragstart	The element has begun to be dragged.			5.0		
	ondrop	The dragged element has been dropped.			5.0		
	onerrorupdate	The data transfer to the element has been cancelled.			4.0		
	onfocus	The element has received the focus.			5.0		
	onfocusin	The element is about to receive the focus.			6.0		
	onfocusout	The form element has just lost the focus.			6.0		
	onhelp	The user has selected online help from the browser.			4.0		
	oninput	Text has just been entered into the form field.			6.0		
	onlosecapture	The element has been captured by the mouse selection.			5.0		
	onmouseenter	The mouse pointer enters the element's boundaries.			5.5		
	onmouseleave	The mouse pointer leaves the element's boundaries.			5.5		
	onmousewheel	The mouse wheel is moved.			6.0		
	onmove	The browser window or element has been moved by the user.			5.5		
	onmoveend	Movement of the element has ended.			5.5		
	onmovestart	The element has begun to move.			5.5		
	onpaste	Data has been pasted from the clipboard into the element.			5.0		
	onpropertychange	One or more of the element's properties has changed.			5.0		
	onreadystatechange	The element has changed its ready state.			4.0		
	onresize	The browser window or element has been resized by the user.			4.0		
	onscroll	The scrollbar position within the element has been changed.			4.0	7.0	7.0
	onselectstart	Selection has begun within the element.			4.0		
	onstop	The page is finished loading.			5.0		

HTML and XHTML Elements and Attributes

The following table contains an alphabetic listing of the elements and attributes supported by HTML, XHTML, and the major browsers. Some attributes are not listed in this table, but are described instead in the general attributes tables presented in the previous section of this appendix.

PAGE	ELEMENT/ATTRIBUTE	DESCRIPTION	HTML	XHTML	IE	NS	OP
10	`<!-- text -->`	Inserts a comment into the document (comments are not displayed in the rendered page)	2.0	1.0	1.0	1.0	2.1
	`<!doctype>`	Specifies the Document Type Definition for a document	2.0	1.0	2.0	1.0	4.0
61	`<a> </a>`	Marks the beginning and end of a link	2.0	1.0	1.0	1.0	2.1
86	`accesskey="char"`	Indicates the keyboard character that can be pressed along with the accelerator key to activate the link	4.0	1.0	4.0	6.0	7.0
	`charset="text"`	Specifies the character encoding of the linked document	4.0	1.0			7.0
154	`coords="value list"`	Specifies the coordinates of a hotspot in a client-side image map; the value list depends on the shape of the hotspot: shape="rect" "left, right, top, bottom" shape="circle" "x_center, y_center, radius" shape="poly" "x1, y1, x2, y2, x3, y3, ..."	4.0	1.0		6.0	7.0
61	`href="url"`	Specifies the URL of the link	3.2	1.0	1.0	2.0	2.1
	`hreflang="text"`	Specifies the language of the linked document	4.0	1.0		6.1	
63	`name="text"`	Specifies a name for the enclosed text, allowing it to be a link target	2.0	1.0	1.0	1.0	2.1
87	`rel="text"`	Specifies the relationship between the current page and the link specified by the href attribute	2.0	1.0	3.0	6.0	7.0
87	`rev="text"`	Specifies the reverse relationship between the current page and the link specified by the href attribute	2.0	1.0	3.0	6.0	7.0
154	`shape="rect|circle| polygon"`	Specifies the shape of the hotspot	4.0	1.0		6.0	7.0
86	`title="text"`	Specifies the pop-up text for the link	2.0	1.0	4.0	6.0	3.0
84	`target="text"`	Specifies the target window or frame for the link	4.0	1.0	3.0	1.0	2.1
	`type="mime-type"`	Specifies the data type of the linked document	4.0	1.0			7.0

PAGE	ELEMENT/ATTRIBUTE	DESCRIPTION	HTML	XHTML	IE	NS	OP
32	`<abbr> </abbr>`	Marks abbreviated text	4.0	1.0		6.0	4.0
32	`<acronym> </acronym>`	Marks acronym text	3.0	1.0	4.0	6.0	4.0
31	`<address> </address>`	Marks address text	2.0	1.0	1.0	1.0	2.1
	`<applet> </applet>`	Embeds an applet into the browser. **Deprecated**	3.2	1.0*	3.0	2.0	3.5

	`align="absmiddle|`
	`absbottom|baseline|`
	`bottom|center`
	`|left|middle`
	`|right|texttop`
	`|top"`
		Specifies the alignment of the applet with the surrounding text	3.2	1.0*	3.0	2.0	3.0

	`alt="text"`	Specifies alternate text for the applet. **Deprecated**	3.2	1.0*	3.0	2.0	
	`archive="url"`	Specifies the URL of an archive containing classes and other resources to be used with the applet. **Deprecated**	4.0	1.0*	4.0	3.0	
	`code="url"`	Specifies the URL of the applet's code/class. **Deprecated**	3.2	1.0*	3.0	2.0	3.5
	`codebase="url"`	Specifies the URL of all class files for the applet. **Deprecated**	3.2	1.0*	3.0	2.0	
	`datafld="text"`	Specifies the data source that supplies bound data for use with the applet	4.0		4.0		
	`datasrc="text"`	Specifies the ID or URL of the applet's data source	4.0		4.0		
	`height="integer"`	Specifies the height of the applet in pixels	3.2	1.0*	3.0	2.0	3.5
	`hspace="integer"`	Specifies the horizontal space around the applet in pixels. **Deprecated**	3.2	1.0*	3.0	2.0	4.0
	`mayscript="mayscript"`	Permits access to the applet by programs embedded in the document				3.0*	
	`name="text"`	Specifies the name assigned to the applet. **Deprecated**	3.2	1.0*	3.0	2.0	3.5
	`object="text"`	Specifies the name of the resource that contains a serialized representation of the applet. **Deprecated**	4.0	1.0*			
	`src="url"`	Specifies an external URL reference to the applet			4.0		3.5
	`vspace="integer"`	Specifies the vertical space around the applet in pixels. **Deprecated**	3.2	1.0*	3.0	2.0	4.0
	`width="integer"`	Specifies the width of the applet in pixels. **Deprecated**	3.2	1.0*	3.0	2.0	3.5

PAGE	ELEMENT/ATTRIBUTE	DESCRIPTION	HTML	XHTML	IE	NS	OP
154	`<area />`	Marks an image map hotspot	3.2	1.0	1.0	2.0	2.1
154	`alt="text"`	Specifies alternate text for the hotspot	3.2	1.0	4.0	3.0	2.1
154	`coords="value list"`	Specifies the coordinates of the hotspot; the value list depends on the shape of the hotspot: shape="rect" "left, right, top, bottom" shape="circle" "x_center, y_center, radius" shape="poly" "x1, y1, x2, y2, x3, y3, ..."	3.2	1.0	1.0	2.0	2.1
154	`href="url"`	Specifies the URL of the document to which the hotspot points	3.2	1.0	1.0	2.0	2.1
154	`nohref="nohref"`	Specifies that the hotspot does not point to a link	3.2	1.0	1.0	2.0	2.1
154	`shape="rect|circle| polygon"`	Specifies the shape of the hotspot	3.2	1.0	1.0	2.0	2.1
84	`target="text"`	Specifies the target window or frame for the link	3.2	1.0*	1.0	2.0	2.1
32	`<b> </b>`	Marks text as bolded	2.0	1.0	1.0	1.0	2.1
76	`<base />`	Specifies global reference information for the document	2.0	1.0	1.0	1.0	2.1
76	`href="url"`	Specifies the URL from which all relative links in the document are based	2.0	1.0	1.0	1.0	2.1
85	`target="text"`	Specifies the target window or frame for links in the document	2.0	1.0*	1.0	1.0	2.1
	`<basefont />`	Specifies the font setting for the document text. **Deprecated**	3.2	1.0*	1.0	1.0	2.1
	`color="color"`	Specifies the text color. **Deprecated**	3.2	1.0*	1.0	1.0	2.1
	`face="text list"`	Specifies a list of fonts to be applied to the text. **Deprecated**	3.2	1.0*	1.0	1.0	2.1
	`size="integer"`	Specifies the size of the font range from 1 (smallest) to 7 (largest). **Deprecated**	3.2	1.0*	1.0	1.0	2.1
	`<bdo> </bdo>`	Indicates that the enclosed text should be rendered with the direction specified by the dir attribute	4.0	1.0	5.0	6.0	4.0
	`<bgsound />`	Plays a background sound clip when the page is opened			2.0		2.1
	`balance="integer"`	Specifies the balance of the volume between the left and right speakers where balance ranges from -10,000 to 10,000			4.0		
	`loop="integer| infinite"`	Specifies the number of times the clip will be played (a positive integer or infinite)			2.0		2.1
	`src="url"`	Specifies the URL of the sound clip file			2.0		2.1
	`volume="integer"`	Specifies the volume of the sound clip, where the volume ranges from -10,000 to 0			4.0		

PAGE	ELEMENT/ATTRIBUTE	DESCRIPTION	HTML	XHTML	IE	NS	OP
32	`<big> </big>`	Increases the size of the enclosed text relative to the default font size	3.0	1.0	3.0	1.0	2.1
	`<blink> </blink>`	Blinks the enclosed text on and off			4.0	1.0	7.0
31	`<blockquote> </blockquote>`	Marks content as quoted from another source	2.0	1.0	1.0	1.0	2.1
19	`align="left|center|right"`	Specifies the horizontal alignment of the content			4.0	4.0	
	`cite="url"`	Provides the source URL of the quoted content	4.0	1.0		6.0	
141	`clear="none|left|right|all"`	Prevents content rendering until the specified margin is clear	3.0*		4.0		4.0
14	`<body> </body>`	Marks the page content to be rendered by the browser	2.0	1.0	1.0	1.0	2.1
	`alink="color"`	Specifies the color of activated links in the document. **Deprecated**	3.2	1.0*	4.0	1.1	7.1
150	`background="url"`	Specifies the background image file used for the page. **Deprecated**	3.0	1.0*	1.0	1.1	2.1
116	`bgcolor="color"`	Specifies the background color of the page. **Deprecated**	3.2	1.0*	1.0	1.1	2.1
	`bgproperties="fixed"`	Fixes the background image in the browser window			2.0		
	`bottommargin="integer"`	Specifies the size of the bottom margin in pixels			2.0		7.0
	`leftmargin="integer"`	Specifies the size of the left margin in pixels			2.0	6.2	7.0
	`link="color"`	Specifies the color of unvisited links. **Deprecated**	3.2	1.0*	1.0	1.1	2.1
	`marginheight="integer"`	Specifies the size of the margin above and below the page				4.0	4.0
	`marginwidth="integer"`	Specifies the size of the margin to the left and right of the page				4.0	4.0
	`nowrap="false|true"`	Specifies whether the content wraps using normal HTML line-wrapping conventions			4.0		
	`rightmargin="integer"`	Specifies the size of the right margin in pixels			4.0		
	`scroll="yes|no"`	Specifies whether to display a scrollbar			4.0		
116	`text="color"`	Specifies the color of page text. **Deprecated**	3.2	1.0*	1.0	1.1	2.1
	`topmargin="integer"`	Specifies the size of the top page margin in pixels			2.0	6.2	7.0
	`vlink="color"`	Specifies the color of previously visited links. **Deprecated**	3.2	1.0*	1.0	1.1	2.1

PAGE	ELEMENT/ATTRIBUTE	DESCRIPTION	HTML	XHTML	IE	NS	OP
38	` `	Inserts a line break into the page	2.0	1.0	1.0	1.0	2.1
141	clear="**none**|left| right|all"	Displays the line break only when the specified margin is clear. **Deprecated**	3.2	1.0*	1.0	1.0	2.1
	`<button> </button>`	Creates a form button	4.0	1.0	4.0	6.0	5.0
	datafld="*text*"	Specifies the column from a data source that supplies bound data for the button			4.0		
	dataformatas="html| plaintext|text"	Specifies the format of the data in the data source bound with the button			4.0		
	datasrc="*url*"	Specifies the URL or ID of the data source bound with the button			4.0		
	name="*text*"	Provides the name assigned to the form button	4.0	1.0	4.0	6.0	5.0
	type="**submit**| reset|button"	Specifies the type of form button	4.0	1.0	4.0	6.0	5.0
	value="*text*"	Provides the value associated with the form button	4.0	1.0	4.0	6.0	5.0
185	`<caption> </caption>`	Creates a table caption	3.0	1.0	2.0	1.1	2.1
185	align="bottom| center|left| right|**top**"	Specifies the alignment of the caption. **Deprecated**	3.0	1.0*	2.0	1.1	2.1
	valign="top|bottom"	Specifies the vertical alignment of the caption			2.0		
31	`<center> </center>`	Centers content horizontally on the page. **Deprecated**	3.2	1.0*	1.0	1.0	2.1
32	`<cite> </cite>`	Marks citation text	2.0	1.0	1.0	1.0	2.1
32	`<code> </code>`	Marks text used for code samples	2.0	1.0	1.0	1.0	2.1
208	`<col> </col>`	Defines the settings for a column or group of columns	4.0	1.0	3.0	6.0	4.0
201	align="left|right| center"	Specifies the alignment of the content of the column(s)	4.0	1.0	4.0		7.0
116	bgcolor="*color*"	Specifies the background color of the column(s)			4.0		
201	char="*char*"	Specifies a character in the column used to align column values	4.0	1.0			
201	charoff="*integer*"	Specifies the offset in pixels from the alignment character specified in the char attribute	4.0	1.0			
208	span="*integer*"	Specifies the number of columns in the group	4.0	1.0	3.0	6.0	7.0
201	valign="top| middle|bottom| baseline"	Specifies the vertical alignment of the content in the column(s)	4.0	1.0	4.0		4.0
197	width="*integer*"	Specifies the width of the column(s) in pixels	4.0	1.0	3.0	6.0	7.0

PAGE	ELEMENT/ATTRIBUTE	DESCRIPTION	HTML	XHTML	IE	NS	OP
208	`<colgroup> </colgroup>`	Creates a container for a group of columns	4.0	1.0	3.0	6.0	4.0
201	`align="left|right center"`	Specifies the alignment of the content of the column group	4.0	1.0	4.0		7.0
116	`bgcolor="color"`	Specifies the background color of the column group			4.0		
201	`char="char"`	Specifies a character in the column used to align column group values	4.0	1.0			
201	`charoff="integer"`	Specifies the offset in pixels from the alignment character specified in the char attribute	4.0	1.0			
208	`span="integer"`	Specifies the number of columns in the group	4.0	1.0	3.0	6.0	7.0
201	`valign="top|middle |bottom|baseline"`	Specifies the vertical alignment of the content in the column group	4.0	1.0	4.0		4.0
197	`width="integer"`	Specifies the width of the columns in the group in pixels	4.0	1.0	3.0	6.0	7.0
28	`<dd> </dd>`	Marks text as a definition within a definition list	2.0	1.0	1.0	1.0	2.1
32	`<del> </del>`	Marks text as deleted from the document	3.0	1.0	4.0	6.0	4.0
	`cite="url"`	Provides the URL for the document that has additional information about the deleted text	3.0	1.0	4.0	6.1	4.0
	`datetime="date"`	Specifies the date and time of the text deletion	3.0	1.0	4.0	6.1	4.0
32	`<dfn> </dfn>`	Marks the defining instance of a term	3.0	1.0	1.0	6.0	2.1
31	`<dir> </dir>`	Contains a directory listing. **Deprecated**	2.0	1.0*	1.0	1.0	2.1
	`compact="compact"`	Permits use of compact rendering, if available. **Deprecated**	2.0	1.0*			
	`<div> </div>`	Creates a generic block-level element	3.0	1.0	3.0	2.0	2.1
	`align="left|center right|justify"`	Specifies the horizontal alignment of the content. **Deprecated**	3.0	1.0*	3.0	2.0	2.1
	`datafld="text"`	Indicates the column from a data source that supplies bound data for the block			4.0		
	`dataformatas="html |plaintext|text"`	Specifies the format of the data in the data source bound with the block			4.0		
	`datasrc="url"`	Provides the URL or ID of the data source bound with the block			4.0		
	`nowrap="nowrap"`	Specifies whether the content wraps using normal HTML line-wrapping conventions	3.0*		4.0		
28	`<dl> </dl>`	Encloses a definition list using the dd and dt elements	2.0	1.0	1.0	1.0	2.1
	`compact="compact"`	Permits use of compact rendering, if available. **Deprecated**	2.0	1.0*	4.0	1.0	
28	`<dt> </dt>`	Marks a definition term in a definition list	2.0	1.0	1.0	1.0	2.1
	`nowrap="nowrap"`	Specifies whether the content wraps using normal HTML line-wrapping conventions			4.0		

PAGE	ELEMENT/ATTRIBUTE	DESCRIPTION	HTML	XHTML	IE	NS	OP
32	`<em> </em>`	Marks emphasized text	2.0	1.0	1.0	1.0	2.1
	`<embed> </embed>`	Places an embedded object into the page			3.0	1.0	3.0
	`align="bottom|left|right|top"`	Specifies the alignment of the object with the surrounding content			3.0	1.0	3.5
	`autostart="true|false"`	Starts the embedded object automatically when the page is loaded			3.0	1.0	3.0
	`height="integer"`	Specifies the height of the object in pixels			3.0	1.0	3.0
	`hidden="true|false"`	Hides the object on the page			3.0	2.0	3.0
	`hspace="integer"`	Specifies the horizontal space around the object in pixels				1.1	4.0
	`name="text"`	Provides the name of the embedded object			4.0	4.0	
	`pluginspage="url"`	Provides the URL of the page containing information on the object			3.0	2.0	3.5
	`pluginurl="url"`	Provides the URL of the page for directly installing the object				4.0	
	`src="url"`	Provides the location of the file containing the object			3.0	1.1	3.5
	`type="mime-type"`	Specifies the mime-type of the embedded object			3.0	3.0	3.5
	`units="text"`	Specifies the measurement units of the object			4.0	3.0	
	`vspace="integer"`	Specifies the vertical space around the object in pixels				1.1	4.0
	`width="integer"`	Specifies the width of the object in pixels			3.0	1.1	3.0
	`<fieldset> </fieldset>`	Places form fields in a common group	4.0	1.0	4.0	6.0	4.0
	`align="left|center|right"`	Specifies the alignment of the contents of the field set			4.0		4.0
	`datafld="text"`	Indicates the column from a data source that supplies bound data for the field set			4.0		
	`dataformatas="html|plaintext|text"`	Specifies the format of the data in the data source bound with the field set			4.0		
	`datasrc="url"`	Provides the URL or ID of the data source bound with the field set			4.0		
116	`<font> </font>`	Formats the enclosed text. **Deprecated**	3.2	1.0*	2.0	1.0	2.1
116	`color="color"`	Specifies the color of the enclosed text. **Deprecated**	3.2	1.0*	2.0	2.0	2.1
119	`face="text list"`	Specifies the font face(s) of the enclosed text. **Deprecated**	3.2	1.0*	2.0	3.0	3.0
122	`size="integer"`	Specifies the size of the enclosed text with values ranging from 1 (smallest) to 7 (largest). A value of +*integer* increases the font size relative to the font size specified in the basefont element. **Deprecated**	3.2	1.0*	2.0	3.0	2.1

PAGE	ELEMENT/ATTRIBUTE	DESCRIPTION	HTML	XHTML	IE	NS	OP
	`<form> </form>`	Encloses the contents of a Web form	2.0	1.0	1.0	1.0	2.1
	`accept="mime-type list"`	Lists mime-types that the server processing the form will handle	4.0	1.0			
	`accept-charset= "char code"`	Specifies the character encoding that the server processing the form will handle	4.0	1.0			
	`action="url"`	Provides the URL to which the form values are to be sent	2.0	1.0	1.0	1.0	2.1
	`autocomplete="on|off"`	Enables automatic insertion of information in fields in which the user has previously entered data			5.0		
	`enctype="mime-type"`	Specifies the mime-type of the data to be sent to the server for processing; the default is "application/x-www-form-urlencoded"	2.0	1.0	1.0	1.0	2.1
	`method="get|post"`	Specifies the method of accessing the URL specified in the action attribute	2.0	1.0	1.0	1.0	2.1
	`name="text"`	Specifies the name of the form	2.0	1.0	1.0	1.0	2.1
	`target="text"`	Specifies the frame or window in which output from the form should appear	4.0	1.0	3.0	2.0	2.1
251	`<frame> </frame>`	Marks a single frame within a set of frames	4.0	1.0*	3.0	2.0	2.1
270	`border="integer"`	Specifies the thickness of the frame border in pixels				4.0*	
270	`bordercolor="color"`	Specifies the color of the frame border			4.0	3.5	
270	`frameborder="1|0"`	Determines whether the frame border is visible (1) or invisible (0); Netscape also supports values of yes or no	4.0	1.0*	3.0	3.5	7.0
D3	`longdesc="url"`	Provides the URL of a document containing a long description of the frame's contents	4.0	1.0*			
255	`marginheight= "integer"`	Specifies the space above and below the frame object and the frame's borders, in pixels	4.0	1.0*	3.0	2.0	2.1
255	`marginwidth="integer"`	Specifies the space to the left and right of the frame object and the frame's borders, in pixels	4.0	1.0*	3.0	2.0	2.1
260	`name="text"`	Specifies the name of the frame	4.0	1.0*	3.0	2.0	2.1
255	`noresize="noresize"`	Prevents users from resizing the frame	4.0	1.0*	3.0	2.0	2.1
255	`scrolling="auto| yes|no"`	Specifies whether the browser will display a scrollbar with the frame	4.0	1.0*	3.0	2.0	2.1
251	`src="url"`	Provides the URL of the document to be displayed in the frame	4.0	1.0*	3.0	2.0	2.1

PAGE	ELEMENT/ATTRIBUTE	DESCRIPTION	HTML	XHTML	IE	NS	OP
248	`<frameset> </frameset>`	Creates a collection of frames	4.0	1.0*	3.0	2.0	2.1
270	`border="integer"`	Specifies the thickness of the frame borders in the frameset in pixels			4.0	3.0	2.1
270	`bordercolor="color"`	Specifies the color of the frame borders			4.0	3.0	
249	`cols="value list"`	Arranges the frames in columns with the width of each column expressed either in pixels, as a percentage, or using an asterisk (to allow the browser to choose the width)	4.0	1.0*	3.0	2.0	2.1
270	`frameborder="1|0"`	Determines whether frame borders are visible (1) or invisible (0); Netscape also supports values of yes or no			3.0	3.5	
	`framespacing="integer"`	Specifies the amount of space between frames in pixels			3.1		
249	`rows="value list"`	Arranges the frames in rows with the height of each column expressed either in pixels, as a percentage, or using an asterisk (to allow the browser to choose the height)	4.0	1.0*	3.0	2.0	2.1
17	`<hi> </hi>`	Marks the enclosed text as a heading, where *i* is an integer from 1 (the largest heading) to 6 (the smallest heading)	2.0	1.0	1.0	1.0	2.1
19	`align="left|center|right|justify"`	Specifies the alignment of the heading text. **Deprecated**	3.0	1.0*	1.0	1.0	2.1
14	`<head> </head>`	Encloses the document head, containing information about the document	2.0	1.0	1.0	1.0	2.1
	`profile="url"`	Provides the location of metadata about the documenta	4.0	1.0			
36	`<hr />`	Draws a horizontal line (rule) in the rendered page	2.0	1.0	1.0	1.0	2.1
37	`align="left|center|right"`	Specifies the horizontal alignment of the line. **Deprecated**	3.2	1.0*	1.0	1.0	2.1
37	`color="color"`	Specifies the color of the line			3.0		
	`noshade="noshade"`	Removes 3-D shading from the line. **Deprecated**	3.2	1.0*	1.0	1.0	2.1
37	`size="integer"`	Specifies the height of the line in pixels or as a percentage of the enclosing element's height. **Deprecated**	3.2	1.0*	1.0	1.0	2.1
37	`width="integer"`	Specifies the width of the line in pixels or as a percentage of the enclosing element's width. **Deprecated**	3.2	1.0*	1.0	1.0	2.1

PAGE	ELEMENT/ATTRIBUTE	DESCRIPTION	HTML	XHTML	IE	NS	OP
14	`<html> </html>`	Encloses the entire content of the HTML document	2.0	1.0	1.0	1.0	2.1
	`version="text"`	Specifies the version of HTML being used	2.0	1.1			
	`xmlns="text"`	Specifies the namespace prefix for the document		1.0	5.0		
32	`<i> </i>`	Displays the enclosed text in italics	2.0	1.0	1.0	1.0	2.1
273	`<iframe> </iframe>`	Creates an inline frame in the document	4.0	1.0*	3.0	6.0	4.0
273	`align="bottom|left |middle|top |right"`	Specifies the horizontal alignment of the frame with the surrounding content. **Deprecated**	4.0	1.0*	3.0	6.0	6.0
	`datafld="text"`	Indicates the column from a data source that supplies bound data for the inline frame			4.0		
	`dataformatas="html| plaintext|text"`	Specifies the format of the data in the data source bound with the inline frame			4.0		
	`datasrc="url"`	Provides the URL or ID of the data source bound with the inline frame			4.0		
273	`frameborder="1|0"`	Specifies whether to display a frame border (1) or not (0)	4.0	1.0*	3.0	6.0	4.0
273	`height="integer"`	Specifies the height of the frame in pixels	4.0	1.0*	3.0	6.0	4.0
273	`hspace="integer"`	Specifies the space to the left and right of the frame in pixels	4.0	1.0*	3.0	6.0	4.0
D3	`longdesc="url"`	Indicates the document containing a long description of the frame's content	4.0	1.0*			
273	`marginheight= "integer"`	Specifies the space above and below the frame object and the frame's borders, in pixels	4.0	1.0*	3.0	6.0	4.0
273	`marginwidth="integer"`	Specifies the space to the left and right of the frame object and the frame's borders, in pixels	4.0	1.0*	3.0	6.0	4.0
273	`name="text"`	Specifies the name of the frame	4.0	1.0*	3.0	6.0	4.0
273	`scrolling="auto| yes|no"`	Determines whether the browser displays a scrollbar with the frame	4.0	1.0*	3.0	6.0	4.0
273	`src="url"`	Indicates the document displayed within the frame	4.0	1.0*	3.0	6.0	4.0
273	`vspace="integer"`	Specifies the space to the top and bottom of the frame in pixels	4.0	1.0*	3.0	6.0	4.0
273	`width="integer"`	Specifies the width of the frame in pixels	4.0	1.0*	3.0	6.0	4.0
	`<ilayer> </ilayer>`	Creates an inline layer used to display the content of external document				4.0*	
	`above="text"`	Specifies the name of the layer displayed above the current layer				4.0*	
	`background="url"`	Provides the URL of the file containing the background image				4.0*	
	`below="text"`	Specifies the name of the layer displayed below the current layer				4.0*	

PAGE	ELEMENT/ATTRIBUTE	DESCRIPTION	HTML	XHTML	IE	NS	OP
	bgcolor="*color*"	Specifies the layer's background color				4.0*	
	clip="*top, left, bottom, right*"	Specifies the coordinates of the viewable region of the layer				4.0*	
	height="*integer*"	Specifies the height of the layer in pixels				4.0*	
	left="*integer*"	Specifies the horizontal offset of the layer in pixels				4.0*	
	pagex="*integer*"	Specifies the horizontal position of the layer in pixels				4.0*	
	pagey="*integer*"	Specifies the vertical position of the layer in pixels				4.0*	
	src="*url*"	Provides the URL of the document displayed in the layer				4.0*	
	top="*integer*"	Specifies the vertical offset of the layer in pixels				4.0*	
	visibility="hide|**inherit**|show"	Specifies the visibility of the layer				4.0*	
	width="*integer*"	Specifies the width of the layer in pixels				4.0*	
	z-index="*integer*"	Specifies the stacking order of the layer				4.0*	
35	**<img> </img>**	Inserts an inline image into the document	2.0	1.0	1.0	1.0	2.1
140	align="left|right|top|texttop|middle|absmiddle|baselines|bottom|absbottom"	Specifies the alignment of the image with the surrounding content. **Deprecated**	2.0	1.0*	1.0	1.0	2.1
35	alt="*text*"	Specifies alternate text to be displayed in place of the image	2.0	1.0	1.0	1.0	2.1
159	border="*integer*"	Specifies the width of the image border. **Deprecated**	3.2	1.0*	1.0	1.0	2.1
	controls="control"	For video images, displays a playback control below the image			2.0		
	datafld="*text*"	Names the column from a data source that supplies bound data for the image			4.0		
	dataformatas="html|plaintext|text"	Specifies the format of the data in the data source bound with the image			4.0		
	datasrc="*url*"	Provides the URL or ID of the data source bound with the image			4.0		

PAGE	ELEMENT/ATTRIBUTE	DESCRIPTION	HTML	XHTML	IE	NS	OP
	`dynsrc="url"`	Provides the URL of a video or VRML file			2.0		2.1
144	`height="integer"`	Specifies the height of the image in pixels	3.0	1.0	1.0	1.0	2.1
143	`hspace="integer"`	Specifies the horizontal space around the image in pixels. **Deprecated**	3.0	1.0*	1.0	1.0	2.1
	`ismap="ismap"`	Indicates that the image can be used as a server-side image map	2.0	1.0	1.0	1.0	2.1
D3	`longdesc="url"`	Provides the URL of a document containing a long description of the image	4.0	1.0		6.1	
	`loop="integer"`	Specifies the number of times the video will play			2.0		2.1
	`lowsrc="url"`	Provides the URL of the low-resolution version of the image			4.1	1.0	
	`name="text"`	Specifies the image name	4.0	1.0*	4.0	3.0	3.0
35	`src="url"`	Specifies the image source file	2.0	1.0	1.0	1.0	2.1
	`start="fileopen|mouseover"`	Indicates when to start the video clip (either when the file is opened or when the mouse hovers over the image)			2.0		2.1
	`suppress="true|false"`	Suppresses the display of the alternate text and the placeholder icon until the image file is located				4.0*	
157	`usemap="url"`	Provides the location of a client-side image associated with the image (not well-supported when the URL points to an external file)	3.2	1.0	1.0	2.0	2.1
143	`vspace="integer"`	Specifies the vertical space around the image in pixels. **Deprecated**	3.2	1.0*	1.0	1.0	2.1
144	`width="integer"`	Specifies the width of the image in pixels	3.0	1.0	1.0	1.0	2.1
	`<input> </input>`	Marks an input field in a Web form	2.0	1.0	1.0	1.0	2.1
	`align="left|right|top|texttop|middle|absmiddle|baseline|bottom|absbottom"`	Specifies the alignment of the input field with the surrounding content. **Deprecated**	2.0	1.0*	1.0	1.0	2.1
	`alt="text"`	Specifies alternate text for image buttons and image input fields	4.0	1.0	4.0	4.0	4.0
	`checked="checked"`	Specifies that the input check box or input radio button is selected	2.0	1.0	1.0	1.0	2.1
	`datafld="text"`	Indicates the column from a data source that supplies bound data for the input field	4.0		4.0		
	`dataformatas="html|plaintext|text"`	Specifies the format of the data in the data source bound with the input field	4.0		4.0		
	`datasrc="url"`	Provides the URL or ID of the data source bound with the input field	4.0		4.0		

PAGE	ELEMENT/ATTRIBUTE	DESCRIPTION	HTML	XHTML	IE	NS	OP
	height="*integer*"	Specifies the height of the image input field in pixels			4.0	1.0	4.0
	hspace="*integer*"	Specifies the horizontal space around the image input field in pixels			5.0	4.0	4.0
	ismap="ismap"	Enables the image input field to be used as a server-side image map	4.0	1.1		6.0	
	maxlength="*integer*"	Specifies the maximum number of characters that can be inserted into a text input field	2.0	1.0	1.0	1.0	2.1
	name="*text*"	Specifies the name of the input field	2.0	1.0	1.0	1.0	2.1
	readonly="readonly"	Prevents the value of the input field from being modified	2.0	1.0	1.0	1.0	2.1
	size="*integer*"	Specifies the number of characters that can be displayed at one time in an input text field	2.0	1.0	1.0	1.0	2.1
	src="*url*"	Indicates the source file of an input image field	2.0	1.0	1.0	1.0	2.1
	type="button|checkbox|file|hidden|image|password|radio|reset|submit|**text**"	Specifies the type of input field	2.0	1.0	1.0	1.0	2.1
	usemap="*url*"	Provides the location of a client-side image associated with the image input field (not well-supported when the URL points to an external file)	4.0	1.0	2.0	2.0	2.1
	value="*text*"	Specifies the default value of the input field	2.0	1.0	2.0	2.0	2.1
	vspace="*integer*"	Specifies the vertical space around the image input field in pixels			5.0	4.0	4.0
	width="*integer*"	Specifies the width of an image input field in pixels			4.0	1.0	4.0
32	**<ins> </ins>**	Marks inserted text	3.0	1.0	4.0	6.0	4.0
	cite="*url*"	Provides the URL for the document that has additional information about the inserted text	3.0	1.0	4.0	6.1	4.0
	datetime="*date*"	Specifies the date and time of the text insertion	3.0	1.0	4.0	6.1	4.0
	<isindex />	Inserts an input field into the document for search queries. **Deprecated**	2.0	1.0*	1.0	1.0	2.1
	action="*url*"	Provides the URL of the script used to process the sindex data			1.0	4.0*	2.1
	prompt="*text*"	Specifies the text to be used for the input prompt. **Deprecated**	3.0	1.0*	1.0	1.0	2.1

PAGE	ELEMENT/ATTRIBUTE	DESCRIPTION	HTML	XHTML	IE	NS	OP
32	`<kbd> </kbd>`	Marks keyboard-style text	2.0	1.0	1.0	1.0	3.5
	`<label> </label>`	Associates the enclosed content with a form field	4.0	1.0	4.0	6.0	4.0
	`datafld="text"`	Indicates the column from a data source that supplies bound data for the label			4.0		
	`dataformatas="html|plaintext|text"`	Specifies the format of the data in the data source bound with the label			4.0		
	`datasrc="url"`	Provides the URL or ID of the data source bound with the label			4.0		
	`for="text"`	Provides the ID of the field associated with the label	4.0	1.0	4.0	6.0	7.0
	`<layer> </layer>`	Creates a layer used to display the content of external documents; unlike the ilayer element, layer elements are absolutely positioned in the page				4.0*	
	`above="text"`	Specifies the name of the layer displayed above the current layer				4.0*	
	`background="url"`	Provides the URL of the file containing the background image				4.0*	
	`below="text"`	Specifies the name of the layer displayed below the current layer				4.0*	
	`bgcolor="color"`	Specifies the layer's background color				4.0*	
	`clip="top, left, bottom, right"`	Specifies the coordinates of the viewable region of the layer				4.0*	
	`height="integer"`	Specifies the height of the layer in pixels				4.0*	
	`left="integer"`	Specifies the horizontal offset of the layer in pixels				4.0*	
	`pagex="integer"`	Specifies the horizontal position of the layer in pixels				4.0*	
	`pagey="integer"`	Specifies the vertical position of the layer in pixels				4.0*	
	`src="url"`	Provides the URL of the document displayed in the layer				4.0*	
	`top="integer"`	Specifies the vertical offset of the layer in pixels				4.0*	
	`visibility="hide|inherit|show"`	Specifies the visibility of the layer				4.0*	
	`width="integer"`	Specifies the width of the layer in pixels				4.0*	
	`z-index="integer"`	Specifies the stacking order of the layer				4.0*	

PAGE	ELEMENT/ATTRIBUTE	DESCRIPTION	HTML	XHTML	IE	NS	OP
	`<legend> </legend>`	Marks the enclosed text as a caption for a field set	4.0	1.0	4.0	6.0	7.0
	`align="bottom|left |top|right"`	Specifies the alignment of the legend with the field set; Internet Explorer also supports the center option. **Deprecated**	4.0	1.0*	4.0	6.0	
24	`<li> </li>`	Marks an item in an ordered (ol), unordered (ul), menu (menu), or directory (dir) list.	2.0	1.0	1.0	1.0	2.1
28	`type="A|a|I|i |1|disc|square |circle"`	Specifies the bullet type associated with the list item: a value of "1" is the default for ordered list; a value of "disc" is the default for unordered list. **Deprecated**	3.2	1.0*	1.0	1.0	2.1
	`value="integer"`	Sets the value for the current list item in an ordered list; subsequent list items are numbered from that value. **Deprecated**	3.2	1.0*	1.0	1.0	2.1
88	`<link />`	Creates an element in the document head that establishes the relationship between the current document and external documents or objects	2.0	1.0	3.0	4.0	3.5
88	`charset="char code"`	Specifies the character encoding of the external document	4.0	1.0			7.0
88	`href="url"`	Provides the URL of the external document	2.0	1.0	3.0	4.0	3.5
	`hreflang="text"`	Indicates the language of the external document	4.0	1.0			
	`media="all|aural| braille|handheld| print|projection| screen|tty|tv"`	Indicates the media in which the external document is presented	4.0	1.0	4.0	4.0	3.5
88	`name="text"`	Specifies the name of the link			4.0		
88	`rel="text"`	Specifies the relationship between the current page and the link specified by the href attribute	2.0	1.0	3.0	4.0	3.5
88	`rev="text"`	Specifies the reverse relationship between the current page and the link specified by the href attribute	2.0	1.0	3.0	4.0	3.5
88	`target="text"`	Specifies the target window or frame for the link	4.0	1.0*	4.0	7.0	
88	`title="text"`	Specifies the title of the external document	2.0	1.0		6.0	7.0
88	`type="mime-type"`	Specifies the mime-type of the external document	4.0	1.0	3.0	4.0	3.5
152	`<map> </map>`	Creates an element that contains client-side image map hotspots	3.2	1.0	1.0	2.0	2.1
152	`name="text"`	Specifies the name of the image map	3.2	1.0*	1.0	2.0	2.1

PAGE	ELEMENT/ATTRIBUTE	DESCRIPTION	HTML	XHTML	IE	NS	OP
	`<marquee> </marquee>`	Displays the enclosed text as a scrolling marquee			2.0	7.0	7.2
	`behavior="alternate |scroll|slide"`	Specifies how the marquee should move			2.0	7.0	7.2
	`bgcolor="color"`	Specifies the background color of the marquee			2.0		7.2
	`datafld="text"`	Indicates the column from a data source that supplies bound data for the marquee			4.0		
	`dataformatas="html| plaintext|text"`	Indicates the format of the data in the data source bound with the marquee			4.0		
	`datasrc="url"`	Provides the URL or ID of the data source bound with the marquee			4.0		
	`direction="down| left|right|up"`	Specifies the direction of the marquee			2.0	7.0	7.2
	`height="integer"`	Specifies the height of the marquee in pixels			2.0	7.0	7.2
	`hspace="integer"`	Specifies the horizontal space around the marquee in pixels			2.0		
	`loop="integer| infinite"`	Specifies the number of times the marquee motion is repeated			2.0		7.2
	`scrollamount= "integer"`	Specifies the amount of space, in pixels, between successive draws of the marquee text			2.0	7.0	7.2
	`scrolldelay="integer"`	Specifies the amount of time, in milliseconds, between marquee actions			2.0	7.0	7.2
	`truespeed="truespeed"`	Indicates whether the scrolldelay value should be set to its exact value; otherwise any value less than 60 milliseconds is rounded up			4.0		
	`vspace="integer"`	Specifies the vertical space around the marquee in pixels			2.0		
	`width="integer"`	Specifies the width of the marquee in pixels			2.0	7.0	7.2
31	`<menu> </menu>`	Contains a menu list. **Deprecated**	2.0	1.0*	1.0	1.0	2.1
	`compact="compact"`	Reduces the space between menu items. **Deprecated**	2.0	1.0*			
	`start="integer"`	Specifies the starting value of the items in the menu list			6.0	4.0	
28	`type="A|a|I|i |1|disc|square| circle|none"`	Specifies the bullet type associated with the list items	3.2	1.0*	1.0	1.0	2.1

PAGE	ELEMENT/ATTRIBUTE	DESCRIPTION	HTML	XHTML	IE	NS	OP
38	`<meta> </meta>`	Creates an element in the document's head section that contains information and special instructions for processing the document	2.0	1.0	2.0	1.0	3.0
38	`content="text"`	Provides information associated with the name or http-equiv attributes	2.0	1.0	2.0	1.0	3.0
38	`http-equiv="text"`	Provides instructions to the browser to request the server to perform different http operations	2.0	1.0	2.0	1.0	3.0
38	`name="text"`	Specifies the type of information specified in the content attribute	2.0	1.0	2.0	1.0	3.0
	`scheme="text"`	Supplies additional information about the scheme used to interpret the content attribute	4.0	1.0			
	`<nobr> </nobr>`	Disables line wrapping for the enclosed content			1.0	1.0	2.1
	`<noembed> </noembed>`	Encloses alternate content for browsers that do not support the embed element			3.0	2.0	3.0
	`<noframe> </noframe>`	Encloses alternate content for browsers that do not support frames	4.0	1.0*	3.0	2.0	2.1
	`<nolayer> </nolayer>`	Encloses alternate content for browsers that do not support the layer or ilayer elements				4.0*	
	`<noscript> </noscript>`	Encloses alternate content for browsers that do not support client-side scripts	4.0	1.0	3.0	3.0	3.0
	`<object> </object>`	Places an embedded object (image, applet, sound clip, video clip, etc.) into the page	4.0	1.0	3.0	6.0	4.0
	`archive="url"`	Specifies the URL of an archive containing classes and other resources preloaded for use with the object	4.0	1.0		6.0	
	`align="absbottom|absmiddle|baseline|bottom|left|middle|right|texttop|top"`	Aligns the object with the surrounding content. **Deprecated**	4.0	1.0*	3.0	6.0	
	`border="integer"`	Specifies the width of the border around the object. **Deprecated**	4.0	1.0*	6.0	6.0	7.0
	`classid="url"`	Provides the URL of the object	4.0	1.0	3.0	6.0	4.0
	`codebase="url"`	Specifies the base path used to resolve relative references within the embedded object	4.0	1.0	3.0	6.0	4.0
	`codetype="mime-type"`	Indicates the mime-type of the embedded objects' code	4.0	1.0	3.0	6.0	4.0

PAGE	ELEMENT/ATTRIBUTE	DESCRIPTION	HTML	XHTML	IE	NS	OP
	`data="url"`	Provides the URL of the object's data file	4.0	1.0	3.0	6.0	4.0
	`datafld="text"`	Identifies the column from a data source that supplies bound data for the embedded object	4.0				
	`dataformatas="html|plaintext|text"`	Specifies the format of the data in the data source bound with the embedded object	4.0				
	`datasrc="url"`	Provides the URL or ID of the data source bound with the embedded object	4.0				
	`declare="declare"`	Declares the object without embedding it on the page	4.0	1.0			
	`height="integer"`	Specifies the height of the object in pixels	4.0	1.0	3.0	6.0	4.0
	`hspace="integer"`	Specifies the horizontal space around the image in pixels	4.0	1.0	3.0	6.0	4.0
	`name="text"`	Specifies the name of the embedded object	4.0	1.0	3.0	6.0	4.0
	`standby="text"`	Specifies the message displayed by the browser while loading the embedded object	4.0	1.0			7.0
	`type="mime-type"`	Indicates the mime-type of the embedded object	4.0	1.0	3.0	6.0	4.0
	`vspace="integer"`	Specifies the vertical space around the embedded object	4.0	1.0	3.0	6.0	4.0
	`width="integer"`	Specifies the width of the object in pixels	4.0	1.0	3.0	6.0	4.0
24	`<ol> </ol>`	Contains an ordered list of items	2.0	1.0	1.0	1.0	2.1
	`compact="compact"`	Reduces the space between ordered list items. **Deprecated**	2.0	1.0*			
	`start="integer"`	Specifies the starting value in the list. **Deprecated**	3.2	1.0*	1.0	1.0	2.1
28	`type="A|a|I|i|1"`	Specifies the bullet type associated with the list items. **Deprecated**	3.2	1.0*	1.0	1.0	2.1
	`<optgroup> </optgroup>`	Contains a group of option elements in a selection field	4.0	1.0	6.0	6.0	7.0
	`label="text"`	Specifies the label for the option group	4.0	1.0	6.0	6.0	7.0
	`<option> </option>`	Formats an option within a selection field	2.0	1.0	1.0	1.0	2.1
	`label="text"`	Supplies the text label associated with the option	4.0	1.0			
	`selected="selected"`	Selects the option by default	2.0	1.0	1.0	1.0	2.1
	`value="text"`	Specifies the value associated with the option	2.0	1.0	1.0	1.0	2.1
21	`<p> </p>`	Marks the enclosed content as a paragraph	2.0	1.0	1.0	1.0	2.1
19	`align="left|center|right|justify"`	Horizontally aligns the contents of the paragraph. **Deprecated**	3.0	1.0*	1.0	1.0	2.1

PAGE	ELEMENT/ATTRIBUTE	DESCRIPTION	HTML	XHTML	IE	NS	OP
	`<param> </param>`	Marks parameter values sent to an object element or an applet element	3.2	1.0	3.0	2.0	3.5
	`name="text"`	Specifies the parameter name	3.2	1.0	3.0	2.0	3.5
	`type="mime-type"`	Specifies the mime-type of the resource indicated by the value attribute	4.0	1.0	6.0		6.0
	`value="text"`	Specifies the parameter value	3.2	1.0	3.0	2.0	3.5
	`valuetype="data|ref|object"`	Specifies the data type of the value attribute	4.0	1.0	6.0		6.0
	`<plaintext> </plaintext>`	Marks the enclosed text as plain text			1.0	1.0	2.1
172	`<pre> </pre>`	Marks the enclosed text as preformatted text, retaining white space from the document	2.0	1.0	1.0	1.0	2.1
	`width="integer"`	Specifies the width of preformatted text, in number of characters. **Deprecated**	2.0	1.0*		6.0	
32	`<q> </q>`	Marks the enclosed text as a quotation	3.0	1.0	4.0	6.0	4.0
	`cite="url"`	Provides the source URL of the quoted content	4.0	1.0		6.0	
32	`<s> </s>`	Marks the enclosed text as strikethrough text. **Deprecated**	3.0	1.0*	1.0	3.0	2.1
32	`<samp> </samp>`	Marks the enclosed text as a sequence of literal characters	2.0	1.0	1.0	1.0	2.1
	`<script> </script>`	Encloses client-side scripts within the document; this element can be placed within the head or the body element or refer to an external script file	3.2	1.0	3.0	2.0	3.0
	`charset="char code"`	Specifies the character encoding of the script	4.0	1.0	3.0	7.0	7.0
	`defer="defer"`	Defers execution of the script	4.0	1.0	4.0		
	`event="text"`	Specifies the event that the script should be run in response to	4.0		4.0		
	`for="text"`	Indicates the name or ID of the element to which the event attribute refers to	4.0		4.0		
	`language="text"`	Specifies the language of the script. **Deprecated**	4.0	1.0*	3.0	2.0	3.0
	`src="url"`	Provides the URL of an external script file	4.0	1.0	3.0	3.0	3.0
	`type="mime-type"`	Specifies the mime-type of the script	4.0	1.0	4.0	4.0	
	`<select> </select>`	Creates a selection field (drop-down list box) in a Web form	2.0	1.0	1.0	1.0	2.1
	`align="left|right|top|texttop|middle|absmiddle|baseline|bottom|absbottom"`	Specifies the alignment of the selection field with the surrounding content. **Deprecated**	3.0*		4.0		

PAGE	ELEMENT/ATTRIBUTE	DESCRIPTION	HTML	XHTML	IE	NS	OP
	`datafld="text"`	Identifies the column from a data source that supplies bound data for the selection field	4.0		4.0		
	`dataformatas="html| plaintext|text"`	Specifies the format of the data in the data source bound with the selection field	4.0		4.0		
	`datasrc="url"`	Provides the URL or ID of the data source bound with the selection field	4.0		4.0		
	`multiple="multiple"`	Allows multiple sections from the field	2.0	1.0	1.0	1.0	2.1
	`name="text"`	Specifies the selection field name	2.0	1.0	1.0	1.0	2.1
	`size="integer"`	Specifies the number of visible items in the selection list	2.0	1.0	1.0	1.0	2.1
32	`<small> </small>`	Decreases the size of the enclosed text relative to the default font size	3.0	1.0	3.0	1.0	2.1
130	`<span> </span>`	Creates a generic inline elment	3.0	1.0	3.0	2.0	2.1
	`datafld="text"`	Identifies the column from a data source that supplies bound data for the inline element			4.0		
	`dataformatas="html| plaintext|text"`	Specifies the format of the data in the data source bound with the inline element			4.0		
	`datasrc="url"`	Provides the URL or ID of the data source bound with the inline element			4.0		
32	`<strike> </strike>`	Marks the enclosed text as strikethrough text. **Deprecated**	3.0	1.0*	1.0	3.5	2.1
32	`<strong> </strong>`	Marks the enclosed text as strongly emphasized text	2.0	1.0	1.0	1.0	2.1
	`<style> </style>`	Encloses global style declarations for the document	3.0	1.0	3.0	4.0	3.5
	`media="all|aural| braille|handheld| print|projection| screen|tty|tv|"`	Indicates the media of the enclosed style definitions	4.0	1.0	4.0	4.0	3.5
	`title="text"`	Specifies the style of the style definitions	4.0	1.0			
	`type="mime-type"`	Specifies the mime-type of the style definitions	4.0	1.0	3.0	4.0	
32	`<sub> </sub>`	Marks the enclosed text as subscripted text	3.0	1.0	3.0	1.1	2.1
32	`<sup> </sup>`	Marks the enclosed text as superscripted text	3.0	1.0	3.0	1.1	2.1

PAGE	ELEMENT/ATTRIBUTE	DESCRIPTION	HTML	XHTML	IE	NS	OP
179	**\<table\> \</table\>**	Encloses the contents of a Web table	3.0	1.0	2.0	1.1	2.1
207	align="left|center|right" **Deprecated**	Aligns the table with the surrounding content. **Deprecated**	3.0	1.0*	2.0	2.0	2.1
206	background="*url*"	Provides the URL of the table's background image			3.0	4.0	5.0
116	bgcolor="*color*" **Deprecated**	Specifies the background color of the table. **Deprecated**	4.0	1.0*	2.0	3.0	2.1
188	border="*integer*"	Specifies the width of the table border in pixels	3.0	1.0	2.0	1.1	2.1
189	bordercolor="*color*"	Specifies the table border color			2.0	4.0	
189	bordercolordark="*color*"	Specifies the color of the table border's shaded edge			2.0		
189	bordercolorlight="*color*"	Specifies the color of the table border's unshaded edge			2.0		
194	cellpadding="*integer*"	Specifies the space between the table data and the cell borders in pixels	3.2	1.0	2.0	1.1	2.1
193	cellspacing="*integer*"	Specifies the space between table cells in pixels	3.2	1.0	2.0	1.1	2.1
	cols="*integer*"	Specifies the number of columns in the table			3.0	4.0	
	datafld="*text*"	Indicates the column from a data source that supplies bound data for the table	4.0		4.0		
	dataformatas="html|plaintext|text"	Specifies the format of the data in the data source bound with the table	4.0		4.0		
	datapagesize="*integer*"	Sets the number of records displayed within the table	4.0	1.1	4.0		
	datasrc="*url*"	Provides the URL or ID of the data source bound with the table	4.0		4.0		
191	frame="above|below|**border**|box|hsides|lhs|rhs|void|vside"	Specifies the format of the borders around the table	4.0	1.0	3.0	6.0	7.1
195	height="*integer*"	Specifies the height of the table in pixels			2.0	1.1	2.1
143	hspace="*integer*"	Specifies the horizontal space around the table in pixels				2.0	
192	rules="**all**|cols|groups|none|rows"	Specifies the format of the table's internal borders or gridlines	4.0	1.0	3.0	7.0	7.1
187	summary="*text*"	Supplies a text summary of the table's content	4.0	1.0		6.1	
143	vspace="*integer*"	Specifies the vertical space around the table in pixels				2.0	
195	width="*integer*"	Specifies the width of the table in pixels	3.0	1.0	2.0	1.1	2.1

PAGE	ELEMENT/ATTRIBUTE	DESCRIPTION	HTML	XHTML	IE	NS	OP
184	**\<tbody\> \</tbody\>**	Encloses the content of the Web table body	4.0	1.0	3.0	6.0	4.0
201	align="left|center |right|justify |char"	Specifies the alignment of the contents in the cells of the table body	4.0	1.0	4.0	6.0	4.0
116	bgcolor="color"	Specifies the background color of the table body			4.0	6.0	
201	char="char"	Specifies the character used for aligning the table body contents when the align attribute is set to "char"	4.0	1.0			
201	charoff="integer"	Specifies the offset in pixels from the alignment character specified in the char attribute	4.0	1.0			
201	valign="baseline| bottom|middle|top"	Specifies the vertical alignment of the contents in the cells of the table body	4.0	1.0	4.0	6.0	4.0
179	**\<td\> \</td\>**	Encloses the data of a table cell	3.0	1.0	2.0	1.1	2.1
	abbr="text"	Supplies an abbreviated version of the contents of the table cell	4.0	1.0			
201	align="**left**|center |right"	Specifies the horizontal alignment of the table cell data	3.0	1.0	2.0	1.1	2.1
206	background="url"	Provides the URL of the background image file			3.0	4.0	4.0
116	bgcolor="color"	Specifies the background color of the table cell. **Deprecated**	4.0	1.0*	2.0	3.0	2.1
189	bordercolor="color"	Specifies the color of the table cell border			2.0		
189	bordercolordark= "color"	Specifies the color of the table cell border's shaded edge			2.0		
189	bordercolorlight= "color"	Specifies the color of the table cell border's unshaded edge			2.0		
201	char="char"	Specifies the character used for aligning the table cell contents when the align attribute is set to "char"	4.0	1.0			
201	charoff="integer"	Specifies the offset in pixels from the alignment character specified in the char attribute	4.0	1.0			
108	colspan="integer"	Specifies the number of columns the table cell spans	3.0	1.0	2.0	1.1	2.1
D8	headers="text"	Supplies a space-separated list of table headers associated with the table cell	4.0	1.0			
197	height="integer"	Specifies the height of the table cell in pixels. **Deprecated**	3.2	1.0*	2.0	1.1	2.1
	nowrap="nowrap"	Disables line-wrapping within the table cell. **Deprecated**	3.0	1.0*	2.0	1.1	2.1
198	rowspan="integer"	Specifies the number of rows the table cell spans	3.0	1.0	2.0	1.1	2.1
D8	scope="col|colgroup |row|rowgroup"	Specifies the scope of the table for which the cell provides data	4.0	1.0			
201	valign="top|**middle** |bottom"	Specifies the vertical alignment of the contents of the table cell	3.0	1.0	2.0	1.1	2.1
197	width="integer"	Specifies the width of the cell in pixels. **Deprecated**	3.2	1.0*	2.0	1.1	2.1

PAGE	ELEMENT/ATTRIBUTE	DESCRIPTION	HTML	XHTML	IE	NS	OP
	`<textarea> </textarea>`	Marks the enclosed text as a text area input box in a Web form	2.0	1.0	1.0	1.0	2.1
	`datafld="text"`	Specifies the column from a data source that supplies bound data for the text area box	4.0		4.0		
	`dataformatas="html|plaintext|text"`	Specifies the format of the data in the data source bound with the text area box	4.0		4.0		
	`datasrc="url"`	Provides the URL or ID of the data source bound with the text area box	4.0		4.0		
	`cols="integer"`	Specifies the width of the text area box in characters	2.0	1.0	1.0	1.0	2.1
	`name="text"`	Specifies the name of the text area box	2.0	1.0	1.0	1.0	2.1
	`readonly="readonly"`	Specifies the value of the text area box cannot be modified	4.0	1.0	4.0	6.0	5.0
	`rows="integer"`	Specifies the number of visible rows in the text area box	2.0	1.0	1.0	1.0	2.1
	`wrap="off|soft|hard"`	Specifies how text is wrapped within the text area box and how that text-wrapping information is sent to the server-side program; in earlier versions of Netscape Navigator, the default value is "off" (Netscape also accepts the values "off", "virtual", and "physical".)			4.0	4.0*	
184	`<tfoot> </tfoot>`	Encloses the content of the Web table footer	4.0	1.0	3.0	6.0	4.0
201	`align="left|center|right|justify|char"`	Specifies the alignment of the contents in the cells of the table footer	4.0	1.0	4.0	6.0	4.0
116	`bgcolor="color"`	Specifies the background color the table body			4.0	6.0	
201	`char="char"`	Specifies the character used for aligning the table footer contents when the align attribute is set to "char"	4.0	1.0			
201	`charoff="integer"`	Specifies the offset in pixels from the alignment character specified in the char attribute	4.0	1.0			
201	`valign="baseline|bottom|middle|top"`	Specifies the vertical alignment of the contents in the cells of the table footer	4.0	1.0	4.0	6.0	4.0
182	`<th> </th>`	Encloses the data of a table header cell	3.0	1.0	2.0	1.1	2.1
	`abbr="text"`	Supplies an abbreviated version of the contents of the table cell	4.0	1.0			
201	`align="left|center|right"`	Specifies the horizontal alignment of the table cell data	3.0	1.0	2.0	1.1	2.1
206	`axis="text list"`	Provides a list of table categories that can be mapped to a table hierarchy	3.0	1.0			

PAGE	ELEMENT/ATTRIBUTE	DESCRIPTION	HTML	XHTML	IE	NS	OP
206	background="url"	Provides the URL of the background image file			3.0	4.0	4.0
116	bgcolor="color"	Specifies the background color of the table cell. **Deprecated**	4.0	1.0*	2.0	3.0	2.1
189	bordercolor="color"	Specifies the color of the table cell border			2.0		
189	bordercolordark="color"	Specifies the color of the table cell border's shaded edge			2.0		
189	bordercolorlight="color"	Specifies the color of the table cell border's unshaded edge			2.0		
201	char="char"	Specifies the character used for aligning the table cell contents when the align attribute is set to "char"	4.0	1.0			
201	charoff="integer"	Specifies the offset in pixels from the alignment character specified in the char attribute	4.0	1.0			
198	colspan="integer"	Specifies the number of columns the table cell spans	3.0	1.0	2.0	1.1	2.1
D8	headers="text"	A space-separated list of table headers associated with the table cell	4.0	1.0			
197	height="integer"	Specifies the height of the table cell in pixels. **Deprecated**	3.2	1.0*	2.0	1.1	2.1
	nowrap="nowrap"	Disables line-wrapping within the table cell. **Deprecated**	3.0	1.0*	2.0	1.1	2.1
198	rowspan="integer"	Specifies the number of rows the table cell spans	3.0	1.0	2.0	1.1	2.1
D8	scope="col|colgroup|row|rowgroup"	Specifies the scope of the table for which the cell provides data	4.0	1.0			
201	valign="top|middle|bottom"	Specifies the vertical alignment of the contents of the table cell	3.0	1.0	2.0	1.1	2.1
197	width="integer"	Specifies the width of the cell in pixels. **Deprecated**	3.2	1.0*	2.0	1.1	2.1
184	**<thead> </thead>**	Encloses the content of the Web table header	4.0	1.0	3.0	6.0	4.0
201	align="left|center|right|justify|char"	Specifies the alignment of the contents in the cells of the table header	4.0	1.0	4.0	6.0	4.0
116	bgcolor="color"	Specifies the background color of the table body			4.0	6.0	
201	char="char"	Specifies the character used for aligning the table header contents when the align attribute is set to "char"	4.0	1.0			
201	charoff="integer"	Specifies the offset in pixels from the alignment character specified in the char attribute	4.0	1.0			
201	valign="baseline|bottom|middle|top"	Specifies the vertical alignment of the contents in the cells of the table header	4.0	1.0	4.0	6.0	4.0
14	**<title> </title>**	Specifies the title of the document, placed in the head section of the document	2.0	1.0	1.0	1.0	2.1

PAGE	ELEMENT/ATTRIBUTE	DESCRIPTION	HTML	XHTML	IE	NS	OP
179	`<tr> </tr>`	Encloses the content of a row within a Web table	3.0	1.0	2.0	1.1	2.1
201	`align="left|center|right"`	Specifies the horizontal alignment of the data in the row's cells	3.0	1.0	2.0	1.1	2.1
206	`background="url"`	Provides the URL of the background image file for the row				4.0	
116	`bgcolor="color"`	Specifies the background color of the row. **Deprecated**	4.0	1.0*	2.0	3.0	2.1
189	`bordercolor="color"`	Specifies the color of the table row border			2.0		
189	`bordercolordark="color"`	Specifies the color of the table row border's shaded edge			2.0		
189	`bordercolorlight="color"`	Specifies the color of the table row border's unshaded edge			2.0		
201	`char="char"`	Specifies the character used for aligning the table row contents when the align attribute is set to "char"	4.0	1.0			
201	`charoff="integer"`	Specifies the offset in pixels from the alignment character specified in the char attribute	4.0	1.0			
197	`height="integer"`	Specifies the height of the table row in pixels			5.0	6.0	4.0
201	`valign="baseline|bottom|middle|top"`	Specifies the vertical alignment of the contents of the table row	3.0	1.0	2.0	1.1	2.1
32	`<tt> </tt>`	Marks the enclosed text as teletype or monospaced text	2.0	1.0	1.0	1.0	2.1
32	`<u> </u>`	Marks the enclosed text as underlined text. **Deprecated**	3.0	1.0*	1.0	3.5	2.1
24	`<ul> </ul>`	Contains an unordered list of items	2.0	1.0	1.0	1.0	2.1
	`compact="compact"`	Reduces the space between unordered list items. **Deprecated**	2.0	1.0*			
28	`type="disc|square|circle"`	Specifies the bullet type associated with the list items. **Deprecated**	3.2	1.0*	1.0	1.0	2.1
32	`<var> </var>`	Marks the enclosed text as containing a variable name	2.0	1.0	1.0	1.0	2.1
	`<wbr />`	Forces a line-break in the rendered page			1.0	1.0	
	`<xml> </xml>`	Encloses XML content (also referred to as a "data island") or references an external XML document			5.0		
	`ns="url"`	Provides the URL of the namespace that the XML content is bound to			5.0		
	`prefix="text"`	Specifies the namespace prefix of the XML content			5.0		
	`src="url"`	Provides the URL of an external XML document			5.0		
	`<xmp> </xmp>`	Marks the enclosed text as preformatted text, preserving the white space of the source document; replaced by the pre element. **Deprecated**	2.0		1.0	1.0	2.1

Glossary/Index

Note: Boldface entries include definitions.

C

caption

  table, HTML 185–186

<caption></caption> tag, HTML E12

cell, table. *See* table cell

cell padding The amount of space between cell contents and cell borders in a Web table. HTML 194–195

cell spacing The amount of space between cells in a Web table. HTML 193–194

 tag, HTML E12

CERN, HTML 5

character entities, HTML, HTML B1–B7

character formatting elements Inline elements that format text characters. HTML 31–33

circular hotspots, HTML 155

<cite></cite> tag, HTML E12

clear style, HTML 138–140, HTML 141

client A device on a network, such as a computer, that requests the resources of a server. HTML 4

client-server network A network consisting of several clients accessing information provided by one or more servers. HTML 4

client-side image map An image map stored locally on a user's computer or device. HTML 152–153

closing tag The tag that identifies the end of a two-sided tag; it uses the form </*element*>, where *element* is the name of the element. HTML 11

<code></code> tag, HTML E12

cognitive disabilities, HTML D1

<col></col> tag, HTML E12

<colgroup></colgroup> tag, HTML E13

color, HTML 108–116

  accessibility, HTML D4–5

  background. *See* background color

  foreground and background of Web pages, HTML 114–116

  frame borders, HTML 270–271

  names, HTML A1–A5, HTML 113–114

  table borders, HTML 189, HTML 190

  transparent, HTML 133

  viewing list, HTML 113–114

  Web-safe, HTML 112

color blindness, HTML D4–5

color value A numeric expression that precisely describes a color in terms of the intensity of its red, blue, and green components. HTML 109–113, HTML A1–A5

column, newspaper-style layout, HTML 217

column group A collection of columns within a Web table. HTML 208–209

column width, table, HTML 197

columnar layout A layout in which the page content is arranged in columns. HTML 210

comment tag A tag that allows you to insert a comment in your HTML code. HTML 12

creating HTML documents, HTML 9–42

  comments, HTML 12

  displaying files, HTML 16–17

  elements. *See* block-level element; elements

  file structure, HTML 14–16

  graphics, HTML 34–36

  horizontal lines, HTML 36–38

  inline elements, HTML 17, HTML 31–33

  links. *See* link

  special characters, HTML 39–42

  tools for, HTML 8–9

  white space, HTML 12–13

D

<dd></dd> tag, HTML E13

definition list An HTML list format; each item consists of a terms followed by its definition. HTML 28–29

<del></del> tag, HTML E13

deprecated feature An HTML feature that is being phased out and which might not be supported in future browsers. HTML 8

design tips, Web pages, HTML 159–160

destination The document that opens when you click a link. HTML 57

deuteranopia, HTML D4

<dfn></dfn> tag, HTML E13

tag, HTML E13

disabilities. *See* accessibility

displaying

  HTML files, HTML 16–17

  inline images, HTML 36

  special characters, HTML 40

dithering The process by which colors are combined to approximate a color not in the available palette. HTML 111–112

 tag, HTML E13

<dl></dl> tag, HTML E13

<!doctype> tag, HTML E8

dpi The number of dots per inch in an output device. HTML 121

<dt></dt> tag, HTML E13

dynamic content, accessibility, HTML D10

E

element A distinct object in an HTML document, such as a paragraph, a heading, or the page's title. HTML 10

  aligning contents, HTML 19

  attributes, HTML 13

  block-level. *See* block-level element

  body, HTML 14

  character formatting, HTML 31–33

  empty. *See* empty element

  head, HTML 14

  id attribute, HTML 58–59

  inline, HTML 17, HTML 31–33

  logical, HTML 33–34

  marking with tags, HTML 11–12

  nesting, HTML 14

  physical, HTML 33–34

  title, HTML 14

em unit A relative unit based on the width of the uppercase letter M. HTML 120

e-mail, spam, HTML 83–84

e-mail harvesters, HTML 83–84

<embed></embed> tag, HTML E14

empty element An element that contains no content. HTML 11, HTML 34–39

  graphics, HTML 34–36

  horizontal lines, HTML 36–38

event

  core, list, HTML E4

  data, list, HTML E5

  document, list, HTML E4

  form, list, HTML E5

  Internet Explorer, list, HTML E6–7

ex unit A relative unit based on the height of the lowercase letter x. HTML 120